ANALOGIES AT WAR

ANALOGIES AT WAR

KOREA, MUNICH, DIEN BIEN PHU, AND THE VIETNAM DECISIONS OF 1965

Yuen Foong Khong

PRINCETON UNIVERSITY PRESS PRINCETON, NEW JERSEY

Published by Princeton University Press, 41 William Street,
Princeton, New Jersey 08540
In the United Kingdom: Princeton University Press,
Chichester, West Sussex

Library of Congress Cataloging-in-Publication Data

Khong, Yuen Foong, 1956–
Analogies at war : Korea, Munich, Dien Bien Phu, and the
Vietnam decisions of 1965 / Yuen Foong Khong.
p. cm.
Includes bibliographical references (p.) and index.
ISBN 0-691-07846-7 — ISBN 0-691-02535-5 (pbk.)
1. Vietnamese Conflict, 1961–1975—United States. 2. United
States—Foreign relations—1963–1969—Decision-making.
3. International relations—Decision-making. I. Title.
DS558.K55 1992
959.704′3373—dc20 91-35162 CIP

This book has been composed in Linotron Caledonia

Princeton University Press books are printed on acid-free paper
and meet the guidelines for permanence and durability of the
Committee on Production Guidelines for Book Longevity of the
Council on Library Resources

Printed in the United States of America

5 7 9 10 8 6 4

Contents

Figures and Tables

FIGURES

TABLES

Acknowledgments

IN WRITING about the role of historical analogies in foreign policy decision-making, I have had the support of many teachers, friends and institutions. My greatest debt is to Stanley Hoffmann and Michael Joseph Smith. They guided the project from its inception and nurtured it as it struggled to become a book. Along the way, Stanley Hoffmann tutored me in international politics, encouraged me to ask big questions, and was always there as a friend and gentle critic. His erudition, wit and personal graciousness have been, and will remain, a constant source of inspiration to me. Michael Smith also rescued me from a less tractable topic early in my career, inculcated in me a respect for the kind of intellectual depth he exemplifies so well, and has continued to be a valued mentor and friend.

For two years, I pondered the detailed and incisive criticisms of Deborah Larson, Michael Shafer, and Jonathan Crystal. Among them, I inherited forty-five pages of single spaced comments on my original manuscript: they were encouraging when I was reasonable, merciless when I was sloppy. In this regard, I should single out Deborah Larson, whose work convinced me of the possibility and richness of using psychological concepts to illuminate important foreign policy decisions. I thank all three for the care they showered on the manuscript, and I hope I have succeeded in meeting their suggestions at least part of the way.

Alexander George, Robert Keohane, Jorge Dominguez, and Joseph Nye also read portions of the manuscript and gave detailed comments, for which I am thankful. More than anyone else I know, Alexander George has stressed the importance of examining the beliefs of foreign policy elites and has gone about it with the highest standards of social scientific rigor. Without his theoretical and methodological leadership, this work would not have been possible. Similarly, Robert Keohane nudged me to incorporate psychological theories into my work in more explicit and systematic ways than I otherwise might have done. I am grateful for his advice. Jorge Dominguez and Joseph Nye also encouraged me by providing detailed comments and suggestions early on. Much of this book was written at the Center for International Affairs, Harvard University, and I would like to thank Joseph Nye, the current director of the Center; Samuel Huntington, the previous director; and Anne Emerson, executive director, for their support and for making the Center a congenial and stimulating place to pursue one's research. Although I have not worked formally with Robert Jervis and Ernest May, their work has influenced my thinking a great deal, as the reader of the following pages will quickly notice. From 1987 through 1989, I participated in George Breslauer and Philip Tetlock's National Academy of Sciences project on learning in U.S. and Soviet foreign policy: I thank them and other members in the project for a superb learning opportunity and for sharing their reactions to my arguments with me.

Many others also read portions of the manuscript, and provided written comments, or argued their points with me over numerous agreeable lunches. Without their advice and indulgence, this would have been a poorer book. Special thanks to Vikram Chand, Houchang Chehabi, Chin Wei Fong, Aaron Friedberg, Jay Greene, Stephan Haggard, Eng Seng Ho, Bill Jarosz, James Jesudason, Hock Guan Lee, Jonathan Mercer, Andy Moravcsik, Ethan Nadelmann, Gregory Noble, Jim Read, Louise Richardson, Deborah Spar, Beth Simmons, Edward Steinfeld, Kenneth Thompson, Steve Weber, and Fareed Zakaria. Ted Megan, Patricia Small and Rina Verma performed invaluable research for the book and I gratefully acknowledge their assistance.

Many of the decision-makers discussed in this study agreed to be interviewed; I am especially grateful to George Ball, McGeorge Bundy, William Bundy, Roger Hilsman, Harry McPherson, John Roche, Walt Rostow, Dean Rusk, Arthur Schlesinger, Jr., William Sullivan, James Thomson, and Leonard Unger for giving generously of their time. Clark Clifford was also kind enough to write a detailed response to a specific question I had.

Fellowships from the Institute for the Study of World Politics, the Graduate School of Arts and Sciences, Harvard University, and the Lyndon Baines Johnson Foundation facilitated my research and made possible its timely completion. David Humphrey and his colleagues at the Lyndon Baines Johnson Library, Austin, Texas, helped make archival research enjoyable and rewarding.

With such good advice and friendly institutional support, the remaining errors to be found in this book must be solely mine.

Portions of this book have been published previously, and they are adapted by permission of Westview Press from *Learning in U.S. and Soviet Foreign Policy*, edited by George W. Breslaur and Philip E. Tetlock, published by Westview Press, 1991, Boulder, Colorado. The minutes of the July meetings reproduced in chapter 5 are adapted from George Kahin, *Intervention: How America Became Involved in Vietnam* (New York: Alfred Knopf, 1986), pp. 370–85, copyright (c) 1986 by George McT. Kahin, reprinted by permission of Alfred A. Knopf, Inc.

From afar, the members of my family have been, as always, a constant source of encouragement and inspiration. Without their unstinting support and unlimited patience, my task would have been much more difficult. And finally, although she joined this project in the middle, Pheak Son Seo has lived with it daily ever since; only she and I know how crucial a co-conspirator she has become in this and hopefully other projects we have in mind. This book is for her.

Yuen Foong Khong
Cambridge, Massachusetts

Abbreviations

AE	Analogical Explanation
ARVN	Army of the Republic of Vietnam
CIA	Central Intelligence Agency
CINPAC	U.S. Command in Chief Pacific
DRV	Democratic Republic of Vietnam
EDC	European Defense Community
FRUS	*Foreign Relations of the United States*
GVN	Government of South Vietnam
ICC	International Control Commission
JCS	Joint Chiefs of Staff
MPAJA	Malayan People's Anti-Japanese Army
NATO	North Atlantic Treaty Organization
NLF	National Liberation Front
NSC	National Security Council
NVN	North Vietnam
POL	Petroleum, Oil, and Lubricants
ROK	Republic of Korea
RVNAF	Royal Vietnamese Air Force
SAC	Strategic Air Command
SAM	Surface-to-Air Missile
SEATO	Southeast Asia Treaty Organization
SNIE	Special National Intelligence Estimate
SVN	South Vietnam
VC	Viet Cong
UN	United Nations
USIA	United States Information Agency

Part I

THE ARGUMENT

CHAPTER 1

Analogical Reasoning in Foreign Affairs: Two Views

AT THE BEGINNING of Werner Herzog's film *Aguirre, the Wrath of God*, a troop of Spanish conquistadors debates whether to continue the dangerous search for El Dorado, the legendary city of gold. The leader of the expedition urges the troop to turn back, but his assistant, Aguirre, argues for continuing the expedition. Aguirre twice invokes the analogy of Mexico—Cortez "founded" Mexico by defying orders to return, and that won him riches and glory—to make his case.[1] Partly through this argument and partly through intimidation, Aguirre succeeds in persuading the entourage to continue. What he and his entourage do not know is that El Dorado is a fiction invented by the Peruvians to entrap their conquerors. There is no El Dorado. Only death and destruction await them.

Aguirre's use of the Mexico analogy brings to mind a National Security Council (NSC) meeting between President Lyndon Johnson and his principal advisers on July 21, 1965. The issue was whether the United States should commit one hundred thousand troops to South Vietnam. George Ball spoke against sending the troops. When Ball finished, McGeorge Bundy, Dean Rusk, and Robert McNamara attacked his arguments in succession. The U.S. ambassador to South Vietnam, Henry Cabot Lodge, delivered the coup de grace. Summarizing his colleagues' analysis as well as their impatience with Ball, Lodge blurted out, "I feel there is a greater threat to start World War III if we don't go in. Can't we see the similarity to our own indolence at Munich?"[2]

Lodge's use of the Munich analogy at a crucial juncture in the deliberative process may be unusually dramatic, but it is hardly unique. Statesmen have consistently turned to the past in dealing with the present. The way they have invoked historical parallels when confronted with a domestic or foreign policy problem has ranged from the implausible to the prescient. In the early months of World War I, for example, Woodrow Wilson feared that Anglo-American disputes over American rights on the seas would lead to war between the two nations. His reasoning

[1] Werner Herzog, *Screenplays*, trans. Alan Greenberg and Martje Herzog (New York: Tanam Press, 1980), p. 38.

[2] Meeting on Vietnam, notes by Jack Valenti, July 21, 1965, Papers of Lyndon Baines Johnson, Meeting Notes File. Unless otherwise noted, all documents cited in the notes are located in the Lyndon Baines Johnson Library, Austin, Texas.

was based on a curious analogy: "Madison and I are the only two Princeton men that have become President. The circumstances of the War of 1812 and now run parallel. I sincerely hope they will not go further."[3]

Less idiosyncratic but more egregious learning from the past includes the "no more summers of 1914" mindset of European leaders. British and French leaders saw World War I as a mistake that resulted from overreaction and rigid diplomacy. This assessment contributed to a conciliatory policy toward Germany throughout the 1930s, culminating in the appeasement of Hitler at Munich.[4] In the United States, the same attitude took the form of "no more 1917s": many believed that the country was "duped" into World War I, whether by British propaganda or by private financiers and arms merchants. To avoid being drawn into another war in Europe, Congress enacted, from 1935 through 1939, four neutrality acts that sought to prevent the United States from following the 1917 path to war.[5] President Franklin Roosevelt shared the public's aversion to American involvement in another war. He did little to strengthen British or French resolve at Munich, and he may have inadvertently given Hitler the green light to proceed with his expansionist policies.[6]

Munich's infamous role in bringing about World War II in turn led to a "no more Munichs" syndrome in the postwar period. In 1950, the Truman administration reversed its assessment that the Korean peninsula was unimportant to U.S. security because President Truman saw North Korea's invasion of South Korea as analogous to the actions of Mussolini, Hitler, and Japan in the 1930s.[7] Similarly, when informed by his superiors that China might enter the war if the United States moved too far north, General Douglas MacArthur refused to reexamine U.S. aims and protested that stopping his troops short of the Yalu amounted to appeasing the Chinese as the British had appeased Hitler.[8] British Prime Minister Anthony Eden also saw a campaign of Hitlerite proportions in Nas-

[3] Charles Seymour, ed., *The Intimate Papers of Colonel House* (Boston: Houghton Mifflin, 1926–1928), 4:303–4.

[4] See Stanley Hoffmann, *Primacy or World Order: American Foreign Policy since the Cold War* (New York: McGraw-Hill, 1978), p. 22; and Robert Jervis, "Cooperation under the Security Dilemma," *World Politics* 30 (1978): 192.

[5] Robert Schulzinger, *American Diplomacy in the Twentieth Century* (New York: Oxford University Press, 1984), pp. 157–61.

[6] See Robert Divine, *Roosevelt and World War II* (New York: Pelican Books, 1970), p. 22; and Stephen Ambrose, *Rise to Globalism* (New York: Penguin Books, 1984), pp. 25–31.

[7] See Harry Truman, *Memoirs* (Garden City, New York: Doubleday, 1955–1956), 2:332–33. The most persuasive account of how the lessons of the 1930s, and of Munich in particular, influenced Truman is to be found in Ernest May's *"Lessons" of the Past: The Use and Misuse of History in American Foreign Policy* (New York: Oxford University Press, 1973), chap. 3. See also Glenn Paige, *The Korean Decision: June 24–30, 1950* (New York: Free Press, 1968), esp. pp. 114–15, 178.

[8] Cited in James Schnabel, *Policy and Direction: The First Year* (Washington, D.C.: Office of the Chief of Military History, United States Army, 1972), pp. 250–51.

ser's seizure of the Suez Canal in 1956. Eden, who was more prescient than most in sizing up the true Hitler in the 1930s, was quick to apply the same schema to Nasser. This perception of the stakes, among other things, convinced him that a British-French response was imperative.[9] President Dwight Eisenhower and his secretary of state, John Foster Dulles, did not accept Eden's characterization of Nasser. Indeed, the Americans were more concerned about antiquated British and French imperial pretensions. The result was that the United States applied strong pressure to force the British and the French to withdraw from Egypt. Misapplying the lessons of history cost Eden and the nation he led dearly.

A happier instance of learning from the past occurred during the Cuban missile crisis. President John F. Kennedy rejected the advice of his more hawkish advisers to remove Soviet missiles in Cuba by an air strike and opted instead for a naval blockade of the island. He rejected the air strike in part because he was worried about repeating the mistakes of 1914; he also did not want the action to be perceived as a Pearl Harbor in reverse.[10] Kennedy's use of the 1914 and Pearl Harbor analogies is an exception: it injected a certain cautiousness into the Executive Committee's deliberations and thus made possible the selection of the naval blockade, a less drastic option that turned out to be effective.

More recent examples of policymakers using history in their decision-making, like most earlier examples, have more ambiguous or unfortunate outcomes. A principal reason for the U.S. intervention in the Dominican Republic in 1965 was avoiding "another Cuba"; subsequent analyses, however, have raised questions about the accuracy of such a diagnosis and about the impact of the intervention on U.S.–Latin American relations.[11] In 1975, President Gerald Ford and his secretary of state, Henry Kissinger, likened the seizure of the U.S. vessel *Mayaguez* by Cambodia to the North Korean seizure of the *Pueblo* of 1968. Both actions were interpreted as designed to humiliate the United States.[12] Ford and Kissinger were anxious to avoid the protracted negotiations that Lyndon

[9] Anthony Eden, *Full Circle: The Memoirs of Anthony Eden* (Boston: Houghton Mifflin, 1960), pp. 481, 492, 519–20.

[10] Robert Kennedy, *Thirteen Days* (New York: New American Library, 1969), pp. 31, 62. George Ball has claimed that he was the one who first expressed reservations about the "Pearl Harbor in reverse" analogy (interview with author, New York City, New York, July 23, 1986). Cf. "Documentation: White House Tapes and Minutes of the Cuban Missile Crisis," *International Security* 10 (1985): 154–203. See also James Blight and David Welch, *On the Brink: Americans and Soviets Reexamine the Cuban Missile Crisis* (New York: Hill and Wang, 1989), pp. 50, 78, 141, 152, 167, 215, 278.

[11] Abraham Lowenthal, *The Dominican Intervention* (Cambridge: Harvard University Press, 1972), esp. pp. 137–39, 160–62.

[12] Richard Neustadt and Ernest May, *Thinking in Time: The Uses of History for Decision-Makers* (New York: Free Press, 1986), pp. 58–62.

Johnson endured; they chose to bring the United States' overwhelming military force to bear in a rescue mission. Although the rescue team was successful in releasing the hostages, an accident during the mission claimed the lives of more U.S. rescuers than there were hostages.

In the early 1980s, the Munich analogy was back in vogue. Officials of the Reagan administration who formulated the policy of using Nicaraguan rebels, the contras, to pressure or overthrow the Sandinista regime saw critics of their policy as "appeasers" of the Sandinistas. Some, like Jeane Kirkpatrick, argued that Munich, not Vietnam, was the appropriate analogue for the challenge in Nicaragua.[13] For many Americans, however, the Munich argument had been discredited by the Vietnam War; the argument that resonated in their minds was that of the "Vietnam syndrome." Thus critics of the Reagan administration's policies in Central America argued that they were likely to lead to "another Vietnam."[14]

A final example of political elites resorting to historical analogies can be seen in Chinese leader Deng Xiaoping's decision to crush the prodemocracy movement in the spring of 1989. Pirated notes from a meeting of Chinese leaders report Deng equating the students' demands for democracy as "altogether the same stuff as what the rebels did during the Cultural Revolution. All they want is to create chaos under the heavens."[15] Having lived through the horror of those chaotic years, Deng could not countenance their possible return. He saw himself as suppressing a new Cultural Revolution.[16]

This book is about how and why policymakers use historical analogies in their foreign policy decision-making and about the implications of their doing so. It builds on previous attempts to understand the role of "learning from history" in international politics.[17] Learning from history is said to occur when policymakers look to the past to help them deal with the present; the principal device used in this process is the historical analogy. The term *historical analogy* signifies an inference that if two or

[13] *New York Times*, April 26, 1985, p. A7.

[14] See David Fromkin and James Chace, "What *Are* the Lessons of Vietnam?" *Foreign Affairs* 63 (1985): 722–46, for an interesting collection of different interpretations of "the lessons of Vietnam" as they pertain to Central America.

[15] Roderick MacFarquhar, "The End of the Chinese Revolution," *New York Review of Books* (July 29, 1989): 8.

[16] Ibid.

[17] The quotation marks indicate the following: (1) the term is borrowed from others, especially Robert Jervis, *Perception and Misperception in International Politics* (Princeton: Princeton University Press, 1976), chap. 6; (2) policymakers may learn the wrong lessons just as frequently as they learn the right lessons; and (3) since it is possible to argue that learning the wrong lessons is not learning at all, I prefer to use a more neutral term to denote the phenomenon I am investigating: "how decision-makers use history." Cf. Philip Tetlock, "Learning in U.S. and Soviet Foreign Policy: In Search of an Elusive Concept," in *Learning in U.S. and Soviet Foreign Policy*, ed. George Breslauer and Philip Tetlock (Boulder, Colorado: Westview Press, 1991), pp. 20–61.

more events separated in time agree in one respect, then they may also agree in another.[18] Analogical reasoning may be represented thus: $AX{:}BX{::}AY{:}BY$. In words, event A resembles event B in having characteristic X; A also has characteristic Y; therefore it is inferred that B also has characteristic Y. The unknown BY is inferred from the three known terms on the assumption that "a symmetrical due ratio, or proportion, exists."[19] The preceding examples of historical analogies invoked by policymakers can be expressed in this form. Consider Lodge's use of the Munich analogy: appeasement in Munich (A) occurred as a result of Western indolence (X); appeasement in Vietnam (B) is also occurring as a result of Western indolence (X). Appeasement in Munich (A) resulted in a world war (Y); therefore appeasement in Vietnam (B) will also result in a world war (Y). The unknown consequences of appeasement in Vietnam (BY) are inferred through the analogy to Munich.[20]

For some, the way Lodge and the other statesmen cited earlier used historical analogies is striking proof of the power of ideas—mistaken or otherwise—in influencing policy decisions. Stanley Hoffmann singles out this propensity on the part of U.S. decision-makers to use historical analogies as part of the American "national style."[21] In *"Lessons" of the Past: The Use and Misuse of History in American Foreign Policy*, Ernest May documents many more instances of American policymakers resorting to historical analogies, argues that their analogies have almost invariably misguided them, and suggests ways in which policymakers might learn to use history better.[22] May's view, which may be called the analytical view, because it is premised on the idea that policymakers use analogies

[18] This definition is adapted from David Hackett Fischer, *Historians' Fallacies* (New York: Harper and Row, 1970), pp. 243–59; see also Mary Hesse, *Models and Analogies in Science* (Notre Dame: University of Notre Dame Press, 1966), pp. 57–100; and Richard Purtill, *Logical Thinking* (New York: Harper and Row, 1972), pp. 70–73. Cf. Max Black, *Models and Metaphors* (Ithaca: Cornell University Press, 1962); and George Lakoff, *Metaphors We Live By* (Chicago: University of Chicago Press, 1980). For an insightful political analysis of the differences between analogies and metaphors, see Elliot Zashin and Philip Chapman, "The Uses of Metaphor and Analogy: Toward a Renewal of Political Language," *Journal of Politics* 36 (1974): 290–326.

[19] Fischer, *Historians' Fallacies*, p. 243.

[20] As another example, consider British Prime Minister Anthony Eden's communication to President Eisenhower in which he compared Nasser to Hitler: Hitler's occupation of the Rhineland (A) and Nasser's seizure of the Suez Canal (B) are both opening gambits in a larger plot (X); Hitler's actions (A) led to "acts of aggression against the West" (Y); Nasser's actions (B) are also likely to lead to future acts of aggression against the West (Y). The unknown (BY)—the consequences of Nasser's actions—was inferred via the analogy to Hitler. See Eden, *Full Circle*, pp. 519–20. This definitional exercise will also be performed on the Korean analogy later.

[21] Stanley Hoffmann, *Gulliver's Troubles, or the Setting of American Foreign Policy*. New York: McGraw-Hill, 1968.

[22] May, *"Lessons" of the Past*, pp. ix–xiv.

to analyze or make sense of their foreign policy dilemmas, has found corroboration in the works of Robert Jervis, Glenn Snyder, Paul Diesing, Yaacov Vertzberger, and Deborah Larson.[23]

Others accept the finding that policymakers often resort to history but are skeptical about the claim that statesmen use analogies for policy guidance or analysis. The problem for these skeptics is aptly summarized by Arthur Schlesinger in his otherwise favorable review of May's book. For Schlesinger, "The past is an enormous grab bag with a prize for everybody. The issue of history as rationalization somewhat diminishes the force of the argument that history is per se a powerful formal determinant of policy."[24] Skeptics argue that analogies are used more for justification and advocacy than for analysis.[25] In this view, Aguirre, Lodge, and Deng were all using the lessons of history to justify and to advocate, before an audience, policy choices they had already made. The issue as Schlesinger sees it is that "the historian can never be sure—the statesman himself cannot be sure—to what extent the invocation of history is no more than a means of dignifying a conclusion already reached on other grounds."[26] If this is the case, one cannot conclude that the analogies policymakers invoke genuinely explain their policy choices. Still other critics—mainly

[23] Robert Jervis, *Perception and Misperception*, chap. 6; Glenn Snyder and Paul Diesing, *Conflict among Nations* (Princeton: Princeton University Press, 1977), chap. 4; Yaacov Vertzberger, "Foreign Policy Decisionmakers as Practical-Intuitive Historians: Applied History and Its Shortcomings," *International Studies Quarterly* 30 (1986): 223–47; and Deborah Welch Larson, *Origins of Containment: A Psychological Explanation* (Princeton: Princeton University Press, 1985), pp. 50–57, 350–51.

[24] Arthur Schlesinger, review of *"Lessons" of the Past*, by Ernest May, *The Journal of American History* 61 (September 1974): 444. The skeptics' position is also ably articulated in Robert Jervis, "Political Decision Making: Recent Contributions," *Political Psychology* 2 (1980): 89–94. Although a major proponent of the analytical view, Jervis uses the skeptics' objections to critique works that simply assume that analogies or beliefs drive policy. His point is that, to be convincing, claims of analogies driving policies require theoretical as well as empirical backing.

[25] Herbert Butterfield, for example, decries "talk in 1919 of the necessity of 'avoiding the mistakes of 1815' " because "those who talked of 'avoiding the mistakes of 1815' were using history to ratify the prejudices they had already" (*History and Human Relations* [London: Collins, 1951], pp. 176–77). For an account sensitive to the use of history as "historical justification" in the Cold War era, see also Bruce Kuklick, "Tradition and Diplomatic Talent: The Case of the Cold Warriors," in *Recycling the Past: Popular Uses of American History*, ed. Leila Zenderland (Philadelphia: University of Pennsylvania Press, 1978), pp. 117, 125, 128, and 131. John K. Fairbank has also written about the susceptibility of American policymakers to exploiting history as a "grabbag from which each advocate pulls out a 'lesson' to prove his point" ("How to Deal with the Chinese Revolution," *New York Review of Books*, February 17, 1966, p. 10). See also Jack Snyder, *Myths of Empire: Domestic Politics and International Ambition* (Ithaca: Cornell University Press, 1991), chaps. 1, 6, and 7.

[26] Schlesinger, review of *"Lessons" of the Past*, p. 443.

political scientists—doubt whether it is necessary to resort to cognitive structures like historical analogies to explain the choices of policymakers when explanations centering on the constraints imposed by the international system might suffice.[27]

I believe the objections of these skeptics are misplaced. However, I also believe that their concerns are legitimate and, perhaps more important, that their questions reveal gaps in the research program on the cognitive sources of foreign policy that subsequent research may fill. The unifying theme of previous works on the relationship between the lessons of history and policy has been that statesmen frequently turn to historical analogies for guidance when confronted with novel foreign policy problems, that they usually pick inappropriate analogies, and as a result, make bad policies.[28] The emphasis has therefore been on documenting instances of such "misuse" in as many issue areas as possible and on devising techniques to enable policymakers to use history more wisely.[29]

This emphasis has had a price, for little attention has been paid to how historical analogies, once invoked, influence the actual selection of policy options. The link between analogies used and options chosen is always implied but seldom rigorously demonstrated in earlier studies. Yet it is precisely this link that the skeptics deny. Earlier studies do not focus on this link because they emphasize and answer a different "how" question: "How well are analogies used?" As I have indicated, "Not very well," has been the dominant answer. For the skeptics, this focus is premature because it avoids the other more basic and therefore important "how" question, namely, how do analogies actually influence the selection of policy options? As a question about mechanism or process, this is logically prior to the "how well" question; unless one first answers the question of whether and how the analogies in question affect the selection of policy, there is not much point in making the assessment that the analogies are

[27] See Arnold Wolfers, *Discord and Collaboration* (Baltimore, Maryland: Johns Hopkins University Press, 1962), pp. 3–23; Kenneth Waltz, *Theory of International Politics* (Reading, Massachusetts: Addison-Wesley, 1979), chap. 8. For excellent discussions and critiques of the "systemic constraints" argument, see also Jervis, *Perception and Misperception*, pp. 14–21; Larson, *Containment*, pp. 18–23; and Ole Holsti, "Foreign Policy Decision-Makers Viewed Psychologically: Cognitive Processes Approached," in *Thought and Action in Foreign Policy*, ed. G. Matthew Bonham and Michael Shapiro (Basel, Stuttgart: Birkhauser, 1977), esp. pp. 21–25.

[28] This is the consensus view among political scientists and historians who have investigated the relationship between the "lessons of history" and policy-making. See May, *"Lessons" of the Past*, esp. pp. ix–xi and chaps. 1–4; Hoffmann, *Gulliver's Troubles*, esp. pp. 124–43; Lowenthal, *The Dominican Intervention*, pp. 153–62; Jervis, *Perception and Misperception*, chap. 6; Snyder and Diesing, *Conflict among Nations*, p. 321; Larson, *Containment*, pp. 332–39; and Vertzberger, "Foreign Policy Decisionmakers," pp. 223–47.

[29] May, *"Lessons" of the Past*, chaps. 5–7, and Neustadt and May, *Thinking in Time*, provide careful and systematic advice on better ways of using history.

used badly.[30] That is, if analogies do not affect the decision outcome, it does not matter if they are used badly or wisely.

Hence the challenge—a challenge that can be inferred from the skeptics' position—to those who posit such a causal link: specify what it is that historical analogies do and demonstrate how, if at all, such tasks influence decision outcomes. I take up this challenge in this book. Taking from earlier works the cue that analogies are used for analysis, I specify what those analytic tasks are and how they are interrelated, and I organize them into a coherent framework. For the sake of brevity, I shall call this the AE (Analogical Explanation) framework. Simply stated, the AE framework suggests that analogies are cognitive devices that "help" policymakers perform six diagnostic tasks central to political decision-making. Analogies (1) help define the nature of the situation confronting the policymaker, (2) help assess the stakes, and (3) provide prescriptions. They help evaluate alternative options by (4) predicting their chances of success, (5) evaluating their moral rightness, and (6) warning about dangers associated with the options.[31]

Since the test of any framework is how well it illuminates concrete issues, the AE framework will be used in chapters 5, 6, and 7 to elucidate American decision-making during the Vietnam War. I provide reasons for this choice, and I elaborate on the decision outcomes I wish to explain in chapter 3; here it suffices to note that in addition to its substantive importance, Vietnam decision-making would seem to be a "most likely" case for the skeptics' hypothesis that analogies are used for justification and advocacy and a "least likely" case for my hypothesis that analogies

[30] Neither is there much point to asking questions such as from where do policymakers get their analogies? How is the "appropriate" analogy cued in a given instance? These questions become interesting only when we succeed in establishing that analogies do affect the decision outcomes.

[31] See Richard Snyder, H. W. Bruck, and Burton Sapin, *Foreign Policy Decision-Making: An Approach to the Study of International Politics* (New York: Free Press, 1962), and Glenn Paige, *The Korean Decision: June 24–30, 1950* (New York: Free Press, 1968), for early discussions that touch on some of these themes. Charles Powell, James Dyson, and Helen Purkitt make an eloquent case for examining such cognitive processes in "Opening the 'Black Box': Cognitive Processing and Optimal Choice in Foreign Policy Decision Making," in *New Directions in the Study of Foreign Policy*, ed. Charles Hermann, Charles Kegley, and James Rosenau (Boston: Allen and Unwin, 1987), pp. 203–20. For more recent discussions on analogies and these functions, see my "Seduction by Analogy in Vietnam: The Malaya and Korea Analogies," in *Institutions and Leadership: Prospects for the Future*, ed. Kenneth Thompson (Lanham, Maryland: University Press of America, 1987), pp. 65–77; Vertzberger, "Foreign Policy Decisionmakers," and Dwain Mefford, "Analogical Reasoning and the Definition of the Situation: Back to Synder for Concepts and Forward to Artificial Intelligence for Method," in Hermann, Kegley, and Rosenau, *New Directions*, pp. 221–44.

influence decision outcomes.[32] This is so because such a large number of analogies were invoked so publicly, frequently, and indiscriminately by Vietnam decision-makers that even those sympathetic to the analogical explanation may want to begin by taking the skeptics' claims seriously.[33]

Yet I shall argue that the AE framework, when applied to the analogies invoked by America's Vietnam decision-makers, succeeds in accounting for the Vietnam decisions of 1965 at a level of precision not achieved by other explanations. Specifically, I suggest that the Korean and Munich analogies—or rather, the lessons the policymakers drew from these historical parallels—predisposed them toward military intervention in Vietnam. In particular, the lessons of Korea had an especially powerful influence on Vietnam decision-making because they not only predisposed the policymakers toward intervention but also predisposed them toward selecting a specific option among the several prointervention options. The Korean analogy, in other words, shaped the *form* as well as the fact of the U.S. intervention.

In this sense, the Korean analogy had a more decisive impact than the Munich analogy in the making of the Vietnam decisions of 1965. If Korea and Munich shaped the perceptions of the most senior decision-makers and predisposed them to favor intervention, the French experience in Vietnam during the 1950s suggested to others that Vietnam was an unwinnable war and that it was therefore essential for the United States to cut its losses and withdraw instead of taking over the fighting from the South Vietnamese. By teasing out the specific analytic tasks performed by these analogies and by showing how, for example, the French, Korean, and Munich analogies led to different policy preferences, the AE framework shows how analogies matter in foreign policy decision-making. Much of this book is devoted to this enterprise.

Insofar as I succeed in demonstrating that historical analogies affected the selection of America's Vietnam options, it becomes meaningful and

[32] Like most researchers who choose small *N* studies, I have been influenced by Harry Eckstein's seminal discussion of how crucial cases can be used for theory building. Eckstein considers the "most likely" and "least likely" cases as crucial cases: the former seem "especially tailored" to invalidation and the latter to confirmation. See Eckstein, "Case Study and Theory in Political Science," in *Handbook of Political Science*, vol. 7, *Strategies of Inquiry*, ed. Fred Greenstein and Nelson Polsby (Reading, Massachusetts: Addison-Wesley, 1975), pp. 113–20. Thus if Vietnam decision-making were a most likely case for the skeptics' hypothesis that analogies are used primarily for justification, finding that analogies actually played a major diagnostic role in policymaking would constitute a decisive invalidation of the skeptics' hypothesis. The same finding, however, would give strong confirmation to the analytical view if Vietnam were a "least likely" case for the analytical view.

[33] This description is applicable to the majority of public speeches and interviews given by senior administration officials from 1965 to 1967. For samples, see the issues of the *Department of State Bulletin* for January 18, 1965, March 21, 1966, and September 18, 1967.

interesting to address a second question: the question of how well analogies were used. As chapters 5, 6, and 7 will show, the way U.S. policymakers picked and used analogies and the way they responded to critics of their analogies suggest that they did not use analogies well. Analogical reasoning during the Vietnam War thus confirms a central finding of previous research on the relationship between history and policy: decision-makers often use history badly.[34] More often than not, decision-makers invoke inappropriate analogues that not only fail to illuminate the new situation but also mislead by emphasizing superficial and irrelevant parallels. Inasmuch as such analogies influence decisions, they are deemed to be at least partially responsible for costly or failed policies. The task now is to explain this observed pattern of poor use of analogies.[35]

An explanation is needed because, for those who see a causal link between analogies and policy, the finding that policymakers are so often misled by their analogies is puzzling. Why are they so easily misled, and if the record is so sorry, why do they continue to rely on historical analogies? For the skeptics, these facts are not in need of explanation. They are consistent with their view that analogies are used to justify and to advocate, not to analyze. Insofar as superficial similarities between the analogy invoked and the new situation exist, what matters from the skeptics' perspective is how effective the analogy will be in convincing others. Therefore it is not surprising that the analogies invoked are often the ones that are the most obvious and the most superficial.

Hence the skeptics' second challenge: explain the observed tendency of policymakers to use analogies poorly and recurrently. The traditional response to the question is that policymakers are poor historians: they do not know enough history, their repertoire of plausible historical parallels is limited, and consequently, they pick and apply the wrong analogies.[36] This answer also implies a certain cure. That is, if only policymakers know more history, if only techniques could be developed to enable policymakers and their staff to identify misleading parallels and to bring them to their superiors' attention, the latter might be able to use history more successfully.[37]

The problem, I suspect, is deeper. For if policymakers of diverse historical depth across administrations seem, on average, to use analogies

[34] See note 28 above.

[35] One may of course argue that because of my selection of Vietnam, the conclusion that analogies were used badly was predetermined. But that is precisely the point: the case of the Vietnam War fits the consensus view that policymakers usually use analogies badly. In choosing an especially vivid case of a general pattern, I can concentrate on examining why rather than whether decision-makers used analogies poorly. I am less interested in dwelling on the normative dangers of the pattern than I am in explaining it.

[36] May, *"Lessons" of the Past*, pp. xi, 18, 50–51, 86, 116–21.

[37] Ibid., esp. chaps. 5–7; Neustadt and May, *Thinking in Time*, is devoted to teaching others how to use history more astutely.

poorly, something systemic—something about the process of analogical reasoning itself—is likely to be at work. My analysis of how analogies figure in the private deliberations of America's Vietnam policymakers supports this notion. It suggests that the issue is only partly how knowledgeable or analytically careful the relevant cast of decision-makers was. Those who dominated Vietnam decision-making in the 1960s were intellectually serious individuals. As a whole, they probably knew more about history and politics than any other comparable group of decision-makers before or after the 1960s. Some of them, including Dean Rusk, McGeorge Bundy, Walt Rostow, Arthur Schlesinger, and James Thomson had taught those subjects before assuming power; others, including George Ball and William Bundy, were certainly more historically conscious than the average career official. For these reasons one of the most perceptive accounts of how America came to be involved in Vietnam refers to the policymakers of the 1960s as "the best and the brightest."[38] Yet these individuals picked and used analogies in ways as confident, undiscriminating, and erroneous as the policymakers cited in the works of May, Jervis, Snyder and Diesing, and Vertzberger.

The second purpose of this book is to explain why policymakers often use analogies poorly, the Vietnam policymakers being cases in point. In contrast to the political explanation provided by the skeptics, and to explanations focusing on deficient historical knowledge, I propose an explanation that focuses on the processes of analogical reasoning. The basic idea is that there is something about the psychology of analogical reasoning that makes it difficult, though not impossible, to use historical analogies properly in foreign affairs.

The psychology of analogical reasoning begins with the idea that human beings are creatures with limited cognitive capacities. As a result, a means by which they cope with the enormous amount of information they encounter is reliance on "knowledge structures" such as analogies or schemas.[39] These knowledge structures help them order, interpret, and simplify, in a word, to make sense of their environment. Matching each new instance with instances stored in memory is then a major way human beings comprehend their world.[40]

[38] David Halberstam, *The Best and the Brightest* (New York: Random House, 1972).

[39] Richard Nisbett and Lee Ross, *Human Inference: Strategies and Shortcomings of Social Judgment* (Englewood Cliffs, New Jersey: Prentice-Hall, 1980), pp. 28–42; Robert Abelson and John Black, introduction, in *Knowledge Structures*, ed. James Galambos, Robert Abelson, and John Black (Hillsdale, New Jersey: Lawrence Erlbaum Associates, 1986), pp. 1–20; Hazel Markus and R. B. Zajonc, "The Cognitive Perspective in Social Psychology," in *The Handbook of Social Psychology*, vol. 1, *Theory and Method*, ed. Gardner Lindzey and Elliot Aronson (New York: Random House, 1985), pp. 142–50.

[40] David Rumelhart and Andrew Ortony, "The Representation of Knowledge in Memory," in *Schooling and the Acquisition of Knowledge*, ed. Richard Anders, Rand Spiro, and

This view of human beings as engaged in continuous analogical reasoning in order to make sense of their world fits hand in glove with the AE framework developed earlier; in fact, it corroborates and encompasses the key assumptions of the framework. The psychological approach's strong point is that its emphasis on the centrality of knowledge structures such as analogies and schemas to human comprehension and its postulates about the systematic biases associated with analogical or schematic information processing are experimentally based.[41] In other words, and in contrast to the skeptics' views, psychological theories suggest that there are compelling cognitive reasons why human beings resort to analogies, for information processing and comprehension, and that there are also identifiable and systematic biases associated with the process. Because these arguments are borne out by rigorous experimental tests, they have greater credence than the plausible but untested view of analogies advanced by the skeptics, namely, that the functions of analogies are limited to justification and advocacy.

In addition to adopting the assumption that to help make sense of reality human beings match new instances with old instances—analogies or schemas—stored in memory, I use two sets of key findings from the social cognitive psychological research program to explain why policymakers often use analogies recurrently and suboptimally. The first set of findings focuses on how analogies are picked or accessed: the key finding here is that people tend to access analogies on the basis of surface similarities. The second set of findings concerns the nature of analogical or schematic processing. Once the analogy or schema is accessed, it (1) allows the perceiver to go beyond the information given, (2) processes information "top-down," and (3) can lead to the phenomenon of perseverance. These two sets of findings suggest that the process of analogical reasoning involves cognitive mechanisms and inferential steps that may lead to simplistic and mistaken interpretations of the incoming stimuli.[42]

Using the psychology of analogical reasoning to explain why policymakers do not use analogies well leads to implications that are at odds with conventional wisdom. They suggest that the problem lies less with a fail-

---

William Montague (Hillsdale, New Jersey: Lawrence Erlbaum Associates, 1977); Terry Winograd, "A Framework for Understanding Discourse," in *Cognitive Processes in Comprehension*, ed. Marcel Just and Patricia Carpenter (Hillsdale, New Jersey: Lawrence Erlbaum Associates, 1977); Markus and Zajonc, "The Cognitive Perspective," p. 169.

[41] For a summary of the major experiments and findings pertaining to schematic processing and analogical problem solving see Markus and Zajonc, "The Cognitive Perspective," and Stella Vosniadou and Andrew Ortony, eds., *Similarity and Analogical Reasoning* (Cambridge: Cambridge University Press, 1989).

[42] To be sure, there are also cognitive mechanisms such as "bottom-up" processing and schema change that might counter or mitigate these effects. They will be discussed in chap. 8.

ure of intellect than with the psychological processes associated with the way humans pick analogies and use them to process information. The problem lies with the very process of analogical reasoning; therefore, attempts to devise techniques to teach policymakers how to use analogies more wisely face greater and more severe obstacles than has been acknowledged.[43]

Throughout this section, I have used the arguments of the skeptics to identify and probe gaps in the existing literature on the relationship between history and policy. I have identified two tasks that are likely to enhance our understanding of the relationship between analogies and policy and that might advance the research program on the cognitive sources of foreign policy. First is the task of specifying precisely what analogies do and applying it to explain a set of important decisions; second is the task of providing an explanation for the finding that policymakers often use analogies badly. I have outlined how I shall attempt to approach these tasks and answer these questions; in the next chapter, I elaborate on my answers.

Some final remarks on the skeptics' position are in order. I claimed earlier that although the questions raised by the skeptics are legitimate, their objections are, in the final analysis, misplaced. I should explain why. The skeptics' arguments are ultimately misplaced because their view of the relationship between analogies and policy is unduly restrictive. Their view of the role of analogies in foreign policy decision-making is strictly instrumental; that is, they claim that policymakers arrive at a decision and then use analogies to dignify or advocate their decision.[44] The view is thus an intensely political one, of decision-makers obliged to persuade others, using analogies as the instruments in that process. The cogency of this view depends in large part on denying that analogies may actually serve a cognitive and/or diagnostic function, i.e., as aids to help analyze and process information and thereby help policymakers arrive at their decisions.

If the cognitive psychologists are correct in their claim that analogical reasoning is central to understanding new situations, the skeptics' denial

[43] Cf. Neustadt and May, *Thinking in Time*; May, *"Lessons" of the Past*.

[44] Even when analogies are used for advocacy and justification, it does not follow that they will have no impact on the decision outcome. Advocacy may in fact help create the consensus that central decision-makers desire and in that sense make certain alternatives more acceptable than others. Similarly, Paul Anderson has found that the need to justify foreign policy decisions (by referring to precedents, for example) constrains what policymakers consider as acceptable policy ("Justifications and Precedents as Constraints in Foreign Policy Decision-Making," *American Journal of Political Science* 25 [1981]: 738–61). Both these phenomena are worthy of investigation; this book, however, focuses on the more fundamental issues of how policymakers come to define and assess the problems they face and how such assessments affect their policy choices.

of a cognitive role for historical analogies is untenable. What is needed is a perspective that allows an independent cognitive role for analogies in decision-making without denying that they may also play an instrumental role in persuading and convincing others in the policy process. The AE framework, buttressed by the findings of cognitive psychology, is such a perspective.

The cogency of the AE view does not depend on denying the use of analogies in justification and advocacy; in fact, it allows it, for policymakers who are influenced by the lessons of history in arriving at their decisions can be expected to use those same lessons to advance their policy preferences. What is critical is that insofar as analogies play a role in informing policymakers' diagnoses of the situation and of their policy options, it becomes possible for the analyst to begin to understand their choices. The fact that policymakers use the same analogies to *justify* their choices does not vitiate the diagnostic role of the analogies in helping the policymakers *arrive* at those choices. Thus Secretary of State Dean Rusk, who used more historical analogies than most others during the Vietnam conflict, spoke of "advocacy with integrity," by which he meant his willingness to use the very lessons of history that informed his thinking about Vietnam to persuade his colleagues and Congress that it was necessary for the United States to fight and to fight in a certain way there. Rusk challenged his critics to find any instance in which he "thought one thing and said another."[45]

Skeptics are right to warn against inferring too much from a policymaker's analogies on the basis of their mere invocation. Arthur Schlesinger's earlier remark that at some point the decision-maker himself may no longer know whether history is used to dignify decisions reached on other grounds is well taken. It suggests the importance of seeking and finding in the empirical record evidence of repeated use of the same set of analogies over time before granting plausibility to the analogical explanation. Such a pattern of use may not always be apparent, since analogies may have played important roles in crisis situations such as the Cuban missile crisis and the Dominican Republic intervention, even though they were invoked sparingly. However, in cases such as Vietnam, when decision-makers had more time and deliberated more often, it is fair to expect repeated private use. Analogies that surface recurrently in the policy formulation and deliberative stages are less likely to be used to "dignify decisions reached on other grounds" than analogies used once or twice in a NSC meeting.

Schlesinger's remark, however, is also telling in ways that he may not have anticipated. It points to a final weakness of the skeptics' position,

[45] Interview with author, Athens, Georgia, August 21, 1986.

that is, that their position begs the question: Just what are these "other grounds"? For those who assume that analogies play diagnostic roles, the grounds on which a decision is reached can be partially inferred from the analogies invoked, when and if they are invoked. When the latter occurs, an analysis of the policymakers' analogies is likely to shed light on their decision-making. Skeptics doubt that the policymakers' analogies tell us much about their decisions, but they (the skeptics) fail to identify the other grounds that supposedly tell us more. Without a theory specifying what those other grounds are, the skeptics' position, is, in the final analysis, unhelpful.

But it may be useful, for the purposes of contrast, to fill in for the skeptics what those "other grounds" might be, given their perspective. In searching for nonanalogical explanations for the Vietnam War, one may pick from a variety of alternatives. In this book I consider four such explanations proposed for the Vietnam decisions of 1965: containment, political-military ideology (along a hawk-dove spectrum), bureaucratic politics, and domestic political considerations. I assume these explanations are the most plausible other grounds that the skeptics can provide. In chapter 7, I contrast each of these explanations with the analogical explanation; the latter is strengthened to the extent that I can show that these "other grounds" cannot explain the decisions of 1965 as well as it can.[46]

I have assumed throughout that there exists a broad category of political scientists and historians who have either voiced the objections of the skeptics or who share their sentiments.[47] The picture of the skeptics I have presented is necessarily a composite one, and it may not fit any particular analyst, but I believe my summary of their positions is representative of the general orientation of those cited; it is certainly representative of the questions raised by many thoughtful students of international relations to earlier versions of my argument. Nonetheless, to the reader who remains doubtful whether anyone or any group really holds

[46] Note, however, that I have not chosen to organize this work around the systematic testing of competing explanations of Vietnam. While I do try to specify what the various competing "theories" claim, infer propositions about what to expect from them, and "test" these propositions against my case study, I consider the exercise more suggestive than conclusive. Explicit and systematic testing of theory is not the purpose of this book in part because the rival "theories" are all underspecified. My main purposes are first, to develop, extend, and revise the analytical view of history's effect on foreign policy first articulated by Hoffmann, May, and others, and second, to spell out the implications of this revised view (the AE framework). I illustrate the utility of my framework by applying it to Vietnam decision-making.

[47] See note 25 above, esp. Snyder, *Myths of Empire*, chaps. 1, 6, and 7.

the views I have labeled as belonging to the skeptics, I suggest that my use of the skeptics' arguments be seen as a heuristic device used to generate a set of questions that I consider worth asking and answering. The significance of the questions and the quality of the answers can be assessed independently of the way the questions were generated.

CHAPTER 2

The AE Framework

> Not ideas, but material and ideal interests, directly govern men's conduct. Yet very frequently the "world images" that have been created by "ideas" have, like switchmen, determined the tracks along which action has been pushed by the dynamic of interest.
> —*Max Weber*, The Social Psychology of the World Religions

WEBER'S SENTIMENT about the importance of ideas has always had a sympathetic, if small, following among contemporary analysts of international politics. What keeps the coterie of analysts who actively pursue this research program small, I suspect, is that while it is easy to acknowledge that ideas and images can guide the tracks of foreign policy action, it is difficult to indicate precisely how ideas translate into decision outcomes.[1] Alexander George's work on the "Operational Code," in my view, comes closest to showing how one might theorize about the precise ways in which ideas affect policy. In his influential 1969 article, "The 'Operational Code': A Neglected Approach to the Study of Political Leaders and Decision-Making," George argued that the systematic study of

[1] Peter Hall summarizes this issue aptly when he writes, "Even those who seek to expose the bare conflicts of interest hidden behind political rhetoric or historical nostalgia admit that ideas play an important role in affairs of state. But that role is not easily described" (Introduction, *The Political Power of Economic Ideas: Keynesianism across Nations*, ed. Peter Hall [Princeton: Princeton University Press, 1989], p. 4). In addition to the Hall volume, some recent works that focus on the role of ideas in the international political economy include Ernst B. Haas, *When Knowledge is Power: Three Models of Change in International Organizations* (Berkeley: University of California Press, 1990); Judith Goldstein, "The Impact of Ideas on Trade Policy: The Origins of U.S. Agricultural and Manufacturing Policies," *International Organization* 43 (1989): 31–72; and John Odell, *U.S. International Monetary Policy* (Princeton: Princeton University Press, 1982). For the role of ideas in the military security sphere, see Aaron L. Friedberg, *The Weary Titan: Britain and the Experience of Relative Decline, 1895–1905* (Princeton: Princeton University Press, 1988); Shafer, *Deadly Paradigms*; and Larson, *Containment*.

the ideological precepts of political leaders could shed much light on their foreign policy behavior.[2] What made the article theoretically important was that George went beyond stating that beliefs influenced behavior; he resurrected the notion of the "Operational Code" from Nathan Leites' *A Study of Bolshevism*, refined and systematized it, and came up with a set of questions by which the Code could be defined.[3]

Five questions, ranging from whether politics was perceived by political elites to be a harmonious or conflictual enterprise, to the role of chance in human affairs, tapped policymakers' philosophical beliefs. A second set of questions, ranging from how best to set one's goals to the best timing of action to advance one's interests, defined the instrumental beliefs of a political leader. According to George, the answers to these questions enables us to tap the policy-relevant beliefs of statesmen and thus to obtain a sense of their policy dispositions.

In this book I do to analogies what George did to *A Study of Bolshevism*. George asked the question, How can the beliefs of the Soviet Politburo, so painstakingly documented in Leites' massive tome, be simplified, organized, and systematized so that it can be used to explain their foreign policy? Following George, I ask the question, How can the numerous ways in which historical analogies have been used by decision-makers, documented so well by May, Jervis, and others, be systematized and simplified so that they can be used to explain foreign policy decisions?

Analogies, I suggest, can be viewed as intellectual devices often called upon by policymakers to perform a set of diagnostic tasks relevant to political decision-making. Six of these tasks are especially important. First and foremost, analogies "help" define the nature of the problem or situation confronting the policymaker by comparing the new situation to previous situations with which the policymaker is more familiar.[4] This comparison highlights the similarities between the two situations and downplays their differences. Once the new situation is partially or wholly defined in terms of a previous situation, the second and third diagnostic tasks follow: analogies give the policymaker a sense of the political stakes

[2] Alexander George, "The 'Operational Code': A Neglected Approach to the Study of Political Leaders and Decision-Making," *International Studies Quarterly* 13 (1969): 190–222.

[3] Nathan Leites, *A Study of Bolshevism* (Glencoe, Illinois: Free Press, 1953).

[4] Cf. Snyder, Bruck, and Sapin, *Foreign Policy Decision-Making*. Snyder, Bruck, and Sapin were among the first to treat "situation definition" as an important variable in understanding foreign policy decision-making; however, they did not specify the possible sources of this variable. See Charles Hermann and Gregory Peacock, "The Evolution and Future of Theoretical Research in the Comparative Study of Foreign Policy," in Hermann, Kegley, and Rosenau, *New Directions*, pp. 22–23.

involved, and they also imply or suggest possible solutions to the problem so defined.[5]

These three tasks and their interrelationships can be easily discerned in the cases of Aguirre and Deng Xiaoping, the first and last examples cited in chapter 1. Aguirre was faced with the dilemma of whether to obey orders to discontinue the expedition or to defy orders and continue on his own. Remembering Cortez's "founding" of Mexico allowed him to liken his situation to that of Cortez's; once that was done, the stakes—personal fame and glory—became clear, as did the implied solution: defy orders and continue, as Cortez did. Similarly, the student demonstrations in Tiananmen reminded Deng Xiaoping of the beginnings of the Cultural Revolution. This assessment of the nature of the situation suggested that the political stakes were extremely high—the violent upheavals of 1966–1976 might return, and Deng might lose power again—and it also implied that suppression might be his only option. The point here is straightforward: the first three diagnostic tasks I attribute to historical analogies—defining the situation, stake assessment, and implicit policy prescription—are connected to or imply one another, with the first normally controlling the content of the second and the third.

The fourth, fifth, and sixth diagnostic tasks all pertain to evaluating the implicit policy prescribed, as well as other possible alternatives. Analogies thus "help" evaluate the implied solution or other alternatives by "predicting" their likelihood of success, "assessing" their moral rightness, and "warning" of dangers associated with them. Thus Aguirre's Mexican analogy does not merely provide an implied solution, but also predicts that this course of action is likely to succeed, since it did so for Cortez. The analogy says nothing about the morality of the action, but it does warn about the hardship and danger of continuing with the expedition. In the case of Deng, the Cultural Revolution analogy says nothing about whether the implied solution, suppression, will work; it does tell Deng that suppressing the students is morally correct (from his point of view), and it also warns of no dangers associated with this course of action.

By breaking down the concept of diagnosis into six distinct but related tasks, we can see how each task "helps" to provide the answers decision-makers need. Summing up over the six tasks, it becomes clear why analogies are such powerful diagnostic tools and why policymakers, for better or worse, are likely to find them attractive and convincing. In other words, when analogies are used to define the situation and evaluate the

[5] Studies of complex organizational decision-making have also found a close connection between problem definition and the generation of solutions. According to Robert Abelson and Ariel Levi, decision-makers "typically developed or identified alternatives *while* diagnosing the decision problem." See Abelson and Levi, "Decision Making and Decision Theory," in Lindzey and Aronson, *Handbook*, p. 272.

options in the ways indicated, they "introduce choice propensities into an actor's decision-making": they predispose the actor toward certain policy options and turn him away from others.[6] If the Mexican and Cultural Revolution analogies performed the diagnostic tasks I claim they did, it should hardly surprise us that Aguirre chose to continue the expedition and Deng Xiaoping chose to suppress the student demonstrations.

The above exercise takes as its point of departure the analytical view's notion that analogies are indeed used for diagnostic purposes by decision-makers. It develops that notion by identifying the tasks analogies perform, isolating the most important few, elaborating on them, and specifying their interrelationships. The result is a framework that identifies with some precision what policymakers are likely to use analogies for and how analogies might affect their policy choices. Of a policymaker's use of historical analogy *X* when faced with situation *Y*, the AE framework suggests that we ask the following questions: (1) How will *X* define situation *Y*? (2) What might *X* say about the stakes in situation *Y*? (3) Does *X* provide an implicit prescription about what to do concerning *Y*? In addition, what does *X* say about (4) the chances of success, (5) the morality, and (6) the risks of its implied prescription or other alternatives put forward to deal with *Y*? Analogy *X* may not provide answers to all of these questions, but it usually answers enough of them to give content to the framework. When it does so, the framework can shed light on the policymaker's dispositions.

A major advantage of this framework is that it captures the versatility and therefore the power of analogical reasoning better than the analytical view. It does so by attributing to analogies multiple diagnostic functions, a notion that is absent or undeveloped in the analytical view. I will illustrate this point by considering one of the best documented and most widely cited instance of how analogies affect policy, Harry Truman's likening North Korea's invasion of South Korea in June 1950 to the events of the 1930s.[7] Before the invasion, the consensus among U.S. policymakers from Truman to Acheson to the Joint Chiefs of Staff was that Korea lay outside the "defense perimeter" of the United States. Why then did Truman reverse stated U.S. policy in the wake of the North Korean invasion? According to Ernest May, Truman's "beliefs about recent history" must have been "determinative."[8] In Truman's own words:

[6] The cited phrase is from Alexander George, "The Causal Nexus between Cognitive Beliefs and Decision-Making Behavior: The 'Operational Code' Belief System," in *Psychological Models in International Politics*, ed. Lawrence Falkowski (Boulder, Colorado: Westview Press, 1979), p. 112.

[7] May, *"Lessons" of the Past*, pp. 81–82; Paige, *The Korean Decision*, pp. 114, 178; Jervis, *Perception and Misperception*, p. 218; and Neustadt and May, *Thinking in Time*, p. 36.

[8] May, *"Lessons" of the Past*, p. 80.

> I had time to think aboard the plane. In my generation, this was not the first occasion when the strong had attacked the weak. I recalled some earlier instances: Manchuria, Ethiopia, Austria. I remembered how each time that the democracies failed to act it had encouraged the aggressors to keep going ahead. Communism was acting in Korea just as Hitler, Mussolini, and the Japanese had acted ten, fifteen, and twenty years earlier. . . . If this was allowed to go on unchallenged it would mean a third world war, just as similar incidents had brought on a second world war.[9]

Informed by the parallel of the 1930s, Truman and his advisers came to the conclusion that "refusal to repel the aggression would be nothing but 'appeasement.' And appeasement, as history has shown, would ultimately lead to war."[10] The analytical view suggests that the lessons of the 1930s convinced Truman that appeasement was bad because it would lead eventually to war. It was this reasoning that led Truman to intervene in Korea.

More can be said about the role of the lessons of the 1930s if one adopts the AE framework. How is the situation defined? In terms of the events of the 1930s. What does that tell us about the stakes as Truman was likely to perceive them? Extremely high, since appeasement led to war before. Is there an implied solution? Yes, to do now what the democracies in the 1930s had failed to do: repel the aggression. What are the chances that this implied solution will work? Good—the assumption among those who took the lessons of the 1930s to heart was that Hitler could have been stopped if the West had been more resolute.[11] Is this solution moral? Undoubtedly. Are there any dangers associated with this solution? The answer is unclear or negative, since intervention was not tried in the 1930s. This series of questions, based on the hypothesis that analogies are capable of performing multiple, interdependent diagnostic tasks, lends a certain order and clarity to the phenomenon of analogical reasoning that is absent or only implicit in the analytical view.

The framework makes the process of analogical reasoning comprehensible in its entirety. Perhaps more important, it also demonstrates the diagnostic powers of the historical analogy, the sum of which seems greater than its parts. By this I mean the lessons of the 1930s did not merely suggest to Truman that appeasement was wrong and therefore needed to be stopped; they also suggested—and this can be teased out

[9] Truman, *Memoirs*, 2:332–33.

[10] Paige, *The Korean Decision*, p. 171.

[11] Dean Rusk, interview with author, Athens, Georgia, August 21, 1986. Whether taking a firm stance against Hitler in 1938 would have actually stopped him and prevented World War II remains a controversial issue. Recent historiography suggests that Hitler might have preferred war earlier (1938) rather than later. See Gerhard Weinberg, "Munich After Fifty Years," *Foreign Affairs* 67 (1988): 165–78.

through the framework above—that the stakes in Korea were exceedingly high, that the North Koreans and their Soviet sponsors could be stopped, and that trying to do just that would be a profoundly moral policy. When the different diagnostic tasks all reinforce the same solution, the power of the analogy can be overwhelming. In fact, if the stakes are high enough and the goal profoundly moral, perhaps it might even be permissible to do more than restore the status quo ante. General Douglas MacArthur thought so. He took the position that stopping his troops short of the Yalu was tantamount to appeasement.[12]

It is important to note that the diagnoses relating to the implied solution, its chances of success, its morality, and its dangers need not always reinforce one another. In the case of the 1930s they did. It is conceivable that, for example, when another analogy is used, its diagnosis of the dangers associated with the solution may be in tension with its diagnosis of its chances of success. In such cases the implied solution may no longer be attractive. A modified and less dangerous form of the solution might become the preferred alternative. The ability to detect such instances is another advantage stemming from differentiating the diagnostic tasks performed by historical analogies. In chapter 5, I rely on such diagnostic tensions to explain the options selected by America's Vietnam policymakers.

THE COGNITIVE DIMENSION OF THE AE FRAMEWORK

Although the above arguments are derived without reliance on the concepts of cognitive psychology, readers familiar with the "cognitive revolution" will be quick to note that my attribution of specific diagnostic functions to analogies converges with some of the major findings of cognitive psychology. The two perspectives meet in the importance they attach to human information processing as the key to understanding behavior, and in the centrality they assign to knowledge structures such as schemas or analogies in human information processing.[13]

Cognitive psychologists have demonstrated that one major way human beings make sense of new situations is by matching them with old situations stored in memory. In the words of Richard Nisbett and Lee Ross, two leading social psychologists, "Objects and events in the phenomenal

[12] Cited in Schnabel, *Policy and Direction*, pp. 250–51.

[13] Richard Lau and David Sears, "Social Cognition and Political Cognition: The Past, the Present, and the Future," in their *Political Cognition* (Hillsdale, New Jersey: Lawrence Erlbaum Associates, 1986), pp. 347–66; Markus and Zajonc, "The Cognitive Perspective," pp. 139–51; Nisbett and Ross, *Human Inference*, pp. 17–42; Abelson and Black, *Knowledge Structures*.

world are almost never approached as if they were *sui generis* configurations but rather are assimilated into preexisting structures in the mind of the perceiver."[14] New events tend to be "assimilated into preexisting structures in the mind" because of the limited cognitive capacities of human beings. George Miller has argued that our awareness at any given moment is limited to seven plus or minus two chunks of information; Herbert Simon disagrees and contends that our short-term memory is actually limited to five plus or minus two chunks of information.[15]

The specific number of chunks need not detain us. The point is that, whether described as "cognitive misers," "satisficers," or people with "bounded rationality," human beings are assumed to have, and have been shown to have, limited computational capacities. This is the hard-core assumption of cognitive psychology.[16] Consequently, human beings have to rely on some sort of simplifying mechanism to cope and to process—to code, store, and recall—the massive amount of information they encounter in their daily lives. One major claim of cognitive psychology is that these simplifying mechanisms are to be found in knowledge structures stored in memory. Schemas, scripts, and analogies are examples of such knowledge structures, and much of cognitive psychology revolves around theorizing and testing in the laboratory propositions about how these knowledge structures are cued, how they process information, and what the implications are thereof.[17]

SCHEMAS AND ANALOGIES

Before turning to schema or script theory to illuminate the way analogies process information, we must make clear what these knowledge structures have and do not have in common. The difference between an analogy and a schema can be easily illustrated by President Truman's reasoning when North Korea invaded South Korea in 1950. For Truman, "this was not the first occasion when the strong had attacked the weak"; he

[14] Nisbett and Ross, *Human Inference*, p. 36.

[15] George Miller, "The Magical Number Seven, Plus or Minus Two: Some Limits on Our Capacity for Processing Information," *Psychological Review* 63 (1956): 81–97; Herbert Simon, "How Big Is a Chunk?" *Science* 183 (1974): 482–88.

[16] Ibid. See also Herbert Simon, *Models of Bounded Rationality*, 2 vols. (Cambridge: MIT Press, 1982); Reid Hastie, "A Primer of Information-Processing Theory for the Political Scientist," in Lau and Sears, ed., *Political Cognition*; and Lau and Sears, "Social Cognition."

[17] See Markus and Zajonc, "The Cognitive Perspective"; Reid Hastie, "A Primer"; and Lau and Sears, "Social Cognition"; and Susan Fiske and Shelley Taylor, *Social Cognition* (Reading, Massachusetts: Addison-Wesley, 1984), chap. 6.

"recalled some earlier instances: Manchuria, Ethiopia, Austria."[18] In each of these cases, the West failed to act and the aggressors continued. From these experiences, Truman arrived at the axiom that aggression unchecked means general war later.

Truman's axiom is called a schema by cognitive psychologists. A schema is a generic concept stored in memory. It may refer to objects, situations, events, or sequences of events and people.[19] A schema may also be viewed as a person's subjective "theory" about how the social or political world works. This subjective "theory" is typically derived, as the case of Truman illustrates, from "generalizing across one's experiences" in the political world.[20] The difference between a schema and an analogy is that an analogy is specific and concrete, while a schema is abstract and generic. Thus, if Truman reasoned that failure to stop North Korea would have the same consequences as Japan's invasion of Manchuria, he would be reasoning by analogy. If he abstracted from the specifics of Manchuria to form the axiom that aggression unchecked means general war later, the axiom would be a schema. As this example indicates, the difference between a schema and an analogy is not easy to discern, because their users constantly shift between the two knowledge structures or the two levels of abstraction. Neither the cognitive psychologists nor the political scientists have seen fit to distinguish strictly between the two structures; in practice, they have been used interchangeably.[21] As Hazel Markus and R. B. Zajonc put it in their review of the field of cognitive social psychology in the 1980s, "The research of the past fifteen years has made it clear. . . . that cognitive structures are more alike than they are different."[22] Schemas, scripts, and historical analogies may thus be considered knowledge structures whose functional similarities are much more impressive and pertinent than their differences. Theories advanced by cognitive psychologists on how schemas are formed, recalled, and used to

[18] Truman, *Memoirs*, 2:332–33.

[19] This is a close paraphrase of Deborah Larson's felicitous definition; see Larson, *Containment*, p. 51. For a review of the various definitions of schema, see Reid Hastie, "Schematic Principles in Human Memory," in *Social Cognition: The Ontario Symposium*, ed. Tory Higgins, C. Herman and M. Zanna (Hillsdale, New Jersey: Lawrence Erlbaum Associates, 1981), 1:39–45.

[20] Markus and Zajonc, "The Cognitive Perspective," p. 145.

[21] John H. Holland, Keith Holyoak, Richard Nisbett, and Paul Thagard, *Induction: Processes of Inference, Learning, and Discovery* (Cambridge: MIT Press, 1986), pp. 292–96; Robert Abelson, "Script Processing in Attitude Formation and Decision-Making," *Cognition and Social Behavior*, ed. John Carroll and John Paye (Hillsdale, New Jersey: Lawrence Erlbaum Associates, 1976); Abelson and Levi, "Decision Making," 1:271–73; Fiske and Taylor, *Social Cognition*, p. 148; Larson, *Containment*, pp. 50–57; and Vertzberger, "Foreign Policy Decisionmakers."

[22] Markus and Zajonc, "The Cognitive Perspective," p. 144.

process information can therefore shed light on the origins, cuing, and functions of historical analogies.

What is most important for our purposes is that research on schemas and analogies confirms the importance of these knowledge structures for apprehending reality. Schema theory, for example, holds that schemas are the "building blocks of cognition." "They are," according to David Rumelhart, "the fundamental elements upon which all information processing depends."[23] Specifically, they are necessary for interpreting sensory data, for retrieving information from memory, and for guiding the flow of processing in the system.[24] There does not yet exist a universally accepted or unified schema theory that accounts for all these aspects of information processing, and this lack has led some observers to argue that there is no such thing as schema theory.[25] In a strict sense, they are right; however, the schema concept has led to enough important and validated findings that, for the sake of convenience, it should be possible to refer to these findings as those of schema theory. More important, there is wide agreement about the centrality of the concept of the schema in modern-day studies of human information processing. In the words of Nisbett and Ross, "It has become increasingly clear to theorists working in almost all areas of psychology that the schema construct is a cornerstone of psychological theory."[26]

The advantage of adding a cognitive psychological dimension to my framework is manifest: the findings of cognitive psychology provide independent corroboration for the assumption that analogies play an important role in information processing. In my earlier discussion of the relative merits of the two contrasting views of policymakers' use of analogies, I claim that the skeptics' view, with its emphasis on justification and advocacy, begs the question of how policymakers arrive at their decisions. The analytical view, in contrast, assumes that analogies help shape policymakers' interpretation of events and in so doing, make certain options more attractive than others.[27]

[23] David Rumelhart, "Schemata: The Building Blocks of Cognition," in *Theoretical Issues in Reading Comprehension*, ed. Rand Spiro, Bertram Bruce, and William Brewer (Hillsdale, New Jersey: Lawrence Erlbaum Associates, 1980), pp. 33–34.

[24] Ibid.

[25] Hastie, "A Primer," pp. 20–22. Although Hastie argues that there is no such thing as schema theory, he acknowledges that the idea of the schema is associated with "a number of theoretical constructs. . . . that are well-defined and in common usage." Joseph Alba and Lynn Hasher are less bashful about using the term *schema theory*. See their "Is Memory Schematic?" *Psychological Bulletin* 93 (1983): 203–31.

[26] Nisbett and Ross, *Human Inference*, p. 36.

[27] There is no implication here that all policymakers will be informed by the same analogies and thus be predisposed in the same way. On the contrary, different policymakers

The notion of the schema provides strong support for the analytical view. If it is true that knowledge structures such as schemas and analogies are the fundamental elements for interpreting sensory data, for retrieving information, and for guiding human information-processing, it follows that the analytical view's assumption that analogies play an important information-processing role in foreign policy decision-making is strongly vindicated. What makes this corroboration strong, and exciting, is that it is independent: it comes from a different theoretical tradition, a tradition with research agendas and questions very different from ours. When such different research traditions, via their own paths, agree on the importance of knowledge structures such as analogies in cognition, the analytical view and, by extension, the AE framework, are buttressed.

The notion of the schema does more than provide independent corroboration for my assumption that analogies perform diagnostic functions. It also characterizes those functions in a way entirely consistent with the AE framework. Not only do schemas help human beings interpret incoming information, but they also allow them to go beyond the information given. The "default values" of the schema fill in for information missing in the incoming stimuli; thus, the schema makes a more complete picture possible.[28] The schema for "bird," for example, will have variables for color, size, beak shape, and so on. When stored in memory, "a schema has default values for all these variables, providing a prototype against which specific examples can be compared."[29] For most individuals, the prototypical bird is a robin.[30] Thus, in attempting to identify a bird, given only information about its size and color, individuals are likely to allow the default values, about beak shape, for example, to fill in for the missing information; if the size and color of the observed bird are similar to that of the robin, individuals may conclude that its beak shape is also that of a robin's and that it is, in fact, a robin.

The relevance of these notions can be seen in our example of Harry Truman pondering the appropriate U.S. response to North Korea's invasion of South Korea. Assume that Truman asked two questions: What is happening, and what is likely to happen next? For Truman, North Korea's behavior was a case of aggression, analogous to the fascist aggres-

may find different analogies salient and thus be predisposed toward different policies. Cf. chap. 5 on Korea, and 6, on Dien Bien Phu.

[28] Markus and Zajonc, "The Cognitive Perspective," p. 162; A. Tesser, "Self-generated Attitude Change," in *Advances in Experimental Social Psychology*, ed. L. Berkowitz (New York: Academic Press, 1978), 11:290; and Larson, *Containment*, pp. 51–52.

[29] Larson, *Containment*, p. 51.

[30] Eleanor Rosch, "On the Internal Structure of Perceptual and Semantic Categories," in Timothy Moore, *Cognitive Development and the Acquisition of Language* (New York: Academic Press, 1973), pp. 111–44.

sions of the 1930s. In the 1930s, appeasement led to general war; in the case of North Korea, therefore, failure to respond *might* lead to World War III.[31] With the information available in June 1950, neither Truman nor anyone could know what might be the repercussions of not stopping North Korea and its perceived sponsor, the Soviet Union. Likening the situation of 1950 to that of the 1930s, however, allowed Truman to go beyond the information given by relying on the default answer supplied by the 1930s schema: aggression unchecked is aggression unleashed.

Schema theory has allowed us to provide a general description of what analogies are capable of doing: going beyond the information given and allowing default values to fill in for missing information. It is nevertheless important to note a significant difference between this general characterization and the AE framework. According to some cognitive psychologists, schema theorists have yet to "clarify their [schemas'] properties or define the type of work they perform."[32] The AE framework goes beyond the findings of schema theorists when it isolates and specifies the six diagnostic tasks of analogies relevant to foreign policy decision-making. The argument that analogies perform such tasks as helping define the situation, assess the stakes, and prescribe policy entails a certain specificity that is absent in the schema literature.

Schema theory's description of some of these diagnostic tasks enriches the AE framework; it is useful to know that among the six tasks I claim analogies perform, many of them, such as stake assessment, implicit policy prescription, and prediction of chances of success of alternative options, will often involve going beyond the information given, thus allowing the default value of the analogy invoked to fill in for the missing information. Truman's assessment of the stakes, of the best response (counter the invasion), and of its chances of succeeding all entailed going beyond the information he had in 1950; the default values of the 1930s schema may well have filled in what information he did not have. The ability of analogies to form such inferences, according to schema theory and the AE framework, is what makes analogies such popular and powerful heuristic tools.

SCHEMAS AND THE PROCESS OF ANALOGICAL REASONING

So far, the findings of schema theorists have been used to do two things. First, to provide independent support for the idea of historical analogies

[31] Truman, *Memoirs*, 2:332–33. See also Stephen Read, "Once Is Enough: Causal Reasoning from a Single Instance," *Journal of Personality and Social Psychology* 45 (1983): 323–34.

[32] Nisbett and Ross, *Human Inference*, p. 36.

as knowledge structures that play an important role in information processing and comprehension. Second, to highlight the idea that analogical reasoning often involves going beyond the information given and using the default values of the analogy invoked to fill in for missing information. It is now possible to use schema theory to explore a third aspect of analogical reasoning in foreign affairs: What explains the recurrent tendency of policymakers to use analogies poorly? Or, more specifically, why did America's Vietnam policymakers have difficulty using analogies well? "Poor use" is defined primarily by process, that is, by the tendency of policymakers to pick the first analogies that come to mind, by their failure to search for and to seriously consider other parallels, by their neglect of potentially important differences between situations being compared, and finally, by their tendency to use analogies as substitutes for proof.[33] Poor use, therefore, implies a pattern of partial or inaccurate assessments of unfolding foreign situations, as well as dubious estimates of the costs of alternative policies. On average and over time, one would expect poor use to be associated with suboptimal policy outcomes.[34]

In focusing on poor use, I do not mean to suggest that policymakers never use analogies well. Earlier, I indicated that the World War I and "Pearl Harbor in reverse" analogies were well used during the Cuban Missile Crisis; later, I will analyze at length Under Secretary of State George Ball's use of the Dien Bien Phu analogy, which is widely regarded as an example of an appropriate and prescient use of history. The point to emphasize, however, is that researchers in this field have documented many more instances of poor use than of good use.[35] Whether the latter implies that poor use is the norm and good use the exception is an interesting question. In either case, it bears only marginally on our explanation. If poor use is the norm, our explanation will have wide applicability; if not, our explanation will be applicable only to Vietnam and to other instances of misuse documented in the literature. "Other in-

[33] The first three criteria are drawn from May, *"Lessons" of the Past*, p. xi and chaps. 1–4; Neustadt and May, *Thinking in Time*, chaps. 3–6, provide extended examples of "poor use"; see also Jervis, *Perception and Misperception*, chap. 6. The fourth criteria, committing the "fallacy of proof by analogy" is discussed in Fischer, *Historians' Fallacies*, pp. 255–57. See also pp. 209–12, 219–20, and 247–48 below.

[34] Although May, Neustadt, Jervis, and most who write about this issue are sensitive to the problem of inferring "poor use" from bad policy outcomes, they do rely, implicitly to some limited extent, on the association between poor use and poor outcomes to "check" or "confirm" their claims about who used analogies poorly when. If there were no positive relationship between poor use and bad policy outcomes, it would not be very interesting to document poor use. That poor use may sometimes still lead to good outcomes need not detract from these authors' arguments; however, if use considered poor leads repeatedly to good outcomes, the criteria and perhaps the concept itself may need to be reconsidered.

[35] See chap. 1, n. 23.

stances of misuse," one need only note, include the vast majority of the cases that *have* been investigated. Inasmuch as corroborated evidence of good analogical reasoning in foreign affairs has not been forthcoming, it is reasonable to consider poor use as the norm, or at least, as the pattern in need of explanation.

It is possible that the pattern of poor use documented by the aforementioned studies are a result of case selection biases rather than a reflection of some underlying reality.[36] That is, researchers may have chosen to examine only those cases in which policymakers picked superficial analogies, made inaccurate assessments, or experienced policy failures. Even if that is true, it will still be necessary and interesting to explain why poor use is so pervasive. However, the possibility of a serious selection bias problem seems remote for two reasons. First, the better studies avoid this pitfall by analyzing policymaking over time; instances of good use are therefore not arbitrarily excluded. Moreover, these works are also judicious in pointing out exemplary usage when it occurs.[37] Second, the most systematic analysis of whether analogies help or hinder policymakers' information processing confirms the findings of earlier studies. In their analysis of international crises from 1898 to 1973, Glenn Snyder and Paul Diesing arrive at the following conclusion about the effect of analogies on policymakers' information processing:

> No examples in our sample or elsewhere in the cases of historical analogies produced a correct interpretation of a message. Jervis's hypothesis that statesmen *usually* draw incorrect or over-generalized inferences from historical analogies is strongly confirmed. In addition, most of the overt instances in our sample are key misinterpretations that provide the initial basis for a mistaken definition of the whole crisis.[38]

The available evidence therefore strongly supports the notion that decision-makers recurrently use analogies poorly. Vietnam is a case in point: virtually all analysts of the Vietnam War agree that the decision-makers of the 1960s were ill-served by their historical analogies.[39] The

[36] I am grateful to Robert Keohane for pointing out this possibility to me.

[37] May's *"Lessons" of the Past* covers chronologically some of the most significant foreign policy events since 1945; Neustadt and May, *Thinking in Time*, chaps. 1–2, carefully notes and analyzes analogies that are well used.

[38] Snyder and Diesing, *Conflict among Nations*, p. 321, emphasis mine. Their cases were selected for possessing characteristics of bargaining behavior, not of analogical reasoning. The issue of selection bias therefore does not arise. The fact that Snyder and Diesing found impressive, though by no means universal, evidence of analogical reasoning in their sample indicates the prevalence of the phenomenon; their conclusion that analogical reasoning distorted information processing strongly reinforces the findings of May, Neustadt and May, Jervis, Vertzberger, and Larson.

[39] Ibid. See also *BDM Corporation Study*, vol. 3, chap. 2 (Lyndon Baines Johnson Li-

task now is to explain why even "the best and the brightest" had trouble using analogies well.

From where do policymakers get their lessons of history? How is the "appropriate" analogy cued in any given instance? Is there something about how analogies process information that makes reasoning by analogy hazardous? The answers to these questions will enable us to construct an explanation, and we will look to schema theory for preliminary answers. If the answers seem plausible, we will have come part of the way toward providing a comprehensive picture of the phenomenon of analogical reasoning in foreign affairs.

A caveat is in order. Though interesting, the findings of cognitive social psychology are not easy to apply to real-world political situations. The laboratory experiments that give psychology the status of a "science" also deny it wide applicability beyond the laboratory. Human beings may deviate from their laboratory behavior when confronted with real-life situations because these situations may not duplicate laboratory conditions and because the stakes involved tend to be higher.[40] Some researchers have claimed, however, that experimental findings on cognitive biases underestimate their pervasiveness in actual situations, because the information given to subjects in the laboratory is unambiguous and controlled, whereas the decision-maker must glean the relevant data from the welter of information present in real situations.[41] All the same, one should be cautious in using the findings of cognitive psychology to illuminate political decision-making. The discussion that follows should not be construed as anything more than highly suggestive.

THE ORIGINS OF THE LESSONS OF THE PAST

From where do policymakers get their historical lessons? Wars, revolutions, and other crucial political events experienced directly or vicariously by the relevant decision-makers seem to be major sources.[42] Particularly strong is the impact of major events such as the most recent war

brary); Paul Kattenburg, *The Vietnam Trauma in American Foreign Policy, 1945–75* (New Brunswick, New Jersey: Transaction Books, 1980), pp. 96–98; Arthur M. Schlesinger, Jr., *The Bitter Heritage: Vietnam and American Democracy, 1941–1966* (Boston: Houghton Mifflin, 1967), chap. 7; and Richard J. Pfeffer, ed. *No More Vietnams? The War and the Future of American Foreign Policy* (New York: Harper and Row, 1968). For a more sympathetic critique, see Leslie Gelb and Richard Betts, *The Irony of Vietnam: The System Worked* (Washington, D.C.: Brookings, 1979), pp. 197–200.

[40] See Nisbett and Ross, *Human Inference*, pp. 251–54 for a discussion of this issue.

[41] Ibid.

[42] Jervis, *Perception and Misperception*, pp. 239–71; Gelb and Betts, *Irony of Vietnam*, p. 197.

or revolution on a generation coming of age.[43] Thus the generation that fought in World War I would be anxious to avoid another "summer of 1914" when they took over the reins of power in the 1930s. Similarly, the generation that saw Munich's effect on Hitler would be attuned to the necessity of ensuring "no more Munichs" when it came to their turn to rule.

This generational hypothesis is an indispensable first cut at the problem. But it has an obvious liability: How does one account for the fact that the members of the same generation may be influenced by different historical analogies? Or for that matter, for the fact that when the members of a given generation look at the same historical event, they may derive different lessons? These questions indicate that it is probably a mistake to view policymakers of any one generation as fixated on any one historical experience. It is necessary to supplement the generational hypothesis with one that allows for some individual variation.

In thinking about how policymakers form their analogies, it is appropriate to begin with the generational analogy, thought of as a historical experience that impresses itself upon an entire generation of individuals. But the generational analogy may be reinforced or modified by or merely coexist with other historical analogies. Policymakers are also affected by lessons from personal and especially career experiences. Thus policymakers of the same generation, while always aware of and attuned to the generational analogy, will also have in store lessons of the past that relate to their individual experiences.

This view of policymakers as possessing repertoires of analogies is consistent with schema theory's assumption that human beings store in their long-term memory numerous schemas.[44] Individuals will be strongly attached to historical lessons in which generational and personal effects reinforce one another.[45] Thus, an entire generation of Europeans will re-

[43] Ibid.

[44] Markus and Zajonc, "The Cognitive Perspective," p. 164.

[45] The more frequently individual experiences reinforce generational experiences, the more likely policymakers are to abstract from them to form general axioms they will apply in a variety of situations. In schema terminology, this means that the "more often one encounters schema-relevant examples, the more abstract the schema becomes, other things being equal. This occurs because people generalize schemata from experience with instances of the category in question" (Fiske and Taylor, *Social Cognition*, p. 173). More abstract schemas, schemas at the top of the abstraction hierarchy, are more likely to be used in a variety of situations. For Keith Holyoak and Paul Thagard, "transfer is facilitated when subjects have the opportunity to form more generalized schematic representations of categories of problems" ("A Computational Model of Analogical Problem Solving," in Vosniadou and Ortony, *Similarity and Analogical Reasoning*, pp. 261–62). When the generational and personal lessons merely coexist or are at odds with one another, they are stored as different schemas and at a lower level of abstraction.

member Munich, but a British cabinet minister of the 1930s who opposed Chamberlain's appeasement policy will be especially attuned to future Munichs. The cabinet minister was of course Anthony Eden, who became prime minister in the 1950s. In the Suez crisis of 1956, it will be recalled, Eden repeatedly equated Nasser's seizure of the Suez Canal with Hitler's campaigns of the 1930s. This perception of the stakes helped convince him that a British-French response was required. When the generational and personal lessons of history reinforce one another, they are likely to overpower the unique characteristics of a new foreign policy situation.

When the generational and personal lessons coexist or contradict one another, there is more potential for analysis. In such cases, there may be more opportunities for matching the parallels and nonparallels of the new situation with the old situation. Alternatively, the contrast between the prescriptions suggested by different and contradictory analogies may alert the policymaker to trade-offs that he might not have otherwise realized. For example, although U.S. military leaders may have shared their commander in chief's and the generational lesson of preventing an Asian Munich during the Korean War, their enthusiasm for preventing Asian Munichs dwindled substantially after China's intervention and after the frustration of fighting a limited war. Many vowed "Never Again," by which they meant they would never allow the United States to fight another limited war in the Asian landmass. When the prospect of another Far Eastern Munich—the defeat of the French at Dien Bien Phu and communist domination of at least the Northern region of Vietnam—appeared in 1954, members of the "Never Again Club" took their personal lessons to President Eisenhower. Although Eisenhower and his civilian advisers did not subscribe to the full set of lessons learned by the "Never Again Club," it is probably fair to assume that they had to weigh their determination to resist aggression against the cost of another protracted land war in Asia. The lessons of Munich had to be weighed against the lessons of Korea. In his memoirs, General Matthew Ridgway, former U.S. Commander of the Eighth Army in Korea and a charter member of the "Never Again Club," takes credit for helping Eisenhower see the danger of intervening in Vietnam, namely, that it might involve the United States in a land war more dangerous and costly than even the Korean War.[46]

The most helpful way to look at the problem, then, is to view each policymaker as having a repertoire of analogies, some shared by the policymakers' generation, others more peculiar to the individual policymaker's career and personal experiences. Since the generational analogies

[46] Matthew Ridgway, *Soldier* (New York: Harper and Row, 1956), chap. 32.

and their lessons will be more widely shared than the personal analogies, it follows that the generational lessons are more likely to be taken seriously in a decision-making context.

RECALL: AVAILABILITY AND REPRESENTATIVENESS

If a decision-maker has a repertoire of historical analogies on which he may rely, the next question becomes, How is one analogy chosen over another in a given situation? To put it in terms of the decision-making of the 1960s: How would the Korean analogy be "activated," given the situation in Vietnam? Why the Korean analogy, with its implication of Soviet-Chinese instigation, instead of the Yugoslavian analogy, which would have portrayed Ho Chi Minh as an Asian Tito with his own political agenda? Historians and political scientists who study how decision-makers "learn" from the past have observed that policymakers tend to rely on the analogies that come most readily to their minds, that they are impressed by superficial similarities, and that they seldom probe more deeply or widely in search of less obvious but perhaps more relevant analogues.[47] In making these observations, the researchers have already provided a partial answer to the question of how analogies are activated. According to cognitive psychologists working on judgment heuristics and analogical problem solving, these characteristics—proclivities toward using analogies most easily recalled and most superficially similar—are also responsible for schema arousal and activation.[48]

When faced with a new situation, individuals turn to their repertoire of historical memories. Which historical event or experience is invoked depends, all other things being equal, on the ease with which it can be recalled. Daniel Kahneman and Amos Tverksy, the two foremost researchers working on judgmental heuristics, have called this the "availability heuristic": it operates when a person estimates the probability of an event by the ease with which similar instances can be recalled.[49] I will

[47] May, *"Lessons" of the Past*, pp. 16–18, 44–51, 86, and 115–21; Jervis, *Perception and Misperception*, chap. 6.

[48] Amos Tversky and Daniel Kahneman, "Judgment under Uncertainty: Heuristics and Biases," and "Availability: A Heuristic for Judging Frequency and Probability," and "Subjective Probability: A Judgment of Representativeness," in Daniel Kahneman, Paul Slovic, and Amos Tversky, eds., *Judgment under Uncertainty: Heuristics and Biases* (Cambridge: Cambridge University Press, 1982). On the importance of "surface similarities" in cuing analogies, see Dedre Gentner, "The Mechanisms of Analogical Learning," and Holyoak and Thagard, "Computational Model," in Vosniadou and Ortony, *Similarity and Analogical Reasoning*, pp. 226–29, 262–64; and Mark T. Keane, *Analogical Problem Solving* (Chichester, West Sussex: Ellis Horwood, 1988), chap. 6.

[49] Kahneman and Tversky, "Judgment under Uncertainty," pp. 11–14.

defer discussion of Kahneman and Tversky's experimental evidence until later in the book, but it is possible to state now that the availability heuristic is consistent with the idea that more recent events are easier to recall. Arguments that the most recent war exercises the most important influence on future wars are based on this recency argument: the more recent events are more "available."[50]

The availability heuristic suggests that within a given repertoire, the more recent events are more likely to be recalled. A second component in the selection of the relevant analogies involves assessing the "fit" between the incoming stimuli and the repertoire of available analogies stored in memory. The perceiver will have to make a similarity judgment, that is, a judgment of the extent to which the memory invoked fits the new situation. Kahneman and Tversky have been able to specify the rule or heuristic that people normally use in making such judgments. They found that people typically assess the probability that *A* (e.g., the challenge in Vietnam) is a *B* (e.g., communist expansionism) by relying on the representativeness heuristic, their assessment of the degree to which *A* resembles *B*. Thus if *A* is highly representative of *B*, the probability that *A* belongs to or is generated by *B* is judged to be high.[51] The question is, of course, How do people come to the judgment that *A* is highly representative of *B*? Kahneman and Tversky are not very explicit on this issue, but researchers working on analogical problem solving have found that "surface commonalities" play a critical role in accessing analogies.[52] Applied to our earlier question of the choice of the Korean analogy instead of the Yugoslavian analogy to assess the situation in Vietnam, the "surface commonalities" hypothesis suggests that the similarities shared by Vietnam and Korea—geographical proximity to China, communist ideology, a North-South divide, and a North bent on unifying the South by force—made the Korean analogy a more likely choice. Notwithstanding the fact that the Korea-Vietnam similarities were superficial and the possibility that there were deeper similarities between Yugoslavia's Tito and Vietnam's Ho Chi Minh, surface similarities seemed to play the more important role in accessing the analogy.[53]

Availability, recency, representativeness, and surface commonalities

[50] Cf. Jervis, *Perception and Misperception*, pp. 266–70.

[51] Kahneman and Tversky, "Judgment under Uncertainty," pp. 4–11.

[52] Dedre Gentner provides operational indicators of "surface similarities" in "Mechanisms," pp. 226–29; see also Holyoak and Thagard, "Computational Model," pp. 262–64.

[53] The Yugoslavian analogy suggests an important similarity between Tito and Ho Chi Minh that policymakers might have taken more seriously as they pondered U.S. options: both were less subject to Soviet influence than commonly assumed, and their independence affected their political strategies. Holyoak and Thagard use the term "structural similarity," as opposed to "surface features," to describe this kind of similarity ("Computational Model," pp. 262–63).

all provide conceptual leads as to which analogies within a given repertoire are more likely to be accessed. Admittedly, these concepts are more difficult to operationalize in real-life situations than in experimental ones. The ambiguity about their meanings in nonexperimental settings notwithstanding, I will try to show in chapter 8 that they can help identify a good number of the historical analogies actually used by decision-makers to analyze the situation in Vietnam.

INFORMATION PROCESSING BY ANALOGY: TOP-DOWN PROCESSING AND PERSEVERANCE

Once cued, analogies affect foreign policy decision-making by performing the information-processing tasks specified by the AE framework. Schema theory points to two aspects of schematic information processing that are especially relevant here: the notion that schematic information processing occurs "top-down" and the idea that schemas persevere even in the face of contradictory evidence. Top-down processing and the phenomenon of perseverance help point to and explain a pattern that has been observed, even if only anecdotally, by political scientists: policymakers are more sensitive to incoming information consistent with their analogies, they seem to have great faith in their analogies, and they persist in using their analogies even when defects have been pointed out to them.[54] This pattern of behavior, it will be seen, occurred regularly in the making of America's Vietnam policy.

The idea of top-down or "theory-driven" processing is that incoming information is compared with or fitted into existing schemas stored in memory. Top-down processing of course is not the only way human beings process information; "bottom-up" or "data-driven" processing happens just as frequently, and there is some controversy among cognitive psychologists as to which of these processes are more important when. That said, it remains true that researchers using the schema construct usually emphasize the theory-driven nature of information processing.[55] Tory Higgins and John Bargh offer the most persuasive synthesis of which process matters when:

> Features of the current environment would appear to activate or "prime" automatically the abstract constructs [schemas] that represent them, no matter what the person's processing goals during priming. . . . Once a social construct is activated by environmental data, however, it constitutes a the-

[54] Jervis, *Perception and Misperception*, chap. 4, uses the consistency principle to explain decision-makers' insensitivity to information inconsistent with their beliefs.

[55] Fiske and Taylor, *Social Cognition*, pp. 140–41.

ory-driven influence on the interpretation of subsequent environmental events.[56]

The significance of top-down processing is that information that does not fit the schema is either ignored or not given the weight it deserves. A classic experiment illustrating this tendency is the one conducted by Harold Kelley in 1950.[57] Subjects were given a seven-adjective description of a guest lecturer. One group received a description that included the word *cold* and another group the word *warm* in an otherwise identical list of traits. This simple manipulation of expectations had a profound influence on the perceptions of the subjects:

> Those expecting a "warm" instructor perceived him to be relatively sociable, informal, even-tempered, friendly and so on, and they responded accordingly by participating more actively in class. In contrast, subjects expecting a cold instructor rated the same person as relatively self-centered, unsociable, and formal, and they showed a corresponding reluctance to participate in class.[58]

The point is not that the subjects were misled by their preconceptions or that they coded the incoming information incorrectly. Rather, the point is that the subjects coded the information according to the schema already invoked. A smile by the lecturer was interpreted as a response to the class by the "warm" group, whereas it was seen as a sign of self-satisfaction by the "cold" group. When the lecturer quickened the pace of his presentation, the "warm" group read it as a sign of enthusiasm, the "cold" group as a sign of impatience.

The parallels between schematic top-down processing and analogical reasoning should be apparent. Like schemas, analogies try to fit incoming information into their mold. Discrepant information tends to be slighted or ignored; ambiguous information tends to be interpreted as supporting the expectations of the analogy. These tendencies on the part of the Vietnam decision-makers will be documented in the chapters that follow. In the absence of psychological theory, it is unclear whether the Vietnam decision-makers were using analogies especially badly or whether they were especially dense. With the help of psychological theory, it seems clear that their way of using analogies was neither especially bad nor dense, but simply in accordance with the way schemas or analogies process information.

The second aspect of schema theory that is essential to understanding

[56] "Social Cognition and Social Perception," *Annual Review of Psychology* 38 (1987): 374.

[57] Harold Kelley, "The Warm-Cold variable in First Impressions of Persons," *Journal of Personality* 18 (1950): 431–39.

[58] Nisbett and Ross, *Human Inference*, p. 68.

analogical reasoning is the perseverance effect. Schema theorists have found that individuals tend to hold on to their schemas even when confronted with contradictory information. This could have been partly anticipated from the assumptions that human beings are cognitive misers and that processing occurs top-down. Susan Fiske and Shelley Taylor explain this perseverance effect eloquently:

> Schemata facilitate information processing, for the most part, by allowing the general case to fill in for a specific example. No single example fits the schema perfectly, but most fit well enough. If people changed their schemata to fit every nuance of every new example, the information-processing advantages of schemata would be substantially lost. The perseverance effect, as it is called, describes a major feature of schemata: they often persist stubbornly even in the face of evidence to the contrary.[59]

The experiment credited for establishing this effect was conducted by Lee Ross and his colleagues in 1975.[60] Subjects were asked to perform a novel task, distinguishing between authentic and unauthentic suicide notes. Subjects were told how well they did after each trial. Later, they were "debriefed": they were informed that the rating of their performance was false. It was found that even after debriefing, subjects who were told that they were successful continued to have a high opinion of their ability at the suicide discrimination task and similar tasks involving social sensitivity. Presumably, their self-schema for social sensitivity was activated by the false rating, and despite debriefing, they continued to cling to the schema. Similarly, those who were called unsuccessful continued to rate themselves that way.

Numerous experiments along the same lines have demonstrated the same point: schemas persist in the face of contradictory evidence.[61] What is true of schemas should also be true of historical analogies: pointing out to policymakers the nonparallels between their favorite analogue and the actual situation is unlikely to erode their faith in their analogy. This phenomenon will be discussed and documented in the chapters that follow. It will be seen that in most cases in which a senior policymaker used a historical analogy, there were others who would question the validity of the analogy by pointing out important differences. None of these efforts had any impact on the senior policymakers. Without the help of psychological theory, their faith in their analogies must appear puzzling. With

[59] Fiske and Taylor, *Social Cognition*, p. 171.

[60] L. Ross, M. R. Lepper, and M. Hubbard, "Perseverance in Self-Perception and Social Perception: Biased Attributional Processes in the Debriefing Paradigm," *Journal of Personality and Social Psychology* 32 (1975): 880–92.

[61] See Nisbett and Ross, *Human Inference*, pp. 167–97, for a summary of the experimental literature.

the help of psychological theory, however, their faith in their analogies in face of evidence to the contrary is neither puzzling nor primarily a result of their denseness; it is simply routine.

In viewing historical analogies as knowledge structures that perform specific diagnostic tasks, the AE framework essentially takes an information-processing approach to understanding decision-making. If the tasks have been properly specified, the analyst should be able to judge the impact of an analogy by tracing its path in the policy process: how it led policymakers to define the situation and evaluate the options, and how those evaluations in turn led to certain policy preferences.

It is useful to conclude with two observations about the schema construct and the cognitive psychological research program from which it is derived. The first observation pertains to how novel or useful the concept is. Robert Jervis and Philip Tetlock have both warned against the uncritical appropriation of the latest psychological concepts to explain political matters. Jervis worries that emphasizing the new may result in the premature abandonment of the older theories.[62] Tetlock wonders whether some of the ways in which the schema construct is being used border on pouring old wine into new bottles.[63] These warnings are sensible and well taken. At times, it does appear that political scientists have too quickly latched on to the latest concepts without assessing their likely payoffs. Some uses of the schema concept do border on being tautological, with little gain in explanatory power.[64]

These cautionary notes are helpful because they invite the analyst to be explicit about the explanatory mileage gained through a concept such as the cognitive schema. What I consider those gains to be should be obvious by now. I use schema theory in the first instance to provide independent corroboration for the notion that analogies can be considered knowledge structures that human beings routinely use to process information. Using schema theory this way shifts the burden of disproof to the skeptics who deny that analogies play any meaningful information-processing or diagnostic role. The burden of proof has been shifted to the skeptics because the finding that knowledge structures such as schemas

[62] "Cognition and Political Behavior," in Lau and Sears, *Political Cognition*, pp. 319–36.

[63] Philip Tetlock, Review of *Political Cognition*, edited by Richard Lau and David Sears, *Political Psychology* 8 (1987): 139–40.

[64] See Lau and Sears, *Political Cognition*. Most of the essays in this pioneering volume use the schema construct to explain issues in American politics. I leave it to the reader to decide which essays succeed and which ones suffer from the problems raised by Jervis and Tetlock. For an early attempt to use the schema construct, see Robert Axelrod, "Schema Theory: An Information Processing Model of Perception and Cognition," *American Political Science Review* 67 (1973): 1248–66.

and analogies are often essential to information processing is based on rigorous experimental tests, while the skeptics' denials remain hypothetical.

In the second instance, drawing from the findings of the schema theorists allows us to characterize in more explicit, full, and informative ways some of the key functions attributed to historical analogies. Thus it is useful to know that when decision-makers rely on analogies to perform some of the tasks specified by the AE framework, they are not only going beyond the information given but are also allowing the default values of the analogies to substitute for missing information. By identifying and describing these inferential mechanisms, schema theory increases our understanding of how analogies process information and where their diagnostic powers lie. Schema theory complements and supplements the AE framework, and enriches it.

Most importantly, findings by cognitive psychologists about how schemas are retrieved and process information are used to explain several tendencies observed by students of analogical decision-making: why policymakers seem to pick superficial analogies, why they seem unreceptive to differences between their analogy and the situation being assessed, and why they cling to their analogy even when its flaws have been pointed out to them. Thus the availability and representativeness heuristics, the notion that schemas process information top-down and the notion that schemas tend to persevere, are used to provide preliminary explanations for these observed tendencies.

To be sure, schema theory does not have a monopoly on explanations for these tendencies. The consistency principle, for example, can also account for such observations as the lack of receptivity to contradictory information and excessive faith in one's own beliefs. Popular in the 1950s and 1960s, the consistency approach postulates that people tend "to behave in ways that minimize the internal inconsistency among. . . . [their] intrapersonal cognitions."[65] The balance principle is held to be an organizing principle of human cognitions; people "feel more comfortable when configurations are balanced. . . . learn them more quickly, remember them better. . . . and interpret new information in such a way as to maintain or increase balance."[66] The emphasis is on the dynamics of maintaining balance instead of the information-processing functions of the belief structures. The cognitive dynamics of seeking balance suggest that incoming information fitting one's preexisting beliefs is assimilated quickly, discrepant information is ignored, and one is likely to continue

[65] William McGuire, "The Current Status of Cognitive Consistency Theories," in *Cognitive Consistency: Motivational Antecedents and Behavioral Consequents*, ed. Shel Feldman (New York: Academic Press, 1966), p. 1.

[66] Robert Jervis, *Perception and Misperception*, p. 118.

to hold on to preexisting beliefs even in the face of contradictory evidence.[67] The consistency or balance principle, then, seems able to account for some of the observations accounted for by the schema notion.[68]

I have chosen, however, to rely only on the schema concept in constructing the explanations provided in this work. The main reason for choosing the schema notion over the consistency notion is that the empirical and theoretical adequacy of the latter has been called into question by subsequent research. Researchers have found that people are often unaware that they are holding contradictory beliefs, that when they are aware they experience little discomfort about the inconsistency, and that achieving a coherent belief system is not necessarily a high priority.[69] It has even been argued that under certain conditions, people are inconsistency seekers.[70] These findings cast doubt on the core assumption of the consistency paradigm, namely, that people are consistency seekers. In a recent review of the field of cognitive social psychology, Markus and Zajonc praise "the balance principle" for generating "direct experimental predictions" that are "quite precise and unambiguous," but they conclude that "the data, unfortunately, did not always agree with the predicted values."[71]

Empirical difficulties, together with the realization that the understanding of internal cognitive dynamics could not advance without an understanding of the "cognitions themselves and how they were *represented or structured*" were in part responsible for the shift, in the 1970s and 1980s, from consistency theories to information-processing theories.[72] In contrast to the assumption of consistency seeking, information-processing approaches rest on the assumption that the mind organizes and processes information around "some type of internal perceptual or

[67] Ibid., pp. 143–44.

[68] Richard Ned Lebow has also used Jervis's formulation of cognitive consistency to analyze international crises. Lebow finds the need for cognitive consistency helpful in explaining decision-making failures but concludes that overall, it is less helpful than models emphasizing the motivational sources of perceptual distortions. See his *Between Peace and War: The Nature of International Crisis* (Baltimore: Johns Hopkins University Press, 1981), pp. 222–28.

[69] Larson, *Containment*, pp. 34, 354. Larson's systematic and superb analysis of the emergence of the Truman administration's Cold War belief system supports some of these assessments. She finds that Truman and James Brynes did not have stable and coherent beliefs about the Soviet Union and that they could hold "incompatible cognitions without discomfort." See also Robert Abelson et al., eds., *Theories of Cognitive Consistency: A Sourcebook* (Chicago: Rand McNally, 1968).

[70] Albert Pepitone, "Some Conceptual and Empirical Problems of Consistency Models," in Feldman, *Cognitive Consistency*, pp. 259–61.

[71] Markus and Zajonc, "The Cognitive Perspective," p. 201.

[72] Ibid., p. 140, emphasis mine.

cognitive structure."[73] The challenge was to settle on a cognitive structure that was consistent with the core assumptions of cognitive psychology—that people have limited cognitive capacities and adopt mental shortcuts—and that could be used as a point of departure for theorizing about mental processes. The schema has emerged as the most widely accepted perceptual structure or unit of cognition; much research in cognitive and social psychology consists of specifying and testing theories about how schemas are "primed" and how they process information. Schemas are presumably agnostic about the consistency principle since inconsistent beliefs may be stored as different schemas; however, once a given schema is primed, it tends to process information top-down, so that discrepant information is likely to be slighted. Schemas do so not because of a need for balance but because it is a simplifying strategy for coping with the massive amount of information they must process.

Since the schema is structurally and functionally so similar to the historical analogy, theoretical findings about how schemas are formed, accessed, and used to process information may be applied to historical analogies. Because many key findings about schematic information processing utilized here—such as going beyond the information given, top-down processing, and perseverance—are consistent with the core assumption that human beings are "cognitive misers" or that they practice "mental economics," schema theory seems not only relevant but potentially fruitful for the purposes at hand.

Our second and final observation pertains to the less than flattering picture of our cognitive capabilities that emerges from the research of the social and cognitive psychologists. This theme may seem initially at odds with our personal experience, since we seem to do reasonably well in the analogical reasoning we perform every day. Psychologists do not deny this. They argue, however, that the very schemas and analogies that seem appropriate in one context may be inappropriate in another.[74] For example, researchers have found simple analogies to be indispensable to learning by children, but they have also found that in the acquisition of advanced knowledge, "simple analogies that help novices to gain a preliminary grasp of difficult, complex concepts may later become serious impediments to fuller and more correct understandings."[75] Rand Spiro and his colleagues found that when analogies were used to introduce medical students to complex concepts, the students were able to grasp the ideas suggested by the parallel (for example, the analogy between

[73] Ibid., p. 143.

[74] Nisbett and Ross, *Human Inference*, chap. 11.

[75] Rand Spiro et al., "Multiple Analogies for Complex Concepts: Antidotes for Analogy-induced Misconception in Advanced Knowledge Acquisition," in Vosniadou and Ortony, *Similarity and Analogical Reasoning*, pp. 498–531.

water pipes and blood vessels was used to illustrate how the radius of the vessel affects impedance to blood flow). However, at a later stage, when students were required to master complex but important details, those analogies hindered their efforts: students had difficulty comprehending features, such as reactance in blood vessels, not suggested by those analogies.[76]

Similarly, a schema that is helpful in illuminating a domestic political situation may be dangerous when applied to a foreign policy problem. Thus Deborah Larson has argued that Truman's use of the Boss Tom Pendergast "machine politician" schema may have helped Truman in American politics, but when Truman applied the same schema to Stalin, it led to less happy consequences.[77] The problem then, is partly one of overextension and misapplication.[78] Robert Jervis summarizes the situation well when he writes that the lessons policymakers learn "will be applied to a wide variety of situations without a careful effort to determine whether the cases are similar on crucial dimensions."[79] Jervis concludes that "often the actor would perceive more accurately had he not undergone the earlier experience."[80]

It is necessary to note, however, that the problem of overuse stems in part from the cognitive allure of reasoning by analogy. Inasmuch as the mental effort and information required to size up new situations is daunting, and inasmuch as analogical reasoning provides a short cut to understanding, through strategies such as going beyond the information given, top-down processing, and perseverance, it should not be surprising that analogies will often be overused and misapplied. The cognitive payoffs, in terms of mental operations saved and simplified, are simply too inviting. Nor should it be surprising that overuse will in turn increase and amplify the cognitive distortions we discussed earlier, distortions associated with simplifying strategies such as top-down processing and the phenomenon of perseverence.

Although there is nothing to suggest that the overuse of analogies will be more prevalent in foreign than in domestic affairs, there are indications that overuse in international affairs will be more difficult to check and correct; the consequences are also likely to be more serious.[81] For if analogies seem to help us make reasonably good inferences in our daily life, it is because we are performing routine tasks in a familiar environment, where feedback about the accuracy of our inferences is often im-

[76] Ibid.

[77] Larson, *Containment*, pp. x, 132–34, and 338.

[78] Nisbett and Ross, *Human Inference*, p. 255.

[79] Jervis, *Perception and Misperception*, p. 228.

[80] Ibid., p. 220.

[81] Nisbett and Ross, *Human Inference*, pp. xii, 15–16, and pp. 250–55.

mediate and clear. The familiar environment and the routineness of our judgmental tasks enable us to judge similarities along crucial dimensions more accurately. Clear and constant feedback serves as a reality check on actions based on our analogical reasoning. On many occasions, the costs of being wrong are also not very palpable; being proven wrong quickly and repeatedly, however, does enable us to update our beliefs, and to discard unhelpful analogies.[82] Natural scientists are even luckier: they use analogies freely in their theorizing, but they always put their inferences to rigorous experimental tests. Upon such usages have major scientific discoveries been made.[83]

The statesman who seeks the help of historical analogies in dealing with foreign situations is in a different position. His task is anything but routine, and he operates in the less familiar but more complex environment of the international setting, where feedback about his analogical inferences, and actions based on these inferences, is costly to obtain, and where, even when such feedback is obtained, it is difficult to interpret. Consider the case of Dean Rusk, who often applied the lessons of Korea to Vietnam. In Rusk's view, the United States faced serious setbacks at the beginning of the Korean War, but eventually it did prevail; one should therefore not be overly pessimistic about setbacks in Vietnam, for eventually the United States might still prevail.[84] What kind of feedback is required to prove or disprove Rusk's inference? One that seems prohibitively costly. The only way to "test" whether the United States could win was through an actual war. If the feedback provided by the first year of fighting suggested that the United States was not winning, Rusk would not necessarily conclude that his inference was wrong. He might point to the high communist casualties and argue that trying even harder might get the United States "the same breaks [as in Korea] down the road."[85] Rusk's deputy, George Ball, argued that the Vietcong did not intend to give the United States such breaks and that it would defeat the United States.

[82] Consider, for example, the inferences we make on meeting new people. On meeting someone who reminds us of an old flame, we might allow the old flame schema to influence our expectations of the new person's demeanor. Whether our expectations are correct will be quickly proven in the course of the meeting; the costs of being wrong on such occasions are usually insignificant, unless of course, it is love at first sight. The example is adapted from Susan Fiske, "Schema-triggered Affect: Applications to Social Perception," in *Affect and Cognition*, ed. Margaret Clark and Susan Fiske (Hillsdale, New Jersey: Lawrence Erlbaum Associates, 1982), pp. 55–78.

[83] See Hesse, *Models and Analogies in Science*; Black, *Models and Metaphors*; and pp. 249–50 below.

[84] Author's interviews with Dean Rusk, August 21, 1986, Athens, Georgia, and George Ball, July 23, 1986, New York City, New York. See also chap. 5.

[85] George Ball, Oral History Interview, 1:33.

Thus, even if feedback is available, it may not be easily interpretable because the international environment is much more complex than our daily environment: many variables at different levels interact to bring about a particular outcome, making it difficult to assess or to agree on the influence of a particular variable on a particular policy. The terms *structural uncertainty* and *decision-making under ambiguity* have been used to characterize this situation.[86] Although these complications actually make analogical reasoning even more irresistible, they do not necessarily make it more appropriate. For without immediate, constant, and usable feedback, it is more difficult to check our analogical inferences and harder to alleviate the problem of misapplication. Foreign affairs being what they are, the consequences of overuse and misapplication of analogies can be potentially destructive to the larger world.

[86] See Holsti, "Foreign Policy Cognitively Viewed"; John Steinbrunner, *The Cybernetic Theory of Decision* (Princeton: Princeton University Press, 1974); and Alexander George, *Presidential Decisionmaking in Foreign Policy: The Effective Use of Information and Advice* (Boulder, Colorado: Westview Press, 1980), chaps. 2–3, for conditions under which cognitive factors such as historical analogies are likely to be influential in decision-making. The term "structural uncertainty" is from Steinbrunner, *Cybernetic Theory*, p. 18.

CHAPTER 3

America's Vietnam Options

> Whatever one's view about the degree to which choices in international affairs are "objectively" determined, the decisions are made by individuals who will be above all conscious of the seeming multiplicity of options.
>
> —*Henry Kissinger*, American Foreign Policy

THE AE FRAMEWORK is based in part on an empirical generalization and in part on a body of deductive theories. The specification of the six diagnostic tasks is based on abstracting from the numerous ways policymakers have used history over time, while the psychological dimension of the framework is derived from the theories and experiments of cognitive social psychology. Regardless of origins, the test of any framework is how much light it sheds on concrete and significant issues in which we are interested. The issue or case I will use the AE framework to elucidate is the making of America's Vietnam policy.

In what follows, I discuss (1) the reasons for choosing the formulation of America's Vietnam policy as my case study, (2) the aspects of American decision-making I seek to explain, and (3) the method I will use to assess the impact of analogical reasoning on decision outcomes.[1]

VIETNAM AS A CASE STUDY OF ANALOGICAL DECISION-MAKING

The major aim of this book is to develop a set of arguments about how policymakers use history and to use those arguments to illuminate an important case of foreign policy decision-making. The case I have chosen to examine is the making of America's Vietnam policy. In particular, I focus on U.S. decision-making on Vietnam in the one-year period be-

[1] I seek to explain two particular aspects of American decision-making: first, the selection and rejection of options tabled in 1965 (chaps. 5–7) and second, why policymakers often use analogies in suboptimal ways (chap. 8). Since the rationale for explaining the latter has been discussed in chap. 2, the discussion of decision-making in this chapter focuses exclusively on the selection of options.

tween the fall of 1964 and the fall of 1965. By the fall of 1964, it was increasingly clear to U.S. policymakers that South Vietnam was in danger of losing the fight with the Vietnamese communists. By the fall of 1965, the Johnson administration had decided to send one hundred thousand U.S. combat troops to help stave off a South Vietnamese defeat. In essence, the United States had taken over the fighting from the Army of the Republic of Vietnam (ARVN). The assumptions underlying American policy, and the arguments in favor of and against the intervention were all debated during this period. In other words, the most critical policy deliberations were all held in this period. Within the case selected, I focus intensively on three historical analogies that were recurrently invoked, and I explore the extent to which they illuminate the two crucial decisions of 1965—the decision to launch an air war in February and the decision to fight a ground war in July.[2]

The substantive importance of the Vietnam decisions is one reason for choosing them as my case study. The decisions of 1965 rank as one of the most fateful of the postwar decisions in American foreign policy, comparable in significance to Truman's declaration of the Cold War, to the Berlin decisions of 1948, and to U.S. decision-making during the Cuban missile crisis. Unlike these other Cold War decisions, which led to policy outcomes congenial to U.S. interests, Vietnam brought the United States its longest war, exacted tens of thousands of American casualties and billions of dollars, and ultimately failed to save South Vietnam. Part of the continuing fascination with the war rests on the puzzle of why a superpower like the United States was unable or unwilling to unleash its full military power against North Vietnam and was thus doomed to failure early on.

Substantive importance and continuing fascination, however, cannot be the only criteria for selecting a case study. For the student of political science, there should also be sound theoretical reasons for picking one's cases. Here, researchers often find Harry Eckstein's and Alexander George's essays about the theoretical promise of case studies instructive.[3] Eckstein's argument about the utility of "critical cases" is especially relevant here.[4] Critical cases are those in which one's arguments are either

[2] Occasionally I stray beyond this time frame to provide a historical context for the issue under discussion or to illustrate an issue's longevity.

[3] Eckstein, "Case Study and Theory," pp. 79–138; George, "The Causal Nexus," pp. 95–124; see also Alexander George and Timothy J. McKeown, "Case Studies and Theories of Organizational Decision Making," *Advances in Information Processing in Organizations* 2 (1985): 21–58.

[4] See Michael D. Shafer, *Deadly Paradigms: The Failure of U.S. Counterinsurgency Pol-*

most likely or least likely to hold. If one's arguments fail to hold up in the most likely case, they must be very weak; conversely, if they hold up in the least likely case, they must be considered promising. For Eckstein, subjecting one's arguments to cases in which they are least likely to hold is perhaps the most theoretically promising feature of the case study.[5]

The case of Vietnam, I argue, approximates a least likely case for my arguments. Those familiar with the incessant barrage of historical analogies that U.S. officials inflicted on the American public in the 1960s are likely to find the skeptics' hypothesis that analogies are used for justification and advocacy much more plausible than my argument that analogies are used for analysis. To begin with, numerous analogies were invoked, apparently without much discrimination. If one were to catalog the different analogies invoked in the one-year period under study, the list would run the gamut from Algeria to Manchuria to Turkey. A strong justificatory tone can often be detected in the way these analogies were used. When Johnson announced to the American public his decision to send combat troops to South Vietnam, he invoked a most accessible analogy to explain the stakes:

> Nor would surrender in Viet-Nam bring peace, because we learned from Hitler at Munich that success only feeds the appetite of aggression. The battle would be renewed in one country and then another country, bringing with it perhaps even larger and crueler conflict, as we have learned from the lessons of history.[6]

In cases like these, it is difficult to deny that there is a strong element of justification and rationalization. Moreover, there is evidence that some officials realized, as far back as 1964, that intervening in Vietnam would mean a protracted and unpopular war. Thus it would be necessary to explain and to justify to both domestic and international audiences the stakes involved.[7] Reference to "the lessons of Munich" or "the lessons of Korea" was likely to be an effective means of doing so. All these factors imply that the case of Vietnam will not favor the interpretation to be

---

icy (Princeton: Princeton University Press, 1988), pp. 14–16, for a succinct discussion of "critical cases."

[5] Eckstein, "Case Study and Theory," pp. 113–20.

[6] *Department of State Bulletin*, August 16, 1965, p. 262.

[7] See *The Pentagon Papers: The Defense Department History of United States Decision-making on Vietnam*, Senator Gravel ed. (Boston: Beacon Press, 1971), 3:594, 648. See also memo, Horace Busby to the President, "Viet Nam News—What's Missing?" July 21, 1965, and memo, Horace Busby to the President, "Impressions, Vietnam Discussion," July 21, 1965, Miscellaneous Vietnam Documents, Reference File. In the former, Busby urges more Churchillesque explanations of why the United States was in Vietnam.

presented in this work. It amounts to being a least likely case for the hypothesis I advance and a most likely case for the rival hypothesis. Under such circumstances, a successful application of the AE framework must be considered powerful substantiation for its core ideas.

One crucial case, two decision outcomes, and three historical analogies—this is the empirical terrain I will cover to make my case. Whether $N = 1$ or 3 here is not the issue; this is a small N study. However, it might be useful to point out a final reason why I have chosen to focus on one case and a few analogies. Previous works on the subject of the "lessons of history" and foreign policy have been large N studies of high quality. May's *"Lessons" of the Past* surveys the entire period after World War II in search of analogies that influenced American foreign policy. Snyder and Diesing's *Conflict among Nations* does not seek, but finds, many instances of analogies influencing policy discussions in international crises between 1898 and 1973. Finally, Jervis's analysis of how decision-makers learn from history in *Perception and Misperception in International Politics* uses anecdotal evidence of numerous cases across different countries and time spans.[8] May and Jervis were interested in demonstrating how persistent, widespread, and prone to error the phenomenon of learning from history is. Snyder and Diesing had a different theoretical agenda, but their findings agree with those of May and Jervis; the point to be made is that they all quite willingly and appropriately traded depth for range.

Subsequent works will probably not advance the research program very far by adducing more examples of poor analogical reasoning and showing how they led to bad policies. Given the high quality of previous work, new research might stand a better chance of uncovering new patterns and generating fresh questions through an intensive analysis of a restricted number of cases. In other words, given that the existing research has range (large N) but lacks depth, it seems worthwhile for new research to reverse the emphasis. In our case, this reversal allows for an intensive analysis of each of the analogies and their impact on the decision outcomes. Intensive analysis makes it possible to focus on the mechanism or process by which analogies affect decisions; it also makes it possible to uncover recurring patterns of policymakers' use of analogies that might otherwise be lost to the researcher. One of the major empirical findings presented in this book—that policymakers' analogies are almost always challenged by colleagues in internal deliberations and that such

[8] May, *"Lessons" of the Past*; Snyder and Diesing, *Conflict Among Nations*, pp. 320–21; Jervis, *Perception and Misperception*, chap. 6.

challenges tend to have little impact on the proposer of the analogies—would not have been possible without intensive analysis of the process of analogical reasoning.

EXPLAINING THE SELECTION AND REJECTION OF OPTIONS

In 1965, President Lyndon Johnson made two crucial decisions with respect to Vietnam. In February he approved the initiation of a graduated air war against North Vietnam, and in July he agreed to send one hundred thousand U.S. combat troops to South Vietnam, a move which meant that the United States would take the major responsibility for conducting a ground war against the Vietnamese communists. Few will deny that these were the two most fateful decisions of the Vietnam War. They committed U.S. power and prestige in an unprecedented way to the conflict in Vietnam.

In choosing to mount a graduated bombing campaign against North Vietnam, Johnson rejected two other options that were tabled:[9] one was to continue the course the United States had been pursuing, namely to respond with retaliatory air strikes whenever the Vietnamese communists launched sizable attacks against U.S. personnel or installations, and the other was to launch a continuous heavy bombing campaign against the North Vietnamese.[10] Similarly, the decision in favor of sending combat troops to South Vietnam meant the rejection of four other options. The four options rejected were withdrawal, continuation of the present course, use of the Strategic Air Command (SAC) to pound the enemy, and a call-up of the reserves and declaration of an emergency.[11] The options presented to President Johnson and his advisers for both decisions can be summarized as follows:[12]

[9] Throughout this book I use the word *tabled* in the British sense, i.e., "presented for consideration."

[10] *Pentagon Papers*, 3:659–60.

[11] Summary of 553d NSC Meeting, July 27, 1965, subject: "Deployment of Additional U.S. Troops to Vietnam," National Security Council History, Deployment of Major U.S. Forces to Vietnam, National Security File (cited hereafter as NSC History—Troop Deployment). This abbreviation follows Larry Berman's *Planning a Tragedy: The Americanization of the War in Vietnam* (New York: W. W. Norton, 1982), p. 154. See also Lyndon B. Johnson, *The Vantage Point: Perspectives of the Presidency, 1963–1969* (New York: Rinehart and Winston, 1971), pp. 145–50.

[12] Options a, b, c, d, and e (ground war) in the original documents have been "relettered" as Options D′, A′, B′, E′ and C′ respectively in this book to facilitate comparisons with Options A, B, and C (air war). Cf. Summary of 553d NSC Meeting, July 27, 1965, NSC History—Troop Deployment.

Air War Options	*Ground War Options*
A: Continue present course	A′: Cut losses/withdraw
B: "Fast squeeze": continuous heavy bombing	B′: Continue present course
C: "Slow squeeze": graduated air attacks	C′: Send 100,000 combat troops
	D′: Use SAC
	E′: Call up reserves, declare emergency

In the case of the air war, Option C was chosen; in the ground war, Option C′ was chosen. I seek to explain these choices. In both cases, the other options tabled were rejected. I also seek to explain why they were rejected.[13] In other words, I am interested in explaining the "why" and the "how": why the United States intervened in Vietnam, and how the United States went about it. Most studies of the Vietnam War do not frame the issue this way. The puzzle for most studies is why the United States intervened in Vietnam. A satisfactory answer is obtained inasmuch as one documents the various factors responsible for the decision to begin the air war or the ground intervention. The first wave of analyses of the Vietnam War were predominantly of this nature.[14]

A second wave of analyses—of more recent vintage—has begun to pay more attention to the actual options presented to the policymakers and has sought to explain why certain options were deemed more acceptable than others by America's decision-makers in the 1960s.[15] Precision made possible by the availability of documents is part of the issue here. First-wave writers, even with access to the *Pentagon Papers*, found it difficult to reconstruct important aspects of the decision-making process. Partly because of this limitation and partly because they were more interested in analyzing U.S. policy over a longer period of time, they were content with explaining the Vietnam decisions of 1965 at an either-or level: Why

[13] The focus is on explaining decision outcomes, not policy outcomes. I am more interested in explaining how the decisions were reached than why the policy failed. The two are related, but they are also mediated by implementation: good decisions poorly implemented will lead to suboptimal policy outcomes, and bad decisions well implemented will still lead to bad policy outcomes.

[14] See, e.g., George McT. Kahin and John W. Lewis, *The United States in Vietnam* (New York: Dial Press, 1967); Ernest May, *"Lessons" of the Past*, chap. 4; and George Herring, *America's Longest War: The United States and Vietnam, 1950–1975* (New York: John Wiley and Sons, 1979).

[15] Gelb and Betts, *Irony of Vietnam*, lies somewhere in between the first and second waves in that it refers to the options rejected and attempts to explain their rejections; however, it is less systematic than the clear second-wave works such as Berman, *Planning a Tragedy*, and George McT. Kahin, *Intervention: How America Became Involved in Vietnam* (New York: Alfred A. Knopf, 1986).

intervention and not withdrawal? To be sure, a successful explanation at this level contributes to our understanding of the Vietnam War. But with the declassification of important memoranda and minutes of meetings not found in the *Pentagon Papers*, it has become possible to address both the "why" and the "how." To put it in terms of the ground war options discussed above, why Option C′ instead of A′, B′, D′, or E′? A successful explanation of the choice of C′ is at once an explanation of why the United States intervened *and* why the intervention took the form that it did.

What are the advantages and disadvantages of framing the question this way? There are four advantages, in increasing order of importance. There is also one disadvantage that needs to be discussed. The first advantage of focusing on options is that it holds the prospect of a richer and more satisfying answer. In addition to indicating why the nonintervention options were rejected, a successful explanation also tells us why, among the prointervention options, one option (say, C′) was chosen over the others (say, D′ or E′). Note that the issue goes far beyond getting the details right. The assumption here is that these options were serious alternatives: which one or which combination of them were chosen matters. Indeed, in the months leading up to the final meetings of July 1965, all five possibilities were live options. George Ball argued strenuously for Options A′ and B′ and felt, until the very end, that he had a fighting chance to convince the president.[16] Clark Clifford, another close adviser to the president, also took Ball's position.[17] Secretary of Defense Robert McNamara, on the other hand, favored Options C′ and E′ combined; the JCS wanted to go further and argued for Option D′ as well. Dean Rusk and the Bundy brothers were more favorably disposed toward Option C′ than to Options A′ or E′.[18] The most satisfactory explanations of Vietnam, it seems to me, are those that can tell us how, given this plethora of conflicting advice and options, which ranged from withdrawing from South Vietnam to using maximum force against North Vietnam, Lyndon Johnson came to choose the option he did.

A second reason for focusing on options is that it reflects the way policymakers actually make decisions. The world of policymakers is a world of options: debates occur when options are developed, when they are tabled, and when they are selected. Advocates of the same policy often disagree about the best option to adopt, if, as is often the case, there is more than one option that will advance the same policy. Moreover, fo-

[16] Interview with author, July 23, 1986, New York City, New York.

[17] Clark Clifford, *Counsel to the President: A Memoir* (Random House: New York, 1991), pp. 410–22.

[18] Memo, McGeorge Bundy to the President, July 1, 1965, NSC History—Troop Deployment.

cusing on options captures the agony of decision-making. In the case of Vietnam, it shows Johnson desperate to find an alternative to intervention, but, for reasons that are the subject of this study, he did not succeed in doing so. This agony and fluidity in the decision-making process suggest that explanations of the U.S. intervention based on the necessities of capitalism or international systemic imperatives are overly deterministic.[19] In fact, as I indicate above, when confronted with the same reality—South Vietnam's impending defeat by North Vietnam and the strategic or systemic implications of such a defeat—those entrusted with protecting the national security of the United States disagreed profoundly on what was to be done.

Third, which option gets chosen has a bearing on the policy outcome: it may mean the difference between success and defeat. The significance of this can be seen in the debate about whether the United States could have "won" the Vietnam War. This debate revolves around the options rejected by the Johnson administration in 1965. Those who argue that Vietnam was an unwinnable war lament the administration's unwillingness to withdraw or to deescalate. They believe none of the harsher options would have worked because they see the North Vietnamese as willing to tolerate high doses of pain to achieve their goal of reunification. The withdrawal option would have saved countless lives; it would also have saved the United States from the humiliation of losing its first conflict.

The opposite view, a view that has gained much attention and influence in the 1980s, holds that the United States could have won, or at least could have "convinced" the North Vietnamese to sign a negotiated settlement earlier, on the assumption that an agreement signed in 1967 would have a better chance of ensuring South Vietnam's survival than one signed in 1973. Many high-ranking civilians and military officers who served in the Johnson administration have argued that if only the harsher options had been chosen at the beginning of the war, South Vietnam would remain independent today. These officials argued for massive continuous bombing (Option B) in the air war and for calling up the reserves and declaring a national emergency on top of sending one hundred thousand troops to South Vietnam (Option E′) in the ground war. Johnson and his advisers were aware that these options had better chances of convincing North Vietnam to stop infiltrating men into South Vietnam. Wil-

[19] See Gabriel Kolko, *Anatomy of a War: Vietnam, the United States, and the Modern Historical Experience* (Pantheon Books: New York, 1985); Waltz, *Theory of International Politics*, chaps. 8–9; Herring, *America's Longest War*, esp. p. x; and Gelb and Betts, *Irony of Vietnam*, for works that emphasize systemic imperatives. Cf. works cited in chap. 1, n. 27 and Charles F. Hermann's recent discussion, "Changing Course: When Governments Choose to Redirect Foreign Policy," *International Studies Quarterly* 34 (1990): 14–20.

liam Bundy and John McNaughton concluded in November 1964 that for the air war, "Option B probably stands a greater chance than either of the other two of attaining our objectives vis-à-vis Hanoi and a settlement in South Vietnam."[20] Similarly, Robert McNamara's assessment in July 1965 that the ground war stood a "good chance" of getting an "acceptable outcome" within a "reasonable time" was premised on pursuing both Options C′ and E′ (calling up 235,000 reserves and National Guardsmen).[21] McNamara "strongly favored" calling up the reserves because of what he "considered to have been the essential role of the Reserves in resolving the 1961 Berlin crisis."[22] Given these assessments about the military superiority of the harsher options, Johnson's decisions to reject them are in need of explanation.

The stakes in the debate as to whether the United States might have succeeded if it had chosen the harsher options are real. How the debate is resolved impinges on what the ultimate lessons of Vietnam are to be for the future decision-makers. Air commanders at the Air War College and the Air Force's Air Command and Staff College are instructing the next generation of officers that the air war could have been won in 1966 if Johnson had only allowed bombing on the massive scale that Richard Nixon would demand in 1972.[23] Similarly, Harry Summer's suggestion that applying a conventional war strategy and taking the strategic offensive could have turned the tide in the 1960s has fallen on receptive ears in military and academic circles.[24] If there is any plausibility to these and other theses about how America could have won, it becomes important to understand why the supposedly more efficacious prointervention options were not chosen. The all-or-nothing approach toward military intervention may be a lesson drawn by recent administrations from the failure of "gradualism" in Vietnam.

A final reason for examining the choice of options is theoretical. Those who believe that decision-making theories are essential to understanding international politics have a rich vein to mine here. I would go further: explaining the choice of options holds more promise of theoretical enrich-

[20] *Pentagon Papers*, 3:663. See also CIA Director John McCone's insistence on Option B and more in his letter to the President, April 1, 1965, NSC History—Troop Deployment.

[21] Memo, Robert McNamara to the President, "Recommendations of Additional Deployments to Vietnam," July 20, 1965, NSC History—Troop Deployment.

[22] Letter from Robert McNamara to Larry Berman, cited in Berman, *Planning a Tragedy*, p. 104. The military shared McNamara's view that a call-up of the reserves was essential to demonstrating U.S. "determination to see this war through." See *Pentagon Papers*, 4:314.

[23] See Mark Clodfelter, *The Limits of Air Power: The American Bombing of North Vietnam* (New York: The Free Press, 1989), pp. ix–x, 206–9.

[24] Harry Summers, *On Strategy: A Critical Analysis of the Vietnam War* (Novato, California: Presidio Press, 1982), chap. 10.

ment than merely explaining "policy." The most systematic expression of the options-based approach is Graham Allison's *Essence of Decision*.[25] Allison's work has become a classic in foreign policy studies in part because it frames the problem ingeniously. Allison does not merely ask why the United States chose force over diplomacy in response to the Soviet emplacement of missiles in Cuba; he goes on to examine why, among the proforce options, the naval blockade was chosen. Put in another way, Allison wants to explain why the blockade option was selected over the other five options. It is this focus on the competing options and their fates in the deliberative process that allows Allison to showcase the strengths and weaknesses of his three models.

One may debate whether Allison's models explain more than the traditional rational-actor model, but it is difficult to deny that focusing on the fates of the various options allows Allison to conduct a theoretically rich investigation.[26] Allison's arguments about how standard operating procedures and turf battles between the Central Intelligence Agency (CIA) and the Air Force successively narrowed the options available to the Executive Committee are theoretically important, even if, as some critics have charged, Allison overemphasizes their impact.[27] Allison's critics dispute the importance of his explanatory models, but none have argued that it was not necessary to explain the choice of the blockade option. In fact, even Allison's strongest critic, Stephen Krasner, accepts the way Allison frames his dependent variable, though he proceeds to show that Allison's models do not explain the selection or rejection of the various options as well as the rational-actor model.[28] Finally, by focusing on options, Allison also shows how conscious the policymakers were of the importance of selecting the "correct" option. There was genuine fear that the "wrong" option might either fail to convince the Soviets to remove the missiles or bring the United States and the Soviet Union closer to nuclear war. If different options have such different hypothesized consequences, understanding why one option is picked over others must be a concern of the analyst.

Admittedly, an exclusive focus on options may result in an analysis that sees the trees but not the forest. This is the danger associated with focusing too narrowly on options. For example, if one were to limit one's analysis to explaining why the blockade option was chosen over the surgical

[25] *Essence of Decision: Explaining the Cuban Missile Crisis* (Boston: Little, Brown and Company, 1971). See also Steinbruner, *The Cybernetic Theory*.

[26] For critiques of Allison, see Stephen Krasner, "Are Bureaucracies Important? Or Allison Wonderland," *Foreign Policy* 7 (1972): 159–79; and Robert Art, "Bureaucratic Politics and American Foreign Policy: A Critique," *Policy Analysis* 4 (1973): 467–90.

[27] Allison, *Essence of Decision*, pp. 118–26; Krasner, "Allison Wonderland," pp. 173–76.

[28] Krasner, "Allison Wonderland," pp. 170–79.

air strike, one would risk neglecting the larger political picture that made it difficult for Kennedy to accept the "do nothing" or diplomatic options.[29] But this danger can be quite easily overcome. An advantage of analyzing options is that one always begins by listing all the options tabled: this means the options will often range from "do nothing" to "use maximum force." In other words, options analysis involves the explicit listing of all conceivable responses and alternatives to a given foreign policy problem. To overcome the danger of narrow focus, it is suggested that the explanations proposed account for as many of the options tabled as possible. In the case of the Cuban missile crisis, an ideal explanation would be one that would show why the three "no force" options—"do nothing," "use diplomacy" and "make a secret approach to Castro"—were rejected and would then go on to show why, among the "force" options, the naval blockade was chosen over the surgical air strike or invasion. In the case of the Vietnam War, the ideal explanation will show why the nonintervention options (A, A′, and B′) were rejected and then, if possible, go on to show why, among the prointervention options, C and C′ were chosen over B (air war) and D′ and E′ (ground war) respectively.

The theoretical payoffs of investigating the Vietnam decisions at the level of options can be seen in the puzzle that this approach raises for traditional explanations of America's intervention in the Vietnam War. One traditional explanation holds that Vietnam was the logical outcome of America's postwar policy of containment.[30] The other traditional explanation, which is essentially the other side of the containment coin, focuses on the importance of U.S. credibility. In this view, the U.S. decision to intervene in Vietnam had to do with the credibility calculations of the decision-makers. It was felt that U.S. credibility was at stake in Vietnam in 1965: failure to intervene would probably result in a communist South Vietnam, and that in turn would lead both allies and enemies to conclude that the United States could not be counted on to live up to its commitments.[31]

How far do the containment and credibility theses take us in elucidating American choices in the ground war, the selection of Option C′ and the rejection of Options A′, B′, D′, and E′? The requirements of containment and credibility calculations can explain why the withdrawal or "do nothing" options (A′ and B′) were unacceptable.[32] But neither cal-

[29] See Ronald Steel's critique of Allison in "Cooling It," *New York Review of Books* (October 19, 1972): 45.

[30] Herring, *America's Longest War*, p. xii; Gelb and Betts, *Irony of Vietnam*, pp. 2, 25.

[31] Gelb and Betts, *Irony of Vietnam*, p. 189; Kahin, *Intervention*, pp. 312–14.

[32] It is necessary to ask why, given the containment policy and the concern for U.S. credibility, the United States rejected the nonintervention options in 1965 whereas it found the nonintervention options acceptable in 1954. I take up this issue in the next chapter.

culation is able to explain why C′ was chosen over D′ or E′. In fact, if one takes the logic of containment or credibility seriously, one would expect options D′ or E′ to be chosen over C′. Options D′ and E′ were the harsher options and the ones widely considered to have better chances of achieving U.S. objectives. Obviously, some factor other than containment or credibility was at work. Containment theorists often turn to domestic or bureaucratic politics to explain why the harsher options were rejected. Although those factors were relevant, the way they are introduced into the argument is rather ad hoc. Why, for example, were they not relevant in deciding between intervention and nonintervention to begin with? Can one specify beforehand where containment ends and domestic politics begin? Moreover, if domestic political costs played an instrumental role in convincing Johnson against the harsher options, what about the domestic political costs of pursuing Option C′ and then losing? These questions suggest that the domestic or bureaucratic politics arguments have not been fully worked out; they seem to function as ad hoc supplements to the containment thesis. They also suggest that if there exists an explanation that accounts for the choice of the intervention over the withdrawal options, *as well as* the choice of Option C′ over the harsher prointervention options, it ought to be preferred on grounds of parsimony and accuracy over the "containment plus domestic and bureaucratic politics" argument. A major claim of this book is that the "lessons" of Korea, as interpreted by the major policymakers, is such an explanation.

ANALOGIES AND OPTIONS

Having made explicit what I hope to explain, I will next discuss the method I will use to demonstrate how analogies affect the choice of options. The method consists of three steps: (1) identification of the most important analogies, (2) specification of what these analogies "teach" and what constitutes acceptable evidence that their lessons were taken seriously, and (3) documentation of the role of each analogy in the policy process and assessment of how consistent (or inconsistent) its lessons are with the options chosen (or rejected).

Which Analogies Matter?

The most important analogies are identified by inspecting the public and the private record. Even a cursory examination of the analogies to Vietnam invoked by senior officials in public in the months prior to the July

1965 decision would have revealed that the Korean, the 1930s, the Greek, and the Malayan analogies were especially relevant. Table 3.1 summarizes the results of a more systematic count of the top ten analogies invoked by senior officials in *public* speeches and briefings from 1950 to 1966. The source used for this count is the *Department of State Bulletin*, which contains the major foreign policy pronouncements of each administration.[33] By this count, Vietnam was most frequently compared to the following five historical cases: the Korean War, the fascist aggressions of the 1930s, the Greek crisis of 1947, the Malayan insurrection of 1948–1960, and the Berlin crises.[34]

Counting the public analogies provides a clue as to which analogies may be significant. The Korean analogy appears to be an order of magnitude more popular than the next two analogies, the lessons of the 1930s and the Greek crisis of 1947. Are these patterns replicated in the private record? Before answering this question, note that for the skeptics, the fact that officials invoke analogies in public would not be surprising, since public speeches are a prime medium of policy justification. It would be rather unusual from the skeptics' perspective to find policymakers con-

[33] The *Department of State Bulletin* is more suitable than the *Public Papers of the President* for foreign policy pronouncements because in addition to presidential speeches, it includes pronouncements and explanations by high-level State Department officials. The count begins in 1950 because the United States began actively siding with the French against Ho Chi Minh that year, and it ends in 1966 because I am interested in explaining the decisions of 1965.

The counting rules are as follows. First, not all references to history qualify as analogies. When a historical event is compared implicitly or explicitly with Vietnam, it counts as an analogy. When it is not explicitly or implicitly comparative, it does not count. For example, there are six analogies in the following statement by Lyndon Johnson: "The challenge we face in Southeast Asia today is the same challenge that we have faced with courage and that we have met with strength in Greece and Turkey, in Berlin and Korea, in Lebanon and in Cuba" (*Department of State Bulletin*, August 5, 1964, p. 260). On the other hand, the following appraisal of Option B, "This course of action has considerably higher risks of major military conflict with Hanoi and possibly Communist China" (*Pentagon Papers*, 3:663) does *not* count as an instance of the Korean analogy. Nothing in the text indicates that its authors were thinking of Korea. Second, each analogy is only counted once per document, regardless of the number of times it is cited. Thus, even though George Ball's October 5, 1964 memo—in which he argues against the air war option—invokes the Korean analogy seventeen times, the analogy itself is only counted once (memo, George Ball to Dean Rusk, Robert McNamara, and McGeorge Bundy, "How Valid Are the Assumptions Underlying our Viet-Nam Policies?" in *The Atlantic Monthly* 320 [July 1972]: 35–49).

[34] The 1930s is a composite analogy composed of one or more of the following events: Japan's invasion of Manchuria, Mussolini's annexation of Ethiopia, Hitler's reoccupation of the Rhineland, the Munich conference, and Hitler's invasion of Czechoslovakia. From the perspective of Dean Rusk and Lyndon Johnson, the two major users of the 1930s analogy, the prototypical event of this period was Munich, which they interpreted as Western appeasement of Hitler, an act that made World War II inevitable. I will use "Munich" and the "1930s" interchangeably in this book.

TABLE 3.1
The Ten Vietnam Analogies Most Frequently Used in Public, 1950–1966

Analogy	*1950–60*	*1961*	*1962*	*1963*	*1964*	*1965*	*1966*	*Total*
Korea	8	1	2	1	7	23	21	63
1930s	1	—	—	—	—	30	11	42
Greece	—	—	—	3	2	13	14	32
Malaya	—	—	1	5	2	9	5	22
Berlin	1	—	—	—	4	6	8	19
Philippines	—	—	—	2	2	8	3	15
Cuba	—	1	—	—	5	5	3	14
Turkey	—	—	—	1	1	3	5	10
World War II	—	—	—	—	—	4	5	9
Germany	1	—	—	1	—	3	3	8

Source: U.S. Department of State, *Department of State Bulletin* (Washington, D.C.: U.S. Government Printing Office).

stantly referring to historical analogies in private, for example, in NSC meetings or in internal memoranda. In such private settings, there is no public to mollify, and there is less need to overstate the case; one may presumably speak one's mind.[35] In other words, finding that policymakers resort to analogies in private recurrently and systematically would do much to undermine the skeptics' notion that analogies are used primarily for public justification.

Again, cursory acquaintance with the "prematurely" declassified *Pentagon Papers* would suggest that Korea, the French experience in Vietnam, Malaya, and Greece were important parallels. A more systematic but by no means scientific count of the analogies invoked in *private* by the major policymakers largely confirms this picture. The sources for this count are the four-volume Senator Gravel edition of *The Pentagon Papers* and declassified documents pertaining to Vietnam decision-making in the 1960s (found in the Kennedy and Johnson libraries) in my possession.[36] Some of these documents were not declassified until the late 1980s. Unlike the public count, this private count is difficult—though not impossible—to replicate because a different analyst may find documents I missed, and new documents are often added to old files as declassification progresses. But that should not invalidate the suggestiveness of table 3.2: since my errors are likely to result in undercounting the absolute frequency of analogy use, it follows that the data presented is a conservative

[35] Even if policymakers invoke analogies in public to justify their policies, the use of the same analogies in private strengthens the presumption that they may have informed the policymakers' assessment of Vietnam.

[36] The Kennedy and Johnson library documents I have consulted are listed in the bibliography.

TABLE 3.2
The Ten Vietnam Analogies Most Frequently Used in Private, 1950–1966

Analogy	*1950–60*	*1961*	*1962*	*1963*	*1964*	*1965*	*1966*	*Total*
Korea	4	3	2	—	6	15	16	46
French Experience	—	4	1	—	3	16	2	26
Malaya	2	3	1	1	2	2	1	12
1930s	1	—	—	—	—	3	6	10
Greece	1	—	—	—	4	2	1	8
Philippines	—	2	—	—	1	2	1	6
World War II	—	—	1	—	—	1	3	5
Berlin	—	1	—	—	2	1	—	4
Cuba	—	—	—	—	2	1	—	3
Turkey	—	—	—	—	1	—	1	2

Sources: *The Pentagon Papers*, Senator Gravel, ed. (Boston: Beacon Press, 1971), vols. 1–4; declassified documents from the Lyndon Baines Johnson Library, Austin, Texas, and the John F. Kennedy Library, Boston, Massachusetts.

estimate of the number of times each analogy was used. Again, the differences in magnitude are revealing.[37] In internal deliberations, Korea was invoked twice as often as the next ranked analogy, the French experience (or Dien Bien Phu), and the latter in turn was twice as popular as the Malayan analogy.[38]

Comparison of tables 3.1 and 3.2 suggests that the overlap between the public and private analogies is impressive. Korea emerges as the most important analogy in public as well as in private. It therefore deserves a special place in our analysis. The 1930s, Malaya, and Greece are also among the top five analogies in both counts. The French experience, however, never invoked in public, was the second most frequently used analogy in private. It therefore also deserves to be analyzed. In addition, the 1930s and Malaya analogies will also figure prominently in this work. In effect, I have chosen to analyze the four most frequently invoked private analogies. The quantitative assessments provided by tables 3.1 and 3.2 are partially responsible for this choice; equally important, however, is a qualitative assessment, based on interviews with former policymakers and a familiarity with the Vietnam documents, of the analogies that seem to matter. A case can be made, for example, for including the Greek analogy in our analysis, since it was among the top five analogies in both the public and private counts. I exclude it because, in private, it became less

[37] I assume that counting errors will not negate the finding that Korea, the French experience in Vietnam, Malaya, the 1930s, and Greece were among the top half-dozen analogies used.

[38] For American policymakers, Dien Bien Phu is the most memorable aspect of the French experience in Vietnam. The village of Dien Bien Phu was the site of the Vietminh's final defeat of the French in the war of 1946 to 1954.

important as the July 1965 decisions approached—it was used less frequently, and mainly by Walt Rostow, who was not a central player until 1966.

What Lessons Do These Analogies Teach, and How Important Are They?

Once the analogies to be analyzed are identified, their contents or the lessons they teach can be teased out by using the AE framework. The six questions listed in chapter 2 are asked of each of the analogies, and the answers to them are determined empirically. Consider for example, the question of defining the nature of the problem. How did the lessons of the 1930s, or Munich, affect policymakers' definition of the situation in Vietnam? It is not enough to deduce that policymakers attuned to the Munich analogy are likely to define the conflict in Vietnam as a case of unjustified external aggression; it is necessary to provide evidence that Lyndon Johnson or Dean Rusk actually posed the issue that way. In providing such evidence, I rely on both their public pronouncements and the declassified record of their private deliberations. There is no reason to dismiss their public analogies prematurely: part of my purpose is to see if there is a correspondence between the public and the private uses of historical analogies.

That said, my case about the importance of the Korean, Munich, and Dien Bien Phu analogies in U.S. decision-making is based primarily on documentary evidence about how these analogies were used in private and on information obtained from interviews with many of the senior policymakers. This approach is doubly helpful. First, the documents provide empirical evidence that those analogies were indeed used in the decision-making process, they reveal who used them, and they indicate what their impact might be. For example, if we find memoranda to the president urging him not to think in terms of another Korea or another Munich in making decisions about Vietnam, we may legitimately infer that he might have been using those historical parallels in his thinking. Moreover, if we find then that the president himself raised concerns about repeating MacArthur's mistake in Korea in several NSC meetings over time, we will have found firm evidence about the importance of the analogy in the president's thinking.

Second, our claims will command greater credence if the inferences we make from the documents can be checked by interviews with the key participants. This will help mitigate the concern that documents may sometimes be written more for posterity, to ensure that the author will look good to future historians, than for analysis. Interviews may help ascertain the importance of analogies compared to other factors, whether the users of the analogies took them seriously, or whether the analogies were just tools for advocacy. To be sure, former policymakers may forget or prevaricate, but one supposes that the passage of time may also allow them a sense of detachment that makes them more forthcoming about what they do remember. Most important, the written record constrains the extent to which their imaginations may roam.

A third source is available to check and to corroborate the evidence I present in this book. I refer to the oral histories given by officials of the Kennedy and Johnson administrations to the respective presidential libraries. In these histories, we find reminiscences by former officials about the president they served and the decisions in which they participated. Unlike my interviews, these were conducted by library historians who had no special interest in how the lessons of history might have affected the Vietnam decisions. If we find different policymakers independently alluding to the importance of certain historical parallels in Vietnam decision-making, then we will have found strong corroboration for the notion that the analogies mattered. I consider the oral histories semiprivate materials: they were usually conducted in the first few years after Kennedy died or after Johnson left office and were not opened to the public until many years later. Some, in fact, are still classified. I occasionally use these materials to check my findings, but I do not put as much weight on them as I do the documents and my interviews.

For all the distinction I make between the public and the private, it will be seen that, with one exception, there is remarkable consistency in the analogies used in the two settings. To be sure, the range and number of analogies used in public was much larger; in that sense the public use of analogies was less discriminating. Yet the most important analogies and the ones analyzed in this book were used in both settings and in basically similar ways. This suggests that the policymakers had no qualms about sharing with the public—informing, explaining, and justifying to their audience—the historical analogies that informed them in private. The only exception is Dien Bien Phu, which was rarely used in public but which was heatedly debated in private. Dien Bien Phu was almost never used by officials in public, because, among other things, it predicted defeat—hardly the kind of message the administration wanted to convey to the American public. Yet, the fact that the analogy played so prominent a role in the internal deliberations suggests the importance of focusing on the private, as opposed to the public, record.

Finally, in documenting how the various analogies influenced policymakers' analyses of Vietnam and their options, I refrain from evaluating the accuracy of their diagnoses. Some of the analogy-based assessments made by policymakers will appear misleading, perhaps even ludicrous, to the reader, yet I shall withhold judgment, at least in part 2 of this work. In so doing, I do not mean to suggest that the policymakers' analogy-based diagnoses were correct. Indeed, in each case, I also document how detractors tried to point out the flaws of those analogies. I join these detractors only in part 3 of this work, where I point to differences between historical situations obscured by the analogies policymakers used and explain why those differences mattered.

Linking the "Lessons of History" and Options Chosen: Process Tracing and the Congruence Method

Suppose that a central lesson of the Munich analogy is, "Aggression unchecked leads to general war later." To argue that the Munich analogy influenced the Vietnam decisions of 1965, one would need to show two things. First, that the analogy was very much on the minds of the central decision-makers and that it was used at important junctures in the policy process. Second, that this lesson of Munich was consistent with the option chosen in Vietnam. The former is basically what George has called *process tracing* and the latter what he has termed the *congruence procedure*.[39] Both methods were developed by George to enable analysts to assess the impact of beliefs on decisional choices in single or small *N* case studies. I rely on both methods to demonstrate how analogies affect decisional choices.[40]

Of the two methods, process tracing is, for George, the "more direct and potentially more satisfactory approach to causal interpretation in single case analysis," because it "takes the form of an attempt to trace the process—the intervening steps—by which beliefs influence behavior." The process traced is of course the policy process. More specifically,

> Process-tracing seeks to establish the ways in which the actor's beliefs influenced his receptivity to and assessment of incoming information about the situation, his definition of the situation, his identification and evaluation of options, as well as, finally, his choice of a course of action.[41]

In George's own work, the beliefs he was most interested in tracing were inferences from policymakers' "Operational Code"; for us the relevant beliefs are the lessons policymakers learn from their analogies.[42] It

[39] My discussion draws primarily on George, "Causal Nexus"; see also George and McKeown, "Case Studies."

[40] George recommends that one begin with the congruence procedure and then use process tracing to refine and check one's findings. For reasons explained below, I find it more helpful to begin with process tracing and end with the congruence procedure to assess the fit between beliefs and options chosen or rejected. A strong distinction between the two methods may not be necessary, for they largely complement one another.

[41] George, "Causal Nexus," p. 113.

[42] Ibid. See also George, " 'Operational Code'." For reasons why I have not used the "Operational Code" in this work, see my "From Rotten Apples to Falling Dominos to Mu-

is probably obvious that our earlier discussion about identifying the salient analogies and documenting their role in policymaking involves process tracing. How else can one determine whether analogies perform the tasks the AE framework claims they do? To return to the example of Munich: it is by process tracing that we determine who was informed by the analogy, how it affected his analysis of the "Vietnam problem," and whether the analogy commanded the belief of others or elicited dismissive rebuttals.[43] In addition to Munich, I also trace the paths of the Korean and Dien Bien Phu analogies in the policy process. For each of these analogies, process tracing should reveal (1) its main advocates, (2) its detractors, (3) how it affected its advocates' definition of the situation and evaluation of options, and (4) the choice propensities of its advocates.[44]

My view about the extent to which process tracing is able to establish how "the actor's beliefs [analogies] influenced. . . . his choice of a course of action" differs slightly from George's. I believe that process tracing can take us far in assessing the relative importance of the various factors behind the Vietnam decisions. For example, process tracing can easily lend doubt to explanations of U.S. policy that focus on the need for markets and raw materials or on the Southeast Asia Treaty Organization (SEATO) requirements.[45] Evidence of such concerns are simply absent in the memos and minutes of meetings leading to the decisions of 1965. Process tracing, however, seldom establishes a direct one-to-one relationship between a given belief and the specific option chosen. Minutes of the meeting in which the decision to intervene was taken are unlikely to reveal Henry Cabot Lodge invoking Munich one minute, the other senior policymakers concurring in the next, and the president's assenting and concluding that the decision is made in the next. What actually happened was more complicated. Munich was indeed invoked by Lodge, America's credibility by Dean Rusk, the French experience in Vietnam by George Ball, and the Korean analogy by President Johnson.[46] Process tracing can show that these factors were important right to the end. It can also tell which of these factors had more weight at the meeting: no one questioned Lodge's analogy, Ball's analogy was criticized as being too pessimistic, and Johnson's preoccupation with Korea had weight simply because he had it and used it at a critical juncture in the meeting. From

nich: The Problem of Reasoning by Analogy about Vietnam" (Ph.D. diss., Harvard University, 1987), pp. 13–22.

[43] Munich is often used as an example *not* because it is the most important analogy in Vietnam decision-making, but because its lessons are the most well known and most universally shared. It is ideal, in other words, for purposes of exposition.

[44] The phrase "choice propensities" is borrowed from George, "Causal Nexus," p. 112.

[45] See Gabriel Kolko, *The Roots of American Foreign Policy: An Analysis of Power and Purpose* (Boston: Beacon Press, 1969), for the economic interpretation; the SEATO rationale can be found in *Department of State Bulletin*, May 24, 1965, p. 817.

[46] See chap. 5 for a fuller account of this meeting.

the way and the context in which these analogies were used in the policy process, one may then infer which ones were particularly influential and which options they might predispose Johnson to choose.

Our process-based inference about a particular analogy leading to a particular decisional choice will be checked by the congruence method. This procedure is useful because it checks against overly subjective interpretations of the raw data. Different readers of the minutes of the meeting described above may disagree about which of the analogies invoked were important or what constituted "critical junctures" in such meetings. Although I believe that fears of such disagreements are often exaggerated, I agree that our inferences will command greater belief if they can be double-checked. This is where George's congruence method is especially helpful.

The idea behind the congruence procedure is simple. The aim is to check for congruence or consistency between a policymaker's beliefs or analogies and his policy choice. According to George,

> The determination of consistency is made deductively. From the actor's . . . beliefs, the investigator deduces what implications they have for decision. If the characteristics of the decision are consistent with the actor's beliefs, there is at least a presumption that the beliefs may have played a causal role in this particular instance of decision-making.[47]

Establishing congruence is merely the first step toward showing that beliefs may have played a causal role. George worries about spurious consistency and overly causal imputation of cause and effect. Since experimental designs are not possible for single-case analysis, George searches for "the functional equivalent of experimental design." To this end, he performs a series of ingenious thought experiments and subjects "causal interpretations in single-case analysis" to these "series of hurdles . . . before granting them plausibility."[48]

The gist of George's "functional equivalent of experimental design" is shown in figure 3.1. Suppose, to continue with the example of the ground war, belief *X* (the lesson of Munich) has been shown to be consistent with the option chosen, C′. One must then ask, Can Munich explain and predict only Option C′? Or would Option D′—not chosen by the decision-maker—also have been consistent with Munich? If so, then Munich "may be part of the explanation, but its ability to discriminate among alternative outcomes and its predictive power are weakened." Next, according to George, it is necessary to ask, Are there any options tabled that would not be consistent with the lesson of Munich? Option A′ for example, may

[47] George, "Causal Nexus," p. 106.
[48] Ibid., p. 105.

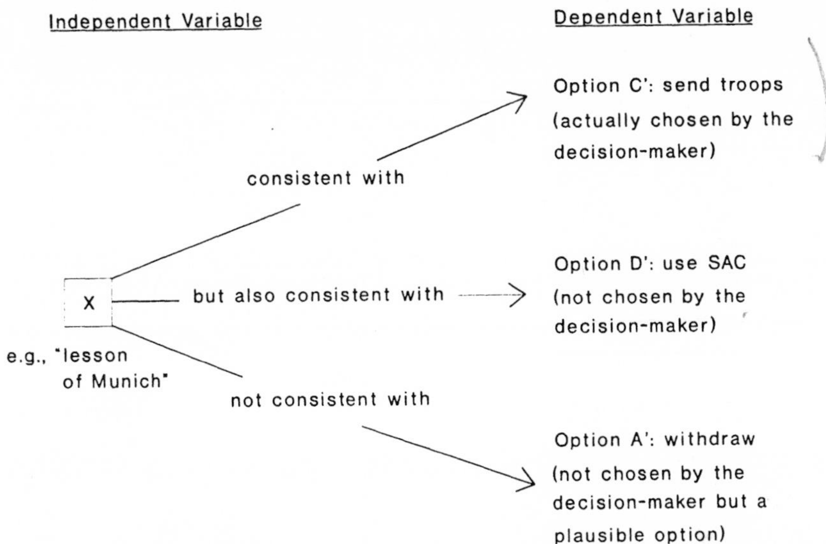

Figure 3.1. The Congruence Procedure Fitted with Experimental Design

Source: Adapted from Alexander George, "The Causal Nexus between Cognitive Beliefs and Decision-Making Behavior: The 'Operational Code' Belief System," in Lawrence Falkowski, ed., *Psychological Models in International Politics* (Boulder, Colo.: Westview Press, 1979), p. 112.

have been proposed by some advisers, but because the option was not consistent with the Munich analogy it was not given a sympathetic hearing. When this happens, "important explanatory and predictive power" can be attributed to Munich "on the grounds that its presence tended to exclude adoption of other policy options" that might have been chosen by other decision-makers having belief *Y* (say, the Dien Bien Phu analogy) rather than *X*.[49]

George is also unwilling to let the relationship among Options A′, C′, and D′ go unexamined. He argues, Suppose C′ differs in some ways from D′, but both options share something in common—both are "hard, refractory" responses to an adversary's actions while A′ is a "conciliatory" response. When such is the relationship among Options A′, C′, and D′, the belief *X*:

> acquires added explanatory and predictive power of a quite useful kind, for it does discriminate between conciliatory and refractory responses (though not by itself between variants of a conciliatory response). In this sense . . . beliefs introduce choice propensities into an actor's decision-making. In

[49] Ibid., pp. 111–12.

other words, the actor's adherence to belief [*X*]. . . . does not determine in a linear, specific way his decision choice, but it does bound and delimit the general range or type of response he is likely to make in a given situation.[50]

In chapters 5 to 7, I demonstrate, by relying on process tracing and the congruence method as outlined above, how the Korean, Dien Bien Phu, and Munich analogies bounded and delimited the U.S. response to the deteriorating situation in South Vietnam. In each chapter, I begin by using the AE framework and process tracing to identify what lessons policymakers drew from these analogies. I then trace the role of the analogy in the policy process by identifying its advocates, its detractors, and its impact on the decision-makers. To ascertain the degree to which the analogy is able to account for the options chosen, I then rely on the congruence procedure. Options inconsistent with the lessons of the analogy should be rejected. Among the remaining options—which should all be basically consistent with the analogy's lessons—I expect the option most fully consistent with most, if not all, of the lessons of the analogy to be the one chosen.

I will also use the congruence test to assess the degree to which competing nonanalogical explanations such as containment and bureaucratic politics are able to account for the options chosen. If they do as well or better than the analogical explanation in accounting for the options selected and rejected, a case can then be made for according them privileged status as explanations of the Vietnam decisions.

The preceding discussion of why Vietnam is an appropriate case study, why it is interesting and important to explain the selection of America's Vietnam options, and how I plan to go about it clears the way for the empirical analysis of the Vietnam analogies and their impact on the decision-making of the 1960s. In part 2 of this work, I shall show how the Korean, Munich, and Dien Bien Phu analogies bounded and delimited the choice propensities of the decision-makers. Because each of these analogies influenced policymakers differently, they predisposed them toward different options. The direction, shape, and form of America's Vietnam policy, therefore, depended very much on which of these analogies were chosen.

[50] Ibid., p. 112.

Part II

THE CASES

CHAPTER 4

Containment, Analogies, and the Pre–1965 Vietnam Decisions

Reasoning by historical analogy became a virtual ritual in the United States under Secretaries of State Acheson (1949–52), Dulles (1953–58) and Rusk (1961–68). . . .
—*Paul M. Kattenburg*, The Vietnam Trauma

IF THERE IS a controlling concept in the scholarly analysis of post–World War II American foreign policy, containment is it. Whatever its origins—political scientists trace it to the bipolar international system while historians attribute it to the lessons of the 1930s—the imperative of containing the extension of Soviet and Chinese communist power has been used to describe and explain many of the most important military security decisions of the postwar era, including the Vietnam decisions of 1965.[1]

Containment is in fact the standard explanation of how America became involved in Vietnam. According to George Herring, a leading historian of the Vietnam conflict,

> The United States' involvement in Vietnam was not primarily a result of errors of judgment or of the personality quirks of the policymakers, although these things existed in abundance. It was a logical, if not inevitable, outgrowth of a world view and a policy, the policy of containment, which Americans in and out of government accepted without serious question for more than two decades.[2]

Similarly, the political scientists Leslie Gelb and Richard Betts see the U.S. intervention in Vietnam as an instance of the pursuit of "the core consensual goal of postwar foreign policy," the containment of communism. For Gelb and Betts, the U.S. involvement in Vietnam is "mainly a story of . . . why U.S. leaders considered it vital not to lose Vietnam by force to communism."[3] There is also agreement why, from the American

[1] Waltz, *Theory of International Politics*, chap. 8; May, *"Lessons" of the Past*, chap. 2; and Gelb and Betts, *Irony of Vietnam*, pp. 197–200.

[2] Herring, *America's Longest War*, p. x.

[3] Gelb and Betts, *Irony of Vietnam*, pp. 2, 25.

perspective, it was important not to lose Vietnam. It was not so much because of territory, industrial potential, or democratic ideals. It was because of credibility: the assumption that "if the United States allowed itself to be challenged successfully in any part of the world, then its determination to resist aggression would be called into question everywhere else."[4]

This explanation of the United States' intervention in Vietnam contains broad essential truths. Policymakers were preoccupied with containing communism and maintaining credibility. Moreover, Vietnam is but one of many postwar cases of the use of force that seem explicable by the containment framework. The other cases are Korea (1950), Guatemala (1954), Lebanon (1958), Cuba (1961), the Dominican Republic (1965), and Grenada (1983). In each of these cases, the United States intervened overtly or covertly to help friendly regimes resist their perceived communist foes and to help domestic groups overthrow procommunist leaders. From the perspective of American policymakers, intervention checked the expansion of Soviet- and Chinese-sponsored communism and maintained the credibility of U.S. power.

Despite these advantages, the correlation between containment and military intervention raises as many questions as it answers. It seems like a sufficient explanation until one observes that in the same period—when the logic of containment supposedly held sway—there were as many cases in which the United States eschewed decisive military action even though friendly regimes were in danger of being overthrown and in many cases were indeed taken over by communists. I refer to Czechoslovakia (1948), China (1949), Vietnam (1954), Cuba (1959), Laos (1961 and 1963), Indonesia (1965) and Nicaragua (1979). The logic or imperative of containment, then, does not necessarily imply that the United States will act decisively or militarily to prevent communist gains.

The case of Indochina is especially telling, even if we disregard all the other cases. From the containment perspective, three pre-1965 decisions pertaining to Indochina appear anomalous or puzzling. They are Eisenhower's decision against intervention in Vietnam in 1954, Kennedy's decision to accept a negotiated settlement in Laos in 1961, and Kennedy's decision later that year to send more aid and advisers instead of combat troops to South Vietnam. Eisenhower's decision meant that the North would most certainly go communist, Kennedy's Laos decision meant that he was willing to accept a negotiated solution and tolerate a communist-dominated coalition government, and the 1961 Vietnam decision merely

[4] Terry L. Deibel and John Lewis Gaddis, eds., *Containing the Soviet Union: A Critique of U.S. Policy* (Washington, D.C.: Pergamon-Brassey, 1987), p. 3. See also Herring, *America's Longest War*, p. 270.

postponed the reckoning in South Vietnam. These decisions are puzzling because if the logic of containment was compelling in 1965—as proponents of the containment thesis claim—it should have been equally if not more compelling in the 1950s and early 1960s. After all, the 1950s and early 1960s, the first decade of the Cold War, were more dangerous than the mid-1960s, when the Sino-Soviet split was apparent to many American officials. One would expect the United States to act more decisively to prevent communist victories in the 1950s and early 1960s, yet this did not happen.

In this chapter I take a closer look at these pre-1965 decisions, in part to provide some historical context for understanding the issues in 1965, but mainly to suggest a way out of this puzzle. I suggest that the need for containment is best viewed as an overarching constant in postwar American diplomacy. It is something of which policymakers are always aware, and it predisposes them to be concerned about communist gains anywhere, but by itself, it cannot explain why policymakers made the choices they did in 1954, 1961, and 1965. The reason why, given containment, we have decisive actions to counter communist gains in one instance (1965) but not in another (1954) has to do with the situation-specific diagnoses and analyses made by policymakers. In other words, the imperative of containment may be the point of departure of postwar administrations, but to understand decision outcomes, one needs to examine the specific judgments made by policymakers about the stakes involved, about the chances of success of various options, and about the dangers involved in any given situation. My claim is that in making these judgments and calculations, historical analogies are often—though by no means always—used and that when they are used, the AE framework proposed in this book can be a helpful guide as to how the issue may be decided.

EISENHOWER'S DECISION AGAINST WAR, 1954

Dwight Eisenhower's decision against military intervention in Vietnam in 1954 poses the most serious problem for the containment thesis because U.S. policymakers knew then that nonintervention would mean, at the very least, a communist North. U.S. willingness to tolerate a communist victory in Southeast Asia at the height of the containment period is an anomaly that needs to be explained.[5] Eisenhower's calculations, his

[5] The Eisenhower administration's willingness to see another spot go communist at this time becomes doubly puzzling, from the containment perspective, in light of McCarthysim and other domestic effects of the Cold War. See also chap. 7.

advisory system, Congress, and the lessons of the Korean War have been some of the more important factors cited for the U.S. decision against war.[6] Different studies have put different emphases on the relative importance of these factors, but there is overall agreement on the essentials. The point to be made is that the perceived need to contain communist expansion—a concern that permeates the record—was overridden by other factors, and one of these was the lessons of Korea.

From 1946 to 1954, it will be recalled, Ho Chi Minh's Vietminh and the French were at war. The Vietminh were fighting to dislodge the French from Vietnam, and the French were fighting to reassert their colonial domination of Vietnam. In this conflict, the United States gradually came to take France's side. Its distaste for colonialism notwithstanding, the United States needed France's cooperation on European security matters, especially on the ill-fated European Defense Community (EDC). Moreover, U.S. distaste for colonialism was exceeded only by its fear of communism. After Mao Zedong came to power in China, the United States began to see wars or revolutions like the one in Vietnam as part of a coordinated strategy by China and the Soviet Union to expand communist power and influence. This view was strongly reinforced by the Korean War. The French knew this and accordingly, they slighted Ho's nationalist credentials and emphasized his communist connections. In 1951, U.S. military, technical, and economic aid to France totaled $448 million, the equivalent of 40 percent of what it cost the French to fight the Vietminh that year. By 1953 and 1954, U.S. aid to France climbed to the equivalent of 80 percent of the cost of fighting the war.[7]

Despite U.S. aid, France was losing. The May 1953 map of the commanding French general, Henri Navarre, showed the Vietminh controlling most of the Tonkin region, half of Annam, and a third of Cochin China.[8] The decisive battle was fought at the village Dien Bien Phu, in the lowlands of northwest Vietnam. Assuming that his superior firepower would allow him to score a decisive victory, Navarre chose to lure the Vietminh there to do battle. He was wrong. Under the direction of General Nguyen Vo Giap, the Vietminh took to the mountains surrounding the French garrison, cut it off from land reinforcements, and launched their attack on March 16, 1954. By then "the French garrison found itself

[6] See George Herring and Richard Immerman, "Eisenhower, Dulles, and Dienbienphu: 'The Day We Didn't Go to War' Revisited," *Journal of American History* 71 (1984): 343–63; Melanie Billings-Yun, *Decision against War: Eisenhower and Dien Bien Phu, 1954* (New York: Columbia University Press, 1988); and John P. Burke and Fred I. Greenstein, *How Presidents Test Reality: Decisions on Vietnam, 1954 and 1965* (New York: Russell Sage Foundation, 1989).

[7] Gelb and Betts, *Irony of Vietnam*, p. 46.

[8] See Kahin, *Intervention*, p. 43, for a reproduction of Navarre's map.

outgunned as well as outnumbered, with Giap's artillery so well ensconced that it was largely impervious to French air strikes."[9]

The Eisenhower administration had followed closely the development of the siege at Dien Bien Phu. Three months before the Vietminh launched their final attack, Eisenhower and his advisers had briefly considered the introduction of American ground troops into Vietnam. In a January 8 NSC meeting, the situation at Dien Bien Phu was considered serious enough for the United States to consider its options, although no decision was to be taken yet. Eisenhower quickly rejected the possibility of unilateral intervention. According to the minutes of the meeting, Eisenhower said that "he simply could not imagine the United States putting ground forces anywhere in Southeast Asia, except possibly in Malaya, which one would have to defend as a bulwark to our off-shore island chain."[10]

After the use of ground forces was rejected, the discussion moved to the use of U.S. air and naval power to relieve the siege at Dien Bien Phu. The chairman of the Joint Chiefs of Staff (JCS), Admiral Arthur Radford, was the chief proponent of doing "everything possible to forestall a French defeat at Dien Bien Phu," including sending an aircraft carrier to help the French defend the garrison or putting "one squadron of U.S. planes over Dien Bien Phu for as little as one afternoon." For Radford, the United States was already "in this thing in such a big way that it seemed foolish not to make the one small extra move which might be essential to success." Eisenhower was much more cautious. He reiterated his wish to keep U.S. troops out of "these jungles" but he also told his advisers that "we could nevertheless not forget our vital interests in Indochina." Still, Eisenhower was reluctant to involve the United States directly; his response to Radford's suggestion was to ask if it could be pursued covertly with "U.S. planes without insignia." The meeting ended without any decision except instructions to the CIA and the Defense Department to report to the NSC on measures the United States could take to help the French.[11]

In the next three months, the Eisenhower administration pursued a "two-track" policy. The first track involved warning the Soviet Union and "its Chinese Communist ally" against imposing their political systems on Southeast Asia. "The United States," according to Dulles, "feels that that possibility should not be passively accepted but should be met by united

[9] Ibid., p. 45.

[10] See U.S. Department of State, *Foreign Relations of the United States, 1952–54*, vol. 13, *Indochina* (Washington, D.C.: U.S. Government Printing Office, 1982), p. 949 (hereafter cited as *FRUS*).

[11] Ibid., p. 953.

action."[12] The key phrase here is "united action." Dulles appeared to suggest that the United States would be joined by its allies—principally France and Britain—in resisting communist gains in Southeast Asia. United action was not primarily meant to deter the communists in Indochina; Dulles was aiming more at affecting the Indochina phase of the upcoming Geneva talks. The United States feared that France and Britain would relinquish too much of Indochina to the Vietminh. As Dulles put it in a private phone conversation with Senate Majority Leader William Knowland, "he had to puncture the sentiment for appeasement before Geneva."[13]

The second track was active consideration of a massive air strike against the Vietminh forces in Dien Bien Phu. This move to save the French garrison was to be conducted jointly with the British and other allies if possible; failing that, the United States might have to do it alone. In early April, as the French position in Dien Bien Phu was about to collapse, Eisenhower decided to get congressional backing for possible unilateral U.S. action. On April 3, Dulles and Radford met with selected congressional leaders to seek authorization for the president to use air and naval power in Indochina. A request for U.S. naval air support to relieve the siege at Dien Bien Phu would arrive from Paris the very next day. Congress, however, demurred. The main reason why it was reluctant to go along was the fear of another Korea. As Dulles's record of the meeting has it, the unanimous feeling among the congressional leaders present was that "we want no more Koreas with the United States furnishing 90% of the manpower."[14] This sentiment was different than that of the "Never Again Club," whose members vowed, after the Korean experience, never to involve the United States in another limited Asian land war. The congressional leaders were not wary of military intervention per se but of *unilateral* U.S. intervention. Why? The answer is implicit in their "no more Koreas" statement. What was especially unappealing about unilateral intervention was the prospect of the United States fighting China basically alone, as in Korea, if intervention in Dien Bien Phu brought China into the war. The United States, after all, did not complain about "furnishing 90% of the manpower" before the Chinese intervened in the Korean War.

Dulles and Radford took pains to assure congressional leaders that they "did not now contemplate the commitment of land forces," but the congressmen replied "that once the flag was committed the use of land forces

[12] *Department of State Bulletin*, April 12, 1954, p. 539.

[13] Cited in William Gibbons, *The U.S. Government and the Vietnam War*, pt. 1: 1945–1960 (Princeton: Princeton University Press, 1986), p. 181.

[14] *FRUS*, 1952–1954, 13:1224.

would inevitably follow."[15] That fear partially explains why the specter of another Korea haunted those present; another relevant factor was the administration's 1954 estimate that "the chances were about even that the Chinese would intervene in the face of an impending Vietminh defeat."[16]

Still, Congress was willing to grant Dulles's request if the secretary of state could multilateralize the effort by getting Britain and other allies to join in the fight. Especially if the British could be cajoled into a joint endeavor, "the consensus [among those present] was that a congressional resolution could be passed, giving the President power to commit armed forces in the area."[17] Eisenhower sought to enlist the British the very next day. His letter to Prime Minister Churchill illustrates how serious the stakes were, from the perspective of the White House:

> [If] Indochina passes into the hands of the Communists the ultimate effect on our and your global strategic position with the consequent shift in the power ratio throughout Asia and the Pacific could be disastrous and, I know, unacceptable to you and me. . . .This had led us to the hard conclusion that the situation in Southeast Asia requires us urgently to take serious and far-reaching decisions. . . .
>
> If I may refer again to history; we failed to halt Hirohito, Mussolini and Hitler by not acting in unit and in time. That marked the beginning of many years of stark tragedy and desperate peril. May it not be that our nations have learned something from that lesson?[18]

Few Englishmen could have been more attuned to the lessons of the 1930s than Churchill and his foreign minister, Anthony Eden. Apparently, neither accepted the comparison. Neither saw the stakes in Dien Bien Phu to be as high as Dulles or Eisenhower did; both also worried about precipitating a war with China should Britain and the United States pursue "united action."[19] Churchill refused to commit his nation. Without commitment from the British, there was no prospect of a congressional resolution. Eisenhower decided against using U.S. forces to save the French at Dien Bien Phu.

Some accounts suggest that Eisenhower was personally so skeptical about the intervention that he let Congress impose conditions that he knew were unlikely to be met.[20] John Burke and Fred Greenstein have argued against this interpretation on the grounds that Eisenhower

[15] Ibid., 13:1225.

[16] Kahin, *Intervention*, p. 46.

[17] *FRUS*, 1952–1954, 13:1225.

[18] Ibid., 13:1239–40; see also *Pentagon Papers*, 1:98–99.

[19] *FRUS*, 1952–1954, 13:1311–12; *Pentagon Papers*, 1:101–6, 477–78.

[20] Billings-Yun, *Decision against War*, p. xii.

showed too much interest in the intervention option. They suggest that it was Eisenhower's advisory system and its encouragement of the vigorous airing of opposing views that allowed the president to base his decision on the best possible advice.[21] Whether Eisenhower dissembled before Congress or whether his advisory system played a critical role in the decision against war need not be settled here. The germane point is that Eisenhower took the multilateral injunction very seriously, as can be seen in the NSC deliberations throughout April. As long as the French garrison in Dien Bien Phu had not surrendered and as long as there were voices within the administration in favor of defending Southeast Asia, the air strike was a live option.

What finally led Eisenhower to reject that option was the issue of multilateralism. In a NSC meeting of April 29, 1954, Eisenhower remarked that it was beyond his comprehension "how the United States, together with the French, could intervene with armed forces in Indochina unless it did so in concert with some other nations." When foreign aid director Harold Stassen argued strenuously for unilateral U.S. intervention "to save Southeast Asia from Communism," Eisenhower voiced his concerns about the risk of "a general war with China and perhaps with the USSR, which the United States would have to prosecute separated from its allies." Thus, for all the importance Eisenhower attached to preventing communist gains in Southeast Asia, he shared the sentiments of the congressional leaders who met with Dulles in early April: the United States must not risk finding itself alone at war with China once more. "No more Koreas" came to mean "no more unilateral interventions close to the Chinese border." In response to Stassen's repeated importunities that Congress and the American people would support unilateral intervention, Eisenhower replied that for him, "the concept of leadership implied associates. Without allies and associates the leader is just an adventurer like Genghis Khan."[22]

Without American military support, the French position at Dien Bien Phu was doomed. The French surrendered to General Giap Vo Nguyen's forces on May 7. It was a timely victory for the Vietnamese communists. The Indochina phase of the Geneva Conference was to begin the next day.[23] The Vietminh's success in the battlefield, however, did not translate into a full victory at the negotiating table. Although the Vietminh controlled three-quarters of the country, the Geneva accords gave them political control of only the territory north of the seventeenth parallel. The area south of the seventeenth parallel was to revert to French con-

[21] Burke and Greenstein, *How Presidents Test Reality*, p. 111, n. 17, and chaps. 5 and 12.

[22] *FRUS*, 1952–1954, 13:1440.

[23] My account of the Geneva Conference draws mainly on Kahin, *Intervention*, pp. 52–65.

trol. This dividing line was not a political boundary, but a provisional line whose purpose was to create two military regroupment zones, with the Vietminh and their sympathizers regrouping north of the seventeenth parallel and the French forces regrouping south of the parallel.[24]

Why did the Vietminh agree to the armistice and settle for an area incommensurate with what they actually controlled? In part, it was because China and the Soviet Union applied strong pressure on the Vietminh. But more significant was the opportunity to transfer the struggle for the control of all of Vietnam from the military to the political realm. The Final Declaration provided for just that by stipulating that elections were to be held in 1956 to reunify the country. This suited the Vietminh. They were confident of their political support, and they were certain that they would win the elections. According to George Kahin, author of perhaps the definitive study of the Vietnam War, the promise of elections was "the heart of the Geneva Agreements" for the Vietminh. British foreign minister and co-chair of the Geneva Conference Anthony Eden had also made the same point: "Without the firm and explicit assurance of national elections aimed at reunifying the country, the Vietminh would never have agreed to the armistice."[25] This is hardly surprising. Even American officials believed the Vietminh would win. Briefing selected congressmen on the Geneva talks in June 1954, Under Secretary of State Bedell Smith predicted that Ho Chi Minh was likely to get 80 percent of the vote if "free elections" were held in Vietnam.[26]

No elections were held in 1956. By then, the French had left South Vietnam. Ngo Dinh Diem, a Catholic, nationalist, and staunch anticommunist backed by the United States, was in power. U.S. policy consisted of ensuring Diem's political survival, in hopes that a de facto southern state, viable on its own, could be established. The United States therefore acquiesced in Diem's refusal to hold the 1956 elections, which he probably would have lost to Ho Chi Minh. In the early years of his rule, Diem appeared capable of building South Vietnam into a viable entity. Soon, however, he alienated important segments of the intelligentsia, the Buddhist clerics and their supporters, by holding rigged elections, adopting anti-Buddhist policies, and arrogating power to only himself and his relatives.[27]

Starting in mid-1955, Diem systematically persecuted and in many cases eliminated former Vietminh members and their supporters, many of whom were not communists, who had remained in the South. This was prohibited by the Geneva agreement. Diem's program was so successful

[24] For the text of the Geneva agreements and the Final Declaration, see Kahin and Lewis, *United States in Vietnam*, appendix 2, pp. 348–69.

[25] Kahin, *Intervention*, p. 61.

[26] *FRUS*, 1952–1954, 13:1732.

[27] Kahin, *Intervention*, chap. 4.

that by 1959, the Vietminh infrastructure in the south was nearly destroyed. The remaining Vietminh obtained permission from Hanoi to begin limited military action against Diem's forces. Two years later, the National Liberation Front (NLF) was created to overthrow the Diem regime.[28] Whether instigated by Diem's attack on former Vietminh members and their sympathizers or by Diem's failure to hold elections in 1956, or whether any instigation might have been necessary at all, the Vietnamese communists decided to shift the struggle from the political arena back to the military one. North and South Vietnam were to be unified by force.

The other legacy left by Eisenhower and Dulles to the incoming administration of John F. Kennedy was SEATO. Created in the aftermath of the Geneva accords, SEATO was the institutional embodiment of the principles of "united action" that Eisenhower and Dulles championed, but could not put into effect, during the Dien Bien Phu crisis. The signatories were Britain, France, Australia, New Zealand, the Philippines, Thailand, Pakistan, and the United States. Although Vietnam, Laos, and Cambodia were prohibited from joining any alliances by the Geneva accords, the U.S. circumvented that restriction with a separate protocol stipulating that they would be covered by the treaty. Other Asian states such as India, Indonesia, and Burma refused to join.

SEATO committed its members to certain actions in case of threats to the peace of the area. Two kinds of threats were specified. In the case of armed aggression against any member state or state covered by the protocol, the other members would "act to meet the common danger in accordance with . . . [their] constitutional processes." If a member state were threatened in "any way other than by armed attack" (i.e., subversion), the others would "consult immediately in order to agree on the measures which should be taken for the common defense."[29] In later years, American policymakers would cite SEATO commitments as a major reason behind the U.S. intervention in Vietnam.

THE KENNEDY ADMINISTRATION AND LAOS

SEATO and an incipient revolution in South Vietnam were two major Vietnam legacies that Eisenhower bequeathed to the Kennedy administration. Laos was the third and the most urgent. Since becoming an independent country in 1954, Laotian politics centered on competition and

[28] Jeffrey Race, *War Comes to Long An* (Berkeley: University of California Press, 1972), chap. 3; William Duiker, *The Communist Road to Power in Vietnam* (Boulder, Colorado: Westview Press, 1981), pp. 186–99.

[29] See article 4 of SEATO treaty, reprinted in Kahin and Lewis, *United States in Vietnam*, appendix 3, pp. 377–81.

coalition building among three factions: a right wing group led by General Phoumi Nosavan (backed by the United States), a centrist group led by Prince Souvanna Phouma, and the communist Pathet Lao (backed by the Soviet Union and Hanoi). In late 1957, the three factions came together to form a delicate coalition government. The coalition broke down in May 1960, when Phoumi's faction sought to expel the Pathet Lao from power sharing and proceeded to incarcerate its leader. Civil war broke out. By late December, the communist Pathet Lao appeared to have the upper hand. Laos, in the view of the departing Eisenhower administration, was perilously and unacceptably close to communist domination.[30]

In his preinaugural briefing for Kennedy, Eisenhower put Laos at the top of the list of problems facing the United States. With "considerable emotion," Eisenhower told Kennedy that the United States could not afford to let the communists take Laos. Laos was the "key to the whole area," and if it fell, "it would be just a matter of time until South Vietnam, Cambodia, Thailand and Burma would collapse." If no political settlement could be reached, Eisenhower concluded, the U.S. "must intervene in concert with our allies. If we were unable to persuade our allies, then we must go it alone."[31]

The seriousness with which Kennedy took Eisenhower's advice has often been overlooked. On at least two occasions, Kennedy came close to intervening in Laos with military force.[32] The first was in April 1961, when the Pathet Lao, supported by some "neutralist" forces, mounted a new offensive. In an April 29 meeting with his foreign policy advisers, Kennedy wanted to find out "not only whether any of Laos could be saved by U.S. forces, but whether the U.S. would stand up and fight." Secretary of Defense Robert McNamara argued that if the United States were to give up on Laos, "we would have to attack the DRV" (Democratic Republic of Vietnam). The consensus among the military and civilian officials present was summed up in Deputy Assistant Secretary of State for the Far East John Steeve's comment that if the United States did not defend Laos, it would be "writing the first chapter in the defeat of Southeast Asia." Dean Rusk agreed:

> The Secretary suggested that Thai and US troops might be placed together in Vientiane and, if they could not hold, be removed by helicopter. Even if

[30] Roger Hilsman, *To Move A Nation* (Garden City, New York: Doubleday, 1967), chaps. 10–12; William Gibbons, *U.S. Government*, pt. 2: 1961–1964, chap. 1.

[31] *Pentagon Papers*, 2:636–37.

[32] Only the first occasion will be discussed here. The second occasion when force was seriously contemplated was May 1962; for details, see Gibbons, *U.S. Government*, pt. 2, pp. 112–19.

they were defeated they could be defeated together and this would be better than sitting back and doing nothing.

More drastic action was suggested by General George Decker, the army chief of staff: "We cannot win a conventional war in Southeast Asia; if we go in, we should go in to win, and that means bombing Hanoi, China, and maybe even using nuclear weapons."[33] After the meeting, the Joint Chiefs ordered the Commander in Chief Pacific (CINPAC) to be prepared to move five thousand U.S. combat troops into Thailand and another five thousand into Vietnam. CINPAC was told that the administration intended to use a "SEATO cover" for these moves.

Two days later, with the situation in Laos worsening, Kennedy and his advisers decided that the United States "had no choice but to threaten to take military action unless a cease-fire was arranged."[34] British Prime Minister Harold Macmillan's account of Washington's dispositions on that day is worth quoting:

> 6 p.m. [London] Meeting on Laos. . . . The Americans, supported by Australia and New Zealand, now want to take the preliminary troop movements for a military intervention. . . . They want to declare the alert at the SEATO meeting tomorrow. Their reason is that the two sides have not yet managed to meet to discuss the cease-fire; that the Pathet Lao are obviously stalling till the whole country had fallen; that they are advancing all the time; that the Thais are getting restless; that only the United Kingdom and France are out of step.[35]

Kennedy never did give the final order for intervention. The Pathet Lao, probably pushed by Moscow and Hanoi, agreed to cease-fire talks. This episode has been interpreted as an instance of successful coercive diplomacy, and it is.[36] But what is more interesting for our purposes is that the United States was willing to countenance a negotiated settlement in Laos, even though Kennedy and his advisers "agreed that the chance for salvaging anything out of the cease-fire and coalition government were slim indeed."[37] The settlement called for the neutralization of Laos and the formation of a coalition government in which the communists would play a major role. The pessimism of the administration stemmed from its perception that the settlement merely gave the Pathet Lao time to consolidate its position and perhaps make another bid for power in the future. For an administration that was every bit as attuned to the logic of

[33] Ibid., pp. 27–28.

[34] Ibid., p. 32.

[35] Ibid., pp. 32–33.

[36] See Alexander George, David Hall, and William Simons, *The Limits of Coercive Diplomacy: Laos, Cuba, and Vietnam* (Boston: Little, Brown and Company, 1971), chap. 2.

[37] *Pentagon Papers*, 2:9.

containment as its predecessors but had vowed to pursue it even more vigorously—to "pay any price, bear any burden," in Kennedy's catchy inaugural phrase—this willingness to settle for a compromise solution is noteworthy. It suggests the following question: If, under containment, a negotiated settlement was acceptable in Laos, why was it unacceptable in South Vietnam?

KENNEDY AND THE VIETNAM DECISIONS OF 1961

Kennedy held his first meeting on Vietnam eight days after his inauguration. An earlier report by General Edward Landsdale had indicated that South Vietnam was in danger of losing its fight against the NLF and that without U.S. help, South Vietnam "will be able to do no more than postpone eventual defeat."[38] Kennedy was extremely concerned and asked pointed questions on what the United States was doing about counterinsurgency during the meeting. After the meeting, Kennedy apparently turned to his advisers and said, "This is the worst one we've got, isn't it? You know, Eisenhower never mentioned it. He talked at length about Laos, but never uttered the word Vietnam."[39]

Throughout much of 1961, the Kennedy administration developed its options on Vietnam. In early February, the joint chiefs were queried about their plans for counterinsurgency training and asked if they had learned from other nations in this matter. The chiefs replied that they had studied the British experience in Malaya and the French experience in Indochina.[40] In May, Vice President Lyndon Johnson was dispatched to South Vietnam, the Staley mission followed a month later, and in October, Maxwell Taylor and Walt Rostow took to the trail. The reports and memos submitted to the president at the end of these trips tended to reinforce one another. The U.S. visitors all had reservations about Diem's effectiveness as a leader, but they saw no acceptable alternative to him. The visits also confirmed the seriousness of the situation in South Vietnam. Moreover, the U.S. visitors also agreed that Vietnam was the place to draw the line. This can be seen in Vice President Johnson's conclusion that "the basic decision in Southeast Asia is here. We must decide whether to help these countries to the best of our ability or throw in the

[38] U.S. Department of Defense, *United States–GVN Relations* (Washington, D.C.: U.S. Government Printing Office, 1972), vol. 2, pt. IV, A.5, pp. 66–77.

[39] Walt W. Rostow, *The Diffusion of Power: An Essay in Recent History* (New York: Macmillan Company, 1972), p. 265.

[40] Chester V. Clinton, Conferences with the President, Joint Chiefs of Staff, February 6, 1961, NSF, Kennedy Library.

towel in the area and pull back our defenses to San Francisco and a 'Fortress America' concept," and in Taylor and Rostow's comment:

> If Vietnam goes, it will be exceedingly difficult if not impossible to hold Southeast Asia. What will be lost is not merely a crucial piece of real estate, but the faith that the United States has the will and the capacity to deal with the Communist offensive in that area.[41]

Given these assessments and strategic imperatives, what were Kennedy's options?[42] The most drastic recommendation came from the military. The JCS and Secretary of Defense Robert McNamara suggested that the United States send up to forty thousand regular troops to fight the NLF and another 205,000 if the North Vietnamese and the Chinese counter-intervened with their armies. The precise troop estimates would fluctuate as the moment of decision arrived, but underlying Defense's approach to Vietnam were two constants: the belief that conventional U.S. forces could defeat the NLF Korea-style, and the conviction that if the United States were to act, it ought to act fast and hard.[43] The latter sentiment is best summarized in Assistant Secretary of Defense for International Security Affairs William Bundy's October 10 memo to McNamara:

> For what one man's feel is worth, mine—based on very close touch with Indochina in the 1954 war and civil war afterwards till Diem took hold—is that it *is* really now or never if we are to arrest the gains being made by the Viet Cong. . . . An early and hard-hitting operation has a good chance (70% would be my guess) of *arresting* things and giving Diem a chance to do better and clean up. Even if we follow up hard, on the lines the JCS are working out after yesterday's meeting, however, the chances are not much better that we will in fact be able to *clean up* the situation. . . . The 30% chance is that we would wind up like the French in 1954; white men can't win this kind of fight.
>
> On a 70-30 basis, I would myself favor going in. But if we let, say, a month go by before we move, the odds will slide. . . . down to 60-40, 50-50, and so on.[44]

A less drastic option, but one still involving the dispatch of U.S. combat forces, was Taylor and Rostow's recommendation to Kennedy that in

[41] *Pentagon Papers*, 2:58, 93.

[42] The following account of the options tabled draws primarily from Lawrence J. Basset and Stephen E. Pelz, "The Failed Search for Victory: Vietnam and the Politics of War," in *Kennedy's Quest for Victory: American Foreign Policy, 1961–1963*, ed. Thomas G. Paterson (New York: Oxford University Press, 1989), pp. 234–39. See also Kahin, *Intervention*, pp. 136–38.

[43] On the Korea-style and all-or-nothing dispositions of the military, see Hilsman, *To Move a Nation*, pp. 143, 146–47, 415–16, and 423.

[44] U.S. Department of Defense, *United States–GVN Relations*, 11:312. Emphasis in original.

addition to increasing military and economic aid to Diem, eight thousand American troops, disguised as a "logistical task force," be introduced in the Delta. Ostensibly, the troops would be there to help repair the damage caused by a recent flood, but in truth, they would also assume combat roles. Committing U.S. troops this way would demonstrate American resolve as well as show the South Vietnamese how to get the job done.[45]

A third option, coming from the State Department, argued against sending U.S. troops to South Vietnam. State was skeptical of, and frustrated with, Diem's regime. Dean Rusk was not sure if Diem was prepared to "take necessary measures to give us something worth supporting." Consequently, Rusk was reluctant to commit additional "American prestige to a losing horse."[46] He recommended sending additional advisers (not combat troops) and aid to Diem with the proviso that Diem be asked to make the necessary reforms that would allow him to fight the NLF effectively. Mike Mansfield, whom Kennedy had also consulted, was also against military intervention. Mansfield argued that if "the necessary reforms have not been forthcoming over the past seven years to stop communist subversion. . . . then I do not see how American combat troops can do it today." Moreover, according to Mansfield, there was risk of Chinese intervention; the United States "must . . . avoid another Korean-type involvement on the Asian mainland." Mansfield's bottom line was to give Diem economic and military aid while keeping the number of military advisers to a minimum.[47]

A fourth option, advocated by Averell Harriman, Chester Bowles, John Kenneth Galbraith, and Abram Chayes, called for the neutralization of Vietnam. Harriman, chief of the U.S. delegation that negotiated the Laotian neutralization settlement, thought that a similar settlement might be possible for Vietnam and would avoid commiting U.S. prestige and forces to South Vietnam.[48]

There is some evidence that Kennedy considered the neutralization option, although he eventually rejected it.[49] This rejection can be understood in light of the historical context. Nineteen-sixty-one was a year of

[45] *Pentagon Papers*, 2:84–92. Cf. Bassett and Pelz, "Failed Search for Victory," pp. 234–35.

[46] Cable, Dean Rusk to (Acting) Secretary of State, November 1, 1961, NSF Countries File—Vietnam, Kennedy Library. See also *Pentagon Papers*, 2:105.

[47] Memo, Mike Mansfield to John F. Kennedy, "The Vietnamese and the Southeast Asian Situation," November 2, 1961, NSF, Countries File—Vietnam, Kennedy Library.

[48] Memo, Averell Harriman to the President, November 11, 1961, NSF, Countries File—Vietnam, Kennedy Library.

[49] Kennedy had discussed the option with Averell Harriman, John Kenneth Galbraith, Dean Rusk, and Indian Prime Minister Jawaharlal Nehru. See Gibbons, *U.S. Government*, pt. 2, p. 82. Roger Hilsman confirms that Kennedy was intrigued by the Laos model and pondered its applicability to the conflict in South Vietnam (interview with author, April 9, 1986, New York City, New York).

foreign policy setbacks for the Kennedy administration. In January, Khrushchev made a strident pledge to support wars of national liberation, and June saw him attempting to browbeat Kennedy at Vienna and making threats about Berlin. In August, the Soviets erected the Berlin Wall. These events put the Kennedy administration on the defensive. Moreover, the policy of containment and U.S. credibility were not enhanced by the Bay of Pigs fiasco and the Laotian crisis. In Laos, as we saw earlier, the United States accepted a negotiated solution resulting in the neutralization of Laos and the formation of a coalition government that included the communists. Given these events, it is quite comprehensible that demonstrating U.S. resolve became such an issue for Kennedy. Neutralizing Vietnam along the lines of Laos would do little to contain communism or shore up U.S. credibility.

But if containment and credibility can explain why Kennedy rejected the neutralization option for Vietnam, they do not seem able to elucidate why Kennedy rejected the two options requiring the introduction of U.S. combat forces and settled instead for the option of more advisers and aid. Add to the logic of containment the above foreign policy setbacks and the perception that "early and hard-hitting" military action was needed to win in Vietnam, one would expect Kennedy to favor Defense's recommendations. His choice of the State Department option is puzzling from the containment perspective and the historical context. Part of the explanation must lie in the military strategy that has been associated with the Kennedy years: flexible response. Flexible response meant giving the United States an array of tools from which it could select the ones most appropriate to counter any perceived threat. The contrast was with massive retaliation, Eisenhower's strategy of countering communist provocation by threatening to respond disproportionately and with nuclear weapons if necessary. In a day when both the United States and the Soviet Union possessed hydrogen bombs, the Kennedy administration believed such threats were no longer credible. Hence the importance of having a spectrum of actions from which the United States could pick the most proportionate and effective to counter a given communist threat.[50]

Although flexible response did not rule out the use of conventional U.S. forces to help defend South Vietnam, it did make the search for less conventional military measures more legitimate. Here, the notion of counterinsurgency and the examples of Malaya and the Philippines are pertinent. They gave Kennedy an opportunity to experiment with unconventional warfare and, at the same time, an excuse not to commit U.S.

[50] See John L. Gaddis, *Strategies of Containment: A Critical Appraisal of Postwar American National Security Policy* (New York: Oxford University Press, 1982), chaps. 5–8, for an excellent discussion of massive retaliation and flexible response.

troops to South Vietnam. Kennedy's interest in counterinsurgency is so well documented that it need not detain us here.[51] What has been less well documented is the extent to which the administration's models of counterinsurgency were derived from the Malaya and the Philippine analogies and how those models might have affected U.S. strategy in Vietnam in the early 1960s.

The four options discussed above may be recast in terms of various historical models. The Defense Department's recommendation to use tens of thousands of troops to battle the NLF and to send another two hundred thousand should North Vietnam and China send their regular troops may be construed as the "Korean" model. The emphasis was on engaging the communists directly and in going to the "source" of the problem if necessary. For many—including Mike Mansfield, Dean Rusk, Roger Hilsman, and as we shall see, the president—this option conjured up images of "another Korea."[52] Harriman's neutralization approach toward Vietnam was of course informed by the Laotian model—getting the principal powers behind the warring parties to disengage from the country, and allowing the parties to work out a coalition government, even if such a government would include the communists. The State Department's recommendation of more aid and advisers but no combat troops was more akin, though not totally similar, to the Greek, Malayan, and Philippine models. The notion here was that by providing military and economic aid and advice, by working closely with the local leaders, and by adopting programs specific to the problems faced by the country concerned (for example, resettling procommunist peasants in Greece and Malaya), it was possible to defeat communist guerrillas as in Greece, Malaya, and the Philippines.[53] What made this model more attractive than the Korean one was that it did not envisage a major role for combat forces; what made it infinitely better than the Laotian model was that it promised a clear-cut defeat of the communists instead of a compromise. Finally, the Taylor and Rostow recommendation of an eight-thousand man "logistical task force" may be seen as a mix of

[51] See Douglas Blaufarb, *The Counterinsurgency Era: U.S. Doctrine and Performance* (New York: Free Press, 1977), chaps. 1–4; Hilsman, *To Move a Nation*, pt. 9; Rostow, *Diffusion of Power*, pp. 273–85; and Shafer, *Deadly Paradigms*, chap. 9.

[52] For Mansfield, see n. 47 above; for Rusk, see memo, McGeorge Bundy to the President, "Notes for Talk with Secretary Rusk," November 15, 1961, NSF Countries File—Vietnam, Kennedy Library; for Hilsman, see n. 43 above. See also memo, Robert Komer to McGeorge Bundy, "The Risks in Southeast Asia," October 31, 1961, NSF, Regional Security—Southeast Asia General, Kennedy Library.

[53] See memo, Walt Rostow to McGeorge Bundy, "Counter-Guerrilla Campaigns in Greece, Malaya, and the Philippines," November 21, 1961, NSF, Meetings and Memoranda File, Walt Rostow, Guerrilla and Unconventional Warfare, Kennedy Library.

the model based on Korea and that based on Greece, Malaya, and the Philippines.

Kennedy's decision to opt for sending more aid and advisers but no combat forces for the time being may thus be seen as a triumph of the Malayan-Greek-Philippine model over the Korean and Laotian models. That this is the case can be seen from statements of the president and his principal advisers on Vietnam. Kennedy's address to the graduating class of the U.S. Military Academy in the spring of 1962 is indicative of his administration's perspective:

> Korea has not been the only battle ground since the end of the Second World War. Men have fought and died in Malaya, in Greece, in the Philippines, in Algeria and Cuba, and Cyprus and almost continuously on the Indo-China Peninsula. No nuclear weapons have been fired. No massive nuclear retaliation has been considered appropriate. This is another type of war, new in its intensity, ancient in its origin—war by guerrillas, subversives, insurgents, assassins, war by ambush instead of by combat; by infiltration, instead of aggression, seeking victory by eroding and exhausting the enemy instead of engaging him. It requires in those situations where we must counter it. . . . a whole new kind of strategy, a wholly different kind of force, and therefore a new and wholly different kind of military training.[54]

Quite apart from the problem of telling the new graduates that their training might have been obsolete, the speech did reflect the president's inner convictions. On the day before the important November 15 meeting in which he made the decision to send more aid and advisers, Kennedy had sent a memo to Rusk and McNamara that among other things asked them to have someone "look into what we did in Greece. How much money and men were involved. How much money was used for guerrilla warfare?"[55] The historian Ernest May found it surprising that documents of the Vietnam debate in 1961 contain few references to the Korean model whereas documents of 1964–1965 contain many.[56] Kennedy's speech explains this "surprise": Malaya, Greece, and the Philippines, not Korea, were his models in 1961.[57]

[54] Reprinted in Donald Robinson, ed., *The Dirty Wars: Guerrilla Actions and Other Forms of Unconventional Warfare* (New York: Delacorte Press, 1968), p. 813.

[55] Note, President Kennedy to Dean Rusk and Robert McNamara, November 14, 1961, NSF, Countries File—Vietnam, Kennedy Library.

[56] May, *"Lessons" of the Past*, p. 96.

[57] Walt Rostow has suggested that Kennedy's "attitude towards Viet Nam was colored strongly by his memories of having seen the French in Viet Nam. . . . He kept coming back to the fact that the French put in more than 250,000 good troops, and were run out" (transcript, Walt Rostow Oral History Interview, p. 81, Kennedy Library). Rostow's recollection is corroborated by Arthur Schlesinger, Jr., who also argues that Kennedy was familiar with the French experience in Vietnam and was anxious to avoid repeating France's

The Korean analogy illustrated the aggressive tendencies of communist regimes well, but it had one shortcoming. The means used by the North Koreans against the South Koreans were a conventional invasion and the U.S.-UN response was also conventional. The situation in Vietnam in the early 1960s was different. Ngo Dinh Diem's government was not threatened by an outright invasion of regular North Vietnamese units but by Hanoi-backed communist guerrillas, many of whom were southerners. Recently declassified notes of the November 15 meeting confirm Kennedy's reluctance to view Vietnam and Korea as analogous. According to the meeting notes, Kennedy "questioned the wisdom of involvement in Viet Nam since the basis thereof is not completely clear. By comparison he noted that Korea was a case of clear aggression which was opposed by the United States and other members of the U.N. The conflict in Vietnam is more obscure and less flagrant."[58]

It should not be surprising then that Greece, Malaya, and the Philippines—the "indirect aggression" or "subterranean warfare" models—were considered more useful in assessing the new kind of war brewing in South Vietnam and in thinking about the appropriate response to such threats. The Malayan analogy deserves special attention here both because of the consternation it would cause the joint chiefs and because the analogy's prescription was eventually adopted by the United States as the "backbone" of South Vietnam's strategy for "countering subversion."[59]

The parallels between Malaya and Vietnam were striking. A British colony since 1874, Malaya was occupied by the Japanese during World War II. The Malayan Communist Party, formed in 1930, reorganized itself during this period as the Malayan People's Anti-Japanese Army (MPAJA) and was the only domestic group that cooperated with the British to mount an armed resistance against the Japanese invaders. MPAJA members—who were mostly ethnic Chinese—mounted guerrilla operations against the Japanese army; although they succeeded in making life difficult for the occupation forces, they were unable to dislodge them.

The MPAJA's "nationalist" reputation succeeded in attracting many followers to the organization, and with Japan's surrender in 1945, the MPAJA emerged as a possible contender for state power. Unlike Ho Chi

---

mistakes (interview with author, April 10, 1986, New York City, New York). Rostow's and Schlesinger's recollections would be consistent with Kennedy's rejection of the Korea-style option, and it also provides a fascinating contrast with 1965. In 1961, Kennedy, suspicious of the Korean precedent but more attuned to the French experience, rejected sending combat troops and sent military advisers instead; in 1965, Johnson, skeptical about the French parallel but very much taken by the Korean analogy, opted for military intervention.

[58] Notes on NSC Meeting, November 15, 1961, Vice Presidential Security File, "National Security Council (II)," NSF.

[59] *Pentagon Papers*, 2:149.

Minh's Vietminh, which took over Hanoi in the aftermath of Japan's defeat, the communists in Malaya were unable to win power. Although the communists did enjoy some support from the Chinese peasants and working class, they could not command the support of the largest ethnic group in Malaya, the Malays. Neither were they popular among the Chinese middle class. Moreover, during the Japanese occupation, the MPAJA had been ruthless toward Malays and middle-class Chinese who refused to cooperate with it. Their actions did much to alienate these two groups from the MPAJA, and since the MPAJA was predominantly Chinese, they also sowed the seeds of antagonism between the Malays and the Chinese.

Upon their return to Malaya, the British quickly and ruthlessly suppressed the communists and their front organizations. Fighting for their political survival, and also reasoning that they did not fight against one imperialist power only to bring in another, the communists launched a major insurrection in 1948. The insurrection began with the ambush and murder of three European rubber estate managers; the guerrillas also killed recalcitrant government officials and terrorized uncooperative peasants. In other words, the subterranean violence that Kennedy spoke about was common during this period. The conflict dragged on for twelve years, but in the end the guerrillas lost.[60]

Robert K. G. Thompson is the individual most often credited for defeating the guerrillas in Malaya. Initially, the British saw the insurrection as a military problem and reacted in kind. They launched large-scale military operations and bombed suspected jungle bases. Two years later, they found that they were worse off than when they began. Thompson concluded that as long as the guerrillas had the support—voluntary or involuntary—of the Chinese peasants, it was impossible to defeat them. He came up with the idea of "New Villages," secure hamlets where the peasants were isolated from the guerrillas. Civic action teams would visit to provide simple government services, and the police would train the peasants in the use of firearms and win their confidence so that communist sympathizers could be identified. The switch from a "search and destroy" strategy to a "clear and hold" strategy contributed greatly to the successful containment of communism in Malaya.[61]

We have no internal documents to establish directly that Kennedy took the Malayan analogy seriously and that it affected his decision-making.

[60] Anthony Short, *The Communist Insurrection in Malaya, 1948–1960* (London: Frederick Mueller, 1975); Gordon P. Means, *Malaysian Politics* (Singapore: Hodder and Stoughton, 1976); Blaufarb, *Counterinsurgency Era*, chap. 2.

[61] Sir Robert Thompson, *Defeating Communist Insurgency: The Lessons of Malaya and Vietnam* (New York: Praeger Books, 1966), esp. pp. 126–27. See also Blaufarb, *Counterinsurgency Era*, pp. 40–51.

We do have indirect evidence, however, suggesting that the analogy was very much on the minds of civilian decision-makers. In October 1961, Chairman of the JCS Lyman Lemnitzer wrote a memo to Kennedy's personal military adviser, Maxwell Taylor, to express his concern that "the success of the counter-terrorist police organization in Malaya has had considerable impact" on the administration's approach to Vietnam.[62] Given the analogy's influence, Lemnitzer felt obliged to point out its defects. He proceeded to list five "major differences between the situations in Malaya and South Vietnam." Lemnitzer's analysis is prescient and important enough to be cited in full:

> **a.** Malayan borders were far more controllable in that Thailand cooperated in refusing the Communists an operational safe haven.
>
> **b.** The racial characteristics of the Chinese insurgents in Malaya made identification and segregation a relatively simple matter as compared to the situation in Vietnam where the Viet Cong cannot be distinguished from the loyal citizen.
>
> **c.** The scarcity of food in Malaya versus the relative plenty in South Vietnam made the denial of food to the Communist guerrillas a far more important and readily usable weapon in Malaya.
>
> **d.** Most importantly, in Malaya the British were in actual command, with all of the obvious advantages this entails, and used highly trained Commonwealth troops.
>
> **e.** Finally, it took the British nearly 12 years to defeat an insurgency which was less strong than the one in South Vietnam.[63]

To be sure, Lemnitzer's critique stemmed as much from his need to protect the institutional prerogatives of the U.S. military as from his intellectual differences with Kennedy and his counterinsurgency advisers. Taking the Malayan analogy seriously would have meant adopting a military strategy antithetical to much of what the U.S. military held dear. American military strategy emphasized direct engagement with the enemy in any conflict and use of superior American firepower to minimize U.S. casualties. In other words, American expertise resided in conventional fighting strategies. A "Korean-type" war is the kind of conflict the American military had been trained to fight. The Malayan or the Greek examples, however, would prescribe a different role for the U.S. military. Instead of fighting, it would be engaged in counterinsurgency activities: training Vietnamese police cadres and civic action teams to win the peasants over, overseeing or helping build villages or "strategic hamlets"

[62] *Pentagon Papers*, 2:650–51.
[63] Ibid., p. 651.

to house forcibly relocated peasants, engaging in counterterrorist police activities, and so on.

Whatever Lemnitzer's motive, his critique of the Malayan analogy is interesting because it appreciates the "on the ground differences" between Malaya and South Vietnam. Lemnitzer took issue with the way the Malayan analogy would have defined the problem in South Vietnam, what it would have prescribed, and what it would have predicted as the result. The Malayan analogy implied that sanctuaries for the Vietcong were not a major issue. Lemnitzer believed the situation in South Vietnam, where the guerrillas could have safe havens in Laos and Cambodia, to be different. He also found the strategy prescribed by the Malayan analogy wanting, with its emphasis on counterterrorist political measures as opposed to military campaigns. Finally, he was less sanguine about the prediction of eventual success than Kennedy's civilian advisers. Lemnitzer's position implied that the Vietnamese communists would be much harder to defeat than the Malayan ones.

The other important point about Lemnizter's critique is that it was ignored. The administration's actions and statements suggest that the Malayan model won the day. The November 1961 decision against sending combat troops is consistent with the approach suggested by the Malayan, Greek, and Philippine models. The subsequent U.S. approval of and backing for Robert Thompson's "Strategic Hamlet Program"—the Vietnam version of the "New Villages" that had worked so well in Malaya—strongly suggests that Kennedy saw the Malayan model as applicable to South Vietnam. The Department of Defense paid for most of the "Strategic Hamlet Kits"—building materials, barbed wire, weapons and communication equipment—and saw to it that these materials were delivered promptly.[64] Roger Hilsman, Kennedy's chief adviser on counterinsurgency, has also written that "the President was impressed with Thompson's ideas and agreed that this was the direction we should go in developing a strategic concept for Vietnam."[65]

In Saigon, CIA Station Chief William Colby encouraged Diem to seek out Robert Thompson and his "British Advisory Mission" to apply the lessons of Malaya to South Vietnam.[66] As far as Thompson and his team were concerned, "we had found nothing new in Vietnam except in scale or intensity. It was to us a matter only of adapting strategy, tactics, and methods to a slightly different environment."[67] Malayan Prime Minister Tunku Abdul Rahman visited Saigon to exchange notes with Diem, with

[64] Ibid., p. 152.

[65] Hilsman, *To Move a Nation*, p. 438.

[66] Gibbons, *U.S. Government*, pt. 2, p. 104.

[67] Sir Robert Thompson, *No Exit from Vietnam* (London: Chatto and Windus, 1969), p. 133.

U.S. Ambassador Frederick Nolting sitting in. Although the Tunku also pointed out that it took Malaya ten years to suppress its insurgency, he felt that the Malayan and Vietnamese cases were so similar that he told Diem, "If you fail here, we will have to start all over again in Malaya."[68]

All these actions were consistent with the administration's public statements. Robert McNamara announced in the summer of 1962 that the United States considered the Strategic Hamlet Program to be the "backbone of President Diem's program for countering subversion directed against his state."[69] Roger Hilsman also argued that the best way to "pull the teeth of the Viet Cong terrorist campaign" was not by killing communists but by protecting the peasants in these hamlets. Hilsman claimed, "This technique was used successfully in Malaya against the Communist movement there."[70] Similarly, in April 1963, U. Alexis Johnson, deputy under secretary of state, suggested that the postwar insurgencies in Burma, Indonesia, Malaya, Indochina, and the Philippines were coordinated by China, but he singled out Malaya as the struggle that "provided valuable lessons which are now being applied in Viet-Nam."[71]

The Strategic Hamlet Program failed to contain the communist insurgency in South Vietnam. Formally initiated as "Operation Sunrise" in Bin Duong Province in early 1962, it failed to survive the deaths of Diem and his brother Nhu in late 1963. The failure of the hamlet program does not mean that the error lay in misapplying the lessons of Malaya to Vietnam. This may be the case, and I shall argue that this is indeed so, but it is always necessary to point out the situational differences that account for dissimilar outcomes. Lemnitzer's memorandum is a first cut in this direction. Although he was not addressing himself to the strategic hamlet program, his observations, if correct, may help explain why it was successful in Malaya but not in Vietnam. Before proceeding further, it is useful to consider the argument that the failure lay more in the execution of the program than in its conception.

Poor implementation of the program contributed to its failure. Hamlets were built in insecure areas, and too many were built in too short a time, with the result that many were poorly equipped and defended. Instead of emphasizing pacification—neutralizing and winning over the peasantry by providing them with security and necessary amenities—

[68] Frederick Nolting, *From Trust to Tragedy* (New York: Praeger Books, 1988), pp. 37–38. For U.S. interest in the Tunku's visit and in learning from Malaya, see Nolting's cable, Saigon to Secretary of State, May 26, 1961, and cable, Saigon to Secretary of State, November 7, 1961, NSF, Countries File—Vietnam, Kennedy Library.

[69] *Pentagon Papers*, 2:149.

[70] *Department of State Bulletin*, July 8, 1963, p. 44.

[71] Ibid., April 29, 1963, p. 636.

Diem and his brother Nhu used the program to exert control over the peasantry. This, coupled with corvee labor, failure to repay the peasants for resettlement losses, and corrupt officials, alienated the peasants.[72] Moreover, it has been suggested recently that the person hand-picked by the Ngos to implement the program, Pham Ngoc Thao, may have been a communist agent all along![73]

These problems point to a deeper malaise: Diem's inability to pursue reform and the United States' "inability to exert leverage" on him to do so. The latter, according to the *Pentagon Papers*, "emerges as the principal cause of failure" of the Strategic Hamlet Program."[74] Diem focused on controlling the peasants instead of winning their hearts and minds because it seemed a surer way of maintaining his tenuous grip on power. Diem could not do without U.S. aid, yet he refused to accede to U.S. demands for reform because he saw reform as compromising his authority and South Vietnam's sovereignty. As the authors of the *Pentagon Papers* put it, "He did not want to give credence to communist claims that he was a puppet of the United States, on one hand, or concentrate the coercive instruments of power in the hand of potential antagonists [his subordinates], on the other."[75] The point is not just that Diem exasperated his fellow generals and American policymakers so much that the United States approved a coup by Diem's generals to remove him and his brother. Rather, it is that the British did not face such a complicated situation in Malaya. As Lemnitzer pointed out, the British were in actual command in Malaya, and even then it took them over a decade to suppress the communist insurrection.

History indicates that the differences Lemnitzer identified in his memo were critical, perhaps even more critical than he himself would have liked. Even with American troops and American command, the NLF could not be subdued. Uncontrollable borders, namely sanctuaries and infiltration routes in Laos and Cambodia, also partially explain the difficulty. So does the difficulty of distinguishing loyal and disloyal peasants in Vietnam. There is also the character of the government being helped, a crucial difference omitted in Lemnizter's analysis. Malaya had a relatively stable and popular government both as a British colony and as a newly independent country in 1957. It was apparent even by the late 1950s that Diem's government was neither popular nor stable. Within the Diem regime, there was constant infighting and jockeying for power, so much so that the only principals Diem could trust were his blood rel-

[72] *Pentagon Papers*, 2:153.

[73] See Truong Nhu Tang, *A Vietcong Memoir* (New York: Harcourt Brace Jovanovich, 1985), pp. 42–62.

[74] *Pentagon Papers*, 2:158.

[75] Ibid., 2:146.

atives. Moreover, Diem was too insecure to encourage the building of more inclusive political institutions to give the various religious sects, nationalist political parties, and restive intellectuals a chance of meaningful political participation in their polity.

As was mentioned earlier, the Strategic Hamlet Program proved to be a failure, and it died with the overthrow and assassination of Ngo Dinh Diem and his brother, Ngo Dinh Nhu. President Kennedy himself was killed by an assassin's bullet in Texas three weeks later. By the mid-1960s, the Vietnam conflict began to evolve from an unconventional guerrilla war to a war with an increasingly conventional character. Perhaps the evolving nature of the war made the Malayan, Greek, and Philippine analogies less tenable. Perhaps the new president of the United States found his personal experiences more pertinent. At any rate, Lyndon Baines Johnson resorted to a different set of historical precedents to think about the conflict in Vietnam.

The aim of the preceding analysis of three pre-1965 Indochina decisions has been to indicate, in a preliminary way, the relationship among containment, analogical reasoning, and decision outcomes. I suggest that containment is best understood as an overarching constant in the postwar period. Given containment, we can always expect American policymakers to be concerned about communist power gains anywhere. From this reasonable premise, however, it would be premature to conclude that containment necessarily implies decisive action on the part of the United States to counter the extension of communist power. Such a conclusion might seem reasonable if one focused exclusively on the correlation between containment and the 1965 decisions to intervene in Vietnam, but with a broader historical perspective, however, it appears tenuous.

Our analysis of three major pre–1965 Vietnam decisions suggests that even at the height of containment, the United States was willing to allow the North to go communist in 1954, and in 1961 to live with a negotiated settlement in Laos, as well as to avoid direct military confrontation with the NLF. In each of these cases, senior policymakers right up to the president believed that if communist advances were not stopped, vital U.S. interests would be adversely affected. Yet the responses varied from Eisenhower's "do nothing" to Kennedy's "limited partnership" with South Vietnam. Containment, therefore, cannot tell us whether U.S. concerns would result in action or not; neither can it tell us the form of the action, if taken.

Given that containment seems to be consistent with such a variety of outcomes, the question arises as to whether other factors might be more helpful in discriminating among decision outcomes. In this chapter, I suggest, but do not prove, that historical analogies may be one such factor. As we have observed, containment notwithstanding, policymakers have to make situation-specific assessments of the costs and benefits of proposed options. My claim is that in making such assessments, analogies are often, though by no means always, relevant. In 1954, a major reason why Congress and Eisenhower were reluctant to intervene unilaterally in Vietnam was that it would be too costly and risky: "no more Koreas," or no more fighting China alone, was on everyone's minds. Congress seemed unwilling to authorize any U.S. action unless the British joined in. If this interpretation is correct, Winston Churchill may not have been completely off the mark when he rejected "united action" on the grounds that "we were being asked . . . to assist in misleading Congress into approving a military operation, which would in itself be ineffective, and might well bring the world to the verge of a major war."[76] Without British participation, Eisenhower decided against unilateral intervention.

Kennedy was also preoccupied with stopping the extension of communist power in South Vietnam, but he rejected the "Korean style" option and settled for the less drastic options and strategies recommended by the Malayan, Philippine, and Greek experiences. I do not mean to suggest that these analogies played a decisive role in convincing Eisenhower and Kennedy to choose the way they did; the documentation is simply too sparse to support such an unqualified assertion. At best, these analogies were one factor among many influencing Eisenhower's and Kennedy's choices. In this sense, this chapter serves as a prelude to the next three chapters, where we begin an intensive analysis of analogies that affected the 1965 decisions, where the evidence of the import of these analogies is much stronger, and where, even if analogies remain one factor among many, that factor is arguably primus inter pares.

[76] Cited in Eden, *Full Circle*, p. 117.

CHAPTER 5

Korea

> I would suggest to you that if we had not gone into Korea, I think it would have been very unlikely that we would have gotten into Vietnam.
>
> —*George Ball, July 1986*

THE HISTORICAL analogy that played the most influential role in the decision-making of the 1960s was that of Korea. This is true not just because George Ball said so, but because however one sifts the record—by quantitative analysis of the public and private use of the analogies, by textual analysis of the documents of the period, or by what former policymakers are now willing to say—the "lessons" of Korea emerge as a preeminent consideration in the minds of those who formulated America's Vietnam policy.

In this chapter, I argue that the Korean analogy—or rather, what U.S. decision-makers considered to be the major lessons of the U.S. experience in the Korean War—can explain why the Johnson administration decided to intervene in Vietnam, as well as why the American intervention took the form that it did. My argument is based on the ways the Korean analogy (1) shaped the administration's definition of the challenge in Vietnam, (2) assessed the political stakes involved, and (3) provided an implicit policy prescription, and on the ways it also "helped" evaluate this and other policy prescriptions by (4) predicting their chances of success, (5) assessing their morality, and (6) warning about their dangers. By defining the situation and evaluating the options in these ways, that is, by performing the diagnostic tasks the AE framework claims for analogies, the Korean analogy introduced choice propensities into the administration's decision-making: it predisposed those who took it seriously toward certain policy options and turned them away from others. In so doing, it played an important role in influencing the decision outcome.

Figure 5.1 shows how frequently (measured quarterly) policymakers used historical analogies in public and in private in the years 1961–1966. Both in public and in private, the most precipitous climb in the use of

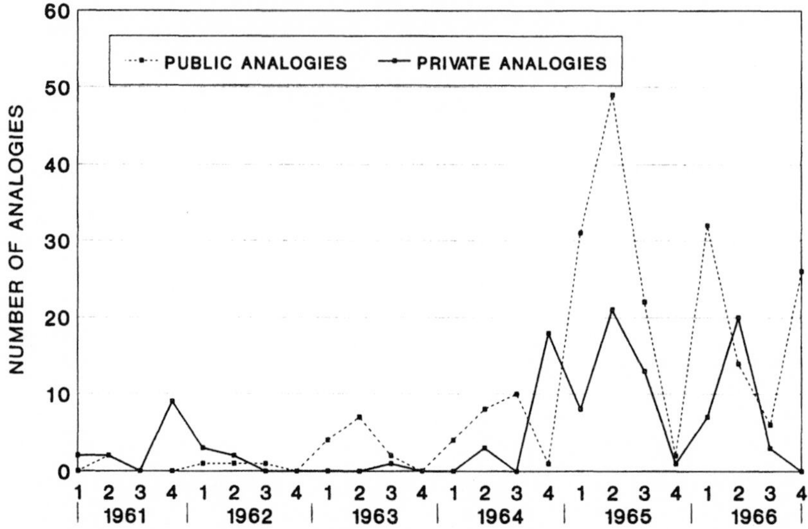

Figure 5.1. Total Number of Most Frequently Used Public and Private Historical Analogies per Quarter, 1961–1966

Source: U.S. Department of State, *Department of State Bulletin* (Washington, D.C.: U.S. Government Printing Office); *The Pentagon Papers*, Senator Gravel, ed., vols. 1–4 (Boston: Beacon Press, 1971); and declassified documents from the Lyndon Baines Johnson Library, Austin, Texas, and the John F. Kennedy Library, Boston, Massachusetts.

analogies occurred during the last quarter of 1964 and the first two quarters of 1965. Not coincidentally, this was the period in which the Johnson administration was most active in formulating its Vietnam options. The pattern of *private* use is especially revealing: it shows that there was a marked increase in the number of analogies used by policymakers in their internal deliberations in the quarter leading up to every major decision on Vietnam. In addition to the peaks of late 1964 (leading to the December–February air war decision) and early 1965 (leading to the July ground war decision), two other peaks can be discerned. The first was in late 1961, coinciding with Kennedy's November decision to send more advisers and aid to South Vietnam, and the second was in 1966, coinciding with Johnson's decision to allow U.S. planes to bomb North Vietnam's Petroleum, Oil, and Lubricants (POL) sites, targets he had prohibited until then.[1]

[1] The June 1966 decision will not be extensively analyzed in this work, although I will have occasion to refer to it. For a sense of the analogies relevant to the decision, see meet-

If the analogies charted in the figures are disaggregated, as was done in tables 3.1 and 3.2, it will be found that the Korean analogy emerges as by far the most often cited; its frequency of use also reached new heights in 1965 and 1966. Two points are worth reiterating: as the decision-makers contemplated intervening militarily in Vietnam, they referred to historical analogies more frequently. Of all the analogies invoked, the Korean analogy was the most popular. This finding suggests that Korea may have played a special role in the analysis or justification of the U.S. role in the Vietnam War; it also supports the notion that the last successful war exercises a major impact on the way a nation looks at the next war.[2]

THE PUBLIC LESSONS OF KOREA

In January 1965, the assistant secretary of state for Far Eastern affairs, William Bundy, shared his thoughts on "American Policy in South Vietnam and Southeast Asia" with the members of the Washington, Missouri, Chamber of Commerce. Like most of his other speeches, this one was long and detailed, but never condescending. Like many of his other speeches, this one referred to the Korean analogy. This speech, however, was distinguished by the systematic manner in which Bundy drew on the lessons of Korea to illuminate the problem in South Vietnam.

Bundy began by surveying the postwar history of the Far East. He described the inability of the United States to prevent China from turning communist in 1949 and lamented its consequences: "There came to power . . . a Communist regime . . . imbued above all with a primitive Communist ideology in its most virulent and expansionist form." Bundy then turned to the case of Korea. In Korea, the United States succeeded in foiling the expansionist plans of North Korea and its backers, China and the Soviet Union, at the cost of 150,000 American casualties and $18 billion. But South Korea remained independent. This historical sketch was necessary to understand American policy toward South Vietnam, for the policy was not the result of "some abstract design from a drawing board," but rather was "the fruit of history and experience." As Bundy put it:

> In essence, our policy derives from (1) the fact of the Communist nations of Asia and their policies; (2) the lessons of the thirties and of Korea; (3) the

ing with Foreign Policy Advisers, January 22, 1966, Meeting Notes File, and esp. notes of NSC Meeting, June 22, 1966, NSC Meetings File, NSF.

[2] See Jervis, *Perception and Misperception*, pp. 266–70.

logical extension of that fact and these lessons to what has happened in Southeast Asia.[3]

By the "fact of the Communist nations of Asia and their policies," Bundy meant primarily China, North Vietnam, and their expansionist tendencies. The lessons of the thirties were nested in the lessons of Korea:

In retrospect, our action in Korea reflected three elements:

—a recognition that aggression of any sort must be met early and head-on or it will have to be met later and in tougher circumstances. We had relearned the lessons of the 1930's—Manchuria, Ethiopia, the Rhineland, Czechoslovakia.

—a recognition that a defense line in Asia, stated in terms of an island perimeter, did not adequately define our vital interests, that those vital interests could be affected by action on the mainland of Asia.

—an understanding that, for the future, a power vacuum was an invitation to aggression, that there must be local political, economic, and military strength in making aggression unprofitable, but also that there must be a demonstrated willingness of major external powers both to assist and to intervene if required.[4]

Applied to the problem of South Vietnam, these lessons suggested that external aggression—by North Vietnam, with the backing of China and the Soviet Union, against South Vietnam—was the issue. The stakes were vital, for if such aggression was not stopped now, it would have to be stopped later under more difficult conditions. Implicit in this definition of the situation and assessment of the stakes was the notion that U.S. military action along the lines of Korea might be necessary to counter communist expansionism.

The thesis of aggression from the North was most forcefully articulated in a White Paper issued by the State Department in February 1965. The report downplayed the parallels between Vietnam and the experiences of Greece, Malaya, and the Philippines. In Greece, the report argued, the guerrillas used a friendly neighbor as a sanctuary; in Malaya, the guerrillas were physically distinguishable from the peasants; in the Philippines, the guerrillas were separated physically from their source of moral and physical support, China. None of these conditions obtained in the case of Vietnam. Korea was a better analogue:

North Vietnam's commitment to seize control of the South is no less total than was the commitment of the regime in North Korea in 1950. . . . Above

[3] *Department of State Bulletin*, February 8, 1965, p. 171.

[4] Ibid., p. 168.

all, the war in Vietnam is not a spontaneous and local rebellion against the established government.[5]

William Bundy's deputy, Leonard Unger, sardonically brushed aside the suggestion that an indigenous revolt was occurring in South Vietnam: "Certainly, they [the Vietcong] are Vietnamese, and the North Koreans who swept across their boundary in 1950 to attack South Korea were also Koreans."[6] Similarly, years after he made the fateful decisions of 1965, Johnson would lecture Doris Kearns on the same point, with the same analogy:

> How . . . can you . . . say that South Vietnam is not a separate country with a traditionally recognized boundary? . . . Oh sure, there were some Koreans in both North and South Korea who believed their country was one country, yet was there any doubt that North Korean aggression took place?[7]

A fundamental lesson of Korea was, therefore, that international communism was at work. In 1950, North Korea, with the backing of the Soviet Union (and by implication China), attempted to invade South Korea. In 1965, North Vietnam, backed by the two communist giants, was trying to take over South Vietnam. This argument fits the definition of analogical reasoning adopted earlier, which can be expressed in the form, *AX*:*BX*::*AY*:*BY*.[8] North Korea (*A*) and North Vietnam (*B*) were similar in that both were communist states (*X*). North Korea (*A*), supported by the Soviet Union and China, tried to invade the South (action *Y*); therefore North Vietnam (*B*) was probably backed in South Vietnam by the same communist giants, with just as aggressive intentions (action *Y*).

The Korean analogy did not just describe the nature of the conflict in Vietnam. By comparing the Vietnam conflict to the Korean War, the analogy also implied that the political stakes in Vietnam were extremely high. Moreover, if aggression on the part of the North Vietnamese was the definition of the situation suggested by the Korean analogy, military action on the part of the United States was the prescription. In 1950, the United States met North Korea early and head-on. In the 1930s no one met Mussolini and Hitler early and head-on; that only postponed the reckoning until later and under tougher circumstances. Applied to Vietnam, this contrast between the path of 1950 and that of the 1930s offered an unambiguous lesson: meet the North Vietnamese now or meet them later in tougher circumstances.

[5] Ibid., March 22, 1965, p. 404.

[6] Ibid., May 10, 1965, p. 712. Leonard Unger also affirmed this view in an interview with the author, Medford, Massachusetts, August 13, 1985.

[7] Doris Kearns, *Lyndon Johnson and the American Dream* (New York: Harper and Row, 1976), p. 328.

[8] See chap. 1 above; see also Fischer, *Historians' Fallacies*, pp. 242–43.

Implicit in the prescription of military intervention now was the prognostication of success without excessive costs. While Korea may have been considered a stalemate in the 1950s, it had by the 1960s, become an example of a successful limited war. This point will be elaborated later; for the moment, the salient point is that to the foreign policy elite of the 1960s, Korea was no longer an "unmentionable victory," and the path of 1950 was considered preferable to the path of the 1930s.[9] The prediction of eventual success was one of the most attractive characteristics of the Korean analogy. Applied to Vietnam, it implied that timely intervention by the United States was likely to succeed in preventing South Vietnam from going communist, much as American intervention in Korea had foiled North Korea's attempt to conquer the South.

Moreover, if Vietnam was analogous to Korea in that northern aggression was to blame, if the stakes were as vital, and if U.S. intervention was likely to work, then it could be argued that the United States was obligated to help South Vietnam.[10] In other words, underlying the picture given by the Korean analogy was a strong normative invocation: it was morally right for the United States to come to the help of South Vietnam.[11] The policy implication of these public lessons of Korea is not hard to deduce: if necessary, the United States would intervene to keep South Vietnam independent.

THE USES OF THE ANALOGIES: DIAGNOSIS, JUSTIFICATION, AND ADVOCACY

Relying on the public statements of policymakers to document what they learned from the American experience in the Korean War and how they applied those lessons to Vietnam is an appropriate point of departure. However, more must be done in order to claim that the Korean analogy influenced decision outcomes, for focusing only on the public analogies makes my argument susceptible to the skeptics' objections: What if the policymakers did not take the Korean and the other analogies they used seriously? What if the analogies were used primarily for justifying and advocating policy instead of analyzing it? These are legitimate objections. If officials used analogies only to justify before the public the wisdom and

[9] Richard Rovere, *Affairs of State: The Eisenhower Years* (New York: Farrar, Strauss, and Cudahy, 1956), pp. 146–50.

[10] For a more involved discussion of the normative component of the Korean analogy, see my "Seduction by Analogy," pp. 65–77.

[11] McGeorge Bundy, a less avid user of analogies than most of his colleagues, nevertheless found this lesson of Korea highly pertinent (interview with author, New York City, New York, April 11, 1986).

rectitude of their policies, then examining their analogies amounts to studying political rhetoric.

To make this analysis more than that, it is necessary to make a distinction between analogies used only in public and those used in private. If analogies were used to persuade the public, then they ought not to show up frequently in the documents and the private deliberations of the policymakers, but as table 3.2 shows and as we shall see again later, historical analogies in fact abound.

Still, it might be argued that even those private historical analogies were used for advocacy, not diagnosis. An experienced bureaucrat might latch on to a salient analogy to advocate a particular policy whether or not he believed in it. However, to the extent that advocacy is an integral part of decision-making, and to the extent that analogies are effective in persuading others, even an analogy used only to back up a choice already favored can influence the decision outcome. Thus, although the advocacy thesis suggests that a policymaker's analogies do not tell us why he may prefer one option over another, it does not deny that those analogies may play a role in persuading others to support his preferences. If analogies do the latter, they become more than rhetoric or convenient figures of speech; they are devices for consensus building and for facilitating decisions. As such they are worthy of study in their own right.

The AE framework claims, of course, that analogies do much more. The point is that the three uses of analogies—justification, policy advocacy and diagnosis—need not be mutually exclusive. Indeed, in practice, these uses are probably difficult to separate. The policymaker who, say, used the Korean analogy to inform his diagnosis of the stakes in Vietnam would have no problem using the same analogy to justify or advocate his preferred policy. For the purposes of our analysis, it can be readily granted that policy advocacy and justification might be at work when a policymaker uses an analogy. What is important is that we also allow for the likelihood that the analogy will also be used for diagnosis. Once that is allowed, an analysis of a policymaker's analogies is also an analysis of his decision-making.

It is the policymaker who uses analogies he personally disbelieves in order to justify or advocate a particular policy who poses a problem for our analysis. This, I take to be the skeptics' argument. Analyzing such analogies would be tantamount to analyzing an epiphenomenon. One might learn something about the properties of analogies that make them such attractive tools of persuasion—not an unimportant task—but one is unlikely to unveil the reasoning behind policy decisions. If, however, policymakers believe in the analogies they use, their use of the same analogies for advocacy and public justification need not detract from the diagnostic role that the analogies may have played in their decision-making. A study of those analogies can be one way to probe the reasoning behind their decisions.

Three arguments are offered in defense of the assumption that America's Vietnam decision-makers believed in the analogies they used. First, it is the simpler and more parsimonious assumption. One need not document deceitful or manipulative practices on the part of the policymakers, as the public persuasion and private advocacy theses must. At the very least, the latter must document inconsistencies between policymakers' analogies and their true beliefs. This is difficult to do. Moreover, since the justification and advocacy theses both focus on how a policymaker sells his favored option, they beg the question of how he comes to favor that option in the first place. It is consequently simpler to assume that a policymaker takes his analogies seriously: it gives an indication of how he arrives at his decision and it also explains why he may use the analogies to sell his policy.

Second, there is strong evidence that those who formulated America's Vietnam policy were serious about the analogies they used. The memoirs and private papers of many of the principals indicate that they used basically the same analogies in public and in private to make sense of the situation in Vietnam. Figure 5.1 strongly supports this point. For example, Robert McNamara has written that one reason he pressured President Johnson to call up the reserves in 1965 was that he believed the reserves played a critical role in resolving the Berlin crisis of 1961.[12] Also, when asked twenty years later whether they believed in the analogies they used, the former policymakers, virtually to a man, asserted that they did.[13]

It would be unusual, it could be claimed, for former policymakers to deny that they had been serious about the analogies they had used. Yet it is possible to perform a check. A policymaker who used an analogy for advocacy without believing in it would grab the most effective analogy to bolster his preferred option. There need be no correlation between the most effective analogy and his personal experience. Yet the most avid users of historical analogies almost always invoked parallels with which they were most familiar. Lyndon Johnson and Dean Rusk, for example, were both deeply affected by the Korean War. As a senator, Johnson was extremely moved by Truman's decisiveness in responding to the attack by North Korea against the South; Rusk, after all, was the person who designated the thirty-eighth parallel as the dividing line between North and South Korea. Johnson would always remember how Truman pro-

[12] Letter from Robert McNamara to Larry Berman, cited in Berman, *Planning a Tragedy*, p. 104.

[13] Author's interviews with Dean Rusk, William Bundy, Leonard Unger, George Ball, and James Thomson, 1985–1986.

tected America's vital interests in Asia; Rusk would subsequently be uncompromising toward those bent on crossing designated "boundaries."[14] Finally, George Ball, who had worked closely with the French, was much more attuned than his colleagues to the similarities between the American and French experiences in Vietnam. Ball was so convinced of the relevance of the French parallel, and its implications, that he continued to use the analogy even when it was obvious that it was not the most effective tool for advocating his preferred policy.[15] Those who have the occasion to consult the oral histories given by these and other former policymakers are also likely to be struck by the frequency with which they each bring up—without prompting—the influence of the lessons of history in general, and of Korea in particular, on the president, their colleagues, and themselves.[16] None of these former officials has suggested that the users of these analogies were anything but serious about them. When different participants allude to the importance of the same set of historical lessons in the Vietnam policy process, the assumption that policymakers took their analogies seriously gains additional credence.

The strongest argument in favor of the assumption that the Vietnam policymakers believed in the analogies they used is to be found in the cognitive dimension of the AE framework. There is no need to reiterate here the arguments of chapters 1 and 2: it suffices to say that schema theory suggests that analogical reasoning is a major way human beings make sense of new situations and that the notion of the schema provides strong theoretical corroboration for the assumption that policymakers take their analogies seriously. In the next section, I examine how some of the principal decision-makers relied on analogies in private to make sense of the challenge in Vietnam.

THE PRIVATE LESSONS OF KOREA

On August 10, 1964, Congress passed the Southeast Asian Resolution, more commonly known as the Tonkin Gulf Resolution, empowering President Johnson to defend U.S. forces against armed attack in the region as well as to "take all necessary steps, including the use of armed force, to

[14] See Johnson, *The Vantage Point*, pp. 31, 47–48, and 115. For Dean Rusk's views, see *Department of State Bulletin*, May 10, 1965, p. 697.

[15] See for example, Ball's memorandum to the President, "Keeping the Power of Decision in the South Viet-Nam Crisis," June 18, 1965, NSF. William Bundy believed that Ball's reliance on the France in the 1950s analogy made him "much less effective" in policy debates (interview with author, Hofstra University, New York, April 11, 1986).

[16] See transcripts of the oral histories of the following: Lyndon Johnson, Dean Rusk, William Bundy, George Ball, Alexis Johnson, John McCormack.

assist any member of protocol states of the Southeast Asia Collective Defense Treaty" in defense of its freedom.[17] The immediate impetus behind the resolution had to do with purported attacks by North Vietnamese torpedo boats against U.S. warships in the gulf, but it was the long-term implications of the resolution that heartened Johnson and his advisers.[18] Armed with the resolution, the administration felt that it needed no further approval from Congress to intervene militarily in South Vietnam when and if the situation required.

The administration immediately moved to reevaluate its Vietnam policy. In August and September, senior officials from State, Defense, and the JCS circulated memos about the next course of action in Vietnam. The thrust of these memos was that the U.S. should do more to "convince Hanoi that they were facing a determined foe and that they should get out of South Vietnam and Laos."[19] By October, a consensus was forming among Johnson's advisers that "doing more" meant going beyond reprisals for specific acts by Hanoi; the idea of launching a systematic air war against North Vietnam became increasingly popular.[20] It was in this context that George Ball wrote a long October 5, 1964, memorandum, in which he expressed his "sceptical thoughts on the assumptions of our Viet-nam policy," to Dean Rusk, Robert McNamara, and McGeorge Bundy.

Entitled "How Valid Are the Assumptions Underlying our Viet-nam Policies?" this document has been hailed by later analysts as "remarkable" and "prescient."[21] Two successive Saturday afternoons were reserved to debate the issues raised by Ball. When it became obvious after the first meeting that Ball's arguments had not made the slightest dent on his superiors' convictions, the second meeting was canceled.[22] Five months later, the memorandum reached the president's desk. Johnson demanded to know why he had not seen it earlier. A meeting was called to discuss Ball's arguments, and Johnson "showed that he had read the document, for he challenged specific points . . . and even remembered the page numbers where those arguments occurred."[23]

Ball's memorandum began with the observation that the political situ-

[17] Kahin and Lewis, *The United States in Vietnam*, appendix 9, p. 404.

[18] See *Pentagon Papers*, 3:182–89; Berman, *Planning a Tragedy*, pp. 32–34; and Kahin, *Intervention*, pp. 219–26.

[19] *Pentagon Papers*, 3:130–31.

[20] See ibid., 3:206, 524–29, 550–64.

[21] Gelb and Betts, *Irony of Vietnam*, p. 111; Neustadt and May, *Thinking in Time*, p. 170. The memo was reprinted in *The Atlantic Monthly* in 1972.

[22] George Ball, interview with author, New York City, New York, July 23, 1986 (cited hereafter as Ball interview).

[23] George Ball, *The Past Has Another Pattern* (New York: W. W. Norton, 1982), p. 392.

ation in Saigon was going from bad to worse. It was obvious that "within the next few weeks, we must face a major decision of national policy."[24] As Ball saw it, the United States had four options. The first option was to continue to support the South Vietnamese effort, in the full realization that it might not be enough. The second option was to take over the war in South Vietnam by introducing U.S. troops. Third, the United States could bomb the north in hope of forcing it to stop supporting the southern insurgency. Bombing might also improve the U.S. bargaining position, making possible a political solution through negotiation. The fourth option was a political settlement through negotiation without direct U.S. military involvement.

Through a comprehensive analysis of the effectiveness and the likely costs of each of the options, Ball dismissed the first three and came out in favor of the fourth. Option one, it was widely acknowledged, would not be enough to prevent the collapse of South Vietnam. Option two, introducing ground troops, was something everyone was keen to postpone for the moment. The main purpose of Ball's memorandum, therefore, was to question the assumptions of those who favored option three. The most important of these assumptions, if Ball's memo is any indication, was the belief that the Korean and Vietnam conflicts were analogous.

In the foreword of the memorandum and under the subheading "South Viet-nam Is Not Korea," Ball warned:

> In approaching this problem, I want to emphasize one key point at the outset: The problem of South Viet-nam is *sui generis*. South Viet-nam is not Korea, and in making fundamental decisions it would be a mistake for us to rely too heavily on the Korean analogy.[25]

He then went on to list five principal differences between the U.S. position in South Vietnam in 1964 and the U.S. position in Korea in 1951:

> **a.** We were in South Korea under a clear United Nations mandate. Our presence in South Viet-nam depends upon the continuing request of the GVN [Government of South Vietnam] plus the SEATO protocol.
>
> **b.** At their peak, United Nation forces in South Korea (other than ours and those of the ROK [Republic of Korea]) included 53,000 infantrymen and 1000 other troops provided by fifty-three nations.
>
> In Viet-nam, we are doing it alone with no substantial help from any other country.

[24] Ball, "How Valid Are the Assumptions," p. 36.

[25] Ibid., p. 36.

c. In 1950, the Korean government under Syngman Rhee was stable. It had the general support of the principal elements in the country. There was little factional fighting and jockeying for power.

In South Viet-nam, we face governmental chaos.

d. The Korean War started only two years after Korean independence. The Korean people were still excited by their newfound freedom; they were fresh for the war.

In contrast, the people of Indochina have been fighting for almost twenty years—first against the French, then for the last ten against the NVN [North Vietnamese]. All evidence points to the fact that they are tired of conflict.

e. Finally, the Korean War started with a massive land invasion by 100,000 troops. This was a classical type of invasion across an established border. It was so reported within twelve hours by the United Nations Commission on the spot. It gave us an unassailable political and legal base for counteraction.

In South Viet-nam, there has been no invasion—only slow infiltration. Insurgency is by its nature ambiguous. The Viet Cong insurgency does have substantial indigenous support. Americans know that the insurgency is actively directed and supported by Hanoi, but the rest of the world is not so sure. The testimony of the ICC [International Control Commission] has been fuzzy on this point—and we have been unable to disclose our most solid evidence for fear of compromising intelligence sources.

As a result, many nations remain unpersuaded that Hanoi is the principal source of the revolt. And, as the weakness of the Saigon Government becomes more and more evident, an increasing number of governments will be inclined to believe that the Viet Cong insurgency, is, in fact an internal rebellion.[26]

Ball's analysis questioned the diagnoses and moral sanction provided by the Korean analogy. There had been no invasion in South Vietnam, Ball claimed. The Vietcong enjoyed substantial indigenous support. Ball came close to saying that the Vietnam conflict was an internal rebellion.[27] Adherents to the Korean analogy, on the other hand, were inclined to discount the indigenous support enjoyed by the Vietcong. From the president down to William Bundy, the problem in South Vietnam was diagnosed as northern communist aggression; the Vietcong's tactics might be different from those of the North Koreans, but they were basically similar in their aggressive designs on the South.

For Ball, a United Nations mandate and non-U.S. troops had accorded international legitimacy to the U.S. role in Korea. The absence of a sim-

[26] Ibid., p. 37.

[27] Ball called the Vietnam conflict a civil war in a July 1, 1965, memorandum to Lyndon Johnson (*Pentagon Papers*, 4:615).

ilar mandate and support for the United States in Vietnam raised questions about the moral legitimacy of a U.S. counteraction against North Vietnam. Ball's point about the absence of a Syngman Rhee in South Vietnam was a less direct but prescient attack against a third lesson of Korea. That the United States succeeded in Korea was partially attributable to Rhee and the stability his government enjoyed; the governmental chaos in South Vietnam throughout 1964 implied that success would probably be more difficult to achieve in Vietnam.

If the differences between Korea and Vietnam mentioned above were political, dissimilarities that Ball identified later in his memorandum focused on military strategy. Bombing North Vietnam, Ball argued, was unlikely to reduce Hanoi's support for the southern insurgency. In fact, the North Vietnamese were likely to retaliate by sending substantially more ground forces into South Vietnam. Since the United States could not "counter [North Vietnamese] ground forces by air power alone, as we quickly learned in Korea," it was important that "we should remember that in South Viet-nam the nature of the terrain reduces the premium on modern firepower and logistic equipment even more than it did in Korea." In short, an air offensive by the United States against the North was likely to lead to a series of escalatory measures terminating in the introduction of U.S. land forces.

Ball then went on to worry about protracted fighting on the ground. China might intervene, and United States forces would begin to take substantial casualties:

> At this point, we should certainly expect mounting pressure for the use of at least tactical nuclear weapons. The American people would not again accept the frustrations and anxieties that resulted from our abstention from nuclear combat in Korea.
>
> The rationalization of a departure from the self-denying ordinance of Korea would be that we did not have battlefield nuclear weapons in 1950—yet we do have them today.[28]

Ball was not speculating in the abstract. It was known that a segment of the military was uninterested in fighting the North Vietnamese Korea-style. As a JCS working group put it in November 1964,

> Certainly no responsible person proposes to go about such a war [against the North Vietnamese and Chinese], if it should occur, on a basis remotely resembling Korea. "Possibly even the use of nuclear weapons at some point" is of course why we spend billions to have them.[29]

[28] Ball, "How Valid Are the Assumptions," pp. 41–42.

[29] *Pentagon Papers*, 3:623.

It was precisely this kind of reasoning that worried Ball. The use of tactical nuclear weapons in Asia was unacceptable to Ball because he believed it would damage the U.S. world position. The United States would be accused of using nuclear weapons only against Asians.

Toward the end of part 1 of his memorandum, Ball came back to the theme that South Vietnam was not another Korea: "As has been repeatedly pointed out in this memorandum, the issues in Indochina are not clearly defined, as they were in Korea." In making this point, Ball sounded very much like John F. Kennedy when he rejected sending combat troops to South Vietnam in 1961. Kennedy had argued in the November 15 NSC meeting that "Korea was a case of clear aggression" whereas the "conflict in Vietnam" was "more obscure and less flagrant."[30] Now it was Ball's turn to argue against those who wanted to bomb North Vietnam into submission. Ball concluded by emphasizing the differences between Vietnam and Korea:

> Let me reiterate once more that Indochina is not Korea. In bombing North Viet-nam, we would *not* be seeking to stop massive and overt aggression south of the Yalu River on behalf of the UN. We would appear instead to be a great power raining destruction on a small power because we accused that small power of instigating what much of the world would quite wrongly regard as an indigenous rebellion.[31]

Who really thought that Vietnam was another Korea? "Practically everybody," was Ball's answer in 1986.[32] Ball elaborated on the theme:

> After all in 1961, when we got involved in this thing, it hadn't been many years since we were in Korea. Naturally the Korea business overhung everything and it was easy for people to say, "Well, look, we fought the Korean War at some cost, we prevailed, nowadays there is a similar challenge in the same part of the world, how could we not pick this challenge up?"[33]

The two most important believers in the Korean analogy were Lyndon Johnson and Dean Rusk. In his memoirs, Johnson states that "when a President faces a decision involving war or peace, he draws back and thinks of the past and of the future in the widest possible terms."[34] To be

[30] Notes on NSC Meeting, November 15, 1961, Vice Presidential Security File, "National Security Council (II)," NSF.

[31] Ball, "How Valid Are the Assumptions," p. 46.

[32] Ball interview. Ball's statement can be checked by consulting the transcripts of the oral history interviews given by the principal participants. See, in addition to the transcripts of Ball's own interview, those of Dean Rusk, Lyndon Johnson, William Bundy, Alexis Johnson, Maxwell Taylor and Chester Cooper.

[33] Ball interview.

[34] Johnson, *The Vantage Point*, p. 151.

sure, Johnson was informed by many lessons of many pasts, but Korea preoccupied him.[35] Perhaps he was inspired by Truman's decisiveness in June 1950, perhaps their geographical proximity made it easy to link Vietnam and Korea together, or perhaps Korea was the last major war fought—and won, according to elite opinion in the mid-1950s—by the United States.[36] Whatever it was that attracted Johnson to the Korean precedent, a major lesson he drew from it was that the United States made a mistake in leaving Korea in June 1949; the withdrawal emboldened the communists, forcing the United States to return to Korea one year later to save the South. Johnson was not disposed toward repeating the same mistake in Vietnam.[37]

Dean Rusk was the other firm believer in the Korean analogy. According to his former deputy, Rusk "was enormously impressed by the analogy of Korea because he had been deeply engaged himself in the Korean War." Rusk was "convinced that what we had done in Korea was a good thing to do and we had finally won in Korea and therefore by applying enough effort and enough time we should be able to prevail in Vietnam as we had in Korea."[38] Yet, according to Ball:

> I don't want to suggest that he was oversimplified in any sense, but he was very much impressed. As he used to say to me, "Why do you take such a gloomy view of the prospects? We had very bad patches in Korea and we finally came through". . . . I think this was a sustaining thought on his part. He saw this fundamentally as an . . . attempt on the part of the major communist powers to extend their influence in Southeast Asia. He never recognized that this was fundamentally a Tonkinese initiative, and that it was a local conflict, and that the great power involvement was peripheral rather than fundamental. . . . he saw the role of North Vietnam fundamentally as an extension of the role of the Chinese and Soviets. This was something which I continually challenged but nevertheless, he has never gotten over the view that this was like the Korean War and . . . the only qualifications

[35] Ibid., pp. 115, 117, 131, and 152–53.

[36] See the following for elite opinion surmising that the Korean War was a victory for the United States: Adlai Stevenson, "Korea in Perspective," *Foreign Affairs* 30 (April 1952): 352; Averell Harriman, "Leadership in World Affairs," *Foreign Affairs* 32 (July 1954): 526; and Dean Rusk, "The President," *Foreign Affairs* 38 (April 1960): 363–64. See also Richard Rovere's early assessment that "history will cite Korea. . . . as the turning point of the world struggle against Communism and as the scene of a great victory for American arms, one the future will celebrate even though the present does not" (*Affairs of State*, p. 145).

[37] Johnson, *The Vantage Point*, pp. 152–53.

[38] Ball interview. See also transcript, George Ball Oral History Interview, pt. 1, pp. 33–34. Ball's views are reinforced by U. Alexis Johnson, who worked under Rusk in 1950: "Dean Rusk felt very, very strongly on Vietnam, in part, because he'd gone through the Korean affair" (Oral History Interview, 1:12).

that he has ever publicly said since then is that he underestimated the staying power of . . . the North Vietnamese.[39]

By Ball's account, the Korean analogy was instructive to Rusk because it suggested that the challenge in South Vietnam was similar to the challenge in South Korea. Just as communist expansionism—backed by China and the Soviet Union—threatened South Korea's political independence in 1950, it was threatening South Vietnam's political independence in the 1960s. Both were cases of unlawful communist aggression against viable political regimes. Rusk's public statements reinforced the seriousness with which he took the comparison:

> The fact that the demarcation line between North and South Viet-nam was intended to be temporary does not make the assault on South Viet-nam any less of an aggression. The demarcation lines between North and South Korea and between East and West Germany are temporary. But that did not make the North Korean invasion of South Korea a permissable use of force.[40]

Ball's memorandum challenged Rusk's reliance on the Korean analogy to diagnose the nature of the conflict in Vietnam. Ball pointed out that in South Vietnam, there was no invasion, only slow infiltration. Moreover, the insurgency had substantial indigenous support. This and other differences that Ball tried to point out were regarded by Rusk, McNamara, and McGeorge Bundy as "nuances" that did not negate the basic similarities between communist aggression in Korea and Vietnam.[41] Similarly, Rusk's assistant secretary for Far Eastern affairs, William Bundy, once asked a subordinate to draft a speech that would, among other things, "dispose of the canard that the Vietnam conflict was a civil war." When the aide replied, "But in some ways, of course, it is a civil war," Bundy reportedly snapped, "Don't play word games with me!"[42]

If the Korean analogy defined the problem in Vietnam as one of external aggression, its implicit solution was of course the use of military force to check communist expansionism. That was the direction in which Ball's colleagues were moving, and the whole purpose of his memo was to question their assumptions. Ball also had to contend with the normative power of the Korean analogy. If North Vietnam's "assault" against South

[39] Ball interview.

[40] *Department of State Bulletin*, May 10, 1965, p. 697. The same point was made by Rusk in an interview with the author, August 21, 1986. Cf. with U. Alexis Johnson's observation: "Having gone through the Korean experience, all . . . felt very deeply that there were matters of principle . . . involved in this Vietnam affair . . ." (Oral History Interview, 1:12).

[41] Ball interview.

[42] James Thomson, interview with author, Cambridge, Massachusetts, October 31, 1986. The incident is also recounted, minus the identity of the assistant secretary of state, in James Thomson, "How Could Vietnam Happen: An Autopsy," *The Atlantic Monthly* (April 1986): 50.

Vietnam was as impermissible a use of force as North Korea's attack against South Korea, it followed that it was just to use force to prevent the North from winning. McGeorge Bundy found this aspect of the Korean analogy particularly instructive.[43]

Even more important than serving as a diagnostic or evaluative aid, the Korean analogy suggested to Dean Rusk and his colleagues that despite bad spells, victory would eventually be possible if the United States would only persevere. The key notions here are perseverance and victory. As the above passages show, Ball believed that both notions had a strong impact on Dean Rusk. Rusk does not deny this. According to Rusk, things looked very dark for the South Koreans and the United States when they were driven to Pusan by the North Koreans: "We did not quickly come to the conclusion that it was hopeless. This influenced our thinking about Vietnam to a degree."[44] This is hardly surprising. Given his experience with the Korean War, the most recent conflict in his memory, in the same part of the world, it was reasonable for him to compare Vietnam with Korea. It would have been unusual for him and his peer group to have refrained from consulting their previous experiences to assess the situation in Vietnam.

What might be surprising to some, however, is how Rusk and his colleagues interpreted the Korean War in the 1960s: "We had finally won."[45] What happened to the notion, popular in the 1950s, that Korea was the "unmentionable victory"?[46] More pointedly, what about the view espoused by the "Never Again Club" and by those who vowed "no more Koreas"? These questions need to be addressed before discussing the sixth and last lesson of Korea, because if Rusk saw Korea as a victory in 1965 but not in the 1950s, then one might ask whether Rusk—and by extension the policymakers of the 1960s—changed the interpretation of Korea to suit current preferences. It could be that Rusk and his colleagues' preference for intervening in Vietnam made it cognitively necessary for them to remember Korea as a victory, or it could be that they wanted to put a more positive light on the Korean conflict so as to make the Korea-Vietnam analogy more inspiring and convincing. If indeed the change was induced by the impending Vietnam War, the new interpretation cannot be used to explain the Vietnam decisions.[47]

[43] Interview with author, April 10, 1986.

[44] Interview with author, August 21, 1986.

[45] Ball interview.

[46] This term was coined by Richard Rovere in July 1953 as he lamented the refusal of Americans to celebrate the Korean armistice. It was also an early reassessment of whether the United States won by an influential journalist. See Rovere, *Affairs of State*, pp. 146–50.

[47] See Jervis, *Perception and Misperception*, pp. 225–27, on the need to rule out "current preferences influencing memories." According to Jervis, such is likely when shifts in mem-

The available evidence suggests, however, that there was little change in Dean Rusk and his colleagues' view of the Korean War. They acknowledge that the United States failed to reunify North and South Korea, but they also argue that U.S. participation in the Korean War succeeded in restoring the status quo ante. Even before Rusk became secretary of state, he praised Truman's decisiveness and the timely action of the United States for helping to achieve the latter objective.[48] Lyndon Johnson also admired Truman for the same reasons. Rusk's summary of his own perceptions is representative of those of his peers:

> Despite the less than satisfactory conclusion to the war—continuing stalemate along the thirty-eight parallel . . . I believe the outcome of the Korean War was a success for American policy and for the United Nations.[49]

What makes Rusk's position believable is that even if Korea had been the unmentionable victory in 1953 for most Americans, it became increasingly mentionable as time passed.[50] In that sense, Rusk and the policy elite were only slightly ahead of public opinion. In October 1952, 56 percent of Americans surveyed felt that the war was a mistake; 32 percent thought it was worthwhile. By September 1956, however, the percentage of those who considered it a mistake dropped to 41 percent; the percentage of those who considered it worthwhile rose to 46. By the mid-1950s, therefore, a plurality of Americans had come to the position that the war was worthwhile. A special poll conducted in Minnesota—a state with a liberal reputation—showed that by March 1965, only 16 percent of those asked thought that the Korean War was a mistake; the overwhelming majority, 67 percent, thought that it was right and worthwhile.[51]

This change in public consciousness also provides a partial explanation for the declining influence of the "Never Again Club." The club's rationale of avoiding another limited Asian land war did not seem, in the 1960s, to have the influence it had in the 1950s. Also, charter members of the club such as General Matthew Ridgway and Robert Lovett were not in the inner councils of power in 1965. Lovett's advice was not sought until 1966, when he began by telling McGeorge Bundy that he was a "charter member of the Never Again Club," and that he wished "we had

---

ories follow shifts in preferences and when the interpretation of the past is strikingly incorrect. Neither of these two conditions hold in the case of the lessons of Korea.

[48] Rusk, "The President," pp. 363–64. For an even earlier positive assessment of Korea, see Stevenson, "Korea in Perspective," pp. 352–53.

[49] Dean Rusk, *As I Saw It* (New York: W. W. Norton, 1990), p. 176.

[50] Note that even in 1953, it was a "victory" for opinion shapers such as Richard Rovere.

[51] The figures are from Hazel Erskine, "The Polls: Is War a Mistake?" *The Public Opinion Quarterly* 34 (1970): 138–41.

never got into Vietnam" because he had "such a painful memory of Korea."[52]

Although members of the "Never Again Club" were not influential in 1965, the same cannot be said of those who believed in "no more Koreas." As was pointed out in chapter 4, the congressional leaders who told Dulles in 1954, "We want no more Koreas with the United States furnishing 90% of the manpower," differed from the "Never Again Club" in that they were not against military intervention per se.[53] By "no more Koreas," the congressional leaders—among whom was Senate Minority Leader Lyndon Johnson—did not mean no more Asian land wars; they meant no more Asian land wars in which the United States might end up *fighting China alone*. By indicating that they were willing to authorize the use of force if Dulles could get the British to join in, the congressional leaders were implicitly saying that if another Asian land war was to be fought, it ought to be fought by a truly multilateral coalition. In 1965, Johnson faced the prospect of involving the United States in another Asian land war, one in which true multilateralism would not be forthcoming. To remain true to the 1954 spirit of "no more Koreas," there was only one thing left for Johnson and his advisers to do if they choose to intervene in Vietnam: concentrate on not drawing the Chinese in. That, in fact, was the last and perhaps most interesting lesson of the Korean War, to which we now turn.

Earlier, we saw how Ball sought to point out the major differences between Korea and Vietnam. Despite Ball's systematic isolation of the key differences between Vietnam and Korea, despite his worry that his superiors might rely too heavily on the Korean analogy in making decisions about Vietnam, there was one lesson that he shared with them. And that was not to provoke China, lest it intervene on behalf of North Vietnam as it had intervened on behalf of North Korea in 1950. Ball dealt at length with this possibility. Although the most recent Special National Intelligence Estimate (SNIE) concluded that China was "unlikely" to intervene by ground or by air, even in the face of sustained U.S. air attacks against North Vietnam, Ball argued that "we would be imprudent to undertake escalation without assuming that there was a *fair chance* that China would intervene. We made a contrary assumption in Korea in October 1950 with highly unfortunate consequences." He then cited liberally from a book detailing the conversation between President Truman and General MacArthur on the possibility of Chinese intervention in Korea.

52 Memo, McGeorge Bundy to the President, January 26, 1966, Miscellaneous Vietnam Documents, Reference File.

53 *FRUS*, 1952–1954, 13:1224. See also chap. 4 above.

The point of the passage was that in spite of MacArthur's assurances, China did cross the Yalu.[54]

As I have suggested above and as his memoirs indicate, Johnson was mindful of this lesson each time he contemplated using force against the North Vietnamese.[55] Ball's passage about the Truman-MacArthur exchange had an impact on Johnson; as will be seen shortly, Johnson would replay the Truman-MacArthur conversation with a difference in two crucial meetings with his advisers. The "China crosses the Yalu" syndrome also had a profound impact on Dean Rusk. Rusk was assistant secretary of state for Far Eastern affairs during the Korean War. He argued for crossing into North Korea in 1950 and even "helped persuade Dean Acheson" to come around to this position. Rusk's account of the decision-makers' calculations is pertinent:

> The possibility of Chinese intervention was discussed at the highest levels of government and was among the major issues of discussion during the October 1950 Truman-MacArthur meeting on Wake Island. . . .
>
> The real failure at the Wake Island meeting was in our assessment of Chinese intentions and of our ability to handle Chinese forces if they actually intervened. On this one MacArthur and the rest of us were all wrong. On October 25 hundreds of thousands of Chinese troops began crossing the Yalu.[56]

Indeed, Rusk regretted his failure to forecast China's entry into the war; a constant thread running through the Vietnam deliberations, as we shall see later, was not to repeat this mistake.[57] The salience of this lesson for Rusk and for the president cannot be overemphasized. In NSC meetings of the period—whether the discussion concerned selecting North Vietnamese bombing targets or sending combat troops—Johnson would repeatedly ask, "Anticipate Chinese coming in?"[58] Similarly, Dean Rusk would volunteer comments like "Sat around the table during Korean War. Was with MacArthur when he made mistake about China coming in," even when the preceding remarks were not about possible Chinese responses to U.S. moves in Vietnam.[59]

William Sullivan, chairman of the Interdepartmental Vietnam Working Group charged with planning the possible escalation of the Vietnam War

[54] Ball, "How Valid Are the Assumptions," pp. 40–41.

[55] Johnson, *The Vantage Point*, pp. 125, 140, and 149.

[56] Rusk, *As I Saw It*, pp. 167–69. See also Thomas Schoenbaum, *Waging Peace and War: Dean Rusk in the Truman, Kennedy, and Johnson Years* (New York: Simon and Schuster, 1988), pp. 214–18.

[57] Halberstam, *The Best and the Brightest*, p. 326.

[58] Meeting with Foreign Policy Advisers, January 22, 1966, Meeting Notes File.

[59] Ibid.

in early 1964, confirms the role played by the Korean analogy in constraining United States military strategy:

> In several instances the precedent of the Korean conflict was evoked to suggest that China would become directly involved in ground combat if United States forces were to strike north of the [seventeenth] parallel. I believed that the prevalence of such a conviction played a major role in determining how the war was actually fought.[60]

The private lessons that Johnson and his advisers drew from Korea and applied to Vietnam may be summarized as follows: like South Korea, South Vietnam was in danger of being taken over by an aggressive North; the stakes in both conflicts, for the United States and for world peace, were extremely high. Moreover, the Korean precedent also suggested that using military force to stop the North Vietnamese was an option, and a morally acceptable one at that. In other words, the Korean analogy was used in private to define the nature of the problem in Vietnam, to assess the stakes of the problem, to prescribe possible responses, and to indicate the morality of those prescriptions.

Thus the policymakers seemed to affirm in private what they said in public. Two other lessons that were implicit in the public use of the Korean analogy became explicit in private. One was the prediction that, as in Korea, the United States would eventually convince the communists that victory was not possible. The second was the lesson of MacArthur: if the United States pushed the North Vietnamese too hard, the Chinese might intervene as they had when MacArthur carried the war to North Korea. The coherence of the public and the private reasoning of the Johnson administration suggests that the Korean analogy was not merely used for public justification; it did inform the thinking of the principal policymakers.

THE FEBRUARY AND JULY DECISIONS OF 1965

The two most important decisions of the Vietnam War were made in 1965. In February, in the face of the deteriorating situation in South Vietnam, Lyndon Johnson was asked to decide whether to launch a major air war against North Vietnam. Five months later, in the face of the imminent collapse of South Vietnam, Johnson was asked to decide whether to launch a ground war in South Vietnam with one hundred thousand United States troops. Assuming that Johnson and his advisers took the

[60] Letter to author, May 5, 1986. Sullivan reiterated the theme in an interview with the author, New York City, New York, July 23, 1986.

Korean analogy seriously, it does not take much to deduce that they were likely to decide in favor of intervention. In what follows, I shall attempt something more interesting and demanding: I shall demonstrate the relevance of the Korean analogy in Vietnam decision-making by using it to explain the actual options selected. This requires the Korean analogy to explain decision outcomes at a very specific or concrete level: it must not only be able to distinguish between prointervention and antiintervention options, but it should also be able to suggest the prointervention option most likely to be chosen. If the Korean analogy passes this demanding test, it acquires added explanatory power; it also adds to the stock of evidence that the analogy played a critical role in the decision-making process. The context of the 1965 decisions needs to be clarified before this test is performed.

Neither Ball's October 5, 1964, memo nor his subsequent memoranda had much effect on the proponents of escalation. Secretary of Defense McNamara thought that Ball was acting with "reckless disloyalty in . . . putting these kind of thoughts in print and in raising the questions."[61] When the president called his principal advisers in to discuss Ball's memorandum on February 24, 1965, McNamara again "responded with a pyrotechnic display of facts and statistics to prove that [Ball] . . . overstated the difficulties . . . and suggesting at least by nuance, that [Ball] . . . was not only prejudiced but ill-informed."[62]

As the situation in South Vietnam grew progressively worse through the fall of 1964, the (William) Bundy Working Group on Vietnam went through successive drafts of "New Courses of Action in Southeast Asia." By late November, the group had settled on three options. Option A was "to continue present policies indefinitely." This meant providing "maximum assistance within South Vietnam"—strengthening the pacification program, improving the police program, the economic program, and so on—but excluding the introduction of U.S. combat troops or a "United States taking over of command." Limited actions in Laos (on the Ho Chi Minh Trail) and covert actions by the South Vietnamese against the North would also be included, as would specific reprisals by the United States against "VC 'spectaculars' such as Bien Hoa."[63]

Option B "would add to present actions a systematic program of military pressures [i.e., air attacks] against the North, with increasing pres-

[61] Ball interview.

[62] Ball, *The Past Has Another Pattern*, p. 392. Although Johnson formally approved Operation Rolling Thunder on February 13, sustained bombing was not initiated until March 2, 1965. The meeting to discuss Ball's memorandum should be understood in this context. See Kahin, *Intervention*, pp. 286–305, for a meticulous analysis of Johnson's reluctance to escalate the war.

[63] *Pentagon Papers*, 3:659–60.

sure actions to be continued at a fairly rapid pace and without interruption" until U.S. objectives were obtained. Option C differed from B in terms of the pace and scale of the air attacks: "The military scenario should give the impression of a steady deliberate approach," beginning with "graduated military moves against infiltration targets, first in Laos and then in the DRV, and then against other targets in North Vietnam." Under Option C, the air war against North Vietnam would be slow-paced and more cautious.[64]

Negotiations would play no role under Options A and B and a minor role under Option C. As the authors of the paper put it, "Basic to this option [A] is the continued rejection of negotiations." Option B would approach negotiations "with absolutely inflexible insistence on our present objectives." Option C, which would include an "orchestration of . . . communications with Hanoi and/or Peiping," and "indicating from the outset a willingness to negotiate" would seem to take negotiations more seriously until the "Early Negotiating Actions" were specified. The United States would insist on three fundamentals: "(a) that the DRV cease its assistance to and direction of the VC; (b) that an independent and secure GVN be re-established; and (c) that there be adequate international supervising and verification machinery."[65] These were precisely the same "present objectives" about which Option B was to be "absolutely inflexible." If these objectives or fundamentals were to be insisted on by Option C as well, negotiations would seem improbable. The United States would give up nothing; the DRV was expected to give up the very things they were fighting for.

After a long NSC meeting on December 1, 1964, Option B was dropped. Options A and C were renamed Phase I and Phase II respectively, suggesting that they were to be conceived of as stages in a two-part plan.[66] A February 7, 1965, memo written by McGeorge Bundy after he witnessed the results of a Vietcong attack on the Pleiku barracks in South Vietnam started a reluctant Johnson on the path of approving Phase II. McGeorge Bundy painted a grim picture: the situation in Vietnam was deteriorating, and without new U.S. action, defeat seemed inevitable within a year. There was not much time to turn things around. "The [U.S.] stakes in Vietnam," according to Bundy, were "extremely high." The chances of success, defined as "changing the course of the contest in Vietnam," were estimated to be between 25 and 75 percent.[67]

On February 10, the Vietcong attacked the U.S. barracks in Qui Nhon,

[64] Ibid.

[65] Ibid., p. 664. My reading of the document suggests that Option C left a little room for the possibility of negotiations. Kahin believes otherwise (*Intervention*, p. 247).

[66] Kahin, *Intervention*, p. 252.

[67] *Pentagon Papers*, 3:687–91.

killing twenty-three U.S. servicemen. Three days later, President Johnson formally gave the go-ahead for Phase II. Turmoil within the South Vietnamese government made it impossible for the United States to obtain the *pro forma* approval from the Vietnamese authorities until nearly two weeks later. On March 2, Option C, now code-named "Operation Rolling Thunder," was launched.

Sustained bombing of North Vietnam failed to change the course of the contest in Vietnam. Morale in South Vietnam did improve, temporarily. Most observers agree that with the decision to bomb North Vietnam, the United States had indicated its willingness to up the ante to keep South Vietnam noncommunist. Hitherto, Hanoi had sent military, technical, and supply cadres—mostly composed of former southerners—into South Vietnam. Hanoi had refrained from sending regular combat units into South Vietnam for fear of instigating a U.S. escalation of the conflict. The launching of Operation Rolling Thunder, according to Kahin, "removed the constraints that had previously kept Hanoi from sending its own ground combat units into the South."[68]

It was the Vietcong, however, who dealt a series of catastrophic defeats to the ARVN during the summer of 1965. In May, a regiment-sized Vietcong unit decimated two ARVN battalions. American officers who witnessed the battle "went away with the distinct impression that the Royal Vietnamese Air Force (RVNAF) were close to collapse."[69] In June, another battalion of ARVN's finest reserves was decimated at Dong Xoai.[70] "The Viet Cong," according to General Westmoreland, were "destroying battalions faster than they can be reconstituted and faster than they were planned to be organized under the buildup program."[71] Moreover, Westmoreland continued, North Vietnam's 325th and 304th Divisions were either already in South Vietnam or close enough to reinforce the Vietcong. In light of this situation, Westmoreland saw "no course of action open to us except to reinforce our efforts in SVN [South Vietnam] with additional United States or Third Country forces as rapidly as is practicable during the critical weeks ahead." On June 7, Westmoreland requested an additional hundred thousand troops from Washington; added to the 75,000 U.S. troops already in South Vietnam or en route, this request would bring U.S. force levels in South Vietnam to 175,000 troops or thirty-four battalions. Another ten battalions were to be supplied by South Korea, Australia, and New Zealand, putting the total allied forces at forty-four battalions. With forty-four battalions, Westmoreland felt, he

[68] Kahin, *Intervention*, p. 306.

[69] *Pentagon Papers*, 3:392.

[70] Ibid.

[71] Ibid., 4:609.

could "successfully take the fight to the VC," and have enough offensive capability "to convince the VC that they cannot win."[72]

The administration's policy toward Vietnam had arrived at a crossroads: granting Westmoreland's request would mean that the United States would be fighting a major land war in Vietnam, with all the dangers that implied; turning down the request might lead, at best, to a negotiated solution involving a coalition government in South Vietnam, and at worst, to the eventual conquest of South Vietnam by the Vietnamese communists. Among senior officials, George Ball was the only one against escalation. Throughout June, he wrote a series of memos, often referring to the French experience in Vietnam, to dissuade Johnson from committing U.S. troops to combat. Ball's use of the French parallel will be analyzed in the next chapter. Two other confidants of Johnson, Clark Clifford and Senator Mike Mansfield, also took Ball's position: Clifford, in particular, warned Johnson that Vietnam was not comparable to Korea because "the political posture of the parties involved, and the physical conditions, including terrain, are entirely different."[73] Dean Rusk, Robert McNamara, McGeorge Bundy, and William Bundy were more favorably disposed toward Westmoreland's request, although Rusk and McGeorge Bundy also initially asked tough questions about the deployment.[74]

Johnson was "deeply affected by the undersecretary's analysis," in part because he himself had reservations about whether the U.S. could win.[75] Yet his other advisers, most of whom outranked Ball, told him that it was necessary to fight. Confronted with such conflicting advice, Johnson sent Robert McNamara once again to Vietnam to assess the situation and to obtain some answers that the president wanted. Should the United States intervene to "prevent the loss of Southeast Asia" to "aggressive forces moving illegally across international frontiers"? Would United States forces be effective fighting the Vietcong in unfamiliar terrain? Would "non-Vietnamese fighting men revive memories of the French colonial years and arouse anti-foreign sentiments"?[76] On his return from South Vietnam, Secretary McNamara answered the first two questions in the

[72] Cable, General Westmoreland, "U.S. Troop Deployment to SVN," June 7, 1965, NSC History—Troop Deployment.

[73] Letter, Clark Clifford to the President, May 17, 1965, NSC History—Troop Deployment. See also Mansfield's memos to the President, June 5 and 9, NSF, Name File, Mike Mansfield.

[74] See Memo, McGeorge Bundy to the President, July 1, 1965, NSC History—Troop Deployment. Berman provides an excellent discussion of the principals' positions in *Planning a Tragedy*, chap. 4.

[75] Berman, *Planning a Tragedy*, p. 75.

[76] Johnson, *The Vantage Point*, p. 144. These three were not the only questions Johnson asked, but McNamara's memorandum seemed to address two of them in particular.

affirmative in a July 20 memorandum to the president. The third question was not answered. More important, McNamara painted an even bleaker picture of the situation in South Vietnam than McGeorge Bundy had six months earlier: "The situation in South Vietnam is worse than a year ago (when it was worse than a year before that)." Despite the bombing campaign, the South Vietnamese government "is liable to provide security to fewer and fewer people in less and less territory." As such, the "DRV/VC seem to believe that SVN is on the run and near collapse; they show no signs of settling for less than complete takeover."

The United States could do one of three things. The first option, to "cut our losses and withdraw under the best conditions that can be arranged" was certain to humiliate the United States and damage its future effectiveness on the world scene. The second option was to "continue at about the present level," but it suffered from the disadvantage that as the U.S. position weakened, the option would "almost certainly confront us later with a choice between withdrawal and an emergency expansion of forces, perhaps too late to do any good." It should not come as a surprise then that McNamara recommended the third option: "Expand promptly and substantially the United States military pressure against the VC in the South. . . . This . . . would stave off defeat in the short run and offer a good chance of producing a favorable settlement in the longer run." Thus the memorandum's answer to Johnson's first two questions were that substantial U.S. forces—one hundred thousand by October, perhaps another hundred thousand in early 1966—were necessary to prevent a takeover and that with these soldiers, the United States had, in the concluding sentence of the memorandum, "a good chance of achieving an acceptable outcome within a reasonable time in Vietnam."[77]

Lyndon Johnson had heard all sides of the argument. If he eventually went along with the recommendations of McNamara, Rusk, and the Bundys, it was not because they misled him; rather, it was because he shared with them some fundamental beliefs about U.S. credibility and about the importance of the lessons of history. The salience of these beliefs, especially those relating to the lessons of history, has been demonstrated earlier, but they can be seen again in two critical meetings held on July 21 and July 22 to debate McNamara's recommendations. These meetings were critical in the sense that many of the major assumptions and fears that informed the central decision-makers were articulated as the principals debated one another; moreover, the president's dispositions were discernable by the end of the first meeting. The most complete account of these meetings, drawing from three sources—NSC files, presidential aide Jack Valenti's record, and NSC aide Chester Cooper's summary—

[77] *Pentagon Papers*, 4:620–22.

has been assembled by George Kahin. The account provided below is adapted from Kahin's, omitting a few extraneous pages and after a cross-check of the original sources.[78]

Present at this meeting were McGeorge Bundy, Chester Cooper, Jack Valenti, and Horace Busby from the White House; Dean Rusk, George Ball, William Bundy, Ambassador to South Vietnam Henry Cabot Lodge, and Ambassador to Thailand Leonard Unger from the State Department; Robert McNamara, Cyrus Vance, and John McNaughton from the Defense Department; General Earle Wheeler, Chairman of the JCS; Admiral William Raborn and Richard Helms of the CIA; and Leonard Marks and Carl Rowan of the United States Information Agency (USIA). The president began with some substantive questions:

PRESIDENT: What I would like to know is what has happened in recent months that requires this kind of decision on my part, What are the alternatives? I want this discussed in full detail, from everyone around this table. Have we wrung every single soldier out of every country that we can? Who else can help us here? Are we the sole defenders in the world? Have we done all we can in this direction? What are the compelling reasons for this call-up? What results can we expect? Again, I ask you what are the alternatives? I don't want us to make snap judgements. I want us to consider all our options. We know we can tell the South Vietnamese we are coming home. Is that the option we should take? What would flow from that? The negotiations, the pause, all the other approaches we have explored, are these enough? Should we try others?

McNamara discussed the situation: the VC has greatly expanded its control of the country, populous areas are now isolated, both the VC and ARVN have been suffering heavy casualties. Unless the United States steps in with additional forces, the VC will push the GVN into small enclaves and become increasingly ineffective. The VC now controls about 25 percent of the population. (CIA Director Raborn estimated that the VC controlled about 25 percent of the population during the day and about 50 percent at night.) A year ago, the VC controlled less than 20 percent.

The president felt that our mission should be as limited as we dare make

[78] See George Kahin, *Intervention*, pp. 370–78. Permission to reprint Kahin's account is granted by Alfred A. Knopf, Inc. See also meeting on Vietnam, July 21, 1965, notes (by Jack Valenti), Meeting Notes File; and meeting with Foreign Policy Advisers, July 21, 1965, memorandum for the record (by Chester Cooper), Meeting Notes File. Larry Berman has suggested that this meeting was staged by Johnson to get a consensus from his advisers (*Planning a Tragedy*, pp. 105–6, 127–28). Kahin disagrees and interprets it as a true decision-making meeting. I agree with Kahin, and in this case, I believe the record speaks for itself. See also Clark Clifford, *Counsel to the President*, pp. 418–21, which argues that Johnson did not make up his mind until after a July 25 meeting at Camp David.

it. General Wheeler agreed, but felt that we should engage in offensive operations to seek out and fight the VC main force units. Although this is difficult because of lack of tactical intelligence we know where these base areas are.

Director Raborn reported the CIA's estimate that the VC will avoid major confrontations with United States forces and concentrate on destroying our LOCs [lines of communication] and on guerrilla war generally. General Wheeler felt that the VC will have to "come out and fight" and that this will probably take place in the highlands where they will probably attempt to establish a government seat.

BALL: Isn't it possible that the VC will do what they did against the French—stay away from confrontation and not accommodate us?

WHEELER: Yes, that is possible, but by constantly harassing them, they will have to fight somewhere.

MCNAMARA: If the VC doesn't fight in large units, it will give the ARVN a chance to resecure hostile areas. We don't know what VC tactics will be when the VC is confronted by 175,000 Americans.

RABORN: We agree. By 1965's end, we expect NVN (North Vietnam) to increase its forces. It will attempt to gain a substantial victory before our buildup is complete.

PRESIDENT: Is anyone here of the opinion we should not do what the memorandum says? If so, I want to hear from them now, in detail.

BALL: Mr. President, I can foresee a perilous voyage, very dangerous. I have great and grave apprehensions that we can win under these conditions. But let me be clear. If the decision is to go ahead, I am committed.

PRESIDENT: But, George, is there another course in the national interest that is better than the one McNamara proposes? We know it is dangerous and perilous, but the big question is, can it be avoided?

BALL: There is no course that will allow us to cut our losses. If we get bogged down, our cost might be substantially greater. The pressures to create a larger war would be irresistible. The qualifications I have are not due to the fact that I think we are in a bad moral position.

PRESIDENT: Tell me then, what other road can I go?

BALL: Take what precautions we can, Mr. President. Take our losses, let their government fall apart, negotiate, discuss, knowing full well there will be a probable take-over by the Communists. This is disagreeable, I know.

PRESIDENT: I can take disagreeable decisions. But I want to know can we make a case for your thoughts? Can we discuss it fully?

BALL: We have discussed it. I have had my day in court.

PRESIDENT: I don't think we have made any full commitment, George. You have pointed out the danger, but you haven't really proposed an alternative course. We haven't always been right. We have no mortgage on victory.

Right now, I am concerned that we have very little alternative to what we are doing. I want another meeting, more meetings, before we take any definitive action. We must look at all other courses of possibility carefully. Right now I feel it would be more dangerous to lose this now, than endanger a greater number of troops. I want this fully discussed.

RUSK: What we have done since 1954 to 1961 has not been good enough. We should have probably committed ourselves heavier in 1961.

ROWAN: What bothers me most is the weakness of the Ky government. Unless we put the screws on the Ky government, 175,000 men will do us no good.

LODGE: There is not a tradition of a national government in Saigon. There are no roots in the country. Not until there is tranquility can you have any stability. I don't think we ought to take this government seriously. There is simply no one who can do anything. We have to do what we think we ought to do regardless of what the Saigon government does. As we move ahead on a new phase, we have the right and the duty to do certain things with or without the government's approval.

PRESIDENT: George, do you think we have another course?

BALL: I would not recommend that you follow McNamara's course.

PRESIDENT: Are you able to outline your doubts? Can you offer another course of action? I think it's desirable to hear you out, truly hear you out, then I can determine if your suggestions are sound and ready to be followed, which I am prepared to do if I am convinced.

BALL: Yes, Mr. President. I think I can present to you the least bad of two courses. What I would present is a course that is costly, but can be limited to short-term costs.

PRESIDENT: Alright, let's meet again at 2.30 this afternoon to discuss George's proposals. Meanwhile, let Bob tell us why we need to risk all these Americans' lives. I don't choose to do that casually.

McNamara and Wheeler proceeded to outline the reasons for more troops. Essentially, they said, 75,000 men [the number of U.S. troops already in South Vietnam at the time of the NSC meeting] are just enough to protect the bases. The extra men, they insisted, would stabilize the situation, and then improve it. It also would give the ARVN a breathing space, they said. We would limit the incursion of more troops to 100,000 because it might not be possible to absorb more in South Vietnam at this time. . . .

PRESIDENT: It seems to me that you will lose a greater number of men. I don't like that.

WHEELER: Not precisely true, Mr. President. The more men we have there, the greater the likelihood of smaller losses.

PRESIDENT: Tell me this. What will happen if we put 100,000 more men and then two, three years later you tell me you need 500,000 more? How would you expect me to respond to that? And what makes you think if we put in

100,000 men, Ho Chi Minh won't put in another 100,000, and match us every bit of the way?

WHEELER: This means greater bodies of men from North Vietnam, which will allow us to cream them.

PRESIDENT: But what are the chances of more North Vietnamese soldiers coming in?

WHEELER: About a fifty-fifty chance. The North would be foolhardy to put one-quarter of their forces in SVN. It would expose them too greatly in the North.

. . . .

The meeting was adjourned at 1:00 P.M. At 2:30 P.M., it reconvened.

PRESIDENT: Alright, George.

BALL: We cannot win, Mr. President. This war will be long and protracted. The most we can hope for is a messy conclusion. There remains a great danger of intrusion by the Chinese. But the biggest problem is the problem of the long war.

The Korean experience was a galling one. The correlation between Korean casualties and public opinion showed support stabilized at 50 percent. As casualties increase, the pressure to strike at the very jugular of North Vietnam will become very great.

I am concerned about world opinion. If we could win in a year's time, and win decisively, world opinion would be alright. However, if the war is long and protracted, as I believe it will be, then we will suffer because the world's greatest power cannot defeat guerrillas.

Then there is the problem of national politics. Every great captain in history was not afraid to make a tactical withdrawal if conditions were unfavorable to him. The enemy cannot even be seen in Vietnam. He is indigenous to the country. I truly have serious doubt that an army of westerners can successfully fight orientals in an Asian jungle.

PRESIDENT: This is important. Can westerners, in the absence of accurate intelligence successfully fight Asians in jungle rice paddies? I want McNamara and General Wheeler to seriously ponder this question.

BALL: I think we all have underestimated the seriousness of this situation. It is like giving cobalt treatment to a terminal cancer case. I think a long, protracted war will disclose our weakness, not our strength.

The least harmful way to cut losses in SVN is to let the government decide it doesn't want us to stay there. Therefore, we should put such proposals to the GVN that they can't accept. Then, it would move to a neutralist position. I have no illusions that after we were asked to leave South Vietnam, that country would soon come under Hanoi control.

What about Thailand? It would be our main problem. Thailand has proven a good ally so far, though history shows it has never been a staunch ally. If we wanted to make a stand in Thailand, we might be able to make it.

Another problem would be South Korea. We have two divisions there now. There would be a problem with Taiwan, but as long as the Generalissimo is there, they have no place to go. Indonesia is a problem, as is Malaysia. Japan thinks we are propping up a lifeless government and are on a sticky wicket. Between a long war and cutting our losses, the Japanese would go for the latter. My information on Japan comes from Reischauer.

PRESIDENT: But George, wouldn't all these countries say that Uncle Sam was a paper tiger, wouldn't we lose credibility breaking the word of three presidents, if we did as you have proposed? It would seem to be an irreparable blow. But I gather you don't think so.

BALL: No, sir. The worse blow would be that the mightiest power on earth is unable to defeat a handful of guerrillas.

PRESIDENT: Then you are not basically troubled by what the world would say about our pulling out?

BALL: If we were actively helping a country with a stable viable government, it would be a vastly different story. Western Europeans look upon us as if we got ourselves into an imprudent situation.

PRESIDENT: But I believe that these Vietnamese are trying to fight. They're like Republicans who try to stay in power, but don't stay there long. Excuse me, Cabot.

BALL: Thieu spoke the other day and said the Communists would win the election.

PRESIDENT: I don't believe that. Does anyone believe that? (His hand circled the table. McNamara, Lodge, Bill Bundy, Leonard Unger all expressed views contrary to Ball's.)

MCNAMARA: Ky will fall soon. He is weak. We can't have elections there until there is physical security, and even then there will be no elections because as Cabot said, there is no democratic tradition. (Wheeler suggested that McNamara was right about Ky, but said, "I am very impressed with Thieu.")

PRESIDENT: There are two basic troublings within me. First, that westerners can even win a war in Asia. Second, I don't see how you can fight a war under direction of other people whose government changes every month. Now, go ahead, George and make your other points.

BALL: The costs, as well as our western European allies, are not relevant to their (European) situation. What they are concerned about is their own security, that is, troops in Berlin have real meaning, troops in Vietnam have none.

PRESIDENT: Are you saying that pulling out of Korea would be akin to pulling out of Vietnam?

MCGEORGE BUNDY: It is not analogous. We had a status quo in Korea. It would not be that way in Vietnam.

BALL: We will pay a higher cost in Vietnam. This is a decision one makes against an alternative. On one hand, a long, protracted war, costly, very costly, with North Vietnam digging in for the long term. This is their life and driving force. The Chinese are taking the long-term view by ordering blood plasma from Japan. On the other hand, there are short-term losses if we pull out. On balance, we come out ahead of the McNamara plan. Of course, it is distasteful either way.

Mr. Bundy [McGeorge] agreed with the McNamara proposals. He felt that no government which could hold power is likely to be one that is likely to invite us out. The basic lesson of Mr. Ball's view is that: 1) The post-monsoon season will not see us in the clear. 2) No single speech will be sufficient to reassure the American people. We will have to face up to the serious ominous implications of our new policy. This is not a continuation of our present approach. . . . There are no early victories in store, although casualties are likely to be heavy.

Mr. Bundy did not believe that Mr. Ball's "cancer analogy" was a good one. Immaturity and weakness, yes. A non-Communist society is struggling to be born. Before we take our decision to the American people, Ambassador Taylor should go back to the GVN and get greater, more positive assurances. There will be time to decide our policy won't work after we have given it a good try. (Mr. Ball disagreed here, feeling that the larger our commitment, the more difficult would be the decision to get out. "We won't get out; we'll double our bet and get lost in the rice paddies.")

Mr. Bundy felt that the kind of shift in US policy suggested by Mr. Ball would be "disastrous." He would rather maintain our present commitment and "waffle through" than withdraw. The country is in the mood to accept grim news.

RUSK: If the Communist world finds out we will not pursue our commitments to the end, I don't know where they will stay their hand. I have to say I am more optimistic than some of my colleagues. I don't believe the VC have made large advances among the Vietnamese people. It is difficult to worry about massive casualties when we say we can't find the enemy. I feel strongly that one dead man is a massive casualty, but in the sense that we are talking, I don't see large casualties unless the Chinese come in.

McNamara felt that Mr. Ball understated the cost of cutting our losses. He agreed with Mr. Rusk on the international effect of such an action at this time. Mr. Ball also overstates the cost of his (McNamara's) proposal. He agreed that it would take at least two years to pacify the country and we must be prepared to increase our forces by another 100,000.

General Wheeler said that it was unreasonable to expect to "win" in a year regardless of the number of US troops involved. We might start to reverse the unfavorable trend in a year and make definite progress in three years.

The president wondered whether we could win without using nuclear weapons if China entered the war.

General Wheeler felt that we could in "Southeast Asia." He believes US forces can operate in the terrains of Southeast Asia. This is the first "war of National Liberation"; if we walk out of this one, we will just have to face others.

The president asked why, when we've been undertaking military efforts for 20 months, this new effort will be successful.

General Wheeler felt that our additional forces will stave off a deteriorating situation.

LODGE: I feel there is a greater threat to start World War III if we don't go in. Can't we see the similarity to our own indolence at Munich? I simply can't be as pessimistic as Ball. We have great seaports in Vietnam. We don't need to fight on roads. We have the sea. Let us visualize meeting the VC on our own terms. We don't have to spend all our time in the jungles. . . . The Vietnamese have been dealt more casualties than, per capita, we suffered in the Civil War. The Vietnamese soldier is an uncomplaining soldier. He has ideas he will die for.

UNGER: I agree this is what we have to do. We have spotted some things we want to pay attention to.

The president stressed his desire to get more third country troops into South Vietnam. He also raised the possibility of a Vietnam Task Force which will meet daily.

The meeting adjourned at 5:30.

Johnson consulted his military advisers the next day, July 22. Present were General Earle Wheeler, chairman of the JCS; General Harold Johnson, army chief of staff; Admiral David McDonald, chief of naval operations; General Wallace Greene, Jr., commandant of the Marine Corps; Harold Brown, secretary of the Air Force; Paul Nitze, secretary of the Navy; Stanley Resor, secretary of the Army; and Eugene Zuckert, assistant secretary of the Air Force. The civilian advisers present were McGeorge Bundy, Robert McNamara, Clark Clifford, Cyrus Vance, and Jack Valenti.[79]

PRESIDENT: I asked Secretary McNamara to invite you here to counsel with you on these problems and the ways to meet them. Hear from the chiefs the alternatives open to you and then recommendations on those alternatives

[79] Adapted from George Kahin, *Intervention*, pp. 379–85. See also meeting on Vietnam, July 22, 1965, Meeting Notes File.

from a military point (of view). Options open to us: one, leave the country—the "bugging out" approach; two, maintain present force and lose slowly; three, add 100,000 men—recognizing that may not be enough—and adding more next year. Disadvantages of number three—risk of escalation, casualties will be high, and may be a long war without victory. I would like you to start by stating our present position and where we can go.

McDONALD: Sending Marines has improved situation. I agree with McNamara that we are committed to the extent that we can't move out. If we continue the way we are, it will be a slow, sure victory for the other side. By putting more men in it will turn the tide and let us know what further we need to do. I wish we had done this long before.

. . . .

PRESIDENT: Paul, what is your view?

NITZE: In that area not occupied by US forces, it is worse, as I observed on my trip out there. We have two alternatives—support Vietnam all over the country or stick to the secure position we do have. Make it clear to populace that we are on their side. Gradually turn the tide of losses by aiding Vietnam at certain points. If we just maintained what we have—more the Pres. problem than ours—to acknowledge that we couldn't beat the VC, the shape of the world will change.

PRESIDENT: What are our chances of success?

NITZE: If we want to turn the tide, by putting in more men, it would be about sixty-forty.

PRESIDENT: If we gave Westmoreland all he asked for, what are our chances? I don't agree that North Vietnam and China won't come in.

NITZE: Expand the area we could maintain. In the Philippines and Greece it was shown that guerrillas (can lose).

PRESIDENT: Would you send in more forces than Westmoreland requests?

NITZE: Yes. Depends on how quickly they. . . .

PRESIDENT: How many? Two hundred thousand instead of 100,000?

NITZE: We would need another 100,000 in January.

PRESIDENT: Can you do that?

NITZE: Yes.

McNAMARA: The current plan is to introduce 100,000—with the possibility of a second 100,000 by first of the year.

PRESIDENT: What reaction is this going to produce?

WHEELER: Since we are not proposing an invasion of North Vietnam, the Soviets will step up material and propaganda—same with the Chicoms. North Vietnam (might) introduce more regular troops.

PRESIDENT: Why wouldn't North Vietnam pour in more men? Also, call on volunteers from China and Russia?

WHEELER: First, they may decide they can't win by putting in the forces they can't afford. At most they would put in two more divisions. Beyond that, they strip their country and invite a countermove on our part. Second, on volunteers—the one thing all North Vietnam fears is the Chinese. For them to invite Chinese volunteers is to invite China taking over North Vietnam. Weight of judgment is that North Vietnam may reinforce their forces, but they can't match us on a buildup. From military view, we can handle, if we are determined to do so, China and North Vietnam.

PRESIDENT: Don't you anticipate retaliation by the Soviets in the Berlin area?

WHEELER: You may have some flare-up but lines are so tightly drawn in Berlin, that it raises the risk of escalation too quickly. Lemnitzer thinks there will be no flare-up in Berlin. In Korea, if Soviets undertook operations it would be dangerous.

PRESIDENT: Admiral, would you summarize what you think we ought to do?

MCDONALD: First, supply the forces Westmoreland has asked for. Second, prepare to furnish more men—100,000—in 1966. Third, commensurate building in air and naval forces, step up attacks on North Vietnam. Fourth, bring in needed reserves and draft calls.

PRESIDENT: Any ideas on what the cost of this would be?

MCNAMARA: Yes. $12 billion dollars in 1966.

PRESIDENT: Any idea what effect this will have on our economy?

MCNAMARA: It would not require wage and price controls in my judgment. The price index ought not go up more than one point or two.

GENERAL MCCONNELL: If you put in these requested forces and increase air and sea effort, we can at least turn the tide to where we are not losing anymore. We need to be sure we get the best we can out of South Vietnam. We need to bomb all military targets available to us in North Vietnam. As to whether we can come to a satisfactory solution with these forces, I don't know. With these forces properly employed, and cutting of their (VC) supplies, we can do better than we are doing.

. . . .

PRESIDENT: Doesn't it really mean if we follow Westmoreland's request we are in a new war? (Isn't) this going off the diving board?

MCNAMARA: This is a major change in US policy. We have relied on South Vietnam to carry the brunt. Now we would be responsible for satisfactory military outcome.

PRESIDENT: Are we in agreement we would rather be out of there and make our stand somewhere else?

GENERAL JOHNSON: The least desirable alternative is getting out. The second least is doing what we are doing. Best is to get in and get the job done.

PRESIDENT: But I don't know how we are going to get that job done. There are millions of Chinese. I think they are going to put their stack in. Is this the best place to do this? We don't have the allies we had in Korea. Can we get our allies to cut off supplying North Vietnamese?

MCNAMARA: No, we can't prevent Japan, Britain, (and the others) to charter ships to Haiphong.

. . . .

PRESIDENT: Are we starting something that in two or three years we simply can't finish?

BROWN: It is costly to us to strangle slowly, but chances of losing are less if we move in.

PRESIDENT: Suppose we told Ky of requirements we need—he turns them down—and we have to get out and make our stand in Thailand.

BROWN: The Thais will go with the winner.

PRESIDENT: If we didn't stop in Thailand, where would we stop?

MCNAMARA: Laos, Cambodia, Thailand, Burma, surely affect Malaysia. In 2–3 years communist domination would stop there, but ripple effect would be great (in) Japan, India. We would have to give up some bases. Ayub [Khan, head of Pakistan government] would move closer to China. Greece, Turkey would move to neutralist positions. Communist agitation would increase in Africa.

GREENE: Situation is as tough as when it started. But not as bad as it could be. Marines in the First Corps area is example of benefits. (Here are the stakes as I see them.) One, national security stake; (it is a) matter of time before we (would have to) go in some place else. Two, pledge we made. Three, prestige before the rest of the world. If you accept these stakes, there are two courses of action. One, get out. Two, stay in and win. How to win? The enclave concept will work. I would like to introduce enough Marines to do this. Two Marine divisions and one air wing. Extend. 28,000 there—(we need an) additional 72,000.

MCNAMARA: Greene suggests these men over and above the Westmoreland's request.

PRESIDENT: Then you will need 80,000 more Marines to carry this out?

GREENE: Yes. I am convinced we are making progress with the South Vietnamese, in food and construction. We are getting evidence of intelligence from the South Vietnamese. In the North, we haven't been hitting the right targets. We should hit pol (petroleum) storage—essential to their transportation. Also, airfields, MiGs and IL28s. As soon as SAM installations are operable.

PRESIDENT: What would they do?

GREENE: Nothing. We can test it by attacking pol storage. Then we should attack industrial complex in North Vietnam. Then we ought to blockade Cambodia—and stop supplies from coming down. How long will it take? Five years, plus 500,000 troops. I think the (American) people will back you.

PRESIDENT: How would you tell the American people what these stakes are?

GREENE: The place where they will stick by you is the national security stake.

GENERAL JOHNSON: We are in a face-down. The solution, unfortunately, is long-term. Once the military (problem) is solved, the problem of political solution will be more difficult.

PRESIDENT: If we come in with hundreds or thousands of men and billions of dollars, won't this cause China and Russia to come in?

GENERAL JOHNSON: No. I don't think they will.

PRESIDENT: MacArthur didn't think they would come in either.

GENERAL JOHNSON: Yes, but this is not comparable to Korea. . . .

PRESIDENT: But China has plenty of divisions to move in, don't they?

GENERAL JOHNSON: Yes, they do.

PRESIDENT: Then what would we do?

GENERAL JOHNSON: If so, we have another ball game.

PRESIDENT: But I have to take into account they will.

GENERAL JOHNSON: I would increase the build-up near North Vietnam and increase action in Korea.

PRESIDENT: If they move in thirty-one divisions, what does it take on our part?

MCNAMARA: Under favorable conditions they could sustain thirty-one divisions and assuming the Thais contributed forces, it would take 300,000 plus what we need to combat the VC.

PRESIDENT: But remember they're going to write stories about this—the Bay of Pigs—and about my advisers. That's why I want you to think very carefully about alternatives and plans. Looking back on the Dominican Republic would you have done any differently, General?

GENERAL JOHNSON: I would have cleaned out part of the city and gone in—with same numbers.

PRESIDENT: Are you concerned about Chinese forces moving into North Vietnam?

GENERAL JOHNSON: There is no evidence of forces—only teams involved in logistics. (They) could be investigating areas which they could control later.

The historical precedents invoked in debate during the July 21 and 22 meetings included the following: France in the 1950s (Ball), Philippines and Greece (Nitze), Munich (Lodge), and most prominently, Korea (Johnson and Ball). That the Vietcong would use the same guerrilla tactics they used against the French seemed likely to Ball. More important was the implication that if the Vietcong used the same tactics, they were likely to defeat the United States just as they had the French. Ball's one-sentence reference to Vietcong strategy against the French must be understood in light of his June 18 memorandum, "Keeping the Power of Decision in the South Viet-Nam Crisis," in which he drew repeatedly on the French experience in Vietnam to warn Lyndon Johnson of the slim prospects of victory.[80]

[80] Memo, George Ball to the President, "Keeping the Power of Decision in the South Viet-Nam Crisis," June 18, 1965, NSC History—Troop Deployment.

Those, like Paul Nitze, who were less pessimistic than Ball found the analogy of the Philippines and Greece more instructive. Nitze invoked it to show that guerrillas could lose when Johnson worried aloud about "our chances of success" even with the extra hundred thousand troops. Nitze's use of the analogy is important because it exemplifies a recurring tendency of the policymakers: the willingness to be guided by analogies predicting desired outcomes. With the exception of the president and George Ball, administration officials in the 1960s, in private and especially in public, used almost exclusively analogies suggesting the probability of victory. Analogies with the slightest hint of defeat were scrupulously avoided.

The most dramatic use of a historical analogy in the meetings was Ambassador Henry Cabot Lodge's remark about Munich and World War III. It is also probably one of the strongest pieces of evidence we have of the influence of the Munich analogy on the decision-makers. The question of Munich is a question of stakes and consequences. "Our [Western?] indolence at Munich" resulted in World War II; our indolence in South Vietnam might bring about an equally disastrous consequence: "I feel there is greater threat to start World War III if we don't go in." With consequences so drastic, stakes so high, it would be difficult to deny Westmoreland's request for the hundred thousand troops.

It might be worth noting that Lodge's remark was the last in a series of blows (following McGeorge Bundy, Rusk, and McNamara) dealt to George Ball's anti-intervention arguments. Of greater significance was what failed to occur after Lodge's reference to Munich. No one questioned his analogy. McGeorge Bundy, resident critic of specious analogies, fell silent. In June, Bundy had signed an incisive nine-page memorandum disputing Ball's French analogy.[81] In the July 21 meeting, he had also rejected Ball's "cancer analogy" and the president's Korea analogy. Bundy's silence in wake of Lodge's Munich remark is interesting but not surprising. Like most of the senior decision-makers present, he was convinced of its appropriateness. In their public speeches, their memoirs, or their writings, the Vietnam policymakers often made the point that Neville Chamberlain's appeasement of Hitler at Munich helped start World War II; for that reason, the United States could not allow Ho Chi Minh to take over South Vietnam, lest that lead to another world war.[82]

[81] Memo, McGeorge Bundy to the President, "France in Vietnam, 1954, and the U.S. in Vietnam, 1965—A Useful Analogy?" June 30, 1965, NSC History—Troop Deployment.

[82] David Halberstam has observed that McGeorge Bundy's "Munich lecture was legendary at Harvard. . . . It was done with great verve, Bundy imitating the various participants, his voice cracking with emotion as little Czechoslovakia fell, the German tanks rolling in just as the bells from Memorial Hall sounded. The lesson was of course interventionism, and the wise use of force" (*The Best and the Brightest*, p. 56).

However, the analogy most frequently and explicitly invoked in these meetings was that of Korea. The president seemed preoccupied with the lessons of Korea. This is in accord with Johnson's memoirs, where he repeatedly refers to the Korean precedent. Johnson believed that the United States did one crucial thing right in 1950, and that was the decision to use American troops to resist aggression in Korea. Johnson was so proud of Truman's decision that he wrote him an admiring letter, praising him for his courage in responding to the challenge in Korea and reaffirming America's capacity for world leadership. Johnson would later look to Truman's decisiveness for inspiration.[83]

But the United States made three mistakes in Korea, according to Johnson. The first mistake in Korea was the withdrawal of U.S. occupation forces in June 1949. One year later, the United states was back in Korea, resisting aggression. When Johnson asked Ball in the July 21 meeting, "Are you saying that pulling out of Korea would be akin to pulling out of Vietnam?" he was trying to draw out the consequences of Ball's position. Ball had earlier maintained that "troops in Berlin have real meaning, troops in Vietnam have none." Johnson believed that a U.S. withdrawal from South Vietnam would allow the North Vietnamese to invade South Vietnam, just as the withdrawal of U.S. occupation forces from South Korea in 1949 encouraged the North Koreans to invade the South in 1950. Ball did not contest the implications of his position as sketched by Johnson; he merely saw it as the lesser of two evils. Johnson, on the other hand, saw withdrawal as the greater of the two evils:

> I could see us repeating the same sharp reversal once again in Asia. . . . but this time in a nuclear world with all the dangers and possible horrors that go with it. Above all else, I did not want to lead this nation and the world into nuclear war or even the risk of such a war.[84]

The second mistake in Johnson's view was Truman's failure to ask Congress for an expression of its backing of the U.S. effort in Korea. With respect to South Vietnam, this problem was solved in 1964 during the Tonkin Gulf incident—Johnson sought, and received, an overwhelming expression of support from Congress in the form of the Tonkin Gulf Resolution. As noted earlier, the Johnson administration began planning the

[83] Johnson, *The Vantage Point*, pp. 47–48. Clark Clifford, who warned Johnson early on that he did not think the situation in Vietnam was "comparable to Korea," confirmed the impact of the Korean war on Johnson in a letter of April 3, 1990, to the author: "As a Senator . . . Johnson carefully followed the war and its impact on President Truman. After becoming President. . . . Johnson reflected back on this period, hoping to learn from Truman's experience." Clifford's May 17, 1965, letter to Johnson disputing the Korean analogy can be found in NSC History—Troop Deployment.

[84] Johnson, *The Vantage Point*, pp. 152–53.

escalation of the Vietnam War less than a week after they were armed with the resolution.

The United States's third mistake in Korea was getting into a protracted war with China. Johnson was determined to avert such an error in Vietnam, as was Secretary of State Rusk. George Ball, like most others, was aware of this and opened the June 21 afternoon session—his last chance to argue against intervention—by explicitly linking the possibility of Chinese intervention in Vietnam to the Korean experience. Ball's opening argument was a point-blank statement: "We cannot win, Mr. President. This war will be long and protracted. . . . There remains a great danger of intrusion by the Chinese." The biggest problem, however, was the problem of a protracted war:

> The Korean experience was a galling one. The correlation between Korean casualties and public opinion showed support stabilized at 50 percent. As casualties increase, the pressure to strike at the very jugular of North Vietnam will become very great.

Ball did not need to explain why it was taboo to hit at the jugular of North Vietnam. Everyone around the table knew. China would intervene. It did so in 1950 when the United States crossed the thirty-eighth parallel and moved in on the jugular of North Korea.

Johnson's concern about Chinese intervention in Vietnam did not surface in his July 21 meeting with his civilian advisers; it occupied centerstage in his meeting with his military advisers the next day. A major theme, at least on the president's part, was concern about Chinese and Russian intervention. Would Hanoi not ask for volunteers from China and Russia in response to the hundred thousand U.S. troops? "There are millions of Chinese. I think they are going to put their stack in. . . . We don't have the allies we had in Korea." By the time General Wallace Greene, commandant of the Marine Corps, spoke about the United States winning in Vietnam by hitting North Vietnam's petroleum storage, airfields, and "industrial complex," as well as by blockading Cambodia, Johnson had had enough. The president asked, "If we come in with hundreds of thousands of men and billions of dollars, won't this cause China and Russia to come in?" To General Harold Johnson's negative reply, Johnson answered, "MacArthur didn't think they would come in either."

That Lyndon Johnson and his civilian advisers were mindful of China is not controversial. In fact, one of the things about which there is a strong consensus among Johnson's former military and civilian advisers is that this last lesson of Korea, the specter of Chinese intervention, constrained American strategy in Vietnam decisively. If the other five lessons of Korea suggested that the United States ought to intervene and win in Vietnam, this sixth lesson reminded the policymakers of the necessity of avoiding another war with China. It was not that the United States would lose such a conflict, but that the human and political costs of such a war would be prohibitive. Moreover, as Ball pointed out, in such a war, there would be strong pressure to use tactical nuclear weapons; it was the administration's perception that if China entered the war, the Soviet Union might be forced to come in on China's side too. Looked at this way, the stakes of avoiding war with China were as high, if not higher than, the stakes in Vietnam.

For many the China factor was lamentable because it doomed the United States to failure; others were relieved that happened. What is most interesting, however, is the extent to which this particular lesson of Korea was invoked in both the December 1964 and the July 1965 meetings. Nor would this be the only time when the ghost of MacArthur would haunt the president. Slightly more than a year after these decisions, when the Vietnam War was going badly and the United States was taking heavy casualties, Johnson wanted General Westmoreland to address the American public. Mindful of General MacArthur's open attack on Truman before Congress in 1951, Johnson warned Westmoreland as the latter was about to face the media, "I hope you don't pull a MacArthur on me."[85]

Process tracing has revealed that the central decision-makers repeatedly sought to apply the lessons of Korea to Vietnam as they pondered the desirability of military intervention. Aghast at the direction in which policy seemed to be moving, George Ball felt obliged to attack the Korean analogy at least ten times in his October 1964 memo to McGeorge Bundy, Robert McNamara, and Dean Rusk.[86] Ball's main target was the latter, whom Ball felt was overly taken by the analogy.[87] Even if Ball had had some success in undermining the "enormous influence" of the analogy on Rusk, he would have had to convince the president.[88] Johnson was equally taken by the analogy. The documents show that he used it in discussing the air war options and used it again during the meetings about the ground war options. Similarly, William Bundy found the analogy extremely instructive in assessing the meaning and stakes of the Vietnam conflict in January 1965, and he has also confirmed the broad impact of the analogy on his superiors in the Vietnam deliberations.[89] The point need not be belabored: the Korean analogy informed the thinking of most of the senior decision-makers and was taken seriously by them. President

[85] William Westmoreland, *A Soldier Reports* (Garden City, New York: Doubleday, 1976), p. 159.

[86] Ball, "How Valid Are the Assumptions."

[87] Ball interview.

[88] The term "enormous influence" is from Ball (Ball interview).

[89] See William Bundy, unpublished ms., chap. 18, pp. 18–32, Papers of William Bundy.

Johnson, Dean Rusk, William Bundy, and McGeorge Bundy were the analogy's main proponents while George Ball was its major critic.

Process tracing also made it possible to demonstrate that the proponents of the analogy used it to perform almost all of the six diagnostic tasks specified by the AE framework. Can the lessons of Korea detailed above be used to explain why the Johnson administration decided in favor of intervention, and why they chose to use force in a graduated rather than a massive manner? Figure 5.2 shows the relationship between the lessons of Korea and the actual options considered by the policymakers in February and July 1965. The December–February options, it will be recalled, were defined by William Bundy's Working Group on Vietnam; the July options were those listed by President Johnson in the final National Security Council Meeting on July 27. Johnson's listing of options differed from McNamara's listing in that it included Options D′ and E′, which he considered but rejected. Including these two options imposes a more demanding test on the Korean analogy, but if the analogy survives the test, its explanatory power will be significantly increased.

These were the two most important decisions of the Vietnam War. The December-February decision launched the air war against North Vietnam; the July decision launched the American ground war in South Vietnam. The timing of the decisions was influenced primarily by the precarious state of South Vietnam; each time it was perceived that South Vietnam was on the verge of collapse, American policymakers agonized over what the United States should do.

THE LESSONS OF KOREA AND THE AIR WAR

The decision to launch an air war against North Vietnam and the decision to adopt a strategy of graduated air attacks were basically made in December 1964. President Johnson, however, did not give his final approval for war until February 1965; the political situation in South Vietnam, he felt, was too precarious to withstand the military retaliation that was to be expected from the North Vietnamese. On February 13, the president finally gave his approval to launch the air war, now known as "Operation Rolling Thunder." In what follows, I shall use the lessons of Korea to suggest (1) why the United States decided in favor of starting an air war, and (2) why Johnson chose the "slow squeeze" over the "fast squeeze" despite the fact that the latter was deemed the more efficacious option. As indicated in chapter 3, I shall rely on the congruence procedure to assess the extent to which the Korean analogy can account for these choices.

The first half of figure 5.2 shows how one can test for congruence be-

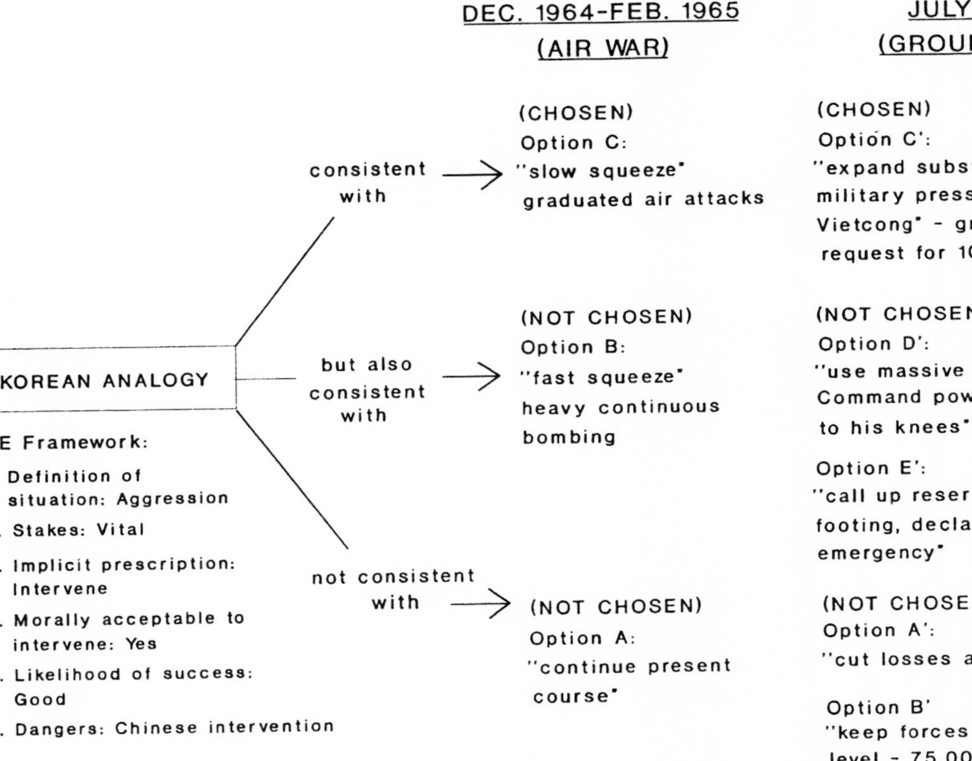

Figure 5.2. The Lessons of Korea and the Option Chosen

tween the lessons of Korea and the air war options. The first five lessons of Korea enumerated are lessons obtained from our earlier discussion of the private lessons of Korea. With knowledge of these lessons, it is easy to see why Option A was rejected.[90] "Continuing the present course" would not have arrested the deteriorating situation in South Vietnam. In a January memorandum to Dean Rusk entitled "Notes on the South Vietnamese Situation and Alternatives," William Bundy offered the "prognosis that the situation in Vietnam is now likely to come apart more rapidly than we had anticipated in November" [1964].[91] Later in the month, McGeorge Bundy told Johnson that he and McNamara were convinced that "our current policy can only lead to disastrous defeat."[92] The implications of Option A were unacceptable. Option A was fundamentally at odds with five of the six lessons of Korea: (1) aggression must not be rewarded, (2) the stakes in Vietnam were extremely high, (3) the implicit solution was to use force to prevent the North from winning, (4) force would work and (5) as in the U.S.-UN intervention in Korea, the United States was morally right. It follows that one would need to go beyond Option A to save South Vietnam.

A believer in the lessons of Korea would find Options B and C to be consistent with his beliefs. Both options entailed starting a sustained air war against North Vietnam; Option B involved heavy, continuous bombing; Option C's pace would be slower and more cautious. It seems that knowing that someone subscribed to the Korean analogy is not enough to predict which of the two options he would choose. In fact, with the Korean analogy's indications about the diagnosis, the high stakes, and the good chance of the United States succeeding, Option B should have been the favored choice. However, the option selected was C. Was something else at work? Can the Korean analogy explain what it was?

It would be possible to infer from the public record that an administration highly attuned to the first five lessons of Korea would also have been alerted to the sixth lesson, that excessive military pressure against the North might provoke Chinese intervention. Dean Rusk's public statements in 1964 and 1965, for example, showed an interesting pattern. Rusk would refer to a string of historical analogies—Korea always among them—to characterize the nature of the conflict and stakes in Vietnam. He would insist that the United States would have to respond to this kind of communist expansionism. He would then point out that the U.S. re-

[90] Option A or Phase I might have been actually tried for a very brief period, but by February, Johnson had to decide whether to go beyond this option. See Kahin, *Intervention*, pp. 252–53, 260–85. Cf. William Bundy, unpublished ms., chap. 18, Papers of William Bundy.

[91] *Pentagon Papers*, 3:685.

[92] Cited in Johnson, *The Vantage Point*, p. 122.

sponse was restrained and that U.S. objectives were limited.[93] In the context of the total military power available to the United States, the U.S. response in Vietnam was in fact restrained. If this restraint is interpreted as an attempt not to appear too provocative to Hanoi and China, one may say this about Korean analogy: while the first five lessons goaded the United States toward a strong response, the sixth—the specter of Chinese intervention—restrained Johnson and his advisers from the "full squeeze."

It is the private record, however, that brings out the restraining function of the Korean analogy most fully. Records of the policy deliberations of 1964 and 1965 suggest that the fear of Chinese military intervention in North Vietnam was instrumental in turning Johnson and his civilian advisers away from Option B. With the exception of the joint chiefs, who accepted all but the sixth lesson of Korea, all of Johnson's advisers were attuned to avoiding MacArthur's mistake in Korea.[94] Thus it is not surprising that the JCS favored using "maximum practicable conventional military power in a short time," a strategy more akin to Option B, to achieve U.S. objectives, while the civilians favored a more graduated response, Option C.[95]

Higher speed and greater intensity differentiates Option B from Option C. Two other differences should also be noted. For William Bundy and John McNaughton, the two officials responsible for developing the options, Option B stood "a greater chance than either of the other two of attaining our objectives vis-a-vis Hanoi and a settlement in South Vietnam." Moreover, the "opening military actions under Option B would be major air attacks on key targets in the DRV, starting with the major Phuc Yen airfield."[96] What this means is that although Option B was considered the more effective option, it was still rejected. I argue below that it was rejected because it did not take the sixth lesson of Korea seriously enough. Similarly, what is interesting about Phuc Yen—North Vietnam's major MiG base—was that it was close to Hanoi and would require a massive air effort to destroy. This raised two problems. George Ball warned Johnson that striking too close to Hanoi increased "the likelihood

[93] See for example, Dean Rusk's "Total Victory for Freedom," in which Rusk reassures the audience that the "United States intends to avoid the extremes. . . . we do not intend to strike out rashly into a major war in that area" (*Department of State Bulletin*, October 5, 1964, p. 466). A few days later, Rusk's assistant secretary of state for Far Eastern affairs went so far as to say that "we do not aim at overthrowing the Communist regime of North Viet-Nam but rather at inducing it to call off the war it directs and supports in South Viet-Nam" (*Department of State Bulletin*, October 19, 1964, p. 537).

[94] Author's interviews with William Sullivan (July 23, 1986), George Ball (July 23, 1986), and John Roche (Medford, Massachusetts, July 5, 1986).

[95] *Pentagon Papers*, 3:679.

[96] Ibid., 3:661–63.

of engagement with the 53 Chinese MiGs sent to Hanoi to defend North Vietnam" and that such an engagement would lead to a series of escalatory steps culminating in a ground war with the Chinese. Ball's projections may have been calculated attempts to urge Johnson to limit the air war, but they were projections based on the analyses of Allen Whiting, head of the Far East division of the State Department's Office of Intelligence and Research. Whiting was the author of the respected *China Crosses the Yalu*, and in 1965, he was assigned to look for signals of Chinese intentions that the United States missed in 1950. Thus Whiting saw the Chinese MiGs, the construction of airfields close to the border, and joint Chinese–North Vietnamese air exercises as indications of growing Chinese concern, and he told his bosses, Dean Rusk and George Ball. They took his message seriously.[97] So did William Bundy. In assessing the risks of striking Phuc Yen in a later period, Bundy wrote:

> As to the Phuc Yen airfield, we believe there is a significant chance that this attack would cause Hanoi to assume that we were going to make their jet . . . airfields progressively untenable. This could significantly and in itself increase the chances of their moving planes to China and all of the interacting possibilities that then arise.[98]

It should not come as a surprise that the president would be just as attuned to this logic. According to Bundy, Ball's warning "persuaded the President to consider the 'China factor' and to limit the bombing program, in particular to avoid bombing the airfield at Phuc Yen near Hanoi."[99] If this is correct, we would expect Johnson to reject Option B.

Recently declassified material about the December 1, 1964, meeting, after which Option B was dropped, portrays Johnson as unwilling to start bombing because of Saigon's weakness. "No point in hitting North if South not together," said Johnson. When Maxwell Taylor, U.S. ambassador to South Vietnam, doubted that Hanoi would "slap back" if the United States "slapped" Hanoi, the president retorted, "Didn't MacArthur say the same?"[100] What is interesting about this exchange is that it did not even refer specifically to the various options. Johnson seemed preoccupied with the Hanoi-Chinese response. By the end of the meeting, however, Option B had basically been rejected. Only Options A and C remained.[101]

[97] Ball interview; see also Allen Whiting, *The Chinese Calculus of Deterrence* (Ann Arbor: University of Michigan Press, 1975), pp. 175–77, 184–88.

[98] *Pentagon Papers*, 4:168.

[99] Cited in Gibbons, *U.S. Government*, pt. 3, pp. 90–91.

[100] Cited in George Kahin, *Intervention*, p. 252.

[101] See Kahin, *Intervention*, p. 252; and Gibbons, *U.S. Government*, pt. 3, pp. 18–23.

Both Dean Rusk's and William Bundy's retrospective accounts of the bombing decision stress the "China factor." For Rusk,

> The bombing was also related to the question as to whether the war would expand and whether Red China would come in. If anyone had asked me in 1963 whether we could have half a million men in South Viet Nam and bomb everything in the North right up to the Chinese border without bringing in Red China, I would have been hard put to say that you could.[102]

Bundy offers a more precise assessment:

> If preserving the independence of South Vietnam had at the end of 1964 . . . a weight of 8 in American policy as a whole, a war between the United States and China had at all times a negative weight of 10. . . . the argument that raged over whether Option B or C involved greater risk of war with China . . . *assumed* that any such war would be a national disaster.[103]

But why this concern about China in the first place? Bundy traces it to "the ghost of the Yalu debacle of 1950," for "if the Chinese came to think the U.S. was out to destroy North Vietnam, would not the situation be essentially similar to MacArthur's advance to the top of North Korea fourteen years before?"[104]

The private record thus shows that the need to avoid MacArthur's mistake of provoking China into a war with the United States was very much on the minds of the major policymakers. With all lessons including this sixth one counted, the Korean analogy is able to account for the choice between Options B and C in the February decision to launch an air war. Although both Options B and C were in the main consistent with the lessons of Korea, Option C was more fully consistent than Option B. Option C took the sixth lesson of Korea seriously; Option B was more cavalier about it.[105]

THE LESSONS OF KOREA AND THE GROUND WAR

The same logic is applicable to the July decision to grant General Westmoreland's request for one hundred thousand troops. Options A′ and B′, as figure 5.2 indicates, were inconsistent with the first five lessons of Ko-

[102] Transcript, Dean Rusk Oral History Interview, p. 24.

[103] William Bundy, unpublished ms., chap. 18, p. 18, Papers of William Bundy.

[104] Ibid., chap. 8, p. 31.

[105] The relative weight of the six diagnostic tasks are determined empirically. In the case of the Korean analogy, the first five lessons predisposed policymakers toward military intervention, but the sixth lesson played a major role in preventing the U.S. from going all out.

rea. Despite or perhaps because of the bombing of North Vietnam, the situation in South Vietnam was "worse than a year ago (when it was worse than a year before that)." The odds were "less than even" that the South Vietnamese government would last out the year. "The DRV/VC seem to believe that South Vietnam is on the run and near collapse; they show no signs of settling for less than a complete takeover."[106] Given this situation, Option B′, continuation of the present course, would not be enough to stave off a South Vietnam and American defeat. Option A′, withdrawal, would guarantee such a defeat. Again, if the stakes in Vietnam were so high, the moral issue so clear, and success so possible (if only the United States tried harder), Options A′ and B′ and their consequences were unacceptable.

Options C′, D′, and E′, on the other hand, were all consistent with the lessons of Korea. As before, the first five lessons on first glance would predisposed their believer toward Options D′ and E′. These were the options in which U.S. military strength and determination would be most unambiguously brought to bear in the Vietnam conflict and would have the greatest likelihood of convincing the North Vietnamese and the NLF to cease and desist. As the record of the July 22 meeting showed, the joint chiefs were very much interested in using SAC's massive air power to decimate North Vietnam's military infrastructure. But once the sixth lesson of Korea is factored into the analysis, it becomes obvious why Option D′ was unacceptable. Crippling Hanoi—bombing its petroleum storage, airfields, MiGs, and IL 28s, as the joint chiefs urged—would have been too provocative to China. As the minutes of the July 22 meeting showed, Johnson referred to MacArthur again when his military advisers wanted to use air power to bring Hanoi to its knees.[107]

The rejection of Option E′ can also be explained with the sixth lesson of Korea factored in. Despite strong pressure from his secretary of defense to call up the reserves because of their "essential role" in "resolving the 1961 Berlin crisis," and despite pressures from the military to "go on a war footing," the president demurred.[108] "The call-up of large numbers of reserves," Johnson realized, "was part of the [pro-intervention] package."[109] McNamara and the military chiefs expected Options C′ *and* E′ to be jointly pursued. Thus McNamara's prediction that the United States had a good chance of achieving its objectives—convincing the VC

[106] *Pentagon Papers*, 4:620.

[107] This concern of Johnson's can also be seen in the 1966 meetings. See meeting with Foreign Policy Advisers, January 22, 1966, Meeting Notes File; and notes of NSC Meeting, June 22, 1966, NSC Meetings File, NSF.

[108] Letter from Robert McNamara to Larry Berman, cited in Berman, *Planning A Tragedy*, p. 104.

[109] Johnson, *The Vantage Point*, p. 146.

and North Vietnam that they could not win—within a reasonable time was premised on granting Westmoreland's request (Option C′) *as well as* calling up 235,000 reserves and National Guardsmen (Option E′).[110] Option E′ was important to McNamara and the military because of the psychological impact it would have on friends and adversaries. Calling up the reserves would demonstrate resolve to friend (e.g., NATO and SEATO) and foe (i.e., Hanoi, Peking, and Moscow), and it would also be a credible signal to all about U.S. willingness to see the Vietnam conflict through.[111] Moreover, there was also a question of manpower and maintaining national security: with 300,000 regular U.S. troops anticipated in Vietnam by the end of 1966, it was necessary to call up 235,000 reserves and national guardsmen "as protection against contingencies" elsewhere.[112]

The importance of signaling resolve and protecting against contingencies notwithstanding, Johnson hesitated; he agonized over the issue, and the final decision, by my reading of the documents, was a close call. What tilted Johnson away from Option E′ was the worry that it might be only too successful. In considering the pluses of indicating determination against the minuses of provoking China and Russia, Johnson gave greater weight to the latter. As he explained in his memoirs, "We would not make threatening noises to the Chinese or the Russians by calling up reserves in large numbers."[113] And as the July meetings show, Johnson's sensitivity to possible Chinese and Soviet intervention in Vietnam was informed in large part by his desire to avoid MacArthur's excesses in Korea. The one option left that was fully consistent with all the lessons of Korea was C′, and that was the option selected.

With the help of the AE framework and process tracing, it has been possible to obtain a detailed understanding of how the Korean analogy "helped" America's decision-makers define the nature of the Vietnam conflict and assess the proposed solutions. By testing for congruence between the lessons of Korea and the actual policy options put forward in February and July 1965, it has been possible to discover which options were likely to be rejected, and indeed, options inconsistent with the ten-

110 Memo, Robert McNamara to the President, "Recommendations of Additional Deployments to Vietnam," July 20, 1965, NSC History—Troop Deployment.

111 See *Pentagon Papers*, 4:314.

112 Memo, Robert McNamara to the President, "Recommendations of Additional Deployments to Vietnam," July 20, 1965, NSC History—Troop Deployment.

113 Johnson, *The Vantage Point*, p. 149. Larry Berman has suggested that another reason Johnson was reluctant to call up the reserves was that the economic and political costs would have been so great that they would have undermined the Great Society (*Planning a Tragedy*, pp. 145–53). I contrast this argument with my analogical explanation in chap. 7.

ets of the Korean analogy were rejected. By combining the various lessons of Korea, it has been further possible to discover which among the remaining options were not fully compatible with the tenets of the Korean analogy. Through this process of elimination, it has been possible to arrive at the actual option selected for the two most important decisions of the Vietnam War. The Korean analogy seems able to shed light on why the Johnson administration decided to intervene in Vietnam, and perhaps even more interesting, it seems able to explain why the interventions took the form that they did, namely Options C and C′.

Although all six lessons identified by the AE framework were relevant, the sixth, the need to avoid drawing China into the war, seems to have been especially influential. The first five lessons were important in that they predisposed the policymakers toward military intervention; the sixth lesson was critical in that it decisively shaped the form of the intervention. It is appropriate to conclude with an observation about the influence of this lesson. Inasmuch as it was very much on the minds of the policymakers, their desire to avoid another war with China needs no further explanation.

What is in need of comment, if not explanation, is the nature of the threshold established by the policymakers, beyond which they felt they could not go. In June 1965, the CIA issued to the decision-makers a briefing paper that dealt prominently with "communist reactions" to "possible courses of U.S. actions." The conditions under which China might intervene in Vietnam with ground forces, that is, the conditions favoring a "Yalu debacle," were specified: short of a U.S. ground invasion of North Vietnam, the CIA believed, the Chinese would *not* intervene. Bombing the industrial and military sectors of North Vietnam would "probably not" bring China in.[114]

None of the harsher or harshest options (B for the air war and D′ and E′ for the ground war) tabled in 1965 entailed a U.S. invasion of North Vietnam. Why then did the civilian decision-makers shy away from them, when they were likely to be more effective than the graduated and ultimately unsuccessful options chosen, and when, according to the best information available, they probably would not have brought China into a ground war?[115] I see no alternative to the idea that their preoccupation with avoiding "MacArthur's mistake" made them extremely cautious—

[114] See CIA (Office of National Estimates) Briefing Paper, June 11, 1965. This paper incorporates the National Intelligence Estimates and SNIEs of the previous year in its findings.

[115] I raise this as an empirical question because it puzzles me as a student of foreign policy decision-making. By no means am I suggesting that the harsher options were the normatively superior options. See chap. 8 below.

overly cautious, some might say.[116] Despite CIA reassurances, the policymakers established their own subjective threshold and Option B for the air war and Options D′ and E′ for the ground war were deemed to be beyond that threshold in 1965. Psychologically, one might say, the decision-makers overcompensated for the ghost of MacArthur.

[116] See memo, Director of Intelligence and Research to Dean Rusk, April 26, 1965, Vietnam Memos, Country File—Vietnam, NSF, for an analysis of the "China factor" that supports the CIA estimate cited above. The charge that the Johnson administration was "overly cautious" is probably most popular among military circles; the view has also gained favor with former officials and a segment of the public. See Clodfelter, *Limits of Air Power*, pp. ix–x, 206–209, as well as William Sullivan's comments cited above.

CHAPTER 6

Dien Bien Phu

The French haven't won a war since Napoleon.
What can we learn from them?
—*an American four-star general, cited in Thomas Thayer*, War without Fronts

Dien Bien Phu, madame . . . Dien Bien Phu . . . history doesn't always repeat itself. But this time it will. We won a military victory over the French, and will win it over the Americans, too. Yes, madame, their Dien Bien Phu is still to come.
—*General Vo Nguyen Giap, interview with Oriania Fallaci*

ANALOGIES MATTER. One way to illustrate this theme is to show the link between the reigning analogy and the policy option chosen. This was done in chapter 5, where I argue that the Korean analogy predisposed policymakers toward choosing Options C and C′, the policies of "restrained" intervention in Vietnam. The argument that analogies matter will be considerably strengthened if it can be shown that a different analogy suggesting different lessons can predispose its believer toward a different option. Finding such an analogy in the decision-making context will strengthen the thesis that analogies matter because it implies that different analogies can lead to different options.[1] This chapter will show that Dien Bien Phu is such an analogy.

Dien Bien Phu, that strategically worthless lowland where the French were defeated by General Vo Nguyen Giap's Vietminh forces, symbolized the frustrating and ultimately abortive attempt by the French to reinstate their colonial domination over all of Vietnam in the 1950s. At its simplest, Dien Bien Phu evoked images of the two-month siege of the French garrison by the Vietminh that ended in the surrender of the French. More broadly, Dien Bien Phu recalled the series of events that

[1] Investigating whether a different analogy will imply a different decision outcome is akin to the method of using "within-case" observations to analyze the causal relationship between variables. See George and McKeown, "Case Studies," pp. 29–31.

led to the siege and its aftermath: the proclamation of independence in 1945, the return of the French after the war, the breakdown of the negotiated settlement, the French-Vietminh war, French war weariness, and the twilight of the French empire. Yet, whether the broad or narrow imagery was evoked, the central message of Dien Bien Phu was unmistakable: the French were defeated.

For a United States contemplating war against the Vietnamese communists in 1965, the bugaboo of Dien Bien Phu was notable in its absence in official public statements. Administration officials who referred freely in public to Malaya and Korea as instances of successful containment, and to Munich, Ethiopia, and Manchuria as instances of the baneful consequences of appeasement, steered clear of Dien Bien Phu. It is possible, however, to infer the lessons Dien Bien Phu might offer policymakers by using the AE framework. How might Dien Bien Phu be used to define the nature of the problem in Vietnam? What does it have to say about the political stakes? Does it provide an implicit prescription? What does it say about the chances of success of the alternative options? Does it touch on the moral rightness of these solutions? And finally, does it warn of any dangers? In the next section, I sketch the answers to these questions provided by the Dien Bien Phu analogy.

Unlike the Korean analogy, which defined the problem in Vietnam as one of Northern aggression, Dien Bien Phu suggests that the problem is one of the Vietnamese fighting colonial domination. The user of the analogy is likely to see any Western nation fighting the Vietnamese communists as taking the position of the French, or the oppressors. It follows that the moral position of such a Western nation is untenable. The political stakes for those fighting the Vietminh/Vietcong are high to medium, but they pertain to the importance of maintaining the grandeur and power of a waning colonial empire. The implicit policy prescription is that one might want to be doubly cautious, especially given the next two lessons. The Dien Bien Phu analogy also suggests that the Vietcong's adversaries would be likely to experience serious internal dissent, just as the French attempt to suppress the Vietminh led to severe internal dissension within France. Finally, the Dien Bien Phu analogy also predicts that the Vietcong's adversary would be unlikely to win.

Not surprisingly, few senior policymakers of the Johnson administration saw the position of the United States in 1965 as analogous to that of France in 1954. The analogy painted a picture too much at variance with the national self-perception of most of the policymakers. The Korean precedent captured their image of themselves and their country better. The handful of individuals who thought the Dien Bien Phu analogy had some pertinent lessons for the United States refrained from using it in public. It would have been too heretical.[2] However, as table 3.2 indicates, the Dien Bien Phu analogy was repeatedly invoked in private. It is therefore necessary to trace its role in the Vietnam policy process in order to identify its users and detractors and to demonstrate how it may have affected the policy dispositions of its proponents.

THE ROLE OF THE DIEN BIEN PHU ANALOGY IN THE POLICY PROCESS

Critics of specious analogies almost always take it upon themselves to propose better ones. George Ball was no exception. His October 1964 memorandum not only provided a sustained critique of the Korean analogy as applied to Vietnam, it also introduced what he considered a more pertinent analogy: the French experience in Vietnam. Ball was worried that introducing ground troops in Vietnam would make "our situation. . . . in the world's eyes, approach that of France in the 1950s." The French, according to Ball, "would take the lead in pointing out that we had . . . clearly put ourselves in the position of France in the early 1950s—with all the disastrous political connotations of such a posture. Asians would not miss the point."[3]

Ball did not elaborate on the specific lessons of the Dien Bien Phu analogy in the October memorandum, for he associated the analogy with a ground war. Aside from some brief remarks about the dangers of a ground war, Ball devoted most of his memo to arguing against the impending air war against North Vietnam. Consequently, the French analogy was not the most appropriate one. Ball preferred a metaphorical warning: "Once on the tiger's back we cannot be sure of picking the place to dismount."[4]

Eight months later, it was clear that bombing had accomplished neither of its objectives. Morale in the South, after a brief upsurge, returned to its usual low. The North Vietnamese continued to send men down the Ho Chi Minh Trail into the South. While his colleagues were contemplating U.S. military intervention to save the South, Ball searched for a

[2] David Nes, deputy chief of mission in Saigon for a few months in 1964, came closest to using the French precedent in public. After being sent back to Washington for raising too many questions in Saigon about the military's optimism, Nes wrote to Senator William Fulbright, explaining why U.S. efforts to obtain an independent noncommunist South Vietnam were likely to fail. Increasing the U.S. military presence and command, according to Nes, would "only hasten the day of total Vietnamese military and administrative collapse. We will then be in virtually the same position as the French in 1954—except that they had several hundred thousand veteran troops on the ground at their disposal" (letter, David Nes to William Fulbright, December 16, 1964, Papers of David Nes).

[3] Ball, "How Valid Are the Assumptions," p. 36.

[4] Ibid., p. 41.

place to dismount. On May 13, 1965, with Dean Rusk abroad, Ball sent "A Plan for a Political Resolution in South Viet-Nam" to Robert McNamara, McGeorge Bundy, and William Bundy. The cover note was one of the tersest by Ball: "Attached is a copy of the memorandum for discussion on Saturday at 11 o'clock," signed, George Ball, Acting Secretary of State.[5]

Ball came close to ordering McNamara and McGeorge Bundy, with whom he now had temporary equality, to discuss his plan for "shifting the struggle from the military to the political arena." The plan involved halting the war in the South and inviting the Vietcong's supporters to participate in the national life of South Vietnam. The United States' objective of an independent South Vietnam was obtainable under this plan, according to Ball. A political solution was preferable to military escalation because the latter might draw the Soviets and Chinese into a general conflict. Equally important, Ball believed, was the fact that U.S. military pressure against the North was unlikely to work. This was so because "the experience of the French from 1945 to 1954 vividly testifies to Viet Cong willingness to submit to heavy punishment rather than give up their long-sought objective of a Communist State covering the whole of Viet-nam."[6]

Ball's pessimism about the utility of military pressure impressed no one. In face of the imminent collapse of South Vietnam, Ball's colleagues and the president seemed inclined toward sending U.S. ground troops to save it. For Ball, this raised the prospect of a protracted and inconclusive ground war. He was sufficiently alarmed and sure that such a war would be against U.S. interests that he sent out a series of memos, all arguing against intervention, to those who would listen.

The first of these memos, "Keeping the Power of Decision," dated June 18, 1965, began with an ominous metaphor by Emerson: "Things are in the saddle, and ride mankind."[7] It was in this memo to the president that Ball fleshed out the France 1954 analogy. Ball argued against expanding the Vietnam conflict into a U.S.-Vietcong ground war because he was not convinced that the United States could win. He leaned toward the view that the United States "may *not* be able to fight the war successfully enough. . . . even with 500,000 Americans."[8] Ball compared the

[5] Memo, George Ball to Robert McNamara, McGeorge Bundy, and William Bundy, May 13, 1965, Country File—Vietnam, NSF.

[6] Ibid.

[7] Memo, George Ball to the President, "Keeping the Power of Decision in the South Viet-Nam Crisis," June 18, 1965, NSC History—Troop Deployment.

[8] Ibid. Maxwell Taylor, U.S. ambassador to South Vietnam, was the other major player who shared Ball's skepticism and analogy. In a February 22, 1965, cable to Washington, Taylor argued against using U.S. troops for offensive missions: "White-faced soldier . . . is not suitable guerrilla fighter for Asian forests and jungles. French tried to adapt their forces to this mission and failed; I doubt U.S. forces could do much better" (cited in *Pentagon*

United States to France, writing with characteristic modesty that a "review of the French experience more than a decade ago may be helpful." Ball went straight to the reason he thought the United States could not win:

> The French fought a war in Viet-nam, and were finally defeated—after seven years of bloody struggle and when they still had 250,000 combat-hardened veterans in the field, supported by an army of 205,000 South Vietnamese.[9]

To be sure, Ball acknowledged that the French were fighting to reinstate colonial domination, while the United States was fighting to thwart aggression. Yet he qualified this diagnosis immediately. This difference would pale into insignificance when substantial U.S. troops were introduced; the appearance would be that of a "white man's war." Anticipating the objections of those who insisted on making a distinction between the United States' and France's motives, Ball claimed that the United States' role in Vietnam was not without its "historical ambiguities." From 1948 until 1954, the United States provided France with $4 billion to fight the Vietminh. The United States had identified itself with the colonial oppressor.[10]

Moreover, Ball continued, many of the current problems and setbacks faced by the United States had been experienced by the French. These included difficulty in collecting intelligence and understanding the enemy, overestimating the "effectiveness of our sophisticated weapons under jungle conditions," and so on. The French also "quoted the same kind of statistics that guide our opinions. . . . the number of Viet Minh killed, the number of enemy defectors, the rate of enemy desertions, etc."; they also came up with successive plans—the DeLattre de Tassigny Plan, the Salan Plan, the Navarre Plan—for winning the war.[11] The ineffectiveness of these tactics, in Ball's view, was "no one's fault." It was in the nature of the struggle.[12]

Ball acknowledged that his comparison of the American and French

---

Papers, 3:419). Taylor continued to resist the deployment of additional U.S. troops until late April, when he was outflanked by McNamara, Westmoreland, William Bundy, McNaughton, Admiral Sharp and JCS Chairman Earle Wheeler. See George Kahin, *Intervention*, pp. 316–19, for a good discussion of a reluctant Taylor capitulating before this "Macedonian phalanx."

[9] Memo, George Ball to the President, June 18, 1965, NSC History—Troop Deployment.

[10] Ibid.

[11] Ball's references to the usefulness of French statistics and plans were thinly veiled critiques of Robert McNamara's fondness for American statistics and new plans (Ball interview).

[12] Memo, George Ball to the President, June 18, 1965, NSC History—Troop Deployment.

efforts did not mean that "*we cannot succeed where the French did not; we have things running for us that the French did not have.*" But the lesson was clear: "We cannot yet be sure that we will be able to beat the Viet Cong without unacceptable costs." The doubts raised by the French analogy led Ball to a novel recommendation: to increase the number of U.S. troops in South Vietnam to an aggregate level of 100,000, but no more, and for a trial period of three months, see how they fare against the Vietcong. Such a "controlled commitment" would "prevent the momentum of events from taking command," for, "on the basis of our experience during that trial period we will then appraise the costs and possibilities of waging a successful land war in South Viet-Nam and chart a clear course of action."[13] Ball was convinced that the trial would confirm his doubts.

Ball's willingness to test the lessons he inferred from the French experience may approximate the way scientists use analogies to make discoveries, but it must have seemed too clinical to Johnson and his other advisers.[14] They seemed more interested in an open-ended commitment that did not tie the United States to artificial troop levels or time constraints. Mostly, they simply failed to see the relevance of the French experience.[15]

On June 29, with the day of decision getting closer, Ball reiterated his doubts in a desperate-sounding memorandum to the principals.[16] It would be "highly imprudent," Ball wrote, to "commit substantially increased American forces to a ground war" without proof that they could locate, engage, and effectively fight the communist guerrillas. Ball turned to the 1950s once more. This time he focused on the dilemma Eisenhower faced in 1954: should the United States intervene to help the beleaguered French garrison at Dien Bien Phu? Ball honed in on General Matthew Ridgway's assessment of the extreme difficulties of

[13] Ibid. The United States had 75,000 troops in South Vietnam when Ball wrote this memo. Ball is thus suggesting adding only 25,000 more—to an aggregate of 100,000—for the three-month trial. This is in contrast to McNamara's July request for 100,000 extra troops—meaning an aggregate of 175,000—for a much more open-ended commitment.

[14] When asked how he could "test" with one hundred thousand lives his belief that the United States would fail as the French had, Ball replied that he saw himself as "fighting a rearguard action." Ball perceived that policy was tending toward intervention; he wanted to argue, "All right, let's do it tentatively and let's make a decision not to go beyond this" (Ball interview).

[15] William Bundy, interview with author, April 11, 1986.

[16] Memo, George Ball to Dean Rusk, Robert McNamara, McGeorge Bundy, William Bundy, and Leonard Unger, "A Plan for Cutting Our Losses in South Viet-Nam," June 29, 1965, NSC History—Troop Deployment. The president was given a seven-page summary of this nineteen-page memo on June 28.

fighting a ground war against the Vietminh, cited the general's reasoning extensively, and enjoined the principals to heed Ridgway's vision:

> We could have fought in Indo-China. We could have won, *if we had been willing to pay the tremendous cost in men and money that such intervention would have required—a cost that in my opinion would have eventually been as great as or greater than, that we paid in Korea. . . .*
>
> When the day comes for me to face my Maker and account for my actions, the thing I would be most humbly proud of was the fact that I fought against, and perhaps contributed to preventing, the carrying out of some harebrained tactical schemes which would have cost the lives of thousands of men. *To that list of tragic accidents that fortunately never happened, I would add the Indo-China intervention.*[17]

If Ball thought the "prognosis" provided by the Dien Bien Phu analogy convincing, others did not. What is interesting and significant is that the latter felt compelled to point out to the president the irrelevance of the Dien Bien Phu analogy. One day after receiving Ball's memo, McGeorge Bundy signed a memorandum to the president entitled, "France in Vietnam, 1954, and the United States in Vietnam, 1965—A Useful Analogy?"[18] The nine-page document answered the question with a resounding no.

[17] Ibid. Emphasis Ball's. The principals' inability to heed Matthew Ridgway's wisdom probably left them with more thankless tasks than did Ridgway's encounter with Vietnam. What Kingsman Brewster said of his close friend McGeorge Bundy is probably applicable to the others as well: "Mac is going to spend the rest of his life trying to justify his mistakes on Vietnam" (cited in David Halberstam, *The Best and the Brightest*, p. 47).

[18] Memo, McGeorge Bundy to the President, June 30, 1965, NSC History—Troop Deployment. Bundy has denied that the memo was written to counter George Ball's use of the French analogy (interview with author, April 10, 1986). Informed of Bundy's denial, George Ball appeared incredulous: "I can't believe that Mac Bundy didn't have my arguments in mind. As a matter of fact the reason he wrote it for Johnson was to. . . . warn Johnson not to take what I was saying too seriously" (Ball interview). Bundy has also denied writing the memo personally. Whether Bundy actually wrote it is not crucial; there is independent evidence that Bundy subscribed to its major tenets. In the draft of a long letter addressed to Donald Graham of *The Harvard Crimson*, Bundy argued against the campus's "underlying opposition to any use of force." Munich, Berlin, Korea and Cuba in 1962 showed the folly of this position, argued Bundy. Bundy then devoted one paragraph to refuting the French analogy. The paragraph most heavily revised (in his handwriting), it is worth quoting in part: "It is our awareness of this basic requirement [that the United States is honestly wanted in South Vietnam] which distinguishes our policy in Vietnam from that of France, and which vitiates the argument that what the French could not do ten years ago no one can do now. We simply are not there as colonialists. . . . The French never earned a similar reputation, and as a consequence they were the inevitable target of Communists and non-Communist nationalists alike. The situation today is quite different. . . . Only a very casual commentator would compare the two experiences as if they were parallel" (letter, McGeorge Bundy to Donald Graham, April 20, 1965, Files of McGeorge Bundy, NSF).

"It has been suggested in some quarters," the memo began, "that the United States today finds itself in a position in Vietnam similar to that of the French in 1954. One implication is that we must expect an outcome to our present policy similar to that which befell the French in their defeat and withdrawal of that year." It was this implication that the rest of the memo sought to refute.[19]

To show the irrelevance of the French precedent, the memo highlighted the difference between (1) the nature of the Vietnam conflict in 1954 and in 1965 and (2) France's domestic political situation in 1954 and that of the United States in 1965. In 1954, the Vietminh were fighting for national independence; the French were fighting to reestablish their colonial rule. France fielded 470,000 men against the Vietminh's 350,000 (a 1.3:1 ratio). French military strategy was static, limited to holding and defensive actions, ensuring that "the prospects for a military victory were nil."[20]

In contrast, the Vietcong were fighting to gain control of South Vietnam in 1965. The Vietcong's tactic was to exploit and appropriate an ongoing noncommunist social and political revolution in the South. This revolution, to be distinguished from the Vietcong insurgency, involved the transfer of power from a Catholic and French-educated elite to a more "militantly nationalistic" group of bonzes and young generals. The United States was in South Vietnam "at the request of successive Saigon governments" to "help resist the Communists" amidst this political turbulence. With a combined U.S./ARVN total of 320,000 troops against the Vietcong's 194,000, the United States enjoyed a 1.6:1 force ratio in its favor. The ARVN was becoming "more effective in guerrilla operations. . . . [and] with continuing U.S. support, has the capacity to prevent a Viet Cong military victory."[21]

Differences between the French and American political scene in the 1950s and 1960s respectively also suggested that the United States could succeed where the French failed. "Two key aspects of France's relation to the Indochina war in 1954," according to the memo, "were the war's acute unpopularity and French political instability." The left actively opposed the war and others used it for their own political ends. Moreover,

> The ambiguous legal status of the conflict enabled French Communists to carry their opposition to the point of sabotage. . . . Successive French governments had to contend with *concerted and organized domestic opposition*;

[19] Ibid. Robert McNamara has also denied the relevance of the French parallel in testimony before the House Armed Services Committee in January 1964 (*Pentagon Papers*, 3:36).

[20] Memo, McGeorge Bundy to the President, June 30, 1965, NSC History—Troop Deployment.

[21] Ibid.

resolutions favoring negotiations and early withdrawal were frequently proposed. . . . Leak and counter leak was an accepted domestic political tactic, and, as a result, even highly classified reports or orders pertaining to the war were often published verbatim.[22]

Politicians like Pierre Mendes-France pushed for negotiations and settlement; "the defeat at Dien Bien Phu made the French Government anxious to disengage as soon as possible." Paris lacked the will to continue fighting. These domestic constraints did not operate for the United States in 1965. Although there was "considerable concern" about the administration's Vietnam policy, "general support" was widespread. The most articulate critics were academics and clergymen, a minority within their own groups; "with the end of the academic year, this protest movement has temporarily subsided." Moreover, the polls indicated that 62 percent of the population approved of the president's management of the Vietnam crisis. Editorials tended to support the president's "determination to keep Vietnam independent." Although congressional critics like Wayne Morse and Ernest Gruening were advocating disengagement, they constituted a tiny minority. The 512 to 2 vote in August 1964 on the Tonkin Gulf Resolution testified to the strong congressional support enjoyed by the president. If Paris had lacked the will, support, and unity to prosecute the war successfully in the 1950s, the United States possessed the determination, support, and unity to do what was necessary in the 1960s.[23]

These perceived differences between France and the United States, and between the Vietnam of 1954 and that of 1965, led to the obvious conclusion: "Despite superficial similarities, the situation faced by France in Vietnam in 1954 is not fundamentally analogous to that faced by the United States in Vietnam in 1965." Therefore the implication that "we must expect an outcome to our present policy similar to that which befell the French in their defeat and withdrawal" was false.[24]

McGeorge Bundy was not the only one unhappy with the Dien Bien Phu analogy. On July 10, it was State's turn to counter it. A telegram sent under Rusk's name to the U.S. Embassy in Saigon stated that "increasing direct U.S. involvement in fighting in Vietnam has led to public comparison [of] U.S. role with that of French in Indochina War." Although arguments refuting this invidious comparison were fairly obvious, there was "special requirement based on high-level interest in subject,

[22] Ibid. It would have been difficult for the author of this memo to foresee what was to happen in America in 1971. Daniel Ellsberg at least could have found solace in knowing that what he did was not unprecedented.

[23] Ibid.

[24] Ibid.

for report contrasting Vietnamese attitudes toward French presence 1945–54 with attitudes toward Americans now." The report had to be in by July 12.[25]

Telegram 117 from Saigon, "Comparison of U.S. Role with Earlier French Involvement," met the deadline. It listed several important differences. Like McGeorge Bundy's memorandum, it emphasized the different political facts: the French obstructed independence, the United States was defending that independence; the French were protecting their commercial interests, the United States, South Vietnamese self-determination. "Knowledgeable Vietnamese" were aware that France was alone during the 1945–1954 war, whereas Australia, Korea, and the Philippines were present alongside the United States in 1965. Compared to the French troops, U.S. troops were perceived to be more restrained and egalitarian. Finally, many Vietnamese considered the French intervention ("albeit unfairly") to be a pursuit of narrow self-interest; the same Vietnamese, however, saw the U.S. role in Vietnam as akin to its role in Korea in the early 1950s. The telegram concluded: "There is essentially no comparison between attitude toward French in period 1945–54 and toward us today."[26]

THE LESSONS OF DIEN BIEN PHU

Using process tracing to analyze the private uses of the Dien Bien Phu analogy leads to some interesting results. Of the six diagnostic functions of analogical reasoning suggested by the AE framework, prognostication was clearly the most important. Ball's reasoning that the United States was unlikely to achieve its objectives in Vietnam by military intervention was based on his reading of the French experience. No one doubted the source or the depth of Ball's conviction. As William Bundy has written:

> Based on his close experience as a lawyer for the French government itself in the period of the First Indochina War . . . Ball was convinced to the depths of his being that white men and Western military techniques simply could not win a guerrilla war against the kind of political/military force Ho had developed.[27]

Bundy has also suggested in a different context that Ball was so convinced that the France precedent was "the germane analogy" that he could not conceive of any differences between France in Vietnam and

[25] Cable, Dean Rusk to Ambassador Taylor, July 10, 1965, Country File—Vietnam, NSF.

[26] Cable, Ambassador Taylor to Dean Rusk, July 12, 1965, "Comparison of U.S. Role with Earlier French Involvement," Country File—Vietnam, NSF.

[27] William Bundy, unpublished manuscript, chap. 17, p. 10, Papers of William Bundy.

America in Vietnam. That made Ball "much less effective in debating."[28] Ball would be the last to deny the centrality of the French experience: "I think that was the one time that I myself was using analogies."[29] More specifically, according to Ball, "Knowing what high hopes they [the French] had of winning and how they were constantly deceived by events certainly played a big role in my thinking."[30]

Ball carried the case of France in the 1950s right to the very day of decision, July 21, 1965. It is worth recalling that Ball's opening statement in that meeting was, "Isn't it possible that the VC will do what they did against the French—stay away from confrontation and not accommodate us?"[31] That was Ball's way of saying the United States could not win. As Horace Busby observed in a memo to the president that evening, Ball's "thinking is influenced by . . . his . . . strong personal involvement. . . . with the French during their fiasco in Indochina. Anyone emotionally involved in those . . . experiences would be cautious, as Ball is cautious."[32] It is also worth recalling that the president took Ball's warning seriously. As Johnson himself remarked during the meeting, one of two "basic troublings within me" is whether "westerners can ever win a war in Asia."[33] The Korean analogy would have predicted a different outcome. Those who doubted the relevance of the Dien Bien Phu analogy, namely Dean Rusk, McGeorge Bundy, and William Bundy, spent most of their intellectual ammunition disputing its gloomy predictions. They believed Ball's prognosis to be premature.

If the main lesson of Dien Bien Phu was the prediction of failure, the other lessons all seemed to reinforce that prediction. Ball initially balked at drawing parallels between the nature of the problem facing the United States in 1965 and that faced by the French in Vietnam earlier. The conclusion would have been that the problem in 1965 was similar to that in 1954: the communists were fighting for national independence, and the United States, like France, was obstructing independence. Ball appeared to reject this diagnosis: "To be sure, the French were fighting a colonial war while we are fighting to stop aggression."[34] Yet, as noted earlier, he

[28] Interview with author, April 11, 1986.

[29] Ball interview.

[30] Ibid. Actually, Ball had also used the Korean analogy to warn his colleagues about the danger of Chinese intervention and the possible domestic repercussions of a protracted war.

[31] July 21, 1965, meeting on Vietnam, notes (by Jack Valenti), Papers of Lyndon Baines Johnson, Meeting Notes File.

[32] Memo, Horace Busby to the President, "Impressions, Vietnam Discussion," July 21, 1965, Miscellaneous Vietnam Documents, Reference File.

[33] July 21, 1965, meeting on Vietnam, notes (by Jack Valenti), Papers of Lyndon Baines Johnson, Meeting Notes File.

[34] Memo, George Ball to the President, "Keeping the Power," June 18, 1965, NSC History—Troop Deployment.

quickly qualified this assertion by focusing on how the world would perceive an extensive U.S. role: "But when we have put enough Americans on the ground in South Vietnam to give the appearance of a white man's war, the distinction as to our ultimate purpose will have less and less practical effect."[35] The Bundy memo passed over the issue of appearances and focused on the differences between U.S. and French intentions. The Taylor telegram reassured the State Department that the South Vietnamese did not see the U.S. role in South Vietnam as analogous to that of the French. If anything, the Vietnamese saw the United States as playing the role it played in Korea.

Differentiating U.S. and French intentions was also essential to counter another implication of the French analogy: that the role of the United States in 1965 was as morally untenable as that of France in 1954. Ball did not question the morality of the American position in such strong terms, but he suggested that the United States was not totally untainted:

> Nor is our position in Viet-nam without its historical ambiguities. From 1948–54 we identified ourselves with the French *by providing almost $4 billions of United States aid to help the French* in Indochina wage war against the Viet Minh. As soon as our aid contributions began to mount, Ho Chi Minh denounced American "imperialism."[36]

The Taylor telegram took strong issue with such suggestions of guilt by association. It dissociated the United States from the French and linked the United States in Vietnam to the United States in Korea: "Many Vietnamese draw analogy between SVN situation and Korean police action in which U.S. came to aid of victims of foreign communist aggression, whereas French intervention here ascribed, albeit unfairly, only to pursuit of narrow self-interest despite Vietnamese aspirations."[37]

Unlike the Korean analogy, Dien Bien Phu did not emphasize external dangers such as the possibility of Chinese intervention. Like the Korean analogy, however, Dien Bien Phu warned of the danger of domestic political turmoil. Domestic opposition to the war was a major reason France chose not to continue fighting in Vietnam. This warning about domestic opposition and its debilitating consequences was of course implicit in Ball's use of the analogy. Yet it is important to note that Ball did not

[35] Ibid. This notion of the United States being considered as colonialist by the Vietnamese was a point that Ball refused to concede. William Bundy believed that Ball's unwillingness to make a distinction between U.S. and French intention was not helpful to Ball in internal debates (interview with author, April 11, 1986).

[36] Memo, George Ball to the President, "Keeping the Power," June 18, 1965, emphasis Ball's.

[37] Cable, Ambassador Taylor to Dean Rusk, July 12, 1965, Country File—Vietnam, NSF.

develop this theme fully in his memo. Perhaps it was too obvious. But he dealt with the issue more directly in the July 21 meeting:

> There is the problem of national politics. Every great captain in history was not afraid to make a tactical withdrawal if conditions were unfavorable to him. The enemy cannot even be seen in Vietnam. He is indigenous to the country. I truly have serious doubts that an army of westerners can successfully fight orientals in an Asian jungle.[38]

However, it should be noted that Ball's conviction of the improbability of a U.S. victory was based just as much on his sense of how the Vietcong's nationalistic élan helped them triumph over the superior firepower of the French as on the domestic repercussions of an unpopular war.[39]

If Ball was content to leave the warning about domestic opposition implicit, McGeorge Bundy was not. Bundy's memo anticipated the warning and sought to refute it. Citing opinion polls, editorial support, and congressional votes, the memo reassured its reader that the warning was premature: domestic political turmoil was unlikely to split the United States as it had France; it was also unlikely to cause the United States to suffer the defeat suffered by France.[40] The point, however, is not what Ball implicitly or what Bundy explicitly did. The point is the French analogy contained a fourth lesson—a warning about the dangers of protracted warfare—that proponents, and especially opponents, could not ignore.

Finally, there was the question of the stakes of the conflict. On one level, the stakes were high for France in the 1950s. The question was whether France would regain control of a former colony. Failure to regain control in Vietnam would further endanger France's position as a colonial power in Algeria and Africa. On another level, however, the stakes were lower. Ball claimed that the French experience also showed that France could withdraw from Vietnam without severe international repercussions. Unsurprisingly, he pointed this out to Johnson. Ball admitted that France "was not a great power and other nations did not depend on France for their own security," while the United States had to "act with the consciousness that if it fails to discharge its role of leader-

[38] July 21, 1965, meeting on Vietnam, notes (by Jack Valenti), Papers of Lyndon Baines Johnson, Meeting Notes File.

[39] Ball interview. In a June 1964 meeting with De Gaulle, the French president had told Ball that Vietnam was a "rotten country" and that "the United States could not win, even though . . . [it] commanded vastly more resources than France." De Gaulle's recounting of the French experience greatly reinforced Ball's conviction that the United States could not win. See Ball, *The Past Has Another Pattern*, pp. 377–78.

[40] Memo, McGeorge Bundy to the President, June 30, 1965, NSC History—Troop Deployment.

ship there is no other free world power capable of taking its place."[41] Despite this caveat, the tone of the memo downplayed the severity of the stakes in Vietnam.

Ball took his own caveat seriously. A few days later, in order to ascertain the U.S. stakes in Vietnam, Ball undertook a country-by-country analysis of the likely consequences of a compromise settlement in South Vietnam. Laos would face increased pressure from the North Vietnamese and the Pathet Lao; Burma and Cambodia would lean more toward Peking; Indonesia would increase its covert aggression against Malaysia. Thailand would "initially see it as a failure of U.S. will," but with time and U.S. military assistance, it would survive as the "foundation rock" of the U.S. "political-military commitment to Southeast Asia." Similarly, Korea's reaction would be "cushioned" by increasing U.S. military and economic aid.[42]

Japan, on the other hand, would not lose confidence in the United States because it preferred "wisdom to valor in an area remote from its own interests." Most important (for Ball at least), "the principal anxiety of our NATO allies is that we have become too preoccupied with an area which seems to them an irrelevance and may be tempted to neglect our NATO responsibilities." Ball concluded that "on balance I believe we would more seriously undermine the effectiveness of our world leadership by continuing the war and deepening our involvement than by pursuing a carefully plotted course toward a compromise solution."[43]

In providing answers to questions about the nature of the challenge in Vietnam, the political stakes, the dangers of intervention, and so on, the Dien Bien Phu analogy seems to have been used by policymakers for most of the diagnostic tasks identified by the AE framework. Another way of saying this is that the AE framework's notion of the function of analogies is a helpful way of lending order and clarity to the numerous ways in which policymakers use analogies. By focusing on six of these tasks, the AE framework makes it possible to get a sense of the policy dispositions of the proponents or detractors of the analogy. Process tracing helps to refine the analysis further by locating, contextualizing, and tracking the various uses or lessons and by indicating the relative significance of the six lessons.

Process tracing reveals that the most salient lesson of the Dien Bien Phu analogy was its estimation that the United States, like France, could not win the war against the Vietnamese communists at an acceptable

[41] Memo, George Ball to the President, June 23, 1965, NSC History—Troop Deployment.

[42] Attachment A to memo, George Ball to the President, July 1, 1965, Country File—Vietnam, NSF.

[43] Ibid.

price. In their own ways, proponents and opponents of the analogy acknowledged the centrality of this lesson. Ball built his case against intervention around that prediction; the Bundys, Rusk, and McNaughton strongly disputed this "French defeat syndrome." Knowledge of the centrality of this lesson to Ball goes a long way toward explaining why he preferred the "cut losses and withdraw" options in 1965. Figure 6.1 shows how the six lessons of Dien Bien Phu acted in unison to predispose Ball toward the nonintervention options: A for the air war and A′ or B′ for the ground war.[44] The lessons of Dien Bien Phu are fundamentally at odds with all the prointervention options of both the air and the ground war. Insofar as Ball's belief in the French analogy predisposed him toward Option A′, while those sympathetic to the Korean precedent preferred Option C′, the proposition that different analogies lead to different policy preferences has been established.

DIEN BIEN PHU, KOREA, AND FOREIGN POLICY INFORMATION PROCESSING

It is probably clear by now that a policymaker who used the French Vietnam experience in the 1950s as a cognitive aid to analysis of the U.S. experience in the 1960s would arrive at conclusions—about the nature of the conflict, the political and moral stakes, the proper solution, the chances of winning, and the dangers involved—very different from those of a policymaker who relied on the Korean analogy. Their different conclusions would lead them to prefer different options.

Why do different analogies lead to different conclusions? The AE framework suggests that it is because they process information differently. The role of the Dien Bien Phu and Korean analogies as "information processors" can be best seen by linking the content of the respective lessons they teach—the "processed information" or "output"—to the "unprocessed" incoming information or "input." Doing so completes the process-tracing procedure. According to Alexander George,

> Process tracing seeks to establish the ways in which actor's *beliefs influenced his receptivity to and assessment of incoming information about the situation*, his definition of the situation, his identification and evaluation of options, as well as, finally his choice of a course of action.[45]

[44] Strictly speaking, Dien Bien Phu should only be used to explain Ball's position in the ground war, since that was the policy context in which he used the analogy. The air-war options are included for illustrative purposes, to indicate that one who took the lessons of Dien Bien Phu seriously would also find Option A more consistent with his beliefs and Options B and C inconsistent with his beliefs.

[45] Alexander George, "The Causal Nexus," p. 113, emphasis mine.

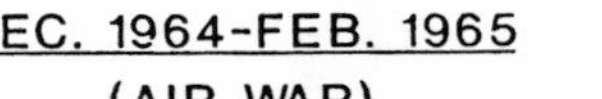

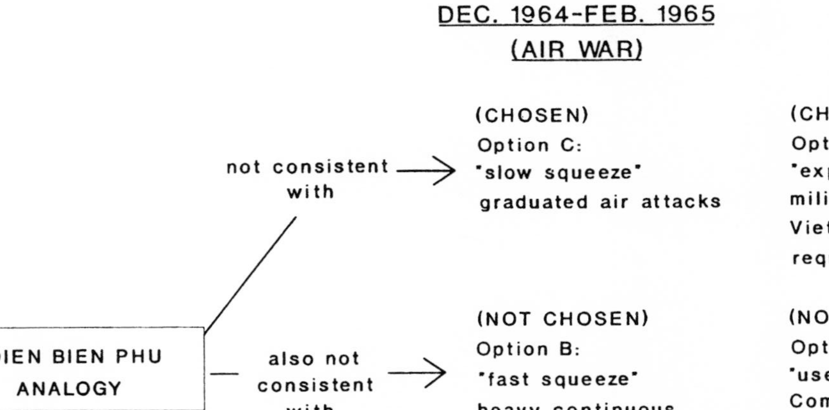

Figure 6.1. The Lessons of Dien Bien Phu and the Option Chosen

Although the analysis so far has dealt with how the Dien Bien Phu analogy influenced Ball's definition of the situation, as well as his identification, evaluation, and choice of options, it has not dealt with this important aspect of the process-tracing procedure: the way the analogy influenced his receptivity to and assessment of incoming information. In other words, the focus up to now has been on the "output" and "outcome" side of the Dien Bien Phu analogy.[46] The "input" or "incoming information" that must be assimilated or rejected by the adherent of the Dien Bien Phu analogy is probably worth examining. For if Dien Bien Phu was the "germane analogy" for Ball, it should have affected his processing of the incoming information in a determinate way.

The analysis can be enriched by an examination of the competing predictions about the likelihood of the United States achieving its objectives in South Vietnam encountered by the adherent of the Dien Bien Phu analogy. The implication here is that presented with three equally plausible but different "incoming" predictions, *X*, *Y*, and *Z*, the believer in the Dien Bien Phu analogy would be likely to be more receptive to the prediction suggesting failure (*X*). Two cognitive steps are involved here. First, if *X*, *Y*, and *Z* were equally plausible and if there was no obvious way to adjudicate among them, Ball would need to go beyond the information given to arrive at his estimate of whether the United States could win in South Vietnam. According to schema theory, this step is facilitated by knowledge structures such as analogies and schemas. The second step involves "top-down processing," in which Ball's Dien Bien Phu schema—"Westerners are unlikely to beat Asians in jungle rice paddies"—would make him more receptive to the pessimistic prediction (*X*) and less receptive to the optimistic predictions (*Y* and *Z*).[47] Conversely, a believer in the Korean analogy would be likely to process the same set of incoming information differently; he would also need to go beyond the information given to arrive at an estimate, but he would be likely to be more receptive to prediction Z (say, success at some cost). Figure 6.2 illustrates the

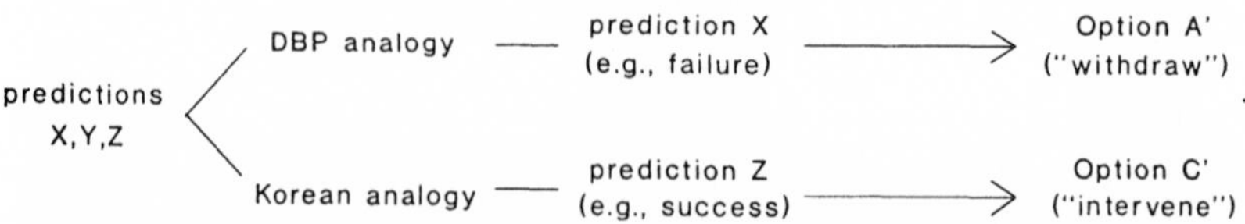

Figure 6.2. Incoming Information Processed by the Dien Bien Phu and Korean Analogies

[46] Chap. 5's discussion of the Korean analogy also focuses primarily on "output."

[47] The quoted interpretation of Dien Bien Phu is Lyndon Johnson's. See July 21, 1965, Meeting on Vietnam, Notes (by Jack Valenti), Meeting Notes File.

role of analogies as information processors; it also shows how different analogies can lead to different policies.

The "receptivity" of the Korean, Dien Bien Phu, and Munich analogies to the same set of incoming information is illustrated in figure 6.3.[48] The assumption is that those charged with formulating America's Vietnam policy were confronted with ambiguous and conflicting information from all sources about most of the critical variables. Evidence for this can be seen in the differing analyses, stake assessments, predictions, and warnings provided by CIA-SNIE, JCS, and NSC documents.[49] That policymakers were given ambiguous and conflicting information about Vietnam is hardly surprising. Uncertainty, more often than not, pervades foreign policy decision-making; it is also a major reason decision-makers look to the past for policy guidance. In fact, political scientists have argued that it is precisely under such conditions of "structural uncertainty" that cognitive variables such as analogies become especially important.[50] What is most interesting, for our purposes, is how different pasts or historical analogies are used to assess and resolve the ambiguities.

To simplify matters, Figure 6.3 presents the incoming information as pairs of conflicting or ambiguous assessments. Two major definitions of the nature of the problem confronting the United States in South Vietnam are discernable. Some believed that South Vietnam was the victim of aggression initiated by North Vietnam; others saw the war in South Vietnam as a civil war with nationalist overtones. Support for both assessments could be found in NSC documents. A NSC Working Group on Vietnam used SNIE reports to arrive at the following assessment of the situation in Vietnam in November 1964: "The primary sources of Communist strength in South Vietnam remain indigenous. . . . the VC enjoys some status as a nationalist movement." At the same time, the working group also noted that "the DRV contribution is substantial. The DRV manages the VC insurrection. . . . we believe that any orders from Hanoi. . . . would in large measure be obeyed by Communist forces in South Vietnam."[51] Given the ambiguity of these assessments, a policymaker who looked to the Korean analogy for guidance would probably

[48] Though Munich is not discussed until the next chapter, I have included the Munich analogy in Figure 6.3 for convenience and to avoid redundancy. The reader may want to skip over the Munich column until he or she has read chapter 7.

[49] Ideally, to minimize the possibility that information presented to policymakers has been preprocessed by the intelligence officer's analogies, these government documents and other sources should not draw historical analogies.

[50] See Steinbruner, *The Cybernetic Theory*, pp. 17–18; Holsti, "Foreign Policy Decision-Makers," pp. 25–26; Powell, Dyson, and Purkitt, "Opening the Black Box"; and George, *Presidential Decisionmaking*, chap. 2.

[51] This document is reproduced in Gareth Porter, ed., *Vietnam: The Definitive Documentation of Human Decisions* (New York: Coleman Enterprises, 1979), 2:326–31.

	CONFLICTING INCOMING INFORMATION	PROCESSED AND RESOLVED BY THE FOLLOWING ANALOGIES: KOREAN	DIEN BIEN PHU	MUNICH
1. Definition of situation:	aggression civil war war of independence	aggression	war of independence	aggression
2. Stakes:	high low to medium	high	medium	high
3. Implicit prescription:	intervene withdraw	intervene	withdraw	intervene
4. Morally acceptable to intervene:	yes no	yes	no	yes
5. Likelihood of success:	likely unlikely	likely	unlikely	likely
6. Dangers:	Chinese intervention domestic turmoil	Chinese intervention, domestic turmoil	domestic turmoil	-

Figure 6.3. How the Korean, Dien Bien Phu, and Munich Analogies Will Resolve Conflicting Incoming Information

emphasize the Northern direction of the insurrection in the South; moreover, if the policymaker read North Korea's intentions in 1950 into North Vietnam's in 1965, he would be likely to resolve any ambiguity in the direction of "outside aggression." On the other hand, a believer in the Dien Bien Phu analogy would be more receptive to the "indigenous" and "nationalist" credentials of the Vietcong and thus be more sympathetic to the civil war thesis.

Similarly, intra-elite or public disagreement about U.S. stakes in Vietnam would be resolved differently by the two analogies. George Ball, James Thomson, and Mike Mansfield did not consider the stakes in Vietnam to be extremely high. Thomson, a China specialist and McGeorge Bundy aide, felt that Vietnam was not worthy of U.S. attention.[52] On the other hand, Lyndon Johnson, the joint chiefs, McNamara, Rusk, and the Bundys saw the stakes as very high. Each side knew about the others' valuation of the stakes, but no compromise was reached. Sensitivity to the Korean precedent would predispose one to seeing high stakes; sensitivity to the French precedent, on the other hand, would imply lower stakes.

Given two conflicting recommendations about the possible courses of action in Vietnam, it also stands to reason that those who took the Korean analogy seriously would be likely to favor intervention because, among other things, the analogy was optimistic about the chances of success. In contrast, those who took the Dien Bien Phu analogy seriously would be likely to be more pessimistic and therefore prone toward the withdrawal option. Similarly, arguments about the moral right of the United States to intervene in Vietnam would be resolved differently. Those who likened Vietnam to Korea would take the position that intervention was just whereas those who likened the American role in Vietnam to that of the French would doubt the justness of military intervention.

The incoming information also contained conflicting assessments of the likelihood of a U.S. victory. A study commissioned by Secretary McNamara asked the JCS to assess the chances of a U.S. victory: "If we do everything we can, can we have assurance of winning in South Vietnam?"[53] McNamara's assistant, John McNaughton, sought to operationalize the terms *assurance* and *winning* for the JCS. His position was that "the degree of 'assurance' should be fairly high—better than 75% (whatever that means)," and "winning" meant that "we succeed in demonstrating to the VC that they cannot win; this, of course, is a victory for us only if it is . . . a way station toward a favorable settlement in South Vietnam." The answer provided by the Goodpaster Study, named after its chair-

[52] Interview with author, October 31, 1986.

[53] *Pentagon Papers*, 4:290–92.

man, General Andrew Goodpaster, was a conditional yes: "Within the bounds of reasonable assumptions. . . . there appears to be no reason we cannot win if such is our will."[54]

McNaughton himself was actually less optimistic but more precise than Goodpaster. His assessment was that the United States chances of winning would be 20 percent by 1966, 40 percent by 1967, and 50 percent by 1968. His assumption was that the United States would commit one hundred thousand troops in 1965, with the number reaching 400,000 and more in 1968.[55] McNamara's position was somewhere between McNaughton's and Goodpaster's: he believed his policy stood "a good chance of achieving an acceptable outcome within a reasonable time in Vietnam."[56]

"Virtually all the [Special National Intelligence] Estimates," on the other hand, "stress Communists confidence in ultimate victory" because the communists saw themselves as fighting a "war of national liberation," "the kind of struggle which they believe they will inevitably win."[57] Obviously one side had to be wrong. In the face of such conflicting assessments, those familiar with the French experience would be likely to give greater stock to the communists' confidence; those more familiar with Korea would be likely to emphasize the ability of the United States to prevail.

Assessments of the risks of U.S. military intervention in Vietnam focused on the possibility of Soviet or Chinese intervention. SNIEs judged Soviet military intervention to be "extremely unlikely." Chinese military intervention was considered probable if the United States invaded North Vietnam, but anything short of that, including U.S. air attacks against industrial and military targets, was deemed unlikely to provoke China.[58]

[54] Winning was defined as "achieving an outcome somewhere between, as a maximum, an end to insurgency . . . and as an acceptable minimum, containment of the insurgency . . . with an end to the need for the presence of substantial U.S. forces." JCS Report, July 14, 1965, Country File—Vietnam, NSF. The most important assumptions were (1) no U.S. or SVN invasion of North Vietnam, (2) no use of nuclear weapons, (3) no mass bombing of population, (4) no Chinese or Soviet intervention, and (5) no subjection of proposed strategy, once approved, to restriction.

[55] Memo, first draft, John McNaughton to Robert McNamara, "Analysis and Options for South Vietnam," July 13, 1965, NSC History—Troop Deployment.

[56] *Pentagon Papers*, 4:622.

[57] CIA Briefing Paper, June 11, 1965, NSC History—Troop Deployment. This document has been heavily sanitized. See also the NSC Working Group document referred to earlier in Porter, *Vietnam*, esp. 2:330.

[58] See intelligence note, Thomas Hughes to Dean Rusk, "Chen Yi on Vietnam," April 26, 1965, Country File—Vietnam, NSF. The Chinese foreign minister's remarks on when China might intervene in Vietnam were considered by the State Department's director of intelligence and research to be "one of the clearest and most succinct statements available

The Korean analogy would obviously hone in on the warning about Chinese intervention. As chapter 5 shows, Lyndon Johnson's extreme sensitivity to the Korean precedent predisposed him to overcompensate: he was reluctant to bomb North Vietnam along the lines of Option B despite CIA estimates that China was unlikely to intervene. The Dien Bien Phu analogy would be insensitive to either danger, for it does not address such international strategic dangers.

SNIE reports had little to say about the dangers of domestic turmoil if the United States decided to fight a ground war in South Vietnam. Interestingly, on this one aspect believers of the Korean and the Dien Bien Phu analogies agreed: regardless of the incoming information, they would expect domestic opposition to increase if the war became protracted.

This exercise indicates that analogies often function as important information processors. They help resolve conflicting incoming information in ways consistent with the expectations of the analogy. Thus, given two different definitions of the situation in Vietnam, policymakers were likely to be more receptive toward the definition that was consistent with the expectations of their analogy. Believers in the Korean or Munich analogies would be more receptive to the aggression thesis, whereas proponents of the Dien Bien Phu analogy would be more receptive to the civil war thesis.

THE CONTINUING SALIENCE OF DIEN BIEN PHU

The thrust of Ball's argument, it will be remembered, was that, like France, the United States was unlikely to achieve its objectives in South Vietnam. McGeorge Bundy's and Dean Rusk's replies disputing the Dien Bien Phu analogy claimed that Ball's prognosis was premature. Bundy and Rusk had a point. The differences they found between the situations were salient and significant. The main problem was that they arrived at the dissimilarities by comparing France and the United States at the wrong points in time.

Ball's prognostications were not based on a comparison between France in 1954 and the United States in 1965; they were based on the conviction that the same revolutionary élan that allowed the communists to outlast the French would also allow them to outlast the Americans. Ball's fear was that after years of protracted and inconclusive fighting, stretching into the early 1970s, the United States would end up in the position of the French in 1954. In 1954, Frenchmen had been fighting

---

of the Chinese Communist position." See also CIA Briefing Paper, June 11, 1965, referred to in n. 57.

and dying in Vietnam for eight years. In 1965, the United States was about to start fighting. The relevant question for those who took the comparison seriously was whether the United States would suffer the same domestic turmoil as France had after years of fighting. Ball believed so; that was one reason he believed that the United States was unlikely to win in Vietnam.

Ball's prescience is stunning in retrospect, yet his reasoning fell on deaf ears. The prevailing analogy was Korea, and its prognostication was eventual success after some costs. Ball's opening salvo, the October 1964 memo, was aimed at the Korean analogy; Dien Bien Phu was introduced as a possible counteranalogy. Later memos elaborated on the lessons to be learned from the French, but they elicited strong rebuttals from Bundy and Rusk.

Bundy and Rusk had a far easier task. No other high-level policymaker had intimate knowledge about, or took seriously, the French experience in Vietnam. Ball lamented understandably that "the lessons of history, to my surprise, were disdained. It was useless for me to point out the meaning of the French experience; they thought that experience without relevance."[59] But he should not have been surprised. The president and his most senior advisers were much more attuned to the Korean and Munich precedents than to the French experience.[60] Moreover, like the general cited at the beginning of the chapter, the policymakers were uninterested in learning from losers. In this context, Ball's efforts, compared to the response of his superiors, must have seemed like small-arms fire.

But if Johnson was not moved by the Dien Bien Phu analogy in 1965, subsequent events made it impossible for him to ignore it. Ball's prognostications came true. The United States became bogged down in a seemingly unwinnable war. Domestic opposition increased. McGeorge Bundy became disillusioned with the war and left the administration in March 1966 to head the Ford Foundation.[61] Ball left shortly thereafter, and McNamara followed in late 1967. Johnson continued to seek Bundy's and Ball's advice after they left. In his capacity as an outside adviser, McGeorge Bundy wrote Johnson a revealing memo in May 1967.[62] Bundy resorted to a variant of the France 1954 analogy to advise Johnson against further escalation. Increased U.S. bombing or military presence, in Bundy's view, was unlikely to "bring the war to a satisfactory conclusion." Hanoi was unlikely to cooperate:

[59] Ball, *The Past Has Another Pattern*, p. 376.

[60] Harry MacPherson, interview with author, Hofstra University, New York, April 11, 1986.

[61] McGeorge Bundy, interview with author, April 10, 1986.

[62] Memo, McGeorge Bundy to the President, "Memorandum on Vietnam Policy," May 4, 1967, Files of John McNaughton, in Papers of Paul Warnke.

> Given their history, they are bound to hold out for a possible U.S. shift in 1969—that's what they did against the French, and they got most of what they wanted when Mendes took power. Having held on for so long this time, and having nothing much left to lose—compared to the chance of victory—they are bound to keep on fighting.[63]

It was an uncharacteristically strong use of the French analogy by its former chief critic. Even Ball did not infer from what the Vietminh did in the 1950s to what they were *bound* to do in the 1960s. By early 1968, Bundy would announce to the "wise men" assembled by Johnson to ponder the course of the war that the United States could not achieve its objectives in Vietnam. Bundy capped his remarks with a generous acknowledgment: "I must tell you what I thought I would never say—that I now agree with George Ball."[64]

It was General Westmoreland, however, who brought the specter of Dien Bien Phu most heavily to bear on Lyndon Johnson. On January 22, 1968, Westmoreland informed Johnson that the Vietcong were planning a decisive campaign in South Vietnam. According to Johnson, Westmoreland saw the threat in Northern I Corps as the most serious. "He thought that the North Vietnamese saw a similarity between the allied base at Khe Sanh and . . . Dien Bien Phu, where the French had suffered a disastrous defeat in 1954."[65] This analysis of the Vietcong's intentions was echoed in the media and by other officials. Marvin Kalb announced that the "historical ghost" of the French defeat was "casting a shadow over Washington." Walt Rostow believed that the Vietcong was trying to "reenact a new Dien Bien Phu."[66]

Westmoreland shared the view that the North Vietnamese attack of Khe Sanh was an attempt to "restage Dien Bien Phu."[67] Where he differed from the Cassandras was in his confidence that the communist attempt would be in vain. To that end, every living French general involved in the defense of Dien Bien Phu was flown to Saigon. The French generals recounted their mistakes at Dien Bien Phu and gave generously of their advice.[68] Westmoreland himself analyzed the parallels between Dien Bien Phu and Khe Sanh meticulously. His conclusion was that the United States would prevail at Khe Sanh because of fundamental differences in geography, military hardware, and firepower.[69]

[63] Ibid.

[64] Cited in Ball, *The Past Has Another Pattern*, p. 408.

[65] Johnson, *The Vantage Point*, p. 381.

[66] Cited in Stanley Karnow, *Vietnam: A History* (New York: Viking Press, 1983), p. 541.

[67] Ibid.

[68] W. Scott Thompson, "Lessons from the French in Vietnam," *Naval War College Review* 27 (1975): 51–52.

[69] Westmoreland, *A Soldier Reports*, pp. 336–39.

The command historian, Colonel Reamer Argo, painted a much gloomier picture. In a special briefing for Westmoreland's staff, Argo suggested that "the besieging force at Dien Bien Phu. . . . succeeded primarily because the defenders lost all initiative."[70] The implication was that the United States might also lose the initiative at Khe Sanh. Westmoreland disagreed vehemently with this prognosis and just before storming out of the briefing, ordered his staff, "We are not, repeat not, going to be defeated at Khe Sanh. I will tolerate no talking or even thinking to the contrary." Westmoreland was convinced that the United States would retain the initiative because of its "tremendous air power," artillery support, and highly mobile ground troops.

President Johnson was less convinced. As the battle raged on, he paced the situation room in the basement of the White House where a sand-table model of Khe Sanh stood. Johnson was so agitated that he demanded from General Earle Wheeler, chairman of the Joint Chiefs, a formal declaration of faith in Westmoreland's ability to hold Khe Sanh. As Johnson was making the demand, he voiced his worst fear: "I don't want any damn Dinbinphoo."[71]

Khe Sanh did not turn out to be another Dien Bien Phu, in part because the Americans managed to hold the fort, and in part because the Vietcong never intended it to be one. As a communist officer who fought at Dien Bien Phu and Khe Sanh claimed: "At Dienbienphu, the French and ourselves massed for what we both expected to be a final battle. The Americans, however, were strong everywhere in the South. Thus we realized from the beginning that we could not beat them decisively in a single encounter like Khesanh."[72] Instead almost all of the communist officers interviewed by the journalist Stanley Karnow saw the "battles at Khesanh and elsewhere in the hinterlands before and during the Tet offensive" as an attempt to "draw the Americans away from South Vietnam's population centers, thereby leaving them naked to [the Tet] assault."[73]

If the thesis of Khe Sanh as diversion is correct, Colonel Argo's warning about initiative takes on a new importance. There is little doubt that American firepower inflicted heavy casualties on the Vietcong at Khe Sanh. But if Khe Sanh was the sideshow for the Vietcong and Saigon was center stage, the Vietcong may have indeed seized the initiative. Khe Sanh distracted Westmoreland. He failed to give the proper weight to intelligence reports that the Vietcong were infiltrating into the cities in large numbers; he saw Saigon as a distraction from Khe Sanh. The Tet

[70] Ibid., p. 338.

[71] Cited in Karnow, *Vietnam*, p. 541.

[72] Ibid., p. 542.

[73] Ibid. Karnow also cites American military experts who concur with this assessment.

offensive of January 1968—the simultaneous Vietcong attacks on virtually all major Southern cities and provincial capitals—therefore caught Westmoreland off guard.

Fifty million Americans watched their televisions in disbelief as they were treated to the spectacle of violence and confusion culminating in the six-hour seizure of the American embassy in Saigon by a handful of Vietcong commandos. Inasmuch as the Tet offensive was a psychological watershed in American attitudes toward the war and Khe Sanh played a role in giving the Vietcong the advantage of tactical surprise in Saigon, it may be said that Westmoreland won the battle at Khe Sanh but lost the Vietnam War. At Dien Bien Phu, the Vietminh needed to defeat the French militarily to win the war; at Khe Sanh, the Vietcong could afford to lose the battle and yet proceed to win the war.

Westmoreland's preoccupation with the reenactment of Dien Bien Phu at the height of American power in Vietnam may have distracted him, but it was not without basis. No account of the Dien Bien Phu analogy is complete without noting General Vo Nguyen Giap's fixation on Dien Bien Phu as the model of how the Vietnamese communists would win the war. As his remarks to Oriania Fallaci cited at the beginning of this chapter reveal, Giap expected a decisive military showdown with and eventual victory over the Americans. The Tet offensive of 1968 may have been a psychological victory for the Vietnamese communists, but it was a military disaster for the Vietcong. They suffered heavy losses, and their infrastructure in the South was nearly decimated by U.S.-ARVN forces. The spring offensive of 1972 was yet another serious military defeat for the Vietcong. In these two instances, Giap was denied his Dien Bien Phu. The same was true in 1975. By the time North Vietnamese tanks rolled into Saigon, American combat troops had been out of South Vietnam for over two years. Of course it was a victory for the Vietnamese communists. But it was hardly a Dien Bien Phu.

CHAPTER 7

Munich and the 1930s

> SENATOR WAYNE MORSE: We hear a lot of comparison of the situation in Vietnam with Munich. Those of us who—somebody sent me an umbrella the other day—. . . are against this escalation. . . . are told, we are a bunch of Chamberlains. Would you give us your view as to what the analogous relationship, if anything, might be between this war and the situation at the time of Munich or between Mao and Hitler?
>
> GEORGE KENNAN: I think they are entirely different things. I think that no episode, perhaps, in modern history has been more misleading than that of the Munich conference. It has given to many people the idea that never must one attempt to make any sort of political accommodation in any circumstances. This is, of course, a fatally unfortunate conclusion. Hitler was, thank heaven, a unique phenomenon.
>
> —*Report on the United States Senate Hearing,* The Truth about Vietnam

IN 1931, the Japanese army invaded Manchuria in hopes of annexing all of North China. Four years later, Benito Mussolini's army took over Ethiopia. Encouraged by the muted international response to these invasions, Adolf Hitler decided to reoccupy the Rhineland in 1936, in blatant violation of both the Versailles Treaty and the Locarno Pact. Austria was Hitler's next victim. Barely after absorbing Austria in March 1938, Hitler began to demand a chunk of Czechoslovakia. The pretext was self-determination for the Sudentenland Germans. Because Czechoslovakia had a Treaty of Mutual Assistance with France and because France was bound by treaty to Britain, Hitler's demands set off a chain of diplomatic consultations throughout the summer and fall of 1938. France and Britain had to decide whether to stand firm against Hitler and face war or appease him. The consultations culminated in the Munich conference of September 30, 1938, in which British Prime Minister Neville Chamberlain and French Premier Edouard Daladier met with Adolf Hitler and Benito Mussolini and signed a document agreeing to Germany's annexation of the Sudenten part of Czechoslovakia. The four leaders returned to their respective capitals as heroes. Chamberlain claimed he had brought peace with honor. Six months later, Hitler took the rest of Czechoslovakia and started issuing ultimatums to Poland. By September 3, 1939, general war had broken out in Europe.[1]

These events of the 1930s were to have a profound effect on an entire generation of American policymakers. From Harry Truman to George Bush, American presidents have consistently thought of the 1930s as they contemplated military action against the nation's major adversaries. The policymakers of the 1960s were no exception. This chapter explores the role of the 1930s analogy in the making of the 1965 decisions. I will argue that memories of the 1930s—and of Munich in particular—foreclosed the nonintervention options suggested by George Ball and the Dien Bien Phu analogy. However, these memories by themselves were too crude to serve as a useful criterion in the selection of the prointervention options, which in the final analysis, was guided by the Korean analogy. Since this chapter also concludes my empirical analysis of the analogies that affected America's Vietnam decision-making, I shall, in the concluding segment, contrast the analogical explanation I have provided with some nonanalogical explanations of the Vietnam decisions of 1965.

THE LESSONS OF MUNICH AND THE 1930S

Manchuria, Ethiopia, the Rhineland, Austria, Czechoslovakia, Munich, Poland, and World War II: from these events, the senior policymakers of the Johnson administration extracted the axiom or the schema that appeasing aggressors only leads to further aggression. Or, put differently, aggression unchecked is aggression unleashed. Aggression unleashed is particularly dangerous because it leads eventually to general war just as the unchecked fascist aggressions of the 1930s led directly to World War II.

One event of the 1930s to impress itself most firmly on the American mindset was Chamberlain's appeasement of Hitler at Munich. As we have already seen, in a revealing moment during the July 21, 1965, NSC meeting on Vietnam, Henry Cabot Lodge argued, "I feel there is a

[1] The most detailed account of the Munich conference is Telford Taylor, *Munich: The Price of Peace* (New York: Vintage Books, 1979), chap. 1–4.

greater threat to start World War III if we don't go in. Can't we see the similarity to our own indolence at Munich?"[2] Since Munich was the prototype of what went wrong in the 1930s, it will be the main object of our analysis.

Lodge was hardly the first or the last American official to invoke the Munich analogy. In 1961, Vice President Lyndon Johnson, on a visit to South Vietnam, hailed President Ngo Dinh Diem as the "Winston Churchill of Asia." In an oral history interview with William Jorden eight years later, Johnson elaborated on his use of the Munich analogy as vice president. The analogy was situated within the context of Johnson's favorite Churchill story, one he repeatedly told the Vietnamese, the U.S. Congress, and the American public. The story began in the 1930s, with "fascism['s] advance and aggression" in Europe:

> [A] great many people started by compromising and by trying to mediate the situation. And Chamberlin [*sic*] came back and thought he had obtained peace in our time, but it remained for Churchill—who had warned all through the years of these great dangers. . . . to rise to the occasion. . . .
>
> I frequently referred to the fact that Churchill standing alone, after the Battle of Britain and after France had fallen, and after it looked like fascism was in the ascendancy—that Churchill almost by himself had provided the courage and the resistance that stopped Hitler.[3]

Johnson felt that Diem "was confronted with a similar situation," with communist Russia, China, and North Vietnam taking the place of fascist Germany. The common theme was aggression and the consequences of not meeting it: "The advance in that area of the world was going to require some strong person to do what Churchill did." Johnson then referred to Churchill's famous line about meeting fascism on the beaches, the alleys, and the streets, with beer bottles if necessary. In telling Diem the story, Johnson made some allowances for local circumstances but the basic lesson for the Vietnamese President was the same:

> So you're going to have to meet them in the bushes, and you're going to have to meet them in the mountains, and you're going to have to meet them in the forests, and if everything else fails, you're going to have to be like Churchill—you're going to have to use your beer bottles on them. Because we cannot let communism take. . . . South Viet-Nam, because it'll be in Thailand, it'll be in Indonesia, and it'll take all the rest of the area, and be back to Honolulu.[4]

[2] July 21, 1965, meeting on Vietnam, notes (by Jack Valenti), Papers of Lyndon Baines Johnson, Meeting Notes File.

[3] Transcript, Lyndon Johnson oral history interview, August 12, 1969, pp. 4–5.

[4] Ibid., p. 6.

Johnson's point was not that Diem had Churchill's character, but that Diem had to avoid being a Chamberlain and instead be a Churchill in standing up to the would-be aggressors. Johnson was serious about the threat posed by communism. In his report to President Kennedy about the trip, Johnson emphasized the stakes: "We must decide whether to help these [Southeast Asian] countries to the best of our ability or throw in the towel in the area and pull back our defenses to San Francisco."[5]

Although the vice president was fond of the Munich analogy, it was not the analogy that other senior members of the Kennedy administration applied to Vietnam. Neither was Korea. It is interesting to note that the two individuals who were most attuned to Munich and Korea, Johnson and Rusk, were not the most influential decision-makers in the Kennedy years. As some have argued, John F. Kennedy wanted to be his own secretary of state, and his brother Robert was probably as if not more influential than Rusk.[6] Kennedy and his counterinsurgency enthusiasts considered Malaya, the Philippines, and Greece to be the more pertinent analogues to Vietnam. Munich was hardly mentioned in public or in private during this period. The administration of fine-tuners fine-tuned their analogies as well.

The assassination of Kennedy meant a return to the more global analogies. With Johnson as president and Rusk as his trusted secretary of state, Munich and Korea came back into vogue.[7] Equally significant was the fact that the nature of the Vietnam conflict was also changing. Although the Vietcong were still using guerrilla tactics, the conflict began to take an increasingly conventional tone. Instead of hit-and-run operations, the Vietcong began to take on entire units of the ARVN. By February 1965, McGeorge Bundy would warn that defeat was unavoidable without U.S. help. Rusk and William Bundy, in speeches about the Vietnam conflict, began imploring their audience not to forget the invasions of Manchuria, Ethiopia, and Czechoslovakia and their role in bringing on World War II.[8] Years later, Rusk explained the connection between these events and Vietnam, as he saw it:

> The principal lesson we learned from World War II is that if a course of aggression is allowed to gather momentum that it continues to build and leads eventually to a general conflict. . . .

[5] Memo, Lyndon Johnson to the President, May 23, 1961, cited in *Pentagon Papers*, 2:58.

[6] See Halberstam, *The Best and The Brightest*, chap. 3.

[7] U. Alexis Johnson, who served both the Kennedy and Johnson administrations, has observed that the latter "lean[ed] on the Secretary [Rusk] more when it came to foreign policy matters." Transcript, U. Alexis Johnson oral history interview, 1:7.

[8] See *Department of State Bulletin*, January 18, 1965, p. 63; February 8, 1965, pp. 169–75; and March 22, 1965, p. 401.

> Our problem is to prevent World War III. . . . If I had thought myself that there was no connection between Viet Nam and preventing World War III, I might have had a different view about Viet Nam.[9]

The 1930s did play a role in the internal deliberations of the period. In a February 1965 meeting with Dwight Eisenhower, Johnson solicited the ex-president's views on the desirability of negotiations with the Vietnamese communists. Johnson mentioned that he had some advisers who favored negotiations and that the British were also encouraging him to try that path. Eisenhower advised Johnson to reject British Prime Minister Harold Wilson's suggestion because, "negotiation from weakness is likely to lead only into deceit and vulnerability." Moreover, Wilson "has not had experience with this kind of problem. We, however, have learned that Munichs win nothing." Therefore, Eisenhower would tell the British, "not now boys."[10] The precise impact of Eisenhower's advice on Johnson is hard to estimate. It probably came too late to have affected Johnson's decision to begin Operation Rolling Thunder, but as one in a stream of recommendations imploring a tough stand against North Vietnam, it could not but have reinforced Johnson's view that an air war was necessary. Even after the air war had begun, the lessons of Munich continued to encourage Johnson to rule out negotiations, as the next example indicates.

In a March 10, 1965, meeting at Camp David with only the president, Rusk, McNamara, and McGeorge Bundy present, Rusk raised the issue of negotiations with the North Vietnamese. At some point, Rusk stated, the United States would have to decide to escalate or to negotiate; Rusk wondered whether the British would help the United States explore the diplomatic track. Johnson's response, according to McGeorge Bundy's handwritten notes of the meeting, was: "Nearly everyone chose to forward this more than LBJ, but I did *cross bridge* in December [1964]. . . . But if you can show me any reasonable out I'll grab it." Johnson also added: "To give in = another Munich. *if not* here—then Thailand."[11] This use of the Munich analogy is significant because, with the air war decision behind him, Johnson had to think about other U.S. options if bombing failed to shore up morale in South Vietnam or force North Vietnam to stop supporting the insurgency. Johnson appeared a truly torn man in this meeting. On the one hand, he wanted a reasonable way out, on the other, he was afraid of giving in, which he saw as tantamount to appeasement. His July decisions indicated that his fears about the latter won out.

[9] Transcript, Dean Rusk oral history interview, p. 22.

[10] Memorandum of Meeting with the President, February 17, 1965, Meeting Notes File.

[11] Papers of McGeorge Bundy, March 10, 1965.

The next significant reference to Munich that can be documented was Henry Cabot Lodge's outburst, already mentioned above, during the July 21 meeting about sending U.S. ground troops to South Vietnam. Six days later, after Johnson had briefed congressional leaders about his decision to intervene, House Speaker John McCormack expressed his support with the same refrain: "I don't think we have any alternatives. Our military men tell us we need more and we should give it to them. The lesson of Hitler and Mussolini is clear. I can see five years from now a chain of events far more dangerous to our country."[12]

The president announced his decision to the nation the following day, and he did not shy away from sharing his private conviction with the American public. "Three times in my lifetime, in two world wars and in Korea," Johnson began, "Americans have gone to far lands to fight for freedom. We have learned at a terrible and brutal cost that retreat does not bring safety and weakness does not bring peace." It was this lesson that impelled the United States to stand in Vietnam. The alternative was surrender, and surrender would not bring peace, "because we learned from Hitler at Munich that success only feeds the appetite of aggression. The battle would be renewed in one country and then another country, bring with it perhaps even larger and crueler conflict, as we have learned from the lessons of history."[13]

Undoubtedly, there was a heavy element of public explanation and justification in this and other public speeches in which Munich and the 1930s were invoked. The analogy was seldom invoked before 1965, and its use correlates strongly with the escalation of the U.S. effort in Vietnam. This is hardly surprising. Political leaders have to explain why a policy is chosen under ordinary circumstances; a decision to initiate war needs even more explanation and greater justification. Citizens need to know why they are asked to risk their lives, especially in a democracy, where the public's support is essential for the success of any long-term policy. Citizens in a democracy may even deny a leader reelection for his policies or his inability to convince them of the appropriateness of the policy.

Compared to Korea and Dien Bien Phu, Munich and the 1930s did not figure as prominently in the Vietnam documents of the period. This absence seems to suggest that its primary role may have been justificatory. Dean Rusk's public statements seem to lend credibility to this view. The stakes in Vietnam were frequently compared to the stakes in Munich (German fascism and expansionism), Manchuria (Japanese fascism and

[12] *Intervention* Meeting with Congressional Leaders, July 27, 1965, Meeting Notes File, NSF.

[13] Lyndon Johnson, "We Will Stand in Vietnam," in *Department of State Bulletin*, August 16, 1965, p. 262.

expansionism), and Ethiopia (Italian fascism and expansionism). This trio, Rusk's famous "lessons of the thirties," would embellish many of the secretary's speeches in the mid-1960s. The following analysis is typical:

> So what is our stake [in Vietnam]? . . . Can those of us in this room forget the lesson that we had in this issue of war and peace when it was only 10 years from the seizure of Manchuria to Pearl Harbor; about 2 years from the seizure of Czechoslovakia to the outbreak of World War II in Western Europe? Don't you remember the hopes expressed those days: that perhaps the aggressor will be satisfied by this next bite. . . . But we found that ambition and appetite fed upon success and the next bite generated the appetite for the following bite. And we learned that, by postponing the issue, we made the result more terrible, the holocaust more dreadful. We cannot forget that experience.[14]

Rusk's rhetoric notwithstanding, it is important not to slight the diagnostic uses of the 1930s analogy. At crucial junctures in the policy process, it ought to be remembered, Munich was invoked: witness Vice-President Johnson's desire that Diem be a Churchill instead of a Chamberlain in 1961, Eisenhower's reference to Munich, Johnson's equation of "giving in" with Munich, Lodge's outburst, and Speaker McCormack's remarks. One reason Munich appeared less frequently than the Korean and Dien Bien Phu analogies may be that its lessons were so widely accepted and internalized by the principals that they were taken for granted. Whenever the analogy was used internally, it was not challenged. This response is quite unlike the reaction that the Korean and Dien Bien Phu analogies elicited.

Both insiders and outsiders have also commented on the seriousness with which Johnson took the Munich analogy. Clark Clifford, a close adviser to the president and McNamara's successor as secretary of defense in 1968, believes that Johnson took the 1930s seriously, in part because he was influenced by his foreign policy advisers:

> President Johnson . . . encountered practically unanimous sentiment among his senior advisers. And they all said, the domino theory is unquestionably so. You will remember if we'd known then what we know now, we never would have permitted Hitler to get started when Hitler went into the Low Countries and into Czechoslovakia and Austria; if he'd been stopped then we might have prevented World War II. . . . so all of this was very much in their minds.[15]

[14] *Department of State Bulletin*, March 22, 1964, p. 401.

[15] Transcript, Clark Clifford oral history interview, p. 16. See also Clifford's *Counsel to the President*, p. 403, where he writes, "Memories of Munich and appeasement were still fresh, especially in the minds of Dean Rusk and Lyndon Johnson." James Reston, the influential *New York Times* columnist, has also expressed similar sentiments about Johnson, his

Johnson hardly needed to be convinced. His more solicitous advisers may have likened him to Churchill and Lincoln at various times, but Johnson himself was already a firm believer.[16] Former Under Secretary of the Air Force Townsend Hoopes has written: "It was my impression that this presidential stance was not empty posturing, but that Lyndon Johnson believed in. . . . the European analogies."[17] Hoopes's position is confirmed by many others who knew the president.[18]

The justification and diagnostic theses are not mutually exclusive. The point cannot be overemphasized. Even analogies used exclusively for analysis will have some justificatory component. Similarly, analogies used exclusively for justification will have some analytical salience. Psychologists warn against making too rigid a separation between justification and analysis, for on the one hand, the policymaker needs to justify or explain to himself the wisdom of his preferred option, and on the other, having used Munich repeatedly to justify his policy, the policymaker might come to believe in the dire consequences predicted by the Munich analogy.[19]

Although the above logic is plausible, one would feel more confident that Johnson and Rusk were not just exploiting Munich to justify their Vietnam policy if there were further evidence that they took its lessons seriously. In this regard, Johnson's intimations to Doris Kearns are especially telling. These revelations were remarkably consistent with his beliefs as he articulated them not only in 1965, but as early as 1961. Hence Johnson's explanation of why he could not get out of Vietnam: "Everything I knew about history told me that if I got out of Vietnam and let Ho Chi Minh run through the streets of Saigon, then I'd be doing what Chamberlain did in World War II."[20] If Ho won, "I would be seen as a coward and my nation would be seen as an appeaser." The lesson Johnson impressed upon Diem in 1961 he imposed on himself in 1965: "Someone had to call Hitler and someone had to call Ho."[21]

It took another occasion for Johnson to flesh out his historical reasoning

---

advisers, and the 1930s analogy. See Townsend Hoopes, *The Limits of Intervention* (New York: David McKay Company, 1969), pp. 100–1.

16 Horace Busby likened Johnson's position to that of Churchill, while Walt Rostow likened it to Lincoln's. See memo, Horace Busby to the President, July 21, 1965, Miscellaneous Vietnam Documents, Reference File; and note, Walt Rostow to the President, March 17, 1967, Memos to the President, Walt Rostow, vol. 24, NSF.

17 Hoopes, *The Limits of Intervention*, pp. 100–1.

18 See Doris Kearns, *Lyndon Johnson*, and Henry F. Graff, *The Tuesday Cabinet: Deliberation and Decision on Peace and War under Lyndon B. Johnson* (Englewood Cliffs, New Jersey: Prentice Hall, 1970).

19 See the discussion of self-perception theory in Larson, *Containment*, pp. 42–50; and Anderson, "Justifications and Precedents," pp. 738–61.

20 Doris Kearns, *Lyndon Johnson*, p. 252.

21 Ibid., p. 321.

in full to Kearns. Angered by her suggestion that the Vietnam War was a civil war, Johnson retorted that he and she "just read different histories, that's all." He then launched into perhaps the most complete exposition of his reading of history and its pertinence to Vietnam:

> It's just perverted history to claim that it's civil war. . . . No understanding of the thirty years before. . . .
>
> I deeply believe we are quarantining aggressors over there [Vietnam] just like the smallpox. Just like FDR and Hitler, just like Wilson and the Kaiser. You've simply got to see this thing in historical perspective. What I learned as a boy in my teens and in college about World War I was that it was our lack of strength and failure to show stamina that got us into that war. . . . Then I was taught in Congress and in committees on defense preparedness and by FDR that we in Congress were constantly telegraphing the wrong messages to Hitler and the Japanese. . . . I remember those days in Congress. . . . I even signed a petition. . . . calling for a popular vote before a war. But then I came to my senses and recognized that Hitler could take over America while we were holding our election, and I felt so silly I ran down and took my name off. I firmly believe we wouldn't have been involved in World War II if it hadn't been for all the vacillation. . . .
>
> So I knew that if the aggression succeeded in South Vietnam, then the aggressors would simply keep going until all of Southeast Asia fell into their hands. . . . Moscow and Peking would be moving to expand their control and soon we'd be fighting in Berlin or elsewhere. And so would begin World War III.[22]

Johnson's final comment to Kearns after finishing his lecture was, "Look, I know you don't agree with me, but you must know that I believe everything I've just said with every bone inside me. You must at least give me that."[23] Most of the historians who know Johnson would have little trouble granting him that.[24]

Born one year before Johnson, Dean Rusk was led to the same conclusions by his formative experiences. When asked in 1986 how important the lessons of history were in policy-making during the Vietnam War, Rusk replied, "One must always think about historical precedents—we are all shaped by the experiences through which we have lived."[25] Rusk saw himself as belonging to that generation of students shaped by World War II. The events of the 1930s were particularly salient:

[22] Ibid., pp. 329–31.

[23] Ibid., p. 331.

[24] Eric F. Goldman, *The Tragedy of Lyndon Johnson* (New York: Alfred A. Knopf, 1969); Graff, *The Tuesday Cabinet*; Hoopes, *The Limits of Intervention*. See also footnote 15.

[25] Interview with author, August 21, 1986.

One must look at the entire context of the sad story of the 1930s. When the League of Nations was discussing sanctions against Mussolini, our Senate Foreign Relations Committee won't let the secretary of state say we'll support sanctions. The Japanese were engaged in a ten-year war against China, yet the U.S. continued to sell scrap metal to Japan. All these things are part of the context through which my generation lived. I mean many of us—members of my generation—were rather angry that the political leaders had allowed World War II to come about. We know that was a war which could have been prevented. Lack of reaction to Manchuria and seizure of Rhineland. . . . If French forces had shown resistance, Hitler's forces would have marched back.[26]

If Johnson's favorite story was of Churchill standing alone against the ascendency of fascism, Rusk's was of the Oxford Union debate of 1933. It was a story he would tell to the American people, Congress, journalists, and researchers across a twenty-five year period:

I was an undergraduate at Oxford Union on the night in 1933 of the debate on the motion, "that this house will not fight for king and country." . . . That motion passed. The motion was quoted by Hitler as an indication that Britain wouldn't fight and therefore his hands were free to pursue his ambitions.[27]

As Rusk also told the journalist Stanley Karnow, "One cannot live through those years and not have some pretty strong feelings . . . that it was the failure of the governments of the world to prevent aggression that made the catastrophe of World War II inevitable."[28]

While admitting that he was very much attuned to the lessons of the 1930s, Rusk took pains to point out that these lessons played only a partial role in the United States' decision to intervene in Vietnam. "Historical analogies can be inaccurate when applied to new situations," Rusk warned; moreover, "one must always think hard about the differences."[29] In the 1960s, however, Rusk's own diagnosis of the threat in Vietnam shied away from the differences:

There are those who object to analogies—that Mao Tse-tung is not a Hitler, that Ho Chi Minh is not a Mussolini. Of course no one supposes they are. But one robber may be named John Doe, another robber may be named Richard Doe—there may be infinite differences between the two, but what they have in common, namely robbery, is what sends them both to prison.[30]

[26] Ibid.

[27] Report on the United States Senate Hearing, *The Truth About Vietnam*, p. 371.

[28] Cited in Karnow, *Vietnam*, p. 179.

[29] Interview with author, August 21, 1986.

[30] See John Henry and William Espinosa, "The Tragedy of Dean Rusk," *Foreign Policy* 8 (Fall 1972): 187.

Countering Kennan's remarks cited at the beginning of this chapter, Rusk argued during the congressional hearings of 1966, "It was said here the other day that Hitler was a unique phenomenon. Well, there were some unique aspects. An Airedale and a Great Dane are different but they are both dogs."[31]

Recent historiography suggests that the assumptions underlying Rusk's and Lodge's interpretations of the 1930s may not be entirely accurate. In 1938, Britain was not so much "indolent" as it was unprepared militarily to confront Hitler; it needed more time to rearm. Neither is it clear whether taking a strong stance against Hitler at Munich would have caused him to back down. According to some of the findings based on new German sources, Hitler had wanted war earlier and may even have viewed the Munich agreement as a setback to his plans.[32] The facts of the 1930s, in other words, were more complicated than most American policymakers in the 1960s allowed. But for our purposes, that is an aside. Although it may be interesting to speculate why the policymakers' interpretations were skewed, it is more important to remember that their decisions were guided less by what the facts really were than by what they thought them to be.

MUNICH, STAKES, AND DOMINOES

The question of Munich is primarily one of stakes. The Munich analogy magnified the stakes of Vietnam for the United States because it envisioned a 1930s syndrome in Southeast Asia. In this sense, the Munich analogy was the intellectual basis of the domino theory.[33] American policymakers from Eisenhower to Nixon remembered the crumbling European dominoes of the 1930s only too well; they were convinced that the spread of communism—the fascism of the 1960s—would lead to a similar catastrophe.[34] Failure to stop the Asian dominoes from falling—with South Vietnam as the Czechoslovakia of the 1960s—would require the United States to fight communism later and under worse conditions; it would also probably cause World War III. With stakes as high as this, it

[31] Report on the United States Senate Hearing, *The Truth About Vietnam*, p. 357.

[32] For three recent revisionist accounts, see J. L. Richardson, "New Perspectives on Appeasement: Some Implications for International Relations," *World Politics* 40 (1988): 289–316; Gerhard Weinberg, "Munich," 165–78; Robert Beck, "Munich's Lessons Reconsidered," *International Security* 14 (1989): 161–91. The notion that Munich was a setback for Hitler is argued by Weinberg.

[33] Gelb and Betts, *Irony of Vietnam*, pp. 197–200.

[34] For Richard Nixon's use of the Munich analogy, see *RN: The Memoirs of Richard Nixon* (New York: Grosset and Dunlap, 1978), p. 462.

is hardly surprising that Johnson and Rusk saw little choice for the United States but intervention.

The other aspects of the Munich analogy reinforced this lesson. Munich suggested that South Vietnam would be the first victim of expansionist communism, just as the Sudentenland had first succumbed to fascism's advance. The moral of the Munich story was how shameful and unwise it was for Chamberlain to appease Hitler; the same moral applied to appeasing Ho Chi Minh and Mao Zedong. Munich may have emphasized how important it was to check Hitler, but it provided no prediction of what might have happened if Chamberlain had done so. The presumption was that Hitler would have backed down, or at the very least, Britain and France would have had the military, industrial, and economic support of Czechoslovakia in fighting Germany.[35] Those who felt that the United States should do in Vietnam what Chamberlain had failed to do in Munich had to assume that by demonstrating sufficient resolve, the United States could force Hanoi to back down. In short, every diagnostic function of the Munich analogy suggests that its proponent would favor intervention.

Figure 7.1 shows how inconsistent Munich would be with the nonintervention options. Although the lessons of Munich help explain why Options A′ and B′ were rejected, they have more trouble explaining why Option C′ was selected. If the stakes were so great, the challenge so direct, and the moral so unambiguous, Options D′ and E′ should have been chosen, inasmuch as they showed greater resolve and seriousness of national purpose and were more likely to work.

MUNICH AND ITS CRITICS

Like the Malayan, Korean, and Dien Bien Phu analogies, Munich had its detractors. Unlike the criticism of the earlier analogies, which came from within, criticism of the Munich analogy came mainly from without, after the decision to intervene with ground troops was made. The importance of these criticisms lay in the response they elicited from Johnson. Invoking instances of hubris by ancient great powers, Senator William Fulbright wrote to Johnson in May 1966 of the United States' "arrogance of power."[36] In his reply to Fulbright, Johnson countered with the Munich analogy:

[35] See Taylor, *Munich*, pp. 983–92; Howard Zinn, *Vietnam: The Logic of Withdrawal* (Boston: Beacon Press), p. 86.

[36] Letter (draft), Lyndon Johnson to William Fulbright, May 25, 1966, Memos to the President, Walt Rostow, vol. 3, NSF.

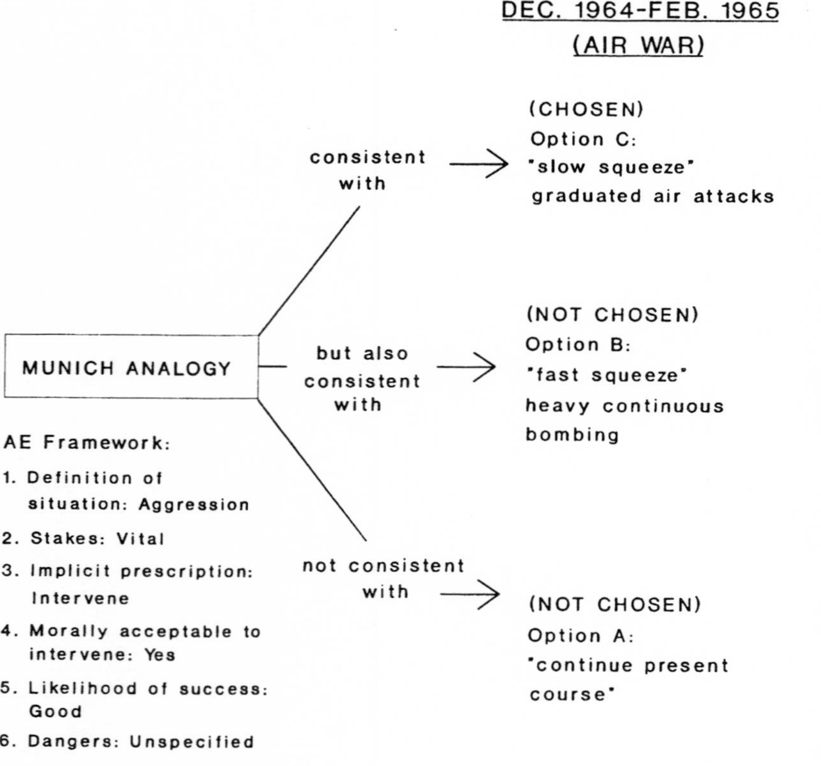

Figure 7.1. The Lessons of Munich and the Option Chosen

> My hope is that we do learn from the past—including the *recent* past. Your analogies of nations in history which were drunk with their own importance are vivid. I also believe there are some very pertinent recent analogies which are applicable, too—and the most significant, as far as I am concerned, is the analogy of what happens when ambitious and aggressive powers are freely permitted in areas where the peace of the world is delicately balanced, to use direct or indirect force against smaller and weaker states in their path.[37]

If the lessons of Munich appear overly broad and categorical, and ultimately shallow, it is because such was the level of discourse held by its proponents, none of whom probed into the reasons Chamberlain and Daladier felt unprepared to fight Hitler in September 1938. Fear of the German Luftwaffe, for example, caused the British and French air staffs to advise against war at almost any cost.[38] Nor did the Vietnam policymakers point out the special worthiness of the Czech government under the able but hapless Eduard Beneš as the reason Czechoslovakia was worth saving.

But the way Johnson, Lodge, and McCormack used the Munich analogy is entirely consistent with the way human beings analogize. Selected aspects of a historical event are made into a schema or script, and a general consensus about the script is formed. Policymakers seldom probed beyond the contours of the consensus script, nor would it probably have much of an impact on the received script had they done so. To probe deeper would have risked revealing significant differences between the situations: the United States had no Vietnamese Luftwaffe to fear, and the rapid succession of corrupt and incompetent South Vietnamese regimes made it difficult to know who it was that the United States had to save. In the words of one historian, "One touches the Munich analogy and it falls apart."[39]

A series of letters between Senate Majority Leader Mike Mansfield and the president approaches a more probing analysis. In a letter to Mansfield, the president invoked the lessons of the thirties and the fifties to argue the "most fundamental . . . question" as to "why we are in Viet-Nam at all": "We are in Viet-Nam for most of the same reasons we were in the Pacific and in Europe during World War II. We have the same reason we had in Korea in 1950. . . . to prevent the success of aggression." For, twenty-five years ago, "the leaders in Germany and Japan had a very different view of the world. The men in Moscow who triggered

[37] Letter (final draft), Lyndon Johnson to William Fulbright, May 27, 1966, Memos to the President, Walt Rostow, vol. 3, NSF.

[38] Taylor, *Munich*, p. xiii.

[39] Zinn, *Vietnam*, p. 88.

the Korean War had a different view 16 years ago. And the men in Hanoi and Peking have a view very different from ours today."[40]

Mansfield took strong exception to the analogies. He replied, "Where is the Hitler or the Mussolini or the Tojo of this conflict? Is it Breshnev [*sic*] or Kosygin? Or Mao Tse-tung? Or Ho Chi Minh?" For Mansfield, Ho was "hardly a Hitler, Mussolini and Tojo rolled into one to his own countrymen—north and south and, in truth, to most of the rest of the world."[41] Johnson's reply to Mansfield was prompt but meek. He posed himself Mansfield's question: "Is it fair to compare Ho Chi Minh to Hitler?" And he answered by attaching a statement by the Prime Minister of Singapore, Lee Kuan Yew![42]

The final documentary evidence of skepticism about Munich is in the meeting notes of a November 1967 meeting between Johnson and the wise men. Dean Acheson, Omar Bradley, and Abe Fortas were all arguing for staying the course and against negotiating with Hanoi. Sensing the resistance to negotiations, former Under Secretary of State George Ball attempted to assuage his colleagues' fears by arguing that "very few Americans really see a political solution as another Munich."[43]

Congressmen and outside commentators were critical of the Munich analogy and raised the best questions about it. Senator Wayne Morse, for example, gave George Kennan a splendid opportunity to point out the flaws in the Munich-Vietnam parallel during the 1966 congressional hearings. The gist of the exchange, cited at the beginning of this chapter, was broadcast live on television. Kennan struck at the heart of the analogy. There was no comparison, he claimed, between Ho and Hitler or Mao. It was in fact "fatal" to conclude from the unique events of the 1930s that one must never accommodate others.[44]

Focusing on the specifics of Vietnam, the historian Howard Zinn pointed to several other important differences. Echoing the consensus today but writing when it was still not the common view, Zinn saw the Vietnam conflict as a civil war. Thus, in 1938, "the main force operating against the Czech status quo was an outside force, Hitler's Germany. . . . the major force operating against the status quo in South Vietnam had been been an inside force. . . . the NLF." In addition, the Czech gov-

[40] Draft memo, Lyndon Johnson to Mike Mansfield, June 16, 1966, Memos to the President, Walt Rostow, vol. 6, NSF.

[41] Letter, Mike Mansfield to Lyndon Johnson, June 25, 1966, Memos to the President, Walt Rostow, vol. 7, NSF.

[42] Letter, Lyndon Johnson to Mike Mansfield, undated, Memos to the President, Walt Rostow, vol. 7, NSF.

[43] Notes, President's Meeting with Foreign Policy Advisers, November 2, 1967, Papers of Lyndon Baines Johnson, Meeting Notes File.

[44] Report on the United States Senate Hearing, *The Truth About Vietnam*, pp. 234–35.

ernment was democratic, "strong, effective, prosperous," whereas the "South Vietnamese government. . . . is a hollow shell of a government, unstable, unpopular. . . . corrupt."[45]

Another historian, A. J. Mayer, agreed that the South Vietnamese insurgency, unlike the Sudenten insurgency, was indigenous. Mayer also found South Vietnam to be of marginal strategic importance compared to Czechoslovakia. Furthermore, China, unlike Hitler Germany, did not seem bent on military expansionism. Most important, for Mayer, the United States, "unlike the Anglo-French allies in 1938, has overwhelming military capabilities in readiness if Peking should, after all, embark on a course of outright military aggression."[46]

Taking off from the last point, Mayer sought to identify and attack "the pivotal assumption" underlying the Munich analogy. Its proponents imply that if Chamberlain and Daladier had stood their ground on Czechoslovakia, Hitler would have backed down and World War II would have been averted. Such counterfactuals, according to Mayer, are impossible to prove. They also beg the question whether it would have been necessary to confront Hitler with a two-front war, "arising from a timely . . . military alliance between the two Western allies and Soviet Russia," in order to persuade him to desist.[47] Mayer's point was that given the West's hostility toward the Soviet Union since 1917, such an alliance was unlikely in 1938. Thus not only was the Munich script unlikely to be played out in Vietnam, the script of what would have happened if Chamberlain had confronted Hitler was a figment of the policymakers' imagination.

The lesson of Munich—the ultimate lesson of the thirties—strongly reinforces the lessons of Korea. As a "worldwide analogy," it dictated the imperative of not giving in to aggression anywhere.[48] It could also emphasize North Vietnamese aggression and deemphasize the civil war aspects of the conflict in Vietnam. But it was too crude to be of much use in choosing among alternative options except in ruling out options favoring "appeasement" or accommodating Ho. Still, to rule out options is to have a significant impact on the policy process. By emphasizing the stakes, Munich lent concrete meaning to the importance of containing communism; the lessons of Korea reinforced that analysis and, perhaps more importantly, suggested that there were options that were likely to contain communism successfully without drawing China or the Soviet

[45] Zinn, *Vietnam*, p. 87.

[46] Arno J. Mayer, "Greece, Not Munich," *The Nation* (March 25, 1968): 408.

[47] Ibid.

[48] The term "worldwide analogy" was used by William Bundy to describe the Munich analogy in contrast to regional analogies like Korea (William Bundy, interview with author, April 11, 1986).

Union into war. The imperative of Munich was clearly intervention. Churchill was to have said to Chamberlain after the Munich conference, "You were given the choice between war and dishonour. You chose dishonour and you will have war."[49] Remembering Churchill's admonishment too well in Vietnam also brought America both, in reverse order.

ALTERNATIVE EXPLANATIONS OF THE VIETNAM DECISIONS OF 1965

The analysis so far has focused on the analogies that informed policymakers' assessments of the challenge in Vietnam as well as their evaluations of the options available to meet the challenge so defined. Once the situation in Vietnam was defined in terms of the challenge of the 1930s, it became difficult to walk away from it. Memories of Munich precluded the withdrawal or negotiation options, options favored by George Ball because his familiarity with the French experience in Vietnam convinced him that the United States would suffer a fate similar to France's. Although Munich can account for the rejection of the nonintervention options, it is unable to suggest why, among the prointervention options, the least harsh one was selected. If the stakes were equal to those of Munich, did it not stand to reason that the response be equal to the challenge?

The Korean analogy seems to take one the farthest in understanding why the Johnson administration acted as it did. The lessons of Korea, like the lessons of Munich, can explain why the withdrawal and negotiation options were unacceptable in 1965. In fact, the Korean and Munich analogies reinforced one another in the most interesting of ways. Both defined the problem as one of international aggression and both defined the stakes as extremely high. Munich underscored, perhaps even more heavily than Korea, the nature of the challenge in Vietnam, the seriousness of the stakes, and the moral necessity of a response.

But Munich was silent about the form of action the United States should take. Neither could it predict the effectiveness or dangers of any action. Munich was less helpful on these points because its implied solutions were counterfactuals. The lessons of Korea, on the other hand, proposed factual answers: military intervention did work, and dangers could be minimized if one limited one's ambitions. Of course, the other reason the Korean analogy had a stronger influence than the Munich analogy was that it had more superficial similarities with Vietnam: both conflicts were in the same part of the world, both had a North-South

[49] Cited in Taylor, *Munich*, p. 978.

divide, and the perceived adversaries, China and the Soviet Union, were the same.[50] All lessons considered, Korea seems able to explain best why the nonintervention options were rejected and why among the prointervention options, Option C for the air war and Option C′ for the ground war were selected.

In providing an analogical explanation of the Vietnam decisions, I do not mean to suggest that other nonanalogical factors were unimportant. Factors such as containment and domestic politics, for example, certainly played a role. I have not focused on them in part because they have been so well covered by, and given such pride of place in, existing accounts of the Vietnam War.[51] In these accounts, the historical analogies used by policymakers are often mentioned, but their precise role in the decision-making process and their relationship to factors such as containment or domestic political calculations are seldom specified. I have reversed the emphasis in this work in order to explore how far the analogical explanation takes us in accounting for the choices of 1965.

At this point in my argument, it is probably useful to consider some of the nonanalogical explanations I have mentioned above. Examining these explanations should highlight the contribution of factors other than analogies to the making of the Vietnam decisions. Contrasting these nonanalogical explanations with the analogical one should showcase the strengths and weaknesses of both types of explanations. In particular, I seek to examine the extent to which the nonanalogical explanations are able to account for the decisions in the way I have, by explaining why the nonintervention options were rejected and explaining why, among the prointervention options, Options C and C′ were selected.

The four nonanalogical arguments to be considered are: (1) containment, (2) political-military ideology, (3) bureaucratic politics, and (4) domestic politics. What each of these explanations lead us to expect will be compared to the explanation given by the Korean analogy.[52] For the sake of brevity, only the ground war decision will be discussed, for arguments applicable to the ground war are also applicable to the air war.

[50] It is interesting to note that "no more Koreas" and "no more Munichs"—and their disparate policy recommendations—were also relevant in 1954, as Eisenhower contemplated intervening in Vietnam. Although both Congress and Eisenhower wanted "no more Koreas," Eisenhower did not refrain from using "no more Munichs" on Churchill to persuade him to join the United States. Churchill was not persuaded that a Vietminh victory at Dien Bien Phu would be "another Munich": in this sense the Korean analogy also triumphed over the Munich analogy in 1954. See chap. 4.

[51] Gelb and Betts, *Irony of Vietnam*; Berman, *Planning a Tragedy*; and Daniel Ellsberg, *Papers on the War* (New York: Simon and Schuster, 1972).

[52] Some of the nonanalogical explanations also address the 1954 decision directly or indirectly. When they do so, their explanations can also be compared to that provided by the lessons of Korea.

CONTAINMENT

The analyst impressed by the basic continuity of America's containment policy might wonder what explanatory mileage has been gained through the analysis provided in part 2. Although a sensitive analyst will differentiate between the initial political-economic phase of containment (1947–1950) and the post-1950 militarization of containment, the question remains: Wouldn't knowing that the United States was willing to use force to contain communism in the period after 1950 be sufficient to explain the decision to intervene in Vietnam?[53] Thus, Gelb and Betts explain the decision in terms of the pursuit of "the core consensual goal of postwar [American] foreign policy," the containment of communism.[54] That is, it was considered vital to America's security that South Vietnam remain noncommunist.[55] The flip side of the containment thesis is the notion that allowing South Vietnam to go communist would seriously undermine the credibility of America's commitments elsewhere. Agreeing with the containment and credibility thesis, Herring has argued that

> the United States involvement in Vietnam was not primarily a result of errors of judgement or of the personality quirks of the policymakers, although these things existed in abundance. It was a logical, if not inevitable, outgrowth of a world view and policy, the policy of containment, which Americans in and out of government accepted without serious question for more than two decades.[56]

The first point to note about the containment thesis is that it shares some of the key premises of the Munich and Korean analogies. All three see the problem in Vietnam as one of communist aggression and expansionism, and all agree on the importance of halting such aggression. The containment thesis will have little trouble dismissing Options A′ and B′: the United States could not choose to withdraw or keep forces at the present level if doing so were likely to lead to the communization of South Vietnam. To this extent, containment is helpful in understanding the 1965 decisions. Beyond this, however, it is less so. It is unable to discriminate among the prointervention options. If the "core consensual goal" of combating communism was decisive, it stands to reason that the

[53] John Lewis Gaddis has argued that the "real commitment to contain communism everywhere originated in the events surrounding the Korean war, not the crisis in Greece and Turkey" ("Was the Truman Doctrine a Real Turning Point?" *Foreign Affairs* 52 [1974]: 386). For the militarization of containment, see James Nathan and James Oliver, *United States Foreign Policy and World Order* (Boston: Little, Brown and Company, 1976), chap. 5.

[54] Gelb and Betts, *Irony of Vietnam*, p. 2.

[55] Ibid., esp. pp. 181–200.

[56] Herring, *America's Longest War*, p. x.

harsher options (D′ and E′) would be preferable over Option C′, since they were potentially more effective. McNamara and the military argued for the harsher options precisely because they were supposed to demonstrate the credibility of the U.S. threat.[57] Yet Johnson chose C′, the least harsh of the prointervention options. It will not do to argue that Johnson chose C′ on the assumption that he could escalate to D′ and E′ if it did not work—the empirical record simply does not support this. Till the end of his presidency, Johnson was reluctant to call up the 262,000 reserves requested by the military; neither did he unleash the full power of the SAC on Hanoi. Moreover, a politician as astute as Johnson would know that choosing Option C′ in July 1965 might lead to domestic and international repercussions that could make it much more difficult for him later to exercise D′ or E′.

Gelb and Betts suggest, however, that although containment may have led to military intervention, domestic political constraints made U.S. policymakers "do the minimally necessary at each stage to keep [pre-1954] *Vietnam and later South Vietnam* out of Communist hands."[58] This argument, however, does not seem applicable to the 1965 decision; it also raises more questions than it answers for the 1954 decision. Gelb and Betts seem aware of the former problem but not the latter. Thus, on Johnson's July 1965 decisions, they write: "Nor were there many domestic constraints by 1965. The real implications of public opinion at that time are unclear and perhaps always will be. But as escalation began in the fall of 1965, 64 percent in a Gallup survey still viewed greater involvement as having been necessary rather than as a mistake."[59] This is a rather permissive majority; it should have given the president room to do more rather than less. In fact, Gelb and Betts also point out that in 1966, 61 percent of those polled supported escalation if Hanoi did not respond to the American bombing pause.[60] Given that public opinion was entirely supportive and that McNamara and the JCS were arguing for Option E′, it is surprising that Johnson chose Option C′, knowing full well that it was less likely to "win."[61]

If containment was the "core consensual goal of postwar foreign policy," how does one explain Eisenhower's decision against intervention in 1954? Gelb and Betts intend their analysis to cover 1954; they imply that Eisenhower did "the minimally necessary . . . to keep Vietnam . . . out of Communist hands." But Eisenhower did *not* do the minimally necessary in 1954, and he did *not* keep Vietnam out of communist hands. The

57 See discussion in chap. 5.

58 Gelb and Betts, *Irony of Vietnam*, p. 25, emphasis mine.

59 Ibid., p. 129.

60 Ibid., pp. 129–30.

61 Ibid., pp. 273–78; see also pp. 144–45 above.

French were defeated, and North Vietnam became communist. Doing the minimally necessary in 1954 would have entailed using U.S. air and naval power to relieve the siege at Dien Bien Phu, an option Eisenhower considered but rejected. The significance of Eisenhower's decision, as I try to show in chapter 4, is that it is in tension with the logic of containment, which stresses the imperative of preventing the extension of communist power. Eisenhower's behavior in 1954 raises a puzzle that we have discussed: if international systemic constraints or containment was so decisive in 1965, why was it not decisive in 1954?

The Korean analogy does not seem to face such empirical difficulties. It is able to explain the rejection of the nonintervention options as well as the selection of Option C′ in 1965. Consider the rejection of Options A′ and B′, the nonintervention options. In 1965, William Bundy put it thus: American policy toward South Vietnam "derives from . . . the fact of the Communist nations of Asia and their [expansionist] policies and . . . the lessons of the thirties and of Korea"; more specifically, "our action in Korea" suggested that "aggression of any sort must be met early and head-on or it will have to be met later and under tougher circumstances."[62] Applied to the conflict in Vietnam, the message of Korea is clear: it is necessary to prevent South Vietnam from falling under communism. In this sense, there is substantial overlap between the containment and explanations based on the lessons of Korea. This overlap should not be surprising because, after all, Korea was an instance of containment and a successful one at that.

To say that Korea was an instance of containment raises an interesting issue: Why not adopt the containment explanation, then, since it appears to be more parsimonious? One need only know that in the postwar period, the United States acted to prevent the spread of communism: hence Vietnam. Using the analogical explanation, on the other hand, requires one to identify the relevant analogy and then to specify its content in order to explain the Vietnam decisions. But as we have seen above, because the containment explanation is parsimonious, it is also underspecified: it can explain the rejection of A′ and B′ but not the selection of C′; nor can it explain the opposite pattern of nonintervention in 1954. In contrast, the Korean analogy can fully explain the choices. Knowing that Johnson wanted to avoid MacArthur's mistake at all costs helps explain why he chose Option C′ over Options D′ and E′ in 1965. It is instructive to note that although Johnson increased the number of U.S. troops in South Vietnam to over five hundred thousand by 1967, he did not escalate to Options D′ or E′, the import of containment notwithstanding.

The Korean analogy also does not encounter the puzzle faced by the

[62] *Department of State Bulletin*, February 8, 1965, pp. 168–71.

containment explanation regarding Eisenhower's 1954 decision. If Korea had not been invoked in 1954, then the analogical explanation would of course be irrelevant. But Korea was invoked in 1954 by both Congress and Eisenhower himself. The very special interpretation they gave to "no more Koreas" made Eisenhower reluctant to intervene, his preoccupation with containment notwithstanding.

This comparison seems to indicate that the Korean analogy can do all the containment thesis does and more. That is, the Korean analogy can explain not only why it was important for the United States to intervene in Vietnam, but also why the intervention took the form that it did. Moreover, the Korean analogy is able to do so without running into the empirical difficulties encountered by the containment thesis. What the Korean analogy loses in parsimony and sweep, it gains in accuracy.

POLITICAL-MILITARY IDEOLOGY

The second nonanalogical explanation to be considered is the argument that the political hawkishness or dovishness of the decision-makers explains their choices. The strong version of this argument goes on to suggest that hawkishness or dovishness may also explain the policymakers' choice of analogies; hawks would choose hawkish analogies and doves dovish ones. Thus, analogies and options may cohere not because the former causes the latter, but because they both are determined by the governing hawk-dove tendency. If this argument is correct, it is possible that the causal relationship between analogies and options suggested in the preceding chapters may be spurious.[63]

The possibility of spuriousness cannot be completely ruled out, but it is possible to raise enough questions about this argument to render it less plausible than the argument presented in this book. To begin with, the hawk-dove argument only gets half of the answer right. Hawks would be prointervention, doves anti-intervention; if hawks constituted a "winning coalition" among the decision-makers, the nonintervention options would be rejected. This was the case in 1965. If the hawks won, one would also expect them to push for the harsher and more effective military options. This was not the case, for the least harsh of the prointervention options was chosen. Hawkishness does not seem to be able to explain the final option chosen.

Equally troubling is the question of what makes one a hawk or a dove

[63] I am grateful to Jonathan Mercer and the members of the National Security Study Group at the Center for International Affairs, Harvard University, for raising and elaborating this point in a seminar discussion in the fall of 1990. Jervis also discusses the issue in *Perception and Misperception*, pp. 246–49.

and how we know which someone was independent of his choices. Was Johnson a dove in 1954 when, as Senate Minority Leader, he counseled the Eisenhower administration against unilateral intervention in Vietnam? Had he become a hawk by 1965? Similarly, was Rusk a dove when he objected to sending U.S. combat troops to South Vietnam in 1961, only to become a hawk in 1965? Was McNamara a dove during the Cuban Missile Crisis, when he argued that "a missile is a missile," and then a hawk on Vietnam?

Political hawkishness, it would seem, matters less than the situation-specific diagnoses made by policymakers. For Johnson and his Republican colleagues invited to the 1954 meeting with Dulles and Radford, "no more Koreas" loomed larger than whatever hawkish tendencies they might have harbored. In 1965, "no more Koreas" remained very much in Johnson's mind, but "no more Munichs" became just as important as the situation in South Vietnam degenerated. These examples suggest that although certain individuals like Barry Goldwater may easily fit the rubric of a hawk, others like Johnson and most of his advisers can be categorized as "hawks" or "doves" only with great difficulty. In fact, one of the clearest themes to emerge from the documentary record of the 1960s is the reluctance, even agony, that characterized Johnson's decision for war.

The problem of identifying hawks can also be seen in the strong form of the political-military ideology argument. Assuming for the moment that the label can be applied to Johnson and his advisers, it helps explain why they favored the Munich analogy. Conversely, "dovishness" helps explain Ball's preference for the Dien Bien Phu analogy. Where does the Korean analogy, the most important analogy in Vietnam decision-making according to our analysis, fit? How could hawks pick an analogy that would severely constrain their military strategy, as the Korean analogy did? Would that not be inconsistent with one of the major traits of hawkishness, the propensity to opt for military means to achieve one's objectives? Perhaps the joint chiefs were the only true hawks, for they consistently dismissed the relevance of the core lesson of Korea; they were the ones pushing for the harsher options, on the grounds that these options were more likely to convince Hanoi to stop sending men South, and they were more willing to risk Chinese intervention in order to increase the chances of achieving U.S. objectives in South Vietnam. The civilians who rejected this reasoning, in full realization that the force they were willing to approve fell short of what the joint chiefs wanted, can only be called hawks with the greatest of difficulty.[64]

[64] David Halberstam writes that a "key moment" in Vietnam policymaking was during a NSC meeting on July 27, 1965, when Johnson obtained JCS Chairman General Earle Wheeler's assent to Option C′ even though "everyone in the room knew Wheeler objected, that the Chiefs wanted more, that they wanted a wartime footing and a call-up of reserves;

Hawkishness or dovishness, instead of explaining the policymakers' choice of analogies, may actually be better explained by those very analogies. At the very least, the causation goes both ways. The hawk-dove argument, like the skeptics' argument, begs the question of what makes one a hawk or a dove to begin with. The analogical argument and the psychological literature suggest that one's generational and career experiences might exercise a strong influence on one's perspectives. Thus, the events of the 1930s and 1950s had a profound impact on the decisionmakers of the 1960s. Johnson and Rusk have repeatedly pointed to the importance of these events in shaping their world political perspectives. The 1930s showed the importance of standing firm against aggressors, and the 1950s reinforced the idea, although they also warned against provoking other major powers into war.

William Bundy said in 1986,

> There's one thing that I don't think any historian has put in writing. . . . it is certainly a peculiar statistical coincidence that of the decision-making group, Johnson, Rusk, McNamara, my brother, Walt Rostow, myself, all of those of us who were of age in 1940–41 were interventionists in the isolationist-interventionist debate. . . . it doesn't show that they all believed in Munich, but they believed that you have to stand up to aggression of some sort.[65]

The statistical coincidence does not demonstrate that the prointerventionists all believed in Munich—we have presented independent evidence of that belief in this chapter—but it does raise the question of the relationship between Munich and the general lesson about the need to "stand up to aggression of some sort." The argument here, based on the policymakers' own recollections and on the argument that schemas are formed by firsthand or vicarious experiences, is simply that the events of the 1930s and the 1950s shaped the policymakers' outlook more than their outlook shaped their interpretations.

BUREAUCRATIC POLITICS

If containment is too underspecified to be helpful in accounting for the final choices of American policymakers, it does not follow that we need to turn immediately to cognitive explanations. Perhaps the logic or requirements of the domestic political system may provide an explanation.

---

the thing they feared most was a partial war and a partial commitment" (*The Best and the Brightest*, pp. 599–600).

[65] Interview with author, April 11, 1986.

I begin by examining the familiar bureaucratic politics approach, which rejects the unitary actor assumption implicit in most studies.[66] The bureaucratic politics approach offers the alternative assumption of many actors representing different governmental organizations, and all of whom have a role in the decision-making process. The proliferation of actors also means a proliferation of various conceptions of the national interest and perhaps even more important, the emergence of organizational, domestic, and personal interests in the decision-making equation. Actors are assumed to look after the interests of their organization by preserving its autonomy and mission—hence the dictum, "Where you stand depends on where you sit." The result of many actors with conflicting stances is that decision-making will be characterized by bargaining among the various actors, decisions will often involve considerable compromise, and as compromises, decision outcomes typically will not reflect any one actor's most preferred option.[67]

The bureaucratic politics approach is helpful in illuminating the nature of the options and their possible sponsors. Thus it would stand to reason that the military would support the prointervention options and among those options, would prefer Options D′ and E′. These preferences would be in line with their organizational missions and their standard operating procedures. One would expect, on the other hand, the nonintervention options, including withdrawal, to be tabled and urged by the State Department. This is, to an extent, true. How far does this take us in explaining the decisions of 1965? Can the bureaucratic politics approach suggest which one of these options might be chosen? On both scores, the answers are not encouraging.

The dictum, "Where you stand depends on where you sit," is one of the approach's more powerful insights; yet this attempt to link organizational roles with policy preferences gives very mixed results when applied to the Vietnam decision-makers. Thus the idea that State Department officials have a proclivity toward diplomatic solutions can help explain Deputy Under Secretary George Ball's anti-intervention, pronegotiation stance; the same idea, however, is at a loss to explain why Secretary of State Dean Rusk was so staunchly prointervention in Vietnam. Similarly, Secretary of Defense Robert McNamara's prointerven-

[66] The following account of bureaucratic politics draws from Graham Allison, *Essence of Decision*; Graham Allison and Morton Halperin, "Bureaucratic Politics: A Paradigm and Some Policy Implications," in *Theory and Policy in International Relations*, ed. Raymond Tanter and Richard Ullman (Princeton: Princeton University Press, 1972); Morton Halperin, *Bureaucratic Politics and Foreign Policy* (Washington, D.C.: Brookings, 1974); and Jerel Rosati, "Developing a Systematic Decision-Making Framework: Bureaucratic Politics in Perspective," *World Politics* 33 (1981): 234–52.

[67] See Allison and Halperin, "Bureaucratic Politics," p. 53.

tion stance can be explained from this perspective, but his Deputy John McNaughton's increasing doubts about the intervention cannot.

More important, the bargaining, compromise, and choice of lowest-common-denominator behavior that the bureaucratic politics model would lead us to expect do not describe the Vietnam deliberations well. With one exception, there was general agreement among the president's advisers on the necessity of intervening. The lone dissident, George Ball, hardly engaged in bargaining with the president and his other advisers. The only actor with whom Ball thought he had a chance was the president himself.[68]

It is difficult to characterize Johnson's decision in favor of military intervention as a compromise solution, as expected by the bureaucratic politics model. Proponents of the bureaucratic politics approach may disagree, but a deeper issue is at stake here, for what constitutes a compromise is extremely vague in the bureaucratic politics literature. In a sense, every foreign policy decision outcome can be construed as a compromise among extreme options. Consider the case of a president presented with three options: A (no war), B (war involving one hundred thousand troops), and C (war involving 100,000 troops and also reserves). In what sense is B the compromise choice? Only in the sense that of the three options, it is the middle one. For proponents of A, the choice of B is anything but a compromise: it is the opposite of their preferred state of affairs, and it is small consolation that the reserves will stay at home. B and A are so much further apart than B and C that to call B a compromise choice violates the meaning we have come to associate with "compromise." The point here is that without *prior* and proper specification of what constitutes a "compromise outcome," the latter concept has a post hoc quality that robs off much of its explanatory utility.

In terms of the 1965 decisions then, I would argue that rejection of the nonintervention options (A′ and B′) did not constitute a compromise: it was a decision to launch a ground war. Among Options C′, D′ and E′, the bureaucratic politics approach has difficulty identifying which would constitute a compromise. Note that the same is not true of the Korean analogy, which does not treat the rejection of Options A′ and B′ as a compromise, but as a war decision. The final selection of Option C′ may be construed as a compromise, albeit one stemming from the need to avoid another conflict with China rather than one stemming from bureaucratic pulling and hauling.

If the notion of compromise is unhelpful in analyzing decision outcomes, the analytic force of the bureaucratic politics approach must shift to the idea that resultant decision outcomes are "distinct from what any

[68] Ball interview.

person or group intended."[69] That is, a compromise solution is one that nobody or few people wanted and fought for but is the only one that everyone could agree on. Such is not the case of the Vietnam decisions of 1965: the decisions to bomb North Vietnam in graduated steps and to commit one hundred thousand troops to South Vietnam were clearly the president's first choices, given his perception of the international constraints.

DOMESTIC POLITICS AND THE GREAT SOCIETY

The final nonanalogical explanation to be explored is also a domestic political explanation. Although this explanation has been presented not as a general approach or model, but as an empirical explanation specific to Vietnam, it is important enough as a plausible rival explanation that it needs to be addressed. This explanation differs from the one presented in this book in the emphasis it places on Johnson's domestic political calculations. The best formulation of this argument is to be found in Larry Berman's *Planning a Tragedy*.[70] Berman argues that Johnson intervened in Vietnam to protect his domestic political agenda. Johnson, according to Berman, "believed that losing Vietnam in the summer of 1965 would wreck his plans for a truly Great Society":[71]

> For while the fundamental fact of international politics in July 1965 was South Vietnam's impending fall to communist control, the overriding concern of domestic politics in July 1965 was Lyndon Johnson's intent that the Great Society reach legislative fulfillment.[72]

The assumption is that if Vietnam had been lost, a divisive debate, similar to the one following the loss of China, would follow, and make it impossible for Johnson to fulfill his plans for the Great Society. This domestic political imperative also explains why Johnson decided against calling up the reserves, according to Berman. By not calling up the reserves, a much more expensive option than just approving Westmoreland's troop request, Johnson gave Congress and the American people the impression that the war would not consume inordinate human and financial re-

[69] Allison, *Essence of Decision*, p. 145.

[70] An early form of the domestic argument can be found in Kearns, *Lyndon Johnson*, chaps. 9–11.

[71] Berman, *Planning a Tragedy*, p. 147.

[72] Larry Berman, "Waiting for Smoking Guns: Presidential Decision-making and the Vietnam War, 1965–67," in *Vietnam as History: Ten Years after the Paris Peace Accords*, ed. Peter Braestrup (Washington, D.C.: University Press of America, 1984), p. 16. See also Berman, *Planning a Tragedy*, pp. 145–53.

sources; he thus bought time and saved money to promote the Great Society.[73] In Berman's words: "He *chose* to avoid a national debate on the war, to keep the Reserves home, and to buy time for a domestic record meriting nothing less than Mount Rushmore."[74]

Domestic political considerations undoubtedly played a role in Johnson's decision to stand in Vietnam and in his decision not to call up the reserves. Few have presented the case as fairly and as rigorously as Berman. Yet I will argue that although Johnson's domestic visions are important in understanding his Vietnam decisions, his foreign policy visions, or illusions, are even more important. My argument is based on the documentary record: although the international and domestic impetus arguments are equally plausible and important, the record more strongly supports the international considerations argument.

If there is one constant in the documents on Vietnam, it is that the international repercussions of a communist South Vietnam were perceived as too potentially damaging for the United States to bear. Lyndon Johnson and his advisers believed that if America did not stand in Vietnam, the rest of Southeast Asia was likely to go communist, and World War III would be a distinct possibility. Their definition of the problem was informed by their experience and reading of the 1930s and 1950s. In contrast, documentary support for the domestic impetus argument is sparse. This lack creates a certain tension in Berman's argument. The conclusion of Berman's book, where he advances the domestic impetus argument, seems at odds with the findings preceding it, for the preceding chapters of his book consist of a fully documented account of the international strategic calculations leading up to the July decisions. Berman writes at the beginning of his conclusion that "the documents show that the principals accepted containment of communism and the domino theory as basic premises for formulating policy and not as hypotheses for analysis." He then cites a study that traces this "cognitive error" to the lessons of history:

> All the presidents had lived through Manchuria, Munich, Poland, Yalta, the "loss" of China, the Korean War, and the McCarthy era. Each drew the lesson that the United States could not afford to be soft on communism, specifically that he [Johnson] could not be the president who permitted the "loss" of Vietnam to communism.[75]

Berman later claims that this explanation is incomplete, and he attempts to fill in "the missing piece of the puzzle," by arguing that "John-

[73] Berman, *Planning a Tragedy*, pp. 146–47.

[74] Ibid., p. 149.

[75] Ibid., p. 131.

son believed that to accept Ball's advice would be political suicide. . . . The domestic repercussion if the United States abandoned its commitment would be too great for a four-year president ever to recoup."[76] Much depends on what Berman means by filling in the missing piece of the puzzle. Does it mean achieving a fuller and more complete picture of the 1965 decisions, or does it mean that without the domestic argument, the 1965 decisions cannot be understood? The former claim is easier to sustain; the domestic argument does add a valuable dimension not captured by the analogical explanation, and in so doing, it helps provide a fuller account of the decisions of 1965. The latter claim, that the Vietnam decisions cannot be understood apart from the domestic argument, is more difficult to sustain. The documentary evidence for the domestic argument cannot bear the weight of so strong a claim. The best illustration of this problem is to be found in Berman's explanation of why Johnson chose Option C′ instead of E′.

Berman's argument relies heavily on one document in which Johnson instructed McGeorge Bundy to strike off one of five reasons the administration was trying to avoid a billion-dollar appropriation in Vietnam.[77] The draft memo, dated July 19, 1965, included the following as reason number three: "It would create the false impression that we have to have guns, not butter—and would help the enemies of the President's domestic legislative program."[78] In the final memo, Johnson eliminated this reason and kept the others. Berman interprets the deletion to mean that Johnson wanted to keep his rationale for rejecting Option E′ a secret: "He sought a pragmatic guns-and-butter solution for avoiding what he believed would have surely been a divisive national debate in order temporarily to protect his Great Society."[79]

Berman's explanation for the rejection of Option E′ is interesting and plausible. It is, however, less convincing than the analogical explanation, for the following reasons. First, even if Berman's domestic explanation is able to eliminate Option E′, it still leaves one with Options D′ and C′. Berman does not use the domestic calculus to explain the rejection of Option D′. The lessons of Korea, on the other hand, can explain the rejection of both Options D′ and E′. Second, the domestic politics explanation portrays Johnson as a president intensely conscious of the domestic sources of his power. It assumes a president astute enough to realize that going beyond Option C′ might jeopardize his Great Society, but it also seems implicitly to assume a president not astute enough to realize

[76] Ibid., p. 146.

[77] In fairness to Berman, he also relies on a letter to him from McGeorge Bundy (*Planning a Tragedy*, pp. 143–45).

[78] Ibid., pp. 147–50.

[79] Ibid., p. 150.

that the failure of Option C′ would be worse: it would destroy his presidency and drive him from office. Which was what happened. As noted earlier, domestic public opinion was permissive rather than restrictive in 1965; Johnson had more leeway to choose more aggressive options in 1965 than in 1968. Yet he did not do so.

Third, if worries about the Great Society legislation prevented Johnson from choosing the harsher options in the summer of 1965, it would stand to reason that after those laws were passed, he would be freer to opt for more decisive military action.[80] Yet in the next two years, Johnson never escalated the war to the extent called for by Options D′ and E′. Worries about provoking China and the Soviet Union remained constant throughout the period, and they provide a more consistent explanation why Options D′ and E′ were never exercised.

Fourth, a different interpretation for the elimination of rationale number three in Bundy's memo is possible: striking it out could mean that, to Johnson, it was irrelevant to his decision-making. There is evidence to support this alternative interpretation. A recently declassified "literally eyes only" cable from Deputy Secretary of Defense Cyrus Vance to Robert McNamara (who was in Saigon) on July 17, 1965, provides an unusual glimpse into the president's mindset. Vance informed McNamara that the president's "current intention" was to "proceed with the 34 battalion plan," that is, to approve Westmoreland's request for one hundred thousand troops. The president, however, was reluctant to ask Congress for more than $300–400 million in 1965, fearing that it might "kill [his] domestic legislative program." Vance believed, however, that through "deficit funding," the administration should be able to get the $750 million necessary to pay for the impending war until the end of the year. The most revealing paragraph of the cable runs as follows:

> I asked highest authority [President Johnson] whether request for legislation authorizing call-up of Reserves and extension of tours of duty would be acceptable in light of his comments concerning domestic program, and he stated that it would.[81]

[80] I do not mean to suggest that these were the ethically superior options; quite the contrary. The question arises because, for the student of decision-making, it is puzzling why Johnson refrained from choosing the harsher (and more efficacious, according to his advisers) options when domestic constraints were minimal—in 1966 and much of 1967, for example—and when what domestic impetus there was favored escalation. See William Lunch and Peter Sperlich, "American Public Opinion and the War in Vietnam," *The Western Political Quarterly* 32 (1979): 22.

[81] This cable was declassified in 1988 at William Gibbons's request, and it is cited in full in his *U.S. Government*, pt. 3, p. 381. In a note on the same page, Gibbons also answers the question of whether Johnson's "current intention" to proceed with the 34-battalion plan meant that the president had already made his decision for war on July 17. Gibbons cites a

In other words, while Johnson was indeed concerned about the negative impact that Option E′ would have on his domestic programs, he was not prepared to reject the option on domestic grounds. On July 17, therefore, the president still found it "acceptable" to proceed with the request for authorization to call up the reserves. On paper, at least, the Great Society was no bar to calling up the reserves.

If protecting the Great Society did not prevent Johnson from pursuing Option E′, what did? The answer provided in this study is that the need to avoid provoking China, and its presumed ally the Soviet Union, into entering the Vietnam War was uppermost in the minds of Johnson and his advisers. This answer finds support in a constant stream of 1964 and 1965 documents, as well as in the minutes of the meetings held in the crucial period of July 21 to July 27, 1965. The need to avoid repeating MacArthur's mistake in Korea is a sentiment that can be repeatedly found in the pages of these documents.

Of the nonanalogical explanations considered above, containment and Larry Berman's argument about Johnson's domestic political concerns are especially insightful. The containment argument emphasizes the strategic context in which the decision-makers found themselves, and it does seem able to explain why the nonintervention options were unacceptable. Berman goes beyond the containment argument when he traces the rejection of Options A′ and B′ to Johnson's concern for his Great Society; he also traces the rejection of Option E′ to the same source. Although he does not explain the rejection of Option D′, he has come closer than most in attempting an explanation for the selection of Option C′.

Berman's focus on domestic politics is a useful complement to the analogical explanation's emphasis on foreign policy considerations. Its emphasis on Johnson's Great Society concerns and its articulation of how those concerns might have affected Johnson's Vietnam choices ring true. The analogical explanation is not inherently incapable of including domestic politics in its explanatory scheme. The fear of the kind of domestic backlash that accompanied the loss of China in 1949 exemplifies an important domestic political factor that could have been potentially important in the making of America's Vietnam policy. Nevertheless, evidence of this fear of "another China" and its effect on Great Society programs does not appear in the documentary record in the manner of the Korean, Dien Bien Phu, and Munich analogies.

---

letter from Cyrus Vance to Fred Greenstein of Princeton University in which the former clarifies the meaning of the president's "current intentions." According to Vance, the latter did not mean that Johnson had decided in favor of war. This point is important because it bears on the issue of whether the July 21–27 deliberations were true decision-making meetings.

There is, of course, a plausible reason for this: politicians are reluctant to reveal, especially in meetings or memos, the domestic factors—whether the fear of backlash or of Congress sabotaging one's domestic programs—that influence their foreign policy decisions. There is much to be said for this argument; it does imply, however, that it is much more difficult to weigh the relative influence of such domestic factors vis-à-vis those strategic-cognitive factors that are better documented. Until decision-makers are willing to leave behind records that indicate the true extent to which domestic politics permeate decisions of war and peace, the role of (perceived) international strategic considerations in foreign policy decision-making will probably be easier to assess.

Part III

THE IMPLICATIONS

CHAPTER 8

The Psychology of Analogical Reasoning

> Whether or not the American officials actually believed their own propositions, they repeated them year after year with a dogged persistence and a perfect disregard for all contradictory evidence. . . . for the American official effort to fit the new evidence into the old official assumptions was something like the effort of the seventeenth century astronomers to fit their observations of the planets into the Ptolemaic theory of the universe.
>
> —*Frances FitzGerald,* Fire in the Lake

In a May 6, 1966, memo to the secretaries of state and defense, Walt Rostow sought to reopen the issue of bombing POL targets in North Vietnam. For six months, the president had resisted the recommendation to extend the bombing to POL targets, but with the resignation of McGeorge Bundy, the option found a new supporter in Walt Rostow, Bundy's successor. Rostow's memo, fully declassified only in November 1985, is entirely consistent with the pattern of analogical reasoning we have observed in earlier chapters; it is also illustration par excellence of the psychology of analogical reasoning. The memo is worth quoting in full:

> I went through an experience in 1944 which may bear on the decision before us.
>
> We used then with respect to the Germans exactly the same analytical methods we are now applying to North Vietnam; that is, we estimated civilian, overall military, and front line military POL requirements. Assuming that they would and could cushion front line military requirements, we told our seniors that attacks on oil would be considerably cushioned and delayed in their impact on the military situation in the field.
>
> We were wrong. From the moment that serious and systematic oil attacks started, front line engine fighter strength and tank mobility were affected. The reason was this: it proved much more difficult, in the face of general oil shortage, to allocate from less important uses than the simple arithmetic of the problem would suggest. When the central sources began to dry up the

effects proved fairly prompt and widespread. What look like reserves statistically are rather inflexible commitments to logistical pipelines.

With respect to North Vietnam we are dealing, of course, with much lower military expenditures of POL in absolute terms; but we are also dealing with a much less sophisticated logistical capacity.

As I remember, the estimate in 1965 was that something like 60% of POL in North Vietnam was for military purposes; 40% for civilian.

We can properly assume that the expansion in recent months is wholly for military purposes. Military requirements may now, therefore, be running at about 80% of total availabilities. This leaves a small civilian cushion, indeed.

With an understanding that simple analogies are dangerous, I nevertheless feel it is quite possible the military effects of a systematic and sustained bombing of POL in North Vietnam may be more prompt and direct than conventional intelligence analysis would suggest.

I would underline, however, the adjectives "systematic and sustained." If we take this step we must cut clean through the POL system—and hold the cut—if we are looking for decisive results.[1]

Rostow was wrong, and conventional intelligence was right. Throughout the second half of 1966, the United States bombed Hanoi's and Haiphong's POL facilities, but bombing failed to achieve its stated goals. As a disillusioned Robert McNamara admitted in his testimony before the Senate Armed Services and Appropriations Committee in January 1967: "I don't believe that the bombing up to the present has significantly reduced, nor any bombing that I could contemplate in the future would significantly reduce, actual flow of men and materiel to the South."[2]

George Ball could have told his colleagues so earlier. In fact, he did. In a January memo to the president, a copy of which was sent to McNamara, Ball wrote,

To bomb the energy sources of North Viet-Nam would threaten the industrial life of the country. Yet, as noted by the Special Memorandum of January 19, 1966, approved by the Board of National Estimates, *none of these attacks*—on the harbor or POL or on the power stations—*would, in itself, have a critical impact on the combat activity of the Communist forces in South Viet-Nam.*[3]

An obvious reason that bombing POL targets was unlikely to change North Vietnam's behavior was the difference between North Vietnam's

[1] Memo, Walt Rostow to the President, May 6, 1966, Memos to the President, Walt Rostow, vol. 2, NSF, emphasis mine.

[2] Cited in *Pentagon Papers*, 4:112.

[3] Memo, George Ball to the President, January 25, 1966, Papers of Paul Warnke—Files of John McNaughton, emphasis Ball's. Ball sent a copy of this memo to McNamara on January 26, 1966.

and Germany's economies: the relatively undeveloped state of North Vietnamese industry meant that it would be less vulnerable to bombing. POL facilities could be dispersed and stored underground, and power disruptions would not have a drastic impact on the morale or economic viability of a peasant economy.[4]

Would Rostow have changed his mind if this point of dissimilarity had been pointed out to him? If the pattern observed in earlier chapters is any indication, the answer is probably no. The contrary argument, that Rostow would have changed his mind when presented with Ball's evidence, overemphasizes the impact of intellectual give-and-take in the decision-making process.[5] It neglects the role of other forces at work. To tease out these other forces, it is helpful to return briefly to Rostow's memo.

Rostow acknowledged that "simple analogies" were dangerous, but nonetheless he believed that the lessons he learned in 1944 were relevant to the issue at hand. In fact, for him, the 1944 analogy was relevant enough to override the conventional intelligence that bombing the POL targets would not seriously dampen Hanoi's will to fight in the South. For Rostow to have fitted the new evidence provided by conventional intelligence into his old assumptions, would have been akin, in Frances FitzGerald's terms, to the "effort of the seventeenth century astronomers to fit their observations of the planets into the Ptolemaic theory of the universe."

This chapter extends and completes the discussion of the psychology of analogical reasoning that began in chapter 2 and has been implicit in the succeeding chapters. In part 2 of the book, I demonstrate the ways policymakers used analogies for cognitive functions such as going beyond the information given, performing the diagnostic tasks specified by the AE framework, and resolving conflicting streams of incoming information. Having completed the empirical analysis of specific analogies' effects on specific individuals, I may now address the psychology of analogical reasoning in a meaningful way.

From what has been observed in the preceding chapters and in the example above, three questions seem interesting. First, from where do policymakers get their analogies? Why were the Korean, Munich, Dien Bien Phu, and Malayan analogies more important in Vietnam decision-making than, say, the Pearl Harbor and Cuban missile crisis analogies? Second, can the pattern of policymakers' use of analogies documented in

[4] *Pentagon Papers*, 4:62–65.

[5] This argument would fit the "Hovland" explanation of attitude change; schema theory, on the other hand, suggests that Rostow's attitude would not change so easily. For an excellent discussion of the different expectations of these and other social psychological theories, see Larson, *Containment*, chap. 1.

part 2 be explained? That is, can we explain why policymakers are insensitive to the differences between situations obscured by their analogies, why they stick to their analogies even when others have pointed out flaws, and why they use analogies as proofs? In a word, why do policymakers use analogies poorly? Third, is there a countervailing pattern to what we have observed? Is there any evidence that policymakers may "break out" of the observed pattern of behavior?

As was suggested in chapter 2, schema theory seems to be able to provide preliminary answers to these questions. The availability and representativeness heuristics can be used to shed light on how schemas or analogies are accessed. Especially suggestive in this respect is the notion that the most representative analogies, defined as those analogies with the most surface commonalities with Vietnam, are likely to be the ones used. The notions that schemas tend to process incoming information top-down and that they tend to persevere help explain the way Johnson, Rusk, the Bundys, Ball, and Rostow used analogies. Finally, schema theory also indicates that there is a countervailing pattern to what has been observed, but the conditions under which it holds are less clearly understood. The remainder of this chapter elaborates on these arguments.

ACCESSING AND RETRIEVING ANALOGIES: THE AVAILABILITY HEURISTIC

When faced with a new situation, individuals turn to their repertoire of historical memories to make sense of it. Which historical event or experience is invoked depends, all else being equal, on the ease with which it can be recalled. Kahneman and Tverksy, the two foremost researchers working on judgment heuristics, have called this heuristic the availability heuristic: it operates when a person estimates the probability of an event by the ease with which similar instances can be recalled.[6] In one of many experiments Kahneman and Tversky performed to illustrate this phenomenon, subjects were asked to judge the relative frequency of words beginning with the letter *r* compared to words with *r* as the third letter. Most people judged words beginning with *r* to be more numerous than words with *r* as the third letter, when in truth—or the absolute frequency—the latter are more numerous. Kahneman and Tversky argue that because it is easier to construct or recall words beginning with *r* than words with *r* as the third letter, people tend to believe that the former are more numerous, when in fact, the latter are far more numerous.[7]

[6] Kahneman, Slovic, and Tversky, *Judgment under Uncertainty*, pp. 11–14.

[7] Kahneman and Tversky, "Availability: A Heuristic for Judging Frequency and Probability," in Kahneman, Slovic, and Tversky, *Judgment under Uncertainty*, pp. 163–78.

The relative ease of recall provides a partial explanation for schema activation. Nisbett and Ross cite two experiments in support of this thesis. The first experiment told subjects they would be divided into different groups for a "learning experiment." One group was exposed to positive words such as "adventurous," "self-confident," "independent," and so on; a second group was given negative words such as "reckless," "conceited," "aloof," and so on; other groups were given other positive or negative words that were not relevant to character evaluation. The groups were then asked to evaluate a young man, Donald, who was characterized as someone with a high opinion of his own abilities, with risky hobbies and limited relations with others. Subjects exposed to the positive words evaluated Donald more kindly than those exposed to negative words; subjects exposed to irrelevant words remained uninfluenced. The experimenters argued that the evaluations were to be explained by the "transient availability" of different "personae" schemas.[8]

In another experiment, H. A. Hornstein and others manipulated the availability of different "schemas for the human race" to subjects who were about to play a prisoner's dilemma game. While waiting for the game to start, subjects were placed in waiting rooms with a piped-in radio program. In one instance, the music was interrupted for a "heart-warming account of someone who offered a kidney to someone whom he did not know who was in need of a transplant."[9] In another instance, subjects heard a morbid account of an urban atrocity. The experimenters found that subjects who heard the heart-warming story played the game much more cooperatively than those who heard about the atrocity. It was the availability of two different schemas, "most people are basically decent and kind" versus "it's dog-eat-dog out there," artificially induced, to be sure, that accounted for the different modes of play.[10]

Do these experiments elucidate which analogies are likely to be used in political decision-making? They do, to a degree. The *r* experiment suggests that not all analogies within a person's repertoire are equal: for whatever reasons, some are more easily recalled than others. A mental experiment along the lines of the *r* experiment can be performed for the policymakers of the 1960s. This mental experiment would begin by asking about the main foreign policy events during the lifetime of the key decision-makers.

[8] T. E. Higgins, W. S. Rholes and C. R. Jones, "Category Accessibility and Impression Formation," *Journal of Experimental Social Psychology* 12 (1976): 422–35, cited in Nisbett and Ross, *Human Inference*, pp. 36–37.

[9] Nisbett and Ross, *Human Inference*, p. 37.

[10] H. A. Hornstein et al., "Effects of Knowledge about Remote Social Events on Prosocial Behavior, Social Conception, and Mood," *Journal of Personality and Social Psychology* 32 (1975): 1038–46, cited in Nisbett and Ross, *Human Inference*, p. 37.

Assume that major world political events from World War I onwards are eligible: Lyndon Johnson was nine, and Dean Rusk and George Ball were eight when the United States entered World War I. Suppose that more recent events are likely to be more "available." In Kahneman and Tversky's experiment, it was the spatial arrangement of the letter *r* that made it easier or harder for the subjects to recall words. In our mental experiment, it seems reasonable to maintain that a temporal dimension will be relevant in determining which analogues decision-makers will recall more easily. Thus, reading backward from 1965, the U.S. intervention in the Dominican Republic, the Cuban missile crisis, the Berlin crises, Korea, Greece, Turkey, Pearl Harbor, and Munich are likely to be more available to the decision-makers of the 1960s than say, the U.S. entry into World War I or U.S. moves in Siberia after the Russian Revolution. With the exception of the intervention in the Dominican Republic, all of these analogues are in fact among the ten analogies most frequently used in public and in private by the Johnson administration (see tables 3.1 and 3.2).

The importance of recency in cuing schemas is also attested to by the Donald and prisoner's dilemma experiments. In both cases, subjects' schemas were primed or made available temporarily; it was these recently primed schemas—compared to other schemas not recently primed—that had a profound effect on how the subjects judged Donald or played the prisoner's dilemma game.[11] Arguments that the latest war exercises the most important influence on future wars are also based on recency.[12]

To say that the more recent is easier to recall still leaves one with a rather broad spectrum of events. Can it be narrowed down? Here the notion of "the coming of political age" is potentially helpful, if it can be more precisely specified than hitherto. Admittedly, different individuals will come of political age at different times, but if the concept is to have any meaning, it is necessary to specify what that age-band is. Otherwise, the coming of age becomes a slippery concept, to be applied to whomever at whatever age so long as it supports the analyst's contentions. I propose that the coming of political age be defined as the age band between twenty and thirty-five years, the former coinciding roughly with early adulthood and voting eligibility, and the latter approximating the time when one's political career responsibilities are likely to increase. If this definition is accepted, the period from the late 1930s to the early 1950s, encompassing events such as Munich, Pearl Harbor, U.S. aid to Greece and Turkey, the Berlin crises, and the Korean War, constitute

[11] See Fiske and Taylor, *Social Cognition*, p. 175.

[12] Cf. Jervis, *Perception and Misperception*, pp. 266–70.

the "formative years" of the key policymakers of the Johnson administration. It follows that these events and their lessons would be especially available to America's Vietnam decision-makers. Events outside this band—such as U.S. entry into World War I, U.S. moves after the Russian Revolution, the Cuban missile crisis, and the intervention in the Dominican Republic—are unlikely to be as available.[13]

ACCESSING AND RETRIEVING ANALOGIES: THE REPRESENTATIVENESS HEURISTIC

The above analysis of the effects of recency and the political coming of age on availability is a first step toward understanding which analogies within the decision-maker's repertoire are likely to be accessed. Not much attention, however, has yet been paid to the events in Vietnam, the stimuli that provoked the search for analogies in the first place. A second component in the selection of the relevant analogies involves assessment of the fit between the incoming stimuli and the repertoire of available analogies stored in memory. The perceiver will have to make a similarity judgment, of, for example, the extent to which the situation in Vietnam matches the memory invoked. Kahneman and Tversky have been able to specify the rule or heuristic that people normally use in making such judgments. They find that people typically assess the probability that *A* (say, the challenge in Vietnam) is a *B* (say, communist expansionism) by relying on the representativeness heuristic, their assessment of the degree to which *A* resembles *B*. Thus, if *A* is highly representative of *B*, the probability that *A* belongs to or is generated by *B* is judged to be high.

Kahneman and Tversky demonstrate how the heuristic works by providing subjects (the similarity group) in their experiment with the following character sketch:

> Tom W. is of high intelligence, although lacking in true creativity. He has a need for order and clarity, and for neat and tidy systems in which every detail finds its appropriate place. His writing is rather dull and mechanical, occasionally enlivened by somewhat corny puns and by flashes of imagina-

[13] Note that this "generational" refinement of the availability/recency hypothesis is not without its ambiguities. It can account for the salience of Munich, since with the exception of McGeorge Bundy, who was nineteen in 1938, all the senior policymakers were between twenty and thirty-five at the time of Munich. It has trouble accounting for Johnson's and Rusk's preoccupation with Korea since by the time the Korean war broke out, Johnson and Rusk were already in their early forties. The war was hardly an "early experience" for them, although it could be counted as such for the Bundys, Walt Rostow, and Robert McNamara, who were all in their late twenties.

> tion of the sci-fi type. He has a strong drive for competence. He seems to have little feel and little sympathy for other people and does not enjoy interacting with others. Self-centered, he nevertheless has a deep moral sense.

The subjects were then asked, "How similar is Tom W. to the typical graduate student in . . . nine fields of graduate specialization?" The subjects ranked computer science and engineering the highest and social science and social work the lowest. A comparable group of subjects (the base-rate group) who were not given the sketch and who were simply asked to guess the percentage of first-year graduate students in each of the nine fields gave rather different answers: they estimated that social science or social work students outnumbered computer science students by at least a factor of two. These results show that the subjects in the similarity group made their judgments on the basis of Tom W.'s similarity to their conception of the typical computer scientist or engineer. They neglected the base rates that would have suggested that in the given population, social science students were likely to be more numerous than computer scientists.[14] This and other experiments showing how people use the representativeness heuristic to make inferences have led some psychologists to the conclusion that

> The representativeness heuristic takes part in the selection of schemas. Indeed, the similarity of the data at hand to some stored representation of objects and events always has been presumed to be the chief determinant of schema arousal and application.[15]

Can the representativeness heuristic shed light on which of the available analogies would be likely to be invoked, given the situation in Vietnam? Since the heuristic attempts to fit an instance into a category, the first question must be whether it is possible to categorize the many analogues available to the policymakers of the 1960s. Assuming that analo-

[14] Kahneman and Tversky, "On the Psychology of Prediction," in Kahneman, Slovic, and Tversky, eds., *Judgment under Uncertainty*, pp. 48–68. Jervis has argued that foreign policy decision-makers often do not neglect base rates because such base rates heavily influence their images of their potential adversaries ("Representativeness in Foreign Policy Judgments," *Political Psychology* 7 (1983): 483–505, esp. nn. 2 and 3). I agree with Jervis. Kahneman and Tversky, however, might consider this argument to conflate base rates, which are objective, with the policymakers' subjective images. Jervis is aware of this objection; it seems to me that Jervis, Kahneman, and Tversky are not in fundamental disagreement. Kahneman and Tversky could easily reinterpret the Tom W. experiment to the effect that the similarity group was using the "best base rate" (their subjective conception of the typical engineer) they had. For my purposes, the important point is that people try to fit incoming stimuli into their preexisting categories.

[15] Nisbett and Ross, *Human Inference*, p. 37. For other experiments involving the representativeness heuristic, see pt. 2 of Kahneman, Slovic, and Tversky, *Judgment under Uncertainty*.

gies from the late 1930s to early 1950s were especially available and that events thereafter had recency and were therefore also easy to recall, four categories of analogues can be distinguished: a fascist aggression schema (Munich, Manchuria, Ethiopia, and Pearl Harbor), a communist expansionism schema (Greece, Turkey, Korea), a superpower confrontation schema (Berlin crises, the Cuban Missile Crisis), and a superpower cooperation schema (the Test Ban Treaty).[16] The specific attributes of the Vietnam conflict—a communist north bent on taking over the south by force, a North Vietnam supported by its ideological brethren, China and the Soviet Union—are more similar to the defining attributes of the communist expansionism and fascist aggression schemas than they are to the superpower confrontation and cooperation schemas. Thus, if the representativeness heuristic played a role in the policymakers' assessments of fit, we should expect the 1930s, Pearl Harbor, Greek, Turkish, and Korean analogies to be especially important.

One might protest that in matching the attributes of the instance or stimulus (Vietnam) to the attributes of the category (the communist expansionism schema), only the most superficial attributes of the former seemed to be used. That is precisely the point, for one of the most interesting findings of researchers working on analogical problem solving is that people pick analogies on the basis of superficial similarities between the prospective analogue and the situation it is suppose to illuminate.[17] In various experiments designed specifically to probe the ways subjects retrieve analogies to solve problems, Dedre Gentner has found that "superficial mere-appearance matches" or "surface commonalities" play "the most important role in access."[18]

In Gentner's experiments, subjects were given one-paragraph stories (and fillers) to read. Later, they were given another set of stories to read with the instructions that "if any of the new stories reminded them of any of the original stories," they were to write out the original stories as fully as possible. The new stories (the target) were designed to match the old stories (the base) in three ways: by "mere appearance," "true analogy," or "false analogy." One-third of the new stories were "mere appearance" matches, one-third "true analogy" matches, and one-third "false analogy" matches. The results of the access experiment were surprising:

> Natural remindings did not produce [sound] analogies. Instead they [subjects] were far more likely to retrieve superficial mere-appearance matches.

[16] These are some of the key foreign policy events in the period under consideration. I have included events that can be inferred from the discussion of "availability" as recency.

[17] Dedre Gentner, "Mechanisms," pp. 226–29; Holyoak and Thagard, "Computational Model," pp. 262–64. The terms "base" and "target" are Gentner's.

[18] Gentner, "Mechanisms," p. 228.

Given mere-appearance matches, subjects were able to access the original story 78% of the time, whereas the true analogies were accessed only 44% of the time, and the false analogies 25% of the time.[19]

Gentner's findings have basically been replicated by others.[20] The findings of Thomas Gilovich are especially pertinent: they deal with how people draw on historical analogies to solve hypothetical crises.[21] Gilovich divided his subjects into three groups and gave each group essentially the same international crisis to solve. The critical difference was that the description of one group's hypothetical crisis included phrases like "Winston Churchill Hall," "minorities fleeing in boxcars" (to elicit the Munich or World War II analogy), another group's description included phrases like "Dean Rusk Hall" and "minorities fleeing in small boats" (to elicit the Vietnam analogy), and the control group's description contained no such obviously evocative phrases. The nature of the crisis was constructed so that the evocations had no bearing on how the crisis was to be solved: for example, "Dean Rusk Hall" was the room where the subject was to be briefed about the crisis. Gilovich nevertheless found that these "irrelevant similarities" encouraged his subjects to draw the expected analogies: those briefed in "Winston Churchill Hall" were more likely to see the crisis as another Munich, and they were more prointervention, whereas those briefed in "Dean Rusk Hall" were more prone toward "a hands-off policy." Gilovich concluded that his subjects drew analogies on the basis of "factors of questionable relevance" and that those analogies affected their policy recommendations.[22]

To be sure, "surface commonalities" have an operational meaning in the psychology laboratory; in real-world situations, the concept is harder to pin down. Yet Gentner's and Gilovich's findings will strike a responsive chord among historians and political scientists. The latter's central lament has been that because statesmen have such a poor repertoire of historical analogies, they often pick the most superficial ones to guide their foreign policy decision-making. But it is not clear that historians and political scientists appreciate the full implications of Gentner's findings. Her findings suggest that even when given a repertoire containing perfect matches with the base analogy, subjects are less likely to pick the perfect matches than the superficial ones. If she is correct, the problem

[19] Gentner, "Mechanisms," p. 228.

[20] See Holyoak and Thagard, "Computational Model," pp. 262–64; and Keane, *Analogical Problem Solving*, chap. 6.

[21] Thomas Gilovich, "Seeing the Past in the Present: The Effect of Associations to Familiar Events on Judgments and Decisions," *Journal of Personality and Social Psychology* 40 (1981): 797–808.

[22] Ibid., pp. 802–6.

lies less in the poor repertoire of analogies possessed by statesmen than in the very process of accessing analogies.[23]

The "surface commonalities" thesis can suggest why the communist and fascist aggression schemas seemed more applicable to Vietnam than the superpower confrontation and cooperation schemas. The latter schemas—generalized from events such as the Berlin crises, the Cuban missile crisis, and the Test Ban Treaty respectively—had fewer surface similarities with Vietnam than the communist and fascist aggression schemas. They were geographically dissimilar, the implied adversary was the Soviet Union instead of China, and they did not suggest the invasion of a contiguous territory.

Finally, if one examines the specific analogies from which the communist and fascist aggression schemas were derived, it is possible to separate out Korea and Munich as the most "superficially similar" to Vietnam. The United States faced no "Pearl Harbor" threat from Hanoi; moreover, the militarization of the conflict in Vietnam rendered the Greece and Turkey analogies less appropriate. Although geographically distant, Munich did capture the image of military expansionism. For better or worse, Korea seemed to have the most surface similarities with Vietnam in the mid-1960s. The Korea-Vietnam similarities ranged from the nature of the challenge (communists bent on taking over a contiguous territory by military force) and its assumed sponsor (China), to the geographic location and its domino implications (East Asia, spreading into Southeast Asia). With so many plausible similarities and the fact that the Korean War was the United States' most recent and somewhat successful war, it should not be surprising that the Korean analogy came to occupy the place that it did in the official mindset.

A PATTERN OF ANALOGICAL REASONING

An identifiable pattern emerges from the way decision-makers used the Korean, Munich, Dien Bien Phu, Malayan, and 1944 (Rostow) analogies. Someone would propose an analogy to Vietnam. Its validity would almost always be questioned. A critic would have little difficulty pointing out differences between the analogy and Vietnam. Witness Ball's critique of the Korean analogy, Mike Mansfield and William Fulbright's skepticism about the relevance of Munich, McGeorge Bundy's attack on Dien Bien Phu, and the joint chiefs' criticism of Malaya. Interestingly, such criticisms and enumerations of differences seldom registered: the proposer of the analogy would either dismiss the differences or pay lip service to

[23] Cf. May, *"Lessons" of the Past*; Neustadt and May, *Thinking in Time*.

them and continue to believe that his analogy was valid. Thus Rusk continued to believe in the salience of Korea, Ball never wavered in his belief in the appropriateness of Dien Bien Phu, and Johnson was quick to insist on the relevance of the 1930s to his former Senate colleagues. Similarly, even as he acknowledged that "simple analogies are dangerous," Rostow dismissed conventional intelligence suggesting that bombing North Vietnamese POL targets would not persuade the North to cease the conflict.

Three facets of this pattern are in need of explanation. The first is why differences between the analogue and Vietnam tended to be neglected, even when they were brought to the attention of the proposer of the analogy. The second is why, even after being informed of the flaws in their analogies, policymakers continued to use and hold on to them. The third is whether these tendencies matter. This last question raises an important issue. If neglecting differences and retaining faith in one's own analogies have no behavioral or policy outcomes, then these aspects of analogical reasoning need no special explanation.

A priori, it is seldom possible to tell whether the differences neglected mattered. Similarly, it is difficult to say whether continuing to believe in one's analogies is necessarily unwise. With hindsight, however, it is possible to argue that, in the case of Vietnam decision-making, not taking differences seriously and clinging to analogies did lead to inaccurate or faulty diagnoses. Policies based on such faulty premises will in turn be costly or be likely to fail or both. If all these can be demonstrated, then it will be worthwhile to explore the psychological processes behind "neglecting differences" and "clinging." I will start by using the concept of top down processing to explain why differences tend to be neglected, continue by using the notion of perseverance to explain "clinging," and finally, demonstrate that these characteristics of schematic processing made it difficult for policymakers to appreciate the local forces at work in Vietnam. This failure of understanding, I argue, contributed to America's failure in Vietnam.

SCHEMAS AND TOP-DOWN INFORMATION PROCESSING

Once formed and stored in memory, analogies play a crucial role in processing incoming information. They make possible and control the characterization of incoming data, the positing of causal relationships among variables, and the prediction of outcomes.[24] If this sounds similar to the uses of historical analogies documented in part 2, it is only because anal-

[24] Rumelhart, "Schemata: The Building Blocks of Cognition," pp. 33–34.

ogies perform essentially the same tasks as schemas. Schema theorists have a favorite experiment to illustrate the importance of schemas in comprehension. Consider the following passage:

> The procedure is actually quite simple. First you arrange things into different groups. Of course, one pile may be sufficient depending on how much there is to do. If you have to go somewhere else due to lack of facilities, that is the next step, otherwise you are pretty well set. It is important not to overdo things. That is, it is better to do too few things at once than too many. . . . After the procedure is completed, one arranges the materials into different groups again. Then they can be put into their appropriate places. Eventually they will be used once more and the whole cycle will then have to be repeated. However, that is part of life.[25]

The passage seems baffling until it is revealed that it is about washing clothes. Once the clothes-washing schema is accessed, the passage becomes understandable. Schemas thus aid comprehension by allowing the perceiver to reconstruct and order the incoming information by fitting it into previously existing categories or experience. The above passage also suggests that facts as such ("bottom-up processing") seldom lend themselves to any meaningful interpretation without an organizing schema. Schema theorists tend to emphasize the top-down nature of human information processing and consider it the norm.[26]

The idea of top-down or theory-driven processing implies that incoming information is compared with or fitted into existing schemas stored in memory. The experiment by Kelly credited for establishing this phenomenon is described in chapter 2. In that experiment, subjects interpreted a standard set of behaviors by the same person differently, and their differing interpretations were explained by the different schemas ("cold lecturer" or "warm lecturer") that were invoked. This top-down view of information processing has been corroborated by subsequent studies.[27]

Inasmuch as schemas and analogies perform largely similar functions, we also should expect analogies to process information top-down. One will tend to interpret ambiguous information in accordance with the expectations of one's chosen analogy, and one will slight or ignore discrepant information. The record seems to bear this out. Consider Walt Rostow's equation of the vulnerability of North Vietnam's POL targets with

[25] John D. Bransford and Marcia K. Johnson, "Consideration of Some Problems of Comprehension," in *Visual Information Processing*, ed. William Chase (New York: Academic Press, 1973), p. 400.

[26] See especially Higgins and Bargh, "Social Cognition," pp. 374–76.

[27] See N. Cantor and W. Mischel, "Traits as Prototypes: Effects on Recognition Memory," *Journal of Personality and Social Psychology* 35 (1977): 38–48; see also Fiske and Taylor, *Social Cognition*, chap. 6, and Nisbett and Ross, *Human Inference*, chap. 4.

that of German POL targets during World War II. Rostow's willingness to slight conventional intelligence suggesting that North Vietnam might be less vulnerable has all the characteristics of top-down processing. Information inconsistent with the expectations of his 1944 analogy was simply not given the weight it deserved.

Similarly, Dean Rusk would acknowledge that the Vietnamese conflict was not completely driven by the North, and that southerners were also fighting to overthrow their own government; these facts, however, did not make Rusk any less attached to his schema, based on the Korean and Munich precedents, that external aggression remained the key problem. In light of the Vietcong's ability to sustain a major insurrection for such a protracted period, Rusk's position might seem incredible or disingenuous to some. Yet his assessment can be easily explained by his failure to give schema-discrepant information the attention it deserved.

Equally interesting is Rusk's inability to see any parallels between the Vietnamese revolution and the American Civil War. In the 1966 congressional hearings, Senator Frank Church expressed skepticism about the Munich and Korean precedents and proceeded to offer his alternative analogy, the American Civil War. Rusk's response was, "Senator, I do not follow the point at all because, whatever you call it, there is aggression from North Vietnam against South Vietnam across the demarcation line."[28] The Vietnam conflict simply did not fit into any of Rusk's civil war schemas; he was perfectly sincere when he retorted that he could not follow Senator Church's point.

Perhaps the closest real-world replication of the Kelley experiment is discussed in chapter 6, in which I try to show how the same set of incoming information was processed differently by the Korean, Dien Bien Phu, and Munich analogies (see figure 6.3). This is very similar to Kelley's experiment, where the same set of gestures was interpreted differently because different schemas were invoked. Thus given one definition of the situation in Vietnam suggesting aggression, and one suggesting a civil war, the believer in the Munich analogy would be more receptive toward the aggression thesis and the believer in the Dien Bien Phu analogy more favorably disposed toward the civil war thesis. Moreover, top down processing, unlike bottom-up or piecemeal processing, which relies on only the information available, allows the perceiver to go beyond the information given.[29] Once the "warm" personality schema was invoked, for example, a host of ambiguous behaviors were interpreted along "warm"

[28] Robinson and Kemp, Report on the United States Senate Hearing, *The Truth about Vietnam*, p. 52.

[29] For more on the notion of "piecemeal processing," see Susan Fiske, "Schema-Based versus Piecemeal Politics: A Patchwork Quilt, but Not a Blanket of Evidence," in Lau and Sears, *Political Cognition*, p. 42.

lines. Similarly, once one had invoked the Dien Bien Phu analogy to assess the U.S. experience in Vietnam, one would not only predict that the United States would probably end up like France; one might also worry about the image of the United States as a colonial power and about the possibility of severe internal dissension.

Without the insight that analogies process information top-down, it would be unclear whether American policymakers were using analogies irresponsibly or were simply obtuse when they neglected the differences between Vietnam and their chosen analogues. With the help of schema theory, we may conclude that their use of analogies was not aberrant; if anything, it was the norm.

PERSEVERANCE

The perseverance effect was defined in chapter 2 as the tendency to persist in believing one's schema even in the face of evidence to the contrary. The experiment of the "authentic" and "inauthentic" suicide notes by Lee Ross and his colleagues is also described there. That experiment demonstrated that individuals who were induced to form a self-schema about their social sensitivity or insensitivity continued to hold that schema even after they had learned that the test on which they had based their judgment was bogus.[30]

Here, it is necessary to cite just one other perseverance experiment even more applicable to our case. In a 1980 study, Anderson, Lepper, and Ross sought to extend their investigation of the perseverance effect to causal "social theories."[31] Their subjects were asked to read case studies suggesting either a positive or negative relationship between risk taking and success as a firefighter. Half of the subjects received case studies suggesting a positive relationship; the other half received case studies suggesting a negative relationship. Subjects were then asked to provide an explanation for the relationship they found. Upon finishing, subjects were told that the data they had been given were totally fictitious and that half of the other subjects had been given data suggesting the opposite pattern of results. The results of this experiment are best described by Nisbett and Ross:

> The degree of belief perseverance among these subjects was substantial. In fact, subjects' belief [after debriefing] in whichever relationship they had

[30] Ross, Lepper, and Hubbard, "Perseverance," pp. 880–92.

[31] Craig A. Anderson, Mark Lepper, and Lee Ross, "Perseverance of Social Theories: The Role of Explanation in the Persistence of Discredited Information," *Journal of Personality and Social Psychology* 39 (1980): 1037–49.

> been encouraged to explain was almost as great as for those subjects who had seen the "data" but neither had explained it nor had been told that it was fictitious! Interviews with subjects who had explained the "data" and then had been debriefed were unsettling. Typically, such subjects justified their views by insisting that, despite the discrediting of the data, it was *obvious* that the particular relationship they had explained was the correct one. Indeed, several expressed surprise that subjects in the other condition had been gullible enough to form the opposite hypothesis.[32]

Quite apart from revealing the mischievousness of the experimenters, these results are highly suggestive for us.[33] The perseverance of the subjects' "theories" in the face of contradictory evidence also seems to have manifested itself in the Vietnam analogies. The fact that someone usually pointed out important flaws in the policymakers' analogies did little to erode their faith. Lyman Lemnitzer pointed to telling differences between Malaya and Vietnam, George Ball elaborated on the differences between Korea and Vietnam in numerous memos to his superiors, McGeorge Bundy attacked the flaws in the Dien Bien Phu analogy, and George Kennan and senators such as Wayne Morse, William Fulbright, and Frank Church repeatedly expressed their skepticism about the Munich analogy. None of these efforts had any impact on Kennedy, Johnson, Ball, and Rusk. They all continued to believe that their analogies captured essential similarities.

American policymakers had better reasons to stick to their analogies than the Stanford undergraduates in the "firefighter" experiment. The latter's theories were subjected to "total evidentiary discrediting" (since the data were fictitious); yet they continued to persevere in their beliefs. In contrast, the Vietnam analogies were simply challenged. No total evidentiary discrediting was possible in 1965; even now, some argue that those analogies were not improper.[34] Thus the fact that Johnson and his advisers stuck to their analogies should not be surprising. If total evidentiary discrediting cannot eliminate perseverance, it would be surprising if challenges on the order of Lemnitzer's, Ball's, and Bundy's memos could.

Without the help of psychological theory, the faith that America's Viet-

[32] Nisbett and Ross, *Human Inference*, p. 185.

[33] Anderson and his colleagues were impressed by the degree of perseverance exhibited by their subjects, but what amazed and perhaps disturbed them even more was that their "subjects' theories were initially grounded in the most minimal of data sets—only two case studies" ("Perseverance of Social Theories," p. 1046). If the Vietnam decision-makers are any indication, statesmen also seem to derive their lessons of history from a limited number of cases and hold on to the lessons just as fervently.

[34] See Norman Podhoretz, *Why We Were in Vietnam* (New York: Simon and Schuster, 1982).

nam policymakers showed in their analogies would appear puzzling. Now, however, their faith in the face of evidence to the contrary should be neither puzzling nor unusual, but only to be expected.

THE ROLE OF AFFECT

The analysis so far has focused exclusively on what psychologists call "cold" cognitive processes. That is, in relying on and clinging to their favorite analogies, U.S. policymakers were assumed to be primarily interested in making sense of the situation they faced, in order to fashion a proper foreign policy response. The phenomena of top-down processing and perseverance, for example, were discussed along these lines. Little reference has been made to the role of "hot cognitions" such as affect, emotions, anxieties, and ego needs, nor have these "hot" factors been incorporated into my explanations.

Although these "hot" factors are not unimportant for understanding analogical reasoning during the Vietnam War, they have been omitted for two reasons. First, the role of affect or emotions in information-processing approaches is only beginning to be systematically explored by psychologists. The information-processing theories of the 1970s and 1980s—including schema theory—consciously shied away from "hot" cognitions, in part because cognitive psychology's model of the mind was informed by the computer analogy. The "cold" aspects of schema theory are thus more developed and better validated than its "hot" aspects. The second reason for focusing on "cold" cognitive processes is theoretical parsimony. Insofar as "cold" factors are sufficient to explain most of our inferential failures and successes, there is only a residual need to resort to "hot" cognitive explanations.[35]

That said, it might still be worthwhile to consider briefly how "hot" cognitions might illuminate some of the issues we have discussed. Of special relevance is the notion of "affect-laden" schemas. In this view, a schema comes prepackaged with affective connotations. As a new event is categorized and the appropriate schema cued, the affect associated with the schema is also felt. Fiske, a major proponent of this thesis, has conducted experiments to test a version of such "schema-triggered" affect.[36] Fiske studied the affective responses of subjects when their "old flame," "politician," and "nerd" schemas were provoked; she found that

[35] Nisbett and Ross, *Human Inference*, pp. 12–13 and chap. 10; Larson, *Containment*, p. 345. Cf. Lau and Sears, "Social Cognition," p. 359.

[36] Susan Fiske, "Schema-triggered Affect: Applications to Social Perception," in *Affect and Cognition*, ed. Margaret Clark and Susan Fiske (Hillsdale, New Jersey: Lawrence Erlbaum Associates, 1982), pp. 55–78.

the first tended to trigger positive feelings, whereas the second and the third tended to trigger negative feelings.[37] When the match was only partial, for example, when subjects were given descriptions of individuals who only partially resembled their old flame, the affect was more moderate than when the match was very good.

For our purposes, the exact sequence or process by which affect is brought into play is not important. It is sufficient to note that affect may accompany the knowledge structure—be it a schema or an analogy—used by policymakers to assess a new person, object, or event. Thus, when Dean Rusk decided that the danger in Vietnam was analogous to that in Korea, the analogy might not only conjure up images of Chinese troops crossing the Yalu river, but also evoke negative feelings about inscrutable Chinese hordes. Rusk's public statements reflected this attitude, and his continual portrayal of Chinese aggressiveness suggested that he harbored strong feelings about communist China. Yet, even if such feelings came with the Korean analogy, they might have been less important than another set of feelings evoked: Rusk's remorse about his failure to anticipate China's intervention in the Korean War.[38] As was argued earlier, this feeling played an influential role in Rusk's determination not to get China involved against the United States in Vietnam.

Affect therefore is potentially helpful in analyzing political decision-making. Yet because it has only been recently incorporated into the research on schematic processing, the findings on it are more tentative and sparse. The systematic incorporation of future, experimentally validated findings about "affect-laden" schemas into the study of analogical reasoning will, I suspect, confirm the general trends noted here. To cite a final possibility, affect should also reinforce the cognitive salience—and thereby contribute to the perseverance effect—of analogies or schemas with which it is associated.

TOP-DOWN PROCESSING, PERSEVERANCE, AND DIFFERENCES NEGLECTED: DID THEY MATTER?

Using the psychological literature to demonstrate that policymakers are likely to be unreceptive to information inconsistent with their schemas is potentially illuminating because it "identifies" a process-based explanation of the pattern observed above. Similarly, knowing that policymakers are not likely to abandon their analogies even when challenged suggests

[37] Ibid. One supposes that for most of the subjects, the parting of ways with their old flames was not unduly painful.

[38] See Halberstam, *The Best and the Brightest*, pp. 325–26; Rusk, *As I Saw It*, p. 169.

that their analogies will continue to play an important role in their information processing. In that sense perseverance and top-down processing reinforce one another. The two observable effects of this reinforcement are the continued salience of the analogies to the policymakers and the tendency to slight information inconsistent with the expectations of the analogy.

If it can be shown that the inconsistent information rejected or the differences neglected by these two mutually reinforcing processes were not just potentially important but were actually so, so that the neglect contributed to suboptimal outcomes, we will have demonstrated that the differences neglected mattered. An argument along these lines will be attempted next.[39] Its basic purpose is to indicate that the neglect of important differences between Vietnam and its purported analogues contributed to judgmental errors on the part of the policymakers and that these errors partially explain why America's Vietnam policy failed.

THE VIETNAM DIFFERENCE

It is possible to cite any number of differences between Vietnam and each of its purported analogues examined in this study. From geography to history to national psychology, there must be hundreds of differences obscured by the Malayan, Korean, Munich, and Dien Bien Phu analogies. General Lemnitzer, in his memo to Maxwell Taylor, pointed out five differences between Malaya and Vietnam. One pertained to geography, another to logistics, and the other three to local historical circumstances. The point on geography is a good illustration of the importance of such differences. According to Lemnitzer, the "Malayan borders were far more controllable in that Thailand cooperated in refusing the Communists an operational safe haven."[40] The implicit contrast was of course to the almost free access enjoyed by the Vietnamese communists along the borders of Laos and Cambodia. The significance of these geographical and political realities became most apparent for the United States in 1969, when President Richard Nixon ordered the secret bombing of Laos and Cambodia, followed by the invasion of Cambodia in April of 1970. Nixon felt that unless these sanctuaries, including the headquarters of the

[39] In an earlier version of my work, I discuss the differences neglected under the logic of analogical reasoning. Without invalidating the role of the logic of analogical reasoning in making the users of analogies neglect differences, I now believe that the psychology of analogical reasoning captures the phenomenon just as well; moreover, it is the more parsimonious explanation. See my "From Rotten Apples to Falling Dominos," chaps. 6 and 7.

[40] Memo, L. L. Leminitzer to Maxwell Taylor, October 12, 1961, in *Pentagon Papers*, 2:650.

NLF in Cambodia, were destroyed, the Vietcong could continue the insurgency with impunity. The absence of such sanctuaries in Malaya made it easier for the British to subdue the communist insurrection there. Even then—as Lemnitzer noted—it took the British twelve years to suppress an insurgency "less strong than the one in South Vietnam."[41]

Those familiar with Vietnamese history and culture are wont to make the point that through the centuries, the Vietnamese have, at great cost to themselves, resisted successive encroachments upon their territory by the Chinese, the French, the Japanese, and then the French once again. As the historian William Turley has observed, a key element of Vietnamese identity was "this image of heroic resistance to foreign rule." Turley elaborates on this theme:

> Leaders who fulfilled this image could extract intense loyalty and enormous sacrifice from a broad spectrum of the population. Those leaders who succumbed to foreign pressure, collaborated with foreign rulers, or accommodated foreigners for personal gain suffered self-doubt and weak support.[42]

Among the policymakers, George Ball realized this peculiarity of Vietnamese history best. It set Vietnam apart from the countries with which it was most frequently compared. Ball was always conscious of the "revolutionary élan" or "atavistic anticolonialism" of the Vietnamese communists, and his memos reflect this insight: he constantly warned about the danger of the United States appearing to be a colonial oppressor to the Vietnamese.[43] According to Ball, even Rusk, who "has never gotten over the view that this [the Vietnam conflict] was like the Korean War," admitted in the end that he "underestimated the staying power" of the Vietnamese communists.[44]

It would serve no useful purpose to list the numerous differences between Vietnam and its analogues. Many of those differences—minor and major—have already been raised by the critics of the analogies analyzed in this book. Instead, I will focus on a few major factors unique to Vietnam that were obscured by all the analogies: the limited role of the Soviet Union and China in the Vietnam conflict, the civil war dimension of the conflict, and finally, the incompetence and illegitimacy of successive

[41] Ibid.

[42] William Turley, *The Second Indochina War* (Boulder, Colorado: Westview Press, 1986), p. 2. See also Timothy Lomperis, *The War Everyone Lost—and Won* (Baton Rouge: Louisiana State University Press, 1984), chaps. 1 and 2.

[43] Ball interview. Ball would occasionally describe the intensity with which Hanoi pursued its goal of national unification as "atavistic anticolonialism." See George Ball, *The Past Has Another Pattern*, p. 422. See also memo, George Ball to the President, "Keeping the Power of Decision," June 18, 1965, NSC History—Troop Deployment.

[44] Ball interview.

South Vietnamese governments. These factors draw the broad contours within which the import of many other differences can be comprehended. Recognition of these factors should have given the decision-makers pause in 1965. Not seeing them or refusing to accord them the weight they deserved made it easier for the United States to intervene and more difficult for it to succeed.

THE ROLE OF EXTERNAL POWERS

A popular view of the origins of the Malayan communist insurrection held that it was directed by the Soviet Union.[45] According to this view, the Soviet Union organized the Calcutta Conference in February 1948 to convey the new Cominform "two-camp" doctrine to its Asian delegates and to instruct them to start violent revolutions. In March, June, and September of the same year, communist-led insurrections broke out in Burma, Malaya, and Indonesia respectively. The Malayan insurrection was therefore one of many wars of liberation instigated by the Soviets as part of their plan to spread world revolution. This view of the insurrection has been questioned by some Southeast Asian specialists on the grounds of insufficient evidence, but it remains generally held.[46]

There is stronger evidence that Soviet and Chinese encouragement played an important role in North Korea's decision to invade the South in 1950.[47] China's entry into the war in 1950 confirmed the solidarity and determination of the communist bloc. Hitler's move for the Sudentenland, in turn, was a pretext for his aggressive designs. Although the desire of some German-speaking people in the Sudentenland to join Germany was genuine, Hitler capitalized on the issue of self-determination to extract concessions that would give his future expansionist goals a firm footing.

To compare the problem in South Vietnam to the Malayan, Korean and Munich precedents is therefore to emphasize the role of external powers in instigating the conflict. Gelb and Betts summarize the U.S. perception of who was doing the instigating in Vietnam:

> In the late 1940s the assumption was that Moscow controlled all Communist advances. . . . After Korea, China was seen as the principal opponent in Asia. This perception stuck through 1968. (An exception was the period of the Laotian crisis and Khrushchev's rhetoric about wars of national libera-

[45] See Lucian Pye, *Guerrilla Communism in Malaya* (Princeton: Princeton University Press, 1956); Means, *Malaysian Politics*; and Blaufarb, *Counterinsurgency Era.*

[46] Ruth McVey, *The Calcutta Conference and the Southeast Asian Uprising* (New York: Cornell University Interim Report Series, 1958).

[47] Marshall Shulman, *Stalin's Foreign Policy Reappraised* (Cambridge: Harvard University Press, 1963), pp. 139–44.

tion, from 1960 to 1962, when the Soviet Union emerged once again as the key source of trouble.) . . . From 1964, high officials could not be sure who was calling the shots in South Vietnam—Moscow or Peking or Hanoi itself.[48]

In November 1964, McGeorge Bundy's assistant on Vietnam affairs, Michael Forrestal, sent a memo to William Bundy in which he sought to clarify the U.S. stakes in Southeast Asia. In Forrestal's view, it was an expansionist China that made the political repercussions of a U.S. withdrawal from Vietnam unacceptable. "As I see it," wrote Forrestal, "Communist China shares the same internal political necessity for ideological expansion today that the Soviet Union did during the time of the Comintern and the period just following the Second World War." The United States therefore "should delay China's swallowing up Southeast Asia (a) until she develops better table manners and (b) the food is somewhat more indigestible."[49]

Similarly, Lyndon Johnson emphasizes the China connection in his memoirs. China and North Vietnam were eager to "absorb" Laos, and an incipient "Djakarta-Hanoi-Peking-Pyongyang axis" was counting on the collapse of South Vietnam. Once that happened, "the entire region would then have been ripe for the plucking."[50] Dean Rusk shared Johnson's and Forrestal's sentiments about China and the Asian dominoes; he also saw the United States as the one power capable of and obligated to prevent China and its ally, the Soviet Union, from succeeding.[51]

The problem with this focus on China and the Soviet Union as instigators is not merely that it overemphasized their role while underemphasizing the domestic roots of the Vietnam conflict. Equally troubling is the fact that it inflated the stakes of the conflict by blowing a civil war over the unification of the Vietnamese nation up into a conflict of Munich-like proportions. To be sure, both China and the Soviet Union provided substantial aid to Hanoi during the course of the first and second Indochina wars but they hardly called the shots. In the absence of the external aggression schema, policymakers might have noticed repeated signals on the part of China and the Soviet Union that, for strategic reasons of their own, they were less than enthusiastic about the reunification of North and South Vietnam.

In a recent work aimed at explaining the drastic rupture of Sino-Vietnamese and Vietnamese-Cambodian relations in the late 1970s, Nayan Chanda traces China's ambivalence toward Hanoi back to the 1950s. Chanda's thesis is that China's approach to Indochina has been "strikingly

[48] Gelb and Betts, *Irony of Vietnam*, pp. 188–89.

[49] *Pentagon Papers*, 3:644.

[50] Johnson, *The Vantage Point*, pp. 135–36.

[51] See Henry and Espinosa, "The Tragedy of Dean Rusk," p. 187.

traditional" from the very start. By that he means China helped North Vietnam not so much out of "ideological expansionism," as Forrestal would have it, but more out of "concern about its own security along the southern border."[52]

Thus, although China provided Hanoi with the military, economic, and technical assistance needed to defeat the French at Dien Bien Phu, it was not particularly anxious to have a unified Vietnam. At the Geneva Conference, Chinese Premier Zhou Enlai told his French interlocutors that China "favored the prolonged existence of two Vietnams and, generally, wanted a multiplicity of states on its borders." Heavy pressure from China and the Soviet Union was instrumental in "persuading" Hanoi to accept the temporary division of the country along the seventeenth parallel. At the Chinese dinner party for the Vietnamese delegates, to which the Bao Dai representative was also invited, Zhou apparently suggested that the South Vietnamese delegate might wish to set up a legation with China. To DRV premier Pham Van Dong's expression of surprise and deep hurt, Zhou quipped, "Of course, Pham Van Dong is closer to us by ideology, but that does not exclude a southern representation. After all, aren't you both Vietnamese and aren't we all Asians?"[53]

China's preference for a settlement at Geneva stemmed in part from its desire to keep the United States out of Indochina and in part from its distrust of the regional intentions of a united and powerful Vietnam. With increasing U.S. involvement in the 1960s, however, "one of the principal rationales for China's moderate posture at Geneva vanished." According to Chanda, between 1965 and 1968, China sent 320,000 noncombat troops to keep Hanoi's transportation system working, to man air defenses, and to provide technical advice.[54] It has been estimated that China gave Hanoi up to $10 billion in aid during the course of the Second Indochina War.[55]

Interestingly enough, with the impending departure of the United States from Vietnam and with the Sino-American rapproachment in the early 1970s, China reverted back to its Geneva posture. Mao reportedly told Pham Van Dong in November 1972, "One cannot sweep very far if the handle of the broom is too short. Taiwan is too far away for our broom to reach. Thieu in South Vietnam is out of reach of your broom, comrade. We must resign ourselves to this situation."[56] More than two years later, when North Vietnam launched its final offensive against Saigon, Peking

[52] Nayan Chanda, *Brother Enemy: The War after the War* (New York: Harcourt Brace Jovanovich, 1986), p. 187.

[53] Ibid., p. 127.

[54] Ibid., p. 128.

[55] See also Lomperis, *The War Everyone Lost—and Won*, p. 75.

[56] Cited in Chanda, *Brother Enemy*, p. 132. See also Karnow, *Vietnam*, p. 43.

warned Hanoi again about the danger of "stretching the broom too far."[57] Hanoi did not take the Chinese metaphor seriously and went on to capture Saigon. Hanoi proved that its broom handle was not too short; in fact, it was long enough to cause China great woe in the years to come.

The Soviet Union did not officially recognize the DRV until 1950, when China did so. Like the Chinese, the Soviets also had their own agenda at Geneva. They were more interested in having the French abandon the EDC than in getting the most favorable settlement for Hanoi. Whether the Soviet Union struck a deal with Mendes-France, in which it would help arrange a cease-fire in Vietnam in return for French rejection of the EDC, remains unresolved. It is well known, however, that the Soviets applied heavy pressure to get Hanoi to accept the "temporary" partition of Vietnam along the seventeenth parallel. When the promised elections of 1956 were not held, the Soviet Union, much to Hanoi's annoyance, did not protest. A year later, it actually proposed that North and South Vietnam be admitted into the United Nations.[58]

Most observers agree that the Soviet support for the Vietnamese in the 1960s was more a function of its rivalry with the United States and its bitter split with China than a function of its desire to spread world revolution. Khrushchev did proclaim in 1961 that the Soviet Union would support wars of liberation, and Kennedy took this announcement as a serious challenge. Yet in the same announcement, Khrushchev cautioned against getting into "local" wars. "And that," according to Michael Tatu, was "precisely what the Vietnamese conflict became, in Soviet terms, once the United States was massively engaged."[59] It was not that the Soviet Union was uninterested in a North Vietnamese victory. The Soviets were more worried about possible escalation of the war and the adverse effect that the war might have on their more urgent diplomatic callings.

At the peak of the war, Soviet aid to Hanoi—mostly in the form of sophisticated weapons and oil—reached $1 billion a year. The North Vietnam spring offensive of 1972 was made possible by Soviet arms, but Soviet leaders were neither informed nor consulted beforehand. The Soviets found the North Vietnamese action, coming three weeks before the U.S.-Moscow summit, "intolerable" because Hanoi "had acted without consulting its protector" and because the action threatened to "obstruct one of the greatest undertakings of postwar Soviet diplomacy—the first visit of an American President to the Soviet Union."[60] When Nixon re-

[57] Cited in Chanda, *Brother Enemy*, p. 133.

[58] Donald Zagoria, *Vietnam Triangle: Moscow/Peking/Hanoi* (New York: Pegasus, 1967), p. 40.

[59] Michael Tatu, "Moscow, Peking, and the Conflict in Vietnam," in *The Vietnam Legacy*, ed. Anthony Lake (New York: Pegasus, 1976), p. 21.

[60] Ibid., p. 32.

sponded to the spring offensive by bombing Hanoi and mining Haiphong harbor, he fully expected the U.S.-Soviet summit to be canceled. Instead, the Soviets issued a brief note of protest and went about business as usual. They were not about to let Hanoi's adventures and the American response postpone or cancel the summit.[61]

Far from directing the North Vietnamese to conquer the South, China and the Soviet Union, as we have seen, were quite prepared to live with two Vietnams. The view of external powers bent on exploiting local conflicts to advance their expansionist aims simply did not characterize Chinese or Soviet behavior toward Vietnam. The help that the Chinese and the Soviets gave Hanoi did not make them masters of the situation there. Curiously, American policymakers did not extend to the communists their own frustration at being held captive by their South Vietnamese clients. Emphasizing the role of external powers also encouraged the policymakers to neglect important domestic realities in Vietnam. Such neglect proved ruinous to American policy because indigenous forces were more powerful in determining the course of the Vietnam conflict. Of the local realities neglected, two were, in my estimation, critical to the communists' success. I refer to the civil war dimension of the conflict and the lack of a stable and legitimate government in the South.

CIVIL WAR

Aggression was the chief diagnosis of the situation in Vietnam provided by the Malayan, Korean, and Munich analogies. The three analogies suggest increasingly overt degrees of aggression. Kennedy, who compared Vietnam to Malaya, diagnosed the problem in Vietnam as indirect aggression. The assumption was that after their failure in Korea, the Soviet Union and China were resorting to less direct means of undermining the government of South Vietnam. Instead of relying on conventional North Vietnamese forces, they relied on the communist guerrillas as their proxies. For Johnson and Rusk, Korea was the better analogue for Vietnam; the aggression was indirect in that it was not a conventional invasion, but it was direct in that North Vietnam was as determined as North Korea to subjugate the South. Munich was, of course, the most blatant and dangerous form of aggression: it suggested that South Vietnam would be taken first, other Southeast Asian nations would follow, and the likely result would be a world war. Without counterforce, communism's appe-

[61] Henry Kissinger, *White House Years* (Boston: Little, Brown and Company, 1979), pp. 1192–95.

tite for violating the territorial integrity and political sovereignty of neighboring countries would know no bounds.

Were these diagnoses correct? If by "aggression" is meant the violation of the territorial integrity and political sovereignty of state *X* by state *Y*, the diagnoses were misleading on two counts. First, as I have argued in the discussion of the role of external powers, China and Soviet Union cannot, by any means, be depicted as states that were using North Vietnam to violate the territorial integrity and political sovereignty of South Vietnam.

Second and perhaps more to the point, the Geneva Conference of 1954 did not create two separate states. The seventeenth parallel was not meant to be a political boundary between North and South Vietnam. As the Final Declaration of the Geneva Agreements put it, the demarcation line divided Vietnam into two zones of regroupment; it was "provisional and should not in any way be interpreted as constituting a political or territorial boundary."[62] What Geneva created was, in George Kahin's words, "two contesting parties within a single national state."[63] The notion of aggression is consequently not very illuminating; the conflict between North and South in Vietnam is better described as a civil war. This indeed is the consensus among serious students of the Vietnam conflict today. Gelb and Betts summarize this view nicely:

> The real struggle in Vietnam was not between sovereign states. It was between Vietnamese. It was a civil war and a war for national independence. . . .
>
> Herein lies one of the paradoxes of and miscalculations about Vietnam. Most American leaders. . . . did not see that the real stake—the question of who would eventually govern Vietnam—was not negotiable. . . . For the Vietnamese, the stakes were their lives and their lifelong political aspirations. . . .
>
> The Vietnam War could no more be settled by traditional diplomatic compromises than any other civil war. President Lincoln could not settle with the South. The Spanish republicans and General Franco's nationalists could not conceivably have mended their fences by elections. None of the post–World War II insurgencies—Greece, Malaya and the Philippines—ended with a negotiated peace. In each of these cases only the logic of war could put these civil differences to rest.[64]

[62] See appendix 2, "Geneva Agreements," in Kahin and Lewis, *United States in Vietnam*, p. 368.

[63] Kahin, *Intervention*, p. 63.

[64] Gelb and Betts, *The Irony of Vietnam*, pp. 338–9. George Kahin, *Intervention*; Nayan Chanda, *Brother Enemy*; and Stanley Karnow, *Vietnam*, also emphasize the national unification aspect of the civil war.

Others may emphasize the social revolutionary aspects of the conflict, as opposed to the goal of national unification, but the general agreement is that the war was between two sides of one state, not between two sovereign states.[65]

Adherents of the Munich, Korean, and Malayan analogies, however, had great difficulty seeing the contest between North and South as a civil war. It was not for lack of information: critics of the Korean and Munich analogies tried to point out the civil war dimension of the conflict to the senior policymakers. George Ball told his superiors in 1964 that the Vietnam conflict was unlike the Korean War, "a classical type of invasion across an established border," because there was no invasion, only slow infiltration in South Vietnam. Moreover, according to Ball, the "Vietcong insurgency does not have substantial indigenous [Southern] support," and many nations see it as "an internal rebellion."[66]

As the July 1965 deliberations approached, Ball threw all bureaucratic caution to the winds and decided to name the Vietnam conflict for what it was, a civil war. In his last major antiescalation memo to the president, Ball cautioned, "No one has demonstrated that a white ground force of whatever size can win a guerrilla war—which is at the same time a civil war between Asians—in jungle terrain in the midst of a population that refuses cooperation with the white forces."[67] Ball was worried that if the United States intervened with troops, the other major powers might also be drawn into the conflict:

> So long as our forces are restricted to advising and assisting the South Vietnamese, the struggle will remain a civil war between Asian peoples. Once we deploy substantial numbers of troops in combat, it will become a war between the U.S. and a large part of the population of South Vietnam, organized and directed from North Vietnam and backed by resources of both Moscow and Peking.[68]

Similarly, during the congressional hearings on the Vietnam War in 1966, Senators William Fulbright and Frank Church repeatedly challenged Dean Rusk's depiction of the Vietnam conflict as a war of aggression. When Rusk resorted to his favorite comparison, the division of Vietnam and the division of Korea, with the suggestion that North Vietnam's action in South Vietnam was analogous to North Korea's invasion of

[65] Those who emphasize the social revolutionary aspect of the civil war include Race, *War Comes to Long An*; Turley, *The Second Indochina War*; and Lomperis, *The War Everyone Lost—and Won*.

[66] Ball, "How Valid Are the Assumptions," 37.

[67] Memo, George Ball to the President, "A Compromise Solution in South Vietnam," July 1, 1965, cited in *Pentagon Papers*, 4:615.

[68] Ibid.

South Korea, Church proposed the counteranalogy of the American Civil War. Rejecting Rusk's claim that it was illegitimate for North Vietnam to unify the South by force, Church embarked on a hypothetical comparison of the conflict in Vietnam with the American Civil War. Church's analysis was more thoroughgoing than all of Rusk's Vietnam-Korea-Munich comparisons combined. It is worth quoting at length:

> I should have thought that it would have been difficult to have ever fought a Civil War in this country had the same doctrine applied a century ago.
>
> At that time, I suppose the southerners felt there had been an invasion of the South from the North, and had England, which favored the South, adhered to the same principle that now seems to govern American policy, and had sent troops in the name of self-determination into the Confederacy, I think the English Government would have been hard put to convince Abraham Lincoln that there should be an election to determine the ultimate outcome of the war.
>
> I mean, I think—without in any way suggesting that our Civil War was an exact parallel—I think these concepts upon which we rest our policy are subject to very serious question. Now you can look at the war in Vietnam as a covert invasion of the South by the North, or you can look at it as some scholars do, as basically an indigenous war to which the North has given a growing measure of aid and abetment, but either way it is a war between Vietnamese to determine what the ultimate kind of government is going to be for Vietnam.
>
> When I went to school that was a civil war. I am told these days it is not a civil war any more.[69]

On this and other occasions, Rusk's response was that he could not follow Church's point.[70]

Clearly, there were policymakers and lawmakers from 1964 to 1966 who saw the Vietnam conflict primarily as a civil war; the current consensus on the aggression–civil war controversy is not based entirely on hindsight. In fact, those who continue to hold that the Vietnam War was one of aggression would argue that hindsight confirms their view. North Vietnamese regulars, not Southern guerrillas, overthrew the Thieu regime in 1975. Although the bloodbath predicted by the aggression theorists failed to occur, unified Vietnam did see the ruthless domination of the South by the North. But these events are not decisive. They, too, are consistent with the civil war hypothesis. Carrying Frank Church's American analogy one step further, upon winning the American Civil War, the northern victors did not hesitate to tear asunder the fabric of southern life. Victors

[69] Report on the U.S. Senate Hearings, *The Truth about Vietnam*, pp. 51–52.
[70] Ibid., p. 52.

in civil wars are neither more nor less benign than those in other kinds of wars. The question is whether the grounds on which the civil war was fought were justifiable, and whether foreign intervention was called for. Prevailing just war theory presumes against foreign intervention in cases of civil war.[71]

Proponents of the aggression thesis also neglect or try to explain away a crucial point that challenges their view of Northern aggression and Southern resistance: the promised but unheld elections of 1956. The importance of this election to Hanoi and to the Vietminh in the South who left their families to regroup in the North cannot be overestimated. From August 1945 to December 1946, the Vietminh had actually ruled Vietnam as a united country. In the ensuing war against the French, the Vietminh lost substantial portions of the South, yet at Geneva, they settled for less than they actually controlled in territory.[72] This they were willing to do in part because of pressure from China and the Soviet Union and in part because they were ready to transfer the fight for unification from the military to the political arena.[73] It is in this context that the Final Declaration of the Geneva Conference—providing for national reunification elections—should be understood.

In countering Rusk's Korean analogy with the hypothetical American Civil War analogy, Frank Church remarked that Britain would have had difficulty convincing Lincoln that there should be an election to settle the outcome of the civil war. The Chinese and the Soviets had apparently less trouble convincing Ho Chi Minh to do the same at Geneva. But if Lincoln could not have been sure of the outcome of such an election, Ho could. According to Eisenhower, "I have never talked or corresponded with a person knowledgeable in Indochinese affairs who did not agree that had elections been held as of the time of fighting, possibly 80 percent of the population would have voted for communist Ho Chi Minh as their leader rather than Chief of State Bao Dai."[74] Perhaps that was why Ho was willing to settle for the temporary partition of the country along the seventeenth parallel. He was convinced that he would win the national reunification elections.[75] According to Anthony Eden, Britain's foreign minister and cochairman of the Geneva Conference, Ho would never

[71] The most thoughtful argument along these lines for the Vietnam conflict is to be found in Michael Walzer, *Just and Unjust Wars: A Moral Argument with Historical Illustrations* (New York: Basic Books, 1977), pp. 96–101.

[72] See Zagoria, *Vietnam Triangle*, p. 41, and Turley, *The Second Indochina War*, p. 5.

[73] Kahin, *Intervention*, p. 61.

[74] Dwight Eisenhower, *Mandate for Change* (New York: Doubleday, 1963), p. 372.

[75] In an intelligence memorandum circulated in May 1965, the CIA explained Hanoi's interest in the 1956 elections in terms of the "fact that in Ho Chi Minh, the Communists had the best known leader in the resistance against France" (intelligence memorandum, CIA, May 11, 1965, Memo [B], Country File—Vietnam, NSF).

have agreed to the Geneva armistice without the assurance of these elections.[76]

Defenders of the aggression thesis have two responses to this argument. One is the constant refrain of officials asked about the elections: the absence of democratic institutions in North Vietnam made it impossible to hold free elections. But there was no provision in the Geneva Agreements saying that elections were contingent upon the existence of such democratic institutions in either regroupment zone. In fact, the Final declaration stated that "fundamental freedoms and democratic institutions" were to be the anticipated results of a unified Vietnam, not the preconditions.[77]

The second response is to cast doubt on the relevance of Eisenhower's statement. Typical is an April 20, 1965, letter from McGeorge Bundy to the influential journalist Walter Lippmann. Lippmann had apparently cited Eisenhower's estimate of the Vietminh's popularity, and Bundy sought to raise doubts about the relevance of that estimate for the period after 1954. Citing Eisenhower's comment, Bundy suggested that it

> clearly applies to the period before the Geneva agreements and not to the period after them. . . . It has to do with the preference of the people of Vietnam as between Ho and Bao Dai at a time of French presence. I think you will agree that this is not at all the same thing as the problem of 1956.[78]

The same point was also made by Dean Rusk and Walt Rostow.[79]

Bundy was being disingenuous. Was the Diem regime so popular and effective that enough of Eisenhower's estimated 80 percent would have transferred their allegiance from Ho to Diem in a two-year period? Such was not the consensus among U.S. intelligence sources and other informed observers. A 1955 State Department Division of Research report concluded that "almost any type of election that could conceivably be held in Vietnam in 1956 would, on the basis of present trends, give the Communists a very significant if not decisive advantage."[80] On the issue of "free elections," the report stated that "maximum conditions of freedom and . . . international supervision might well operate to Communist advantage and allow considerable Communist strength in the South to

[76] Cited in Kahin, *Intervention*, p. 61.

[77] See appendix 2, "Geneva Agreements," in Kahin and Lewis, *The United States in Vietnam*, p. 368.

[78] Letter, McGeorge Bundy to Walter Lippman, April 20, 1965, Country File—Vietnam, NSF.

[79] For Rusk, see Michael Charlton and Anthony Moncrieff, *Many Reasons Why: The American Involvement in Vietnam* (New York: Hill and Wang, 1978), p. 49. Rostow made the point in an interview with the author, Austin, Texas, November 17, 1986.

[80] Cited in Kahin, *Intervention*, p. 89.

manifest itself at the polls." Many years later, American officials would explain that the United States supported Diem in opposing elections because the elections would not have been free. What they did not explain was that if the elections had been free, the Communists would have won.

Ho Thong Minh, a defense minister in Diem's cabinet in the 1950s, acknowledged the likelihood of a Northern victory and more:

> Many observers were of the opinion that if they [the 1956 elections] had taken place, the North would have won. I also thought so, because the North had a firm grip on the population. . . . In the main, though, the population was probably going to vote in favor of the Communists. That is why our idea was to try and consolidate the South and then to renegotiate with the North. . . . we were widening, if possible, the terms of the Geneva Agreement on this specific point, while at the same time, of course, respecting the spirit of the Geneva Agreement.[81]

Minh was forthright and actually quite ingenious: the North would have won, and that was why the South did not want elections. The South violated the letter of the Geneva Agreements, but at least it tried to live by the spirit of Geneva!

Minh's boss, Diem, was not interested in such distinctions. He was concerned, first and foremost, with consolidating his power. After all, if the majority of Southerners would have voted for Ho Chi Minh, Diem had reason to be concerned. He began by removing Bao Dai as chief of state through a national referendum in which he "won" 98 percent of the vote, even though his American advisers had suggested that a 60-percent majority would be ample.[82] From mid-1955 until 1960, against the prohibitions of the Geneva Agreements, Diem embarked on a systematic program to ferret out, incarcerate, and in many cases eliminate Vietminh members and their sympathizers who had remained in the South. Writing about the 1956–1959 period, Joseph Butinger estimated that "thousands of Communists as well as non-Communist sympathizers of the Vietminh were killed and many more thrown into prisons and concentration camps." And "all of this happened more than two years before the Communists began to commit acts of terror against local government officials."[83]

George Kahin has rigorously documented Hanoi's reluctance to approve military action against Diem from 1956 to 1959.[84] Diem's repression of ex-Vietminh supporters reached such heights in 1959 that Hanoi

[81] See Charlton and Moncrieff, *Many Reasons Why*, p. 49.

[82] Kahin, *Intervention*, p. 95.

[83] Joseph Butinger, *Vietnam: The Unforgettable Tragedy* (New York: Horizon Press, 1977), p. 48.

[84] See Kahin, *Intervention*, pp. 96–117.

decided to approve limited military action against the Diem government, lest it risk losing influence over the remaining Vietminh in South Vietnam. As Jeffrey Race put it, "the [Lao Dong] Party" decided "it was then or never."[85] With the formation of the NLF in 1961, a full-scale insurrection to overthrow the Diem government was approved. The question of who would rule a unified Vietnam was to be decided by force. In other words, the civil war had started.

GOVERNMENTAL CHAOS IN THE SOUTH

American policymakers who remembered Colonel Edward Lansdale's success with Philippine President Ramon Magsaysay in crushing the Hukbalahap communist insurgency in the early 1950s were constantly looking for a Magsaysay in South Vietnam. Shortly after the Geneva Conference, John Foster Dulles reportedly gave Lansdale the following marching orders: "Do [in South Vietnam] what you did in the Philippines."[86] The material that Lansdale had to work on unfortunately was quite different. Like Magsaysay, Diem had personal integrity and was strongly anticommunist. Unlike Magsaysay, who was a folk hero among the peasants, Diem was a shy, arrogant, mandarin aristocrat who neither understood nor had much rapport with the Vietnamese peasants. To be sure, Diem had been anti-French, but his nationalist credentials were questioned by some Vietnamese, for he had been willing to work with the Japanese during their occupation of Vietnam.[87]

Diem had great burdens to bear. As we have seen, Vice-President Lyndon Johnson wanted Diem to be a Winston Churchill. Without a Southeast Asian Churchill, Johnson felt, no one would check communism's advance in Asia. Those more familiar with the Korean analogy, however, wanted to see in Diem a Syngman Rhee.[88] Ironically, after an abortive coup against Diem in late 1960, Diem began to compare himself increasingly to Syngman Rhee, for he believed that the successful coup against Rhee in South Korea was inspired by the United States, and he became increasingly cautious and intransigent in his dealings with the United States.[89]

[85] Race, *War Comes to Long An*, p. 110.

[86] Cited in Kahin, *Intervention*, p. 81.

[87] Ibid., p. 79.

[88] Eisenhower, lamenting about Bao Dai's lack of leadership, cited approvingly a remark made to him by a Frenchman: "What Vietnam needs is another Syngman Rhee, regardless of all the difficulties the presence of such a personality would entail" (Eisenhower, *Mandate for Change*, p. 372).

[89] Kahin, *Intervention*, p. 125.

It is interesting to note briefly how Richard Nixon and Henry Kissinger, with their greater attachment to the great men of history, regarded Diem's successors. A recent account of South Vietnamese President Nguyen Van Thieu's last years in office portrays a man who was constantly bristling at Kissinger's contempt. It was thoroughly unbecoming of a mere NSC adviser not to accord the Vietnamese mandarin the rights and privileges he deserved. Right until the very end, Thieu refused to believe that Nixon would have done the same and continued to live in the fantasy that if he could have bypassed Kissinger and dealt directly with Nixon, both he and his country would have been treated better.[90]

One need only make the most cursory acquaintance with Kissinger's writings to see why Thieu would not have fared favorably in his books. Bismark unified states to build Germany; Thieu could not even protect his little one without massive outside help.[91] Metternich was a great statesman in part because he had no problem reconciling what was just with what was possible.[92] Thieu, in Kissinger's view, was completely oblivious to such trade-offs, the best example being Thieu's refusal to give his assent to the Paris Peace Accords. It is extremely unlikely that Kissinger would have even begun the comparison outlined here, and that actually may have been to Thieu's advantage. Throughout his presidency, Thieu was obsessed with the fear that when America grew tired of him, it would approve a coup against him that would end with his death.[93] He might well fear, for he was a major participant in the coup against Diem in 1963, which ended with the assassinations of Diem and Diem's brother Nhu. Whatever else Kissinger and Nixon may have done in Vietnam, they did not make the mistake of ascribing to Thieu qualities he lacked. With lower expectations, it may have proved easier to endure the Thieu regime.

The point need not be belabored: South Vietnam suffered from a succession of unstable, authoritarian, incompetent governments. Moreover, the extent to which these governments and leaders were beholden to the United States made it impossible for them to steal the mantle of nationalism from the communists. As the historian William Turley observes, leaders who were perceived to have succumbed to foreigners "suffered self-doubt and weak support."[94] To be sure, a major source of the problem was that South Vietnamese society was much more divided along religious, rural-urban, and political lines than North Vietnam ever was.

[90] See Nguyen Tien Hung and Jerrold Schecter, *The Palace File* (New York: Harper and Row, 1986).

[91] See Kissinger, *White House Years*, pp. 905, 997 and 1089.

[92] Henry Kissinger, *A World Restored* (Boston: Houghton Mifflin, 1957).

[93] Hung and Schecter, *The Palace File*, pp. 74–77.

[94] Turley, *The Second Indochina War*, p. 2.

Any leader would have found it difficult to satisfy the conflicting political demands of the Buddhist majority, the Catholic minority, and members of sects like the Cao Dai and Hoa Hao, not to mention the expectations of the military, the intelligentsia, and other noncommunist nationalist groups. To compete with the well-organized and dedicated communists for the support of the peasants and the urban middle classes would have required an unusually strong and able government.[95]

No such government was forthcoming. Beginning with Diem and right up to Thieu, the major concern of successive presidents was how to stay in power. It is hardly surprising that many devoted their time to suppressing their noncommunist political opponents while rewarding trusted but incompetent aides with important positions.[96] Many officials stayed long enough to enjoy the perquisites of power, including the accumulation of wealth before being replaced by the next cohort. In the one year after Diem's assassination, for example, there was a succession of seven coups and countercoups. In the December 1, 1964, meeting with his advisers on Operation Rolling Thunder, President Johnson was reluctant to give the go-ahead because of governmental instability in the South. He even wished for a "new Diem":

> Most essential is a stable government. . . . Basic to everything is stability. No point in hitting North if South not together. . . . Why not say, "this is it!"? . . . Hesitant to sock neighbor if fever 104 degrees. . . . We've never been in position to attack. . . . If need be create a new Diem, so when tell Wheeler to slap we can take slap back.[97]

It was after this meeting that Ambassador Maxwell Taylor had his famous confrontation with the South Vietnamese "Young Turks." Air Vice Marshal Nguyen Cao Ky, Rear Admiral Chung Tan Cang, Commander of I Corps Nguyen Chan Thi, and Commander of IV Corps Nguyen Van Thieu were summoned to the U.S. embassy just as they were about to launch a coup against the sitting prime minister, Tran Van Huong. Talking to the group "as errant schoolboys who had been caught stealing apples from an orchard," an exasperated Taylor bawled:

> Do all of you speak English? Well, I told you all clearly . . . that we Americans are tired of coups. Apparently I have wasted my words. . . . Maybe there is something wrong with my French because you evidently didn't un-

95 Ibid., pp. 7–8.

96 The nepotism and insecurity that plagued Nguyen Van Theiu's regime is described in Hung and Schecter, *The Palace File*.

97 December 1, 1964, Meeting with Foreign Policy Advisers on Vietnam, Papers of Lyndon Baines Johnson, Meeting Notes File.

derstand. I thought I made it clear that all our military plans depend on government stability.[98]

"Governmental chaos" was the term that George Ball used to characterize South Vietnam. In the memo attacking the Korean analogy, Ball pointed out that "the Korean Government under Syngman Rhee was stable. It had the general support of the principal elements of the country. There was little factional fighting and jockeying for power."[99] In contrast, "we face governmental chaos" in South Vietnam. Ball liked to remind his boss, Dean Rusk, of this reality: "Look, you've got no government. It's impossible to win in a situation where you've got this totally fragile political base. These people are clowns." And Rusk would retort:

> Don't give me that stuff. You don't understand that at the time of Korea that we had to go out and dig Singman [*sic*] Rhee out of the bush. . . . there was no government in Korea either, and we were able to come through. We're going to get the same breaks down the road. One of these days something is going to happen, and this thing is going to work, just as it did in Korea.[100]

That day never arrived, and Ball's characterization of South Vietnam remained apt until 1975. Governmental chaos also differentiated South Vietnam from Czechoslovakia in the 1930s and Malaya in the 1950s. The Czech government under Beneš and Masaryk had been democratic and effective.[101] Moreover, had Britain and France decided against surrendering the Sudetenland and decided instead to fight Hitler, Czechoslovakia's well-trained divisions and its industrial power could have been harnessed against Hitler.

In Malaya, as General Lemnitzer pointed out, the British were in full control. They were ruthlessly efficient in maintaining stability, and they succeeded in obtaining the cooperation of a majority of Malays and non-Malays. Their intelligence sources were exceptional. When the British granted independence to Malaya in 1957, the communist insurrection was still alive but under control. Tunku Abdul Rahman, the first prime minister of independent Malaya, enjoyed the support of the overwhelming majority of the country's Malays, Chinese, and Indians. An aristocrat and lawyer, the Tunku ran an efficient, clean, and stable government. Under these conditions, it took the British and the postindependence government a total of twelve years to end an insurgency much smaller than that in Vietnam.[102]

[98] Nguyen Cao Ky gives a full account of this meeting in his memoirs, *Twenty Years and Twenty Days* (New York: Stein and Day, 1976), pp. 53–55.

[99] Ball, "How Valid are the Assumptions," 37.

[100] Transcript, George Ball oral history interview, pt. 1, p. 33.

[101] Zinn, *Vietnam*, pp. 86–87.

[102] Means, *Malaysian Politics*.

In relying on the Malayan, Korean, and Munich analogies to make sense of the Vietnam conflict, American policymakers vastly overrated the role of China and the Soviet Union. The diagnoses provided by these analogies also made it difficult for the policymakers to appreciate the civil war dimension of the conflict, and (to a lesser degree) the ineptitude of the governments in Saigon. It is of course not possible to attribute America's failure in Vietnam solely to these three factors. Other factors were important, too. The revolutionary élan of the communists, according to George Ball, was a crucial factor in allowing them to outlast the United States.[103] Dwight Eisenhower made essentially the same point to Johnson in quoting Napoleon: "In war morale is to the material element as three is to one."[104] Another important factor was the progressive erosion of the will of the United States to fight in Vietnam. As the war became more protracted and as American casualties rose, public opinion turned against the war. Once that happened, it became increasingly difficult for the decision-makers to stay the course.

The reason for not providing an extensive analysis of these and other factors is that they can be subsumed under the three main factors discussed in this chapter. Ball's and Eisenhower's point about élan, for example, is best understood in the context of a civil war. The Vietcong saw themselves as fighting a war of reunification, and for that reason they were willing to endure severe hardship and enormous sacrifices. Many peasants in the South supported the Vietcong because they did not perceive the Vietcong as invaders but as social reformers and nationalists. Similarly, America's loss of will can be understood in terms of the three factors. What Ho Chi Minh told the French in the 1940s is also applicable to the Americans: "You can kill ten of my men for every one I kill of yours and even at this odds, you will lose and I will win."[105] If the communists' desire for reunification was so fanatical, and if successive Southern regimes were so weak, it should not be surprising that the United States—insofar as it did not have an equally fanatical goal—would eventually disengage from Vietnam.

Herring has arrived at basically the same explanation of America's failure in Vietnam by a slightly different route. The three factors discussed in this chapter also figure prominently in his analysis:

> By wrongly attributing the Vietnamese conflict to external sources, the United States drastically misjudged its internal dynamics. By intervening in what was essentially a local struggle, it placed itself at the mercy of local

[103] Ball interview.

[104] Memorandum of Meeting with the President, February 17, 1965, Papers of Lyndon Baines Johnson, Meeting Notes File.

[105] Cited in Karnow, *Vietnam*, p. 17.

forces, a weak client, and a determined adversary. It elevated into a major international conflict what might have remained a localized struggle. By raising the stakes into a test of its own credibility, it perilously narrowed its options. A policy so flawed in its premises cannot help but fail, and in this case the results were disastrous.[106]

Herring attributes U.S. misjudgments to the policy of containment and the excessive concern for credibility. In contrast to Herring's, my explanation of the policymakers' misjudgments in the 1960s focuses on a slightly different source: the specific schemas that informed the decisionmakers and the top-down processing that made it difficult for them to correctly judge the "internal dynamics," the "local forces," and the "determined adversary" arrayed against them.

A COUNTERVAILING PATTERN? BOTTOM-UP PROCESSING, SCHEMA CHANGE, AND REALITY TESTING

If the preceding discussion paints an exceedingly bleak picture of the psychology of analogical reasoning and its implications, it is because most cognitive psychologists have been interested in explaining our inferential failures.[107] Psychologists focus on our judgmental errors not because they enjoy pointing out our cognitive foibles, but because they want to emphasize that the cognitive processes responsible for our routine successes are the same ones that are responsible for our inferential failures. Similarly, I have focused on aspects that contribute to inferential failures because they pertain most directly to the way most policymakers used analogies in Vietnam. It is important, however, to guard against an overly pessimistic portrait of our ability to reason schematically or analogically.

Schema theory argues that individuals tend to make the data fit the schema instead of the other way round. But schema theory also concedes that individuals may be cautious about applying a given schema when the fit is only partial. How individuals assess the quality of fit is not completely clear, but there is accumulating evidence that incoming information is not always processed in a top-down manner; bottom-up or data-driven processing also occurs.[108] Bottom-up processing occurs in a piecemeal fashion: it "particularizes the person, event, or issue, instead of

[106] Herring, *America's Longest War*, p. 270.

[107] The works of Kahneman, Tversky, Nisbett, and Ross cited in this book are representative of this tradition. See Fiske and Taylor, *Social Cognition*, for an approach that emphasizes successes as well as failures.

[108] See esp. Fiske, "Schema-Based versus Piecemeal Politics," pp. 44–53. See also Abelson and Black, *Knowledge Structures*, pp. 4–6. In using the representativeness heuristic to explain how schemas are cued, I am also suggesting that bottom-up processes are at work.

treating it as merely another example of an already familiar category."[109] George Ball's ability to contrast the particulars of Korea and Vietnam without completely dismissing the Korean precedent can probably be explained in terms of such piecemeal processing.[110] Schematic processing is consequently more complex than I suggest earlier: there is continual interplay between top-down and bottom-up processing. The nature of this interplay, however, has been barely investigated by schema theorists, because most of them are committed to the assumption that the dominant mode of processing remains top-down.[111] There is a reason for this: presumably, top-down processing is simpler and requires less cognitive effort than bottom-up processing; it is therefore more consistent with the hardcore assumption of the cognitive research program, the notion that human beings are "cognitive misers."[112]

Schema change can also be triggered by a lack of fit between the incoming data and the schema stored in memory. Psychologists have proposed several models of schema change. One model depicts change as a gradual process, in which each discrepant encounter erodes the schema a little, while another model argues that a single "concentrated encounter" can change a schema suddenly. A third model proposes that incongruity leads the perceiver to incorporate exceptions into the overall schema without abandoning it.[113] McGeorge Bundy's willingness to take the French experience more seriously after 1966, for example, may be explained by the gradual change model. By then he had come to the conclusion that "this damned war is much tougher—and very different from—World War II and Korea."[114] It took two years worth of "discrepant encounters" to erode McNamara's confidence in the efficacy of bombing, whereas no number of "discrepant encounters" were able to detach Rostow from his 1944 analogy.

If schematic processing or analogical reasoning does not always lead to inferential errors, the following questions become pertinent: When is an-

[109] Fiske, "Schema-Based versus Piecemeal Politics," p. 42.

[110] Ball did not reject the Korean analogy in toto because he accepted the warning that if the United States pushed Hanoi too hard, China might intervene in Vietnam, as it did in Korea.

[111] Abelson and Black, *Knowledge Structures*, p. 4; Fiske, "Schema-Based versus Piecemeal Politics," pp. 41–42.

[112] Abelson and Black, *Knowledge Structures*; on the nature of research programs, see Imre Lakatos, "Falsification and the Methodology of Scientific Research Programmes," in *Criticism and the Growth of Knowledge*, ed. Imre Lakatos and Alan Musgrave (Cambridge: Cambridge University Press, 1970), esp. pp. 116–22.

[113] Fiske and Taylor, *Social Cognition*, p. 177.

[114] Memo, McGeorge Bundy to the President, March 22, 1968, Miscellaneous Vietnam Documents, Reference File. Cf. memo, McGeorge Bundy to the President, "Memorandum on Vietnam Policy," May 4, 1967, Files of John McNaughton, Papers of Paul Warnke.

alogical reasoning helpful, and when is it a hindrance? How can the latter problem, especially in foreign policy decision-making settings, be mitigated? The question is especially difficult to answer at the level of psychological processes. Psychologists have not been able to specify precisely when the perturbations of top-down processing, the perseverance effect, representativeness, availability, and affect, lead us astray and when they are counterbalanced by bottom-up processing and schema change. The best synthesis is perhaps offered by Higgins and Bargh when they suggest that bottom-up processing may be more influential in activating schemas but that once activated, schemas tend to process information in a top-down manner.[115] Even this emphasis on bottom-up activation, however, may need to be qualified by Gentner's finding that the superficial commonalities play a major role in accessing schemas.[116] It follows that a reasonable point of departure is to regard reasoning by analogy in foreign policy, and its results, with caution, if not skepticism.

It is both possible and necessary to go beyond mere caution. Those who formulated America's Vietnam policy regarded all analogies except their own with great skepticism. Even George Ball succumbed to this tendency when he proposed the Dien Bien Phu analogy. Although Ball showed little skepticism about his own analogy, he did something that none of the other users of analogies did: he suggested to Johnson that the inferences from his analogy be put to a test. That, I suggest, is probably the only way to mitigate the problem of reasoning by analogy in foreign affairs. The historian David Fischer summarizes the logic behind testing succinctly:

> Analogical inference alone is powerless to resolve the critical problem of whether any particular point is a point of similarity or dissimilarity. It can never *prove* that because A and B are alike in respect to X, they are therefore alike in respect to Y. Proof requires either inductive evidence that Y exists in both cases, or else a sound deductive argument for the coexistence of X and Y. If either of these attempts at proof is successful, then the argument becomes more than merely analogical. If neither is successful, there is no argument at all.[117]

Since policymakers often resort to analogies precisely because they lack "inductive evidence," and since even when there is evidence it is often ambiguous and subject to all the psychological distortions discussed above, it is difficult to prove Y inductively. A "sound deductive argument for the coexistence of X and Y" is equally elusive because in international

115 Higgins and Bargh, "Social Cognition," p. 374. See also chap. 2 above.

116 Gentner, "Mechanisms," pp. 226–29.

117 Fischer, *Historians' Fallacies*, p. 259.

affairs, there are few relationships as invariant as "whenever X, therefore Y." The proof of Y must therefore lie in the testing.

The Y that Ball sought to prove with the Dien Bien Phu analogy was that the United States, like France, would lose. In Ball's own words, "We may *not* be able to fight the war successfully enough. . . . even with 500,000 Americans."[118] This conclusion might seem obvious in hindsight, but in June 1965, most would have found McGeorge Bundy's list of dissimilarities between the United States and France impressive. The question of whether the United States would win or lose in Vietnam could never be settled by analogical inference. Ball seemed to realize this. As mentioned in chapter 6, Ball acknowledged that his comparison of the American and French efforts did not mean that "*we cannot succeed where the French did not; we have things running for us that the French did not have.*" He proposed to the president that he use the upcoming monsoon season "as a *test period*" to "appraise our chances for military success in the South." Specifically, Ball urged the president to

> 1. *Decide* now to authorize an increase of American forces in South Viet-Nam [from 75,000] to an aggregate level of 100,000—but no more—additional forces. These should be deployed as rapidly as possible in order to deal with the Viet Cong offensive during the rainy season.
> 2. *Instruct* your top advisers—limited in this case, for security reasons, to the Secretaries of State and Defense (and possibly also Chairman of the Joint Chiefs):
> (a) that you are *not* committing US forces on an open-ended basis to an all-out land war in South Viet-Nam;
> (b) that instead you are making a *controlled commitment* for a *trial period* of three months;
> (c) that on the basis of our experience during that trial period we will then appraise the costs and possibilities of waging a successful land war in South Vietnam and chart a clear course of action accordingly.[119]

If Johnson had taken Ball's advice, the U.S. would probably have bogged down and taken heavy casualties—just as it would later—without making any serious dent on the will of the communist guerrillas to continue their "war of liberation." The prognostication suggested by the French experience would have been vindicated and that suggested by the Korean analogy put into doubt. To be sure, such tests exact a heavy cost, and it sounds almost callous to speak approvingly of testing Ball's analogical inference with 100,000 lives—until one considers the alterna-

[118] Memo, George Ball to the President, "Keeping the Power of Decision in the South Viet-Nam Crisis," June 18, 1965, NSC History—Troop Deployment.

[119] Ibid.

tive. Fortified in part by other analogies suggesting the likelihood of victory, other policymakers were about to commit a total of 175,000 troops to South Vietnam in an open-ended, possibly escalatory and protracted, engagement.

Ball's way of using analogies has its analogue in the scientific community. It is well known that scientists routinely rely on analogies to help them discover new facts and theories. Thus Galileo reasoned that the motion of a pendulum might resemble that of a lamp swinging on its chain in the campanile of Pisa; Thomas Edison patterned the motion-picture projector after the phonograph; Lord Kelvin "saw" similarities in the way heat and electricity were conducted; and James Maxwell began his investigation of electromagnetism by likening it to light waves.[120]

What Ball had in common with the scientists is that they all proceeded to test their inferences by experimentation. They used analogies for the purpose to which they are most suited: that of heuristic devices for discovering new phenomena or explanations. The existence of the posited phenomena or the validity of the explanation suggested by analogy are always checked by an experimental test.

To be sure, tests are easier to devise, conduct, and interpret in science than in politics. Moreover, in international politics, tests exact an inordinate cost measured in lives saved or lost or hurt. Even if Johnson had heeded Ball's advice and found American troops fighting to a stalemate at the end of a three-month test, it is not clear how he might have interpreted the outcome. He might have concluded from the limited experience that the United States could never win in Vietnam. Or he might have decided that more troops were all that was needed to balance in favor of the United States.

The reluctance to give up one's presuppositions in the face of contradictory evidence is not confined to politics. It also happens in science. As Thomas Kuhn has indicated, scientists have often continued to hold on to a theory even when experimental tests have indicated many discrepancies.[121] Albert Michelson and Edward Morley, for example, reasoned that if light waves behaved in some ways like water and sound waves, they might also require a medium analogous to water or air in order to travel through space. They postulated that "ether" was the medium. Although their theory was disconfirmed by a much-heralded experiment

[120] See Fischer, *Historians' Fallacies*, p. 244; Robert Hoffman, "Metaphor in Science," in *Cognition and Figurative Language*, ed. Richard Honeck and Robert Hoffman (Hillsdale, New Jersey: Lawrence Erlbaum Associates, 1980), pp. 393–418; Mary Hesse, *Models and Analogies in Science* (Notre Dame, Indiana: University of Notre Dame Press, 1966).

[121] Thomas Kuhn, *The Structure of Scientific Revolution* (Chicago: University of Chicago Press, 1962).

they themselves conducted, and although that disconfirmation led scientists to ask new questions that paved the way for Einstein's work, Michelson apparently never ceased to believe in the existence of ether. When Einstein made his last visit to the dying Michelson, Michelson's daughter requested that Einstein not raise the subject of ether.[122] If the psychological hold of analogies can be so powerful in science, where the standards of verification are clear and universally held, its psychological grasp must be even more powerful and ominous in international politics, where the evidence is often ambiguous but the passions strong.

[122] *New York Times*, April 28, 1987, section C.

CHAPTER 9

Conclusion

The chief practical use of history is to deliver us from plausible historical analogies.
—*James Bryce*

THE VIETNAM WAR was a debacle for the United States. Fifty-eight thousand deaths, over three hundred thousand casualties and $150 billion later, the United States still failed to prevent the fall of South Vietnam to communism. Reunifying their country cost the Vietnamese communists 950,000 lives and countless wounded; over two hundred thousand members of the South Vietnamese army were killed and about half a million wounded. Vietnam suffered the physical and environmental devastation of having more bombs dropped on it than on all the other countries combined in World War II.[1]

In the United States, the Vietnam War shattered the post–World War II consensus about America's role in international affairs. Ole Holsti and James Rosenau's massive study of the impact of the Vietnam War on the American foreign policy elite concluded that "propositions that for two decades prior to Vietnam were regarded as virtually self-evident truths about international affairs . . . are now among the most contentious points in discussions of American foreign policy."[2] Almost twenty years after America's withdrawal from Vietnam, the adverse effects of this dissension continue to plague the American polity. From disputes over the necessity of a strong U.S. presence in the world arena to legislative-executive quarrels over prerogatives in foreign policy making to fights over the wisdom of supporting anticommunist groups in El Salvador, Nicaragua, and Mozambique in the 1980s, the lack of a consensus has hobbled and rendered incoherent the foreign policy of the United States.

THE AE FRAMEWORK AND ITS IMPLICATIONS

It has not been my purpose to argue that the lessons learned from the Korean and Munich experiences by America's decision-makers were the

[1] The figures are from Turley, *The Second Indochina War*, pp. 195–96.

[2] Ole Holsti and James Rosenau, *American Leadership in World Affairs: Vietnam and the Breakdown of Consensus* (Boston: Allen and Unwin, 1984), p. 249.

sole factors responsible for bringing about the Vietnam War and its consequences. It would be sufficient for my purposes that the lessons of history be considered one of several major factors behind the Vietnam decisions; my aim has been to explore the workings of this one factor and to determine the extent to which it can explain the decision outcomes of 1965. I conclude by recapitulating the central themes of this study and then spelling out their implications.

Because policymakers often encounter new foreign policy challenges and because structural uncertainty usually infuses the environment in which responses to such challenges must be forged, policymakers routinely turn to the past for guidance. When they do so, it behooves us to take the historical analogies they invoke seriously: these analogies do matter. The whole point of the AE framework is to indicate how. According to the framework, analogies matter because they "help" policymakers arrive at inferences—about the nature of the problem confronting them, about the stakes of the problem, and about dangers and prospects of alternative solutions—without which decision-making might well prove impossible. In shaping the content of these inferences, analogies exert their impact on the decision-making process; they make certain options more attractive and others less so.

There is, of course, a point of view highly skeptical of the notion that historical analogies have, or are used because of, such diagnostic or inferential capabilities. According to these skeptics, analogies are primarily used to justify and to advocate the policy options decision-makers have already chosen through other means. Throughout this study, I have sought to show that this view is unduly restrictive, and in the final analysis mistaken. To begin with, the skeptics' position is at odds with the findings of cognitive psychologists who tell us that decision-makers routinely resort to analogies or schemas to interpret the complex and uncertain environment in which they operate and to which they respond. The cognitive psychological perspective, then, provides independent corroboration for the assumptions of the AE framework, while it also raises questions about the theoretical and empirical adequacy of a view that denies the information-processing capabilities of analogies and schemas.

Although cognitive psychology supports the AE view, the true test of the two views must lie in the "deciding": Can it be shown, in a crucial case, that analogies are used for more than justificatory or advocative purposes? Can it be shown that these extrajustificatory purposes affected the decision outcomes? The answer to both questions is affirmative if our analysis of the way America's Vietnam decision-makers used historical analogies is correct. Application of the AE framework to the analogies used by the Vietnam policymakers has revealed that the Korean and Munich analogies did much to shape the inferences drawn by the Johnson administration. The conflict in Vietnam was defined as a case of external aggression; the political stakes were considered to be as high as those in Munich and Korea; military intervention was deemed appropriate and likely to succeed. If these were the inferences drawn, it should hardly be surprising that military intervention was deemed necessary. The Korean analogy, it was found, is especially illuminating, because it can not only explain why military intervention was the favored course, but also why, among the prointervention options, Option C for the air war and Option C′ for the ground war were chosen. Finally, it has also been shown that the Dien Bien Phu analogy led George Ball to infer that, like France, the United States would lose in Vietnam. That inference predisposed Ball toward the withdrawal options.

Thus, for the policymakers in question, analogies did perform the diagnostic or inferential tasks specified by the AE framework, and in so doing, they played a causal role in affecting decision outcomes. These findings constitute the core of my argument. In addition, they demonstrate that the public use of the Korean and Munich analogies to justify and defend the administration's policies need not worry us. The skeptics' error is to infer that because these analogies were used so crudely and indiscriminately in public, they must have played only a minor role in the decision-making process. Inasmuch as the reverse is true, we arrive at a less restrictive and more informative view about the relationship between policymakers and their analogies: the analogies that informed their private assessments are often also used in public to explain and to justify their choices.

Three implications follow from this application of the AE framework. First, we seem able to identify the point in the decision-making process when analogies play the greatest role. They matter most during the selection and rejection of policy options, and they exert their impact by influencing the assessments and evaluations that policymakers must make in order to choose between alternative options. The Korean analogy illustrates this point most vividly: Lyndon Johnson wanted to win the war, yet he was reluctant to approve the harsher options that had a better chance of achieving that goal because his reading of the lessons of Korea warned him against choosing them, although CIA estimates indicated that even the harshest options tabled in 1965 would not have brought China into the war. According to the CIA, only a U.S. ground invasion of Vietnam would have provoked China to enter the war.[3] Yet Johnson and his senior advisers repeatedly fell back on their subjective notion of the limits they had to observe in order to avoid "MacArthur's mistake" in Vietnam. The importance attached to this imperative goes a long way

[3] See CIA Briefing Paper, June 11, 1965, NSC History—Troop Deployment.

toward explaining the selection of Option C′ and the rejection of Options D′ and E′ in the summer of 1965.

Second, our analysis also indicates that a major source of the power of historical analogies is their heuristic or diagnostic versatility. The ability of analogies to perform several diagnostic functions at once allowed policymakers who used them to arrive at a comprehensive picture of the Vietnam problem. Moreover, the portrait often came with its own implied solution, as the use of the Korean and Munich analogies to assess the Vietnam conflict indicate. George Ball's attempt to learn from the French experience of the 1950s may also be used to illustrate this point. The Dien Bien Phu analogy had a profound impact on Ball, not only because it suggested that the United States would lose in Vietnam, but also because it suggested to Ball that the challenges and stakes in Vietnam were much smaller than his colleagues assumed, that military intervention was ethically questionable, and that it might bring about domestic strife. Moreover, because these suggestions all pointed to the high costs and low returns of military intervention, their combined effect would prove especially compelling to Ball. The same may be said of the combined impact of the lessons of Munich and, of course, the lessons of Korea, on Ball's colleagues, except that in those instances, their impact would tend toward military intervention.

Third, using the lessons of Korea, Munich, and Dien Bien Phu to analyze America's Vietnam decision-making has allowed us to explain decision outcomes at a level of precision not obtained by other approaches. To be sure, these lessons were salient in part because the international and domestic political context made it difficult for American policymakers to discount them. Still, explanations focusing on international systemic or domestic political constraints do not take one very far: they are underspecified, riddled with anomalies, and do less well than the analogical explanation in accounting for the options selected and rejected. In contrast, the analogical approach explains what the contextual approach explains, it also explains what the contextual approach does not, and finally it also provides solutions to the empirical puzzles raised by the contextual explanations. Although less parsimonious and more contingent, the analogical explanation is more accurate and more satisfying.

THE PSYCHOLOGY OF ANALOGICAL REASONING AND ITS IMPLICATIONS

In addition to corroborating the claim that analogies can be viewed as knowledge structures on which decision-makers rely to interpret their world, the findings of cognitive social psychology have also allowed us to understand how psychological the process of analogical reasoning is. More important, by borrowing concepts such as the cognitive schema and the vocabulary and insights associated with it, I have been able to identify psychological mechanisms or processes that help explain why, though they were "the best and the brightest," America's Vietnam policymakers also used history sloppily. The final payoff of focusing on these psychological processes is best grasped by a comparison of the policy implications of our approach with those of less explicitly psychological works on the same topic.

Lyndon Johnson once wrote that in making major foreign policy decisions, he and other American presidents liked to consult the past, as well as anticipate the future in the widest possible ways.[4] Similar sentiments abound in the memoirs of other statesmen.[5] Existing research suggests that in the majority of the cases examined, the past misinforms much more than it informs. Scholars and policymakers have therefore devoted much effort to dissecting the errors made by policymakers; in so doing, they perform a valuable service. Almost invariably, the same analysts also suggest how the past could have been better used: such policy advice often consists of the proposal of more appropriate analogies or of suggestions of what the "true" lessons of Korea or Vietnam should have been. Presumably, better analogical reasoning at the time would have led to better decisions and happier policy outcomes.

The spirit and the substance of this approach can be found in Neustadt and May's *Thinking in Time: The Uses of History for Decision Makers*. This work builds on May's earlier analysis of policymakers' misuse of history in the making of postwar American foreign policy.[6] *Thinking in Time* documents many more "horror stories" of the misuse of history in foreign as well as domestic policy. The most novel aspects of the book are the techniques devised by Neustadt and May to enable decision-makers to use history better. They suggest that whenever a decision-maker maintains that *A* is analogous to *B*, aides should make it a habit to separate what is clearly "known" about the relationship from what is "unclear" and "presumed." The policymaker's assistants should also make a list of the similarities and differences between *A* and *B* and whenever possible inspect the history of the issue. Through such thorough and meticulous analysis, decision-makers and their aides should be better equipped to ferret out fallacious analogies and perhaps even propose better ones.[7] Neustadt and May are modest about the potential returns of their rec-

[4] Johnson, *The Vantage Point*, p. 151.

[5] See sources cited in May, *"Lessons" of the Past*; Neustadt and May, *Thinking in Time*; and Jervis, *Perception and Misperception*.

[6] May, *"Lessons" of the Past*.

[7] Neustadt and May, *Thinking in Time*, pp. 34–48, 273–83.

ommendations, but they argue convincingly that such marginal improvements are worth seeking. Above all, they deserve credit for acting on the assumption that decision-makers will continue to use historical analogies, and that as policy analysts, they should try to devise ways to help policymakers use history more responsibly.

What is absent from the above approach is the psychological element inherent in analogical reasoning: the focus on techniques diverts attention from the more fundamental psychological processes at work. The underlying assumption seems to be that reasoning by analogy is primarily an intellectual enterprise: if decision-makers were more aware of their limited repertoire of analogies, they would be more careful, and perhaps they would seek out other parallels; if the differences between their favorite analogy and the actual situation were systematically revealed, they would listen and perhaps change their policy preferences. Yet if my arguments about the psychology of analogical reasoning are correct, this assumption is problematic.

The assumption is problematic because, surprising as it may seem, many of the actions recommended by Neustadt and May were taken before and after the U.S. decision to intervene in Vietnam. Lyman Lemnitzer pointed out major differences between Malaya and Vietnam to Kennedy officials in 1961; George Ball systematically dissected the Korean analogy for all the top officials in his October 1964 memo; throughout 1965 and 1966, the joint chiefs disputed Johnson's worry about repeating MacArthur's mistake in Vietnam, and finally, Senators Mike Mansfield and Frank Church consistently raised serious questions, both privately and publicly, about the Munich analogy.

All these efforts came to nought. Kennedy, Hilsman, Johnson, and Rostow held on to their favorite analogies. Rusk, McGeorge Bundy, and McNamara told George Ball he was trying to "create distinctions" and unnecessary "nuances" when he tried to discuss the differences between Korea and Vietnam noted in his October 1964 memo.[8] Rusk took exception to Senator Church's questions about the Munich analogy and claimed he could not follow the alternative analogies proposed to diagnose the conflict in Vietnam. To Church's suggestion that the threat in Vietnam was different from the threat posed by Hitler, Rusk replied, "There are differences but there are also enormous similarities, Senator."[9] Rostow admitted that "simple analogies are dangerous," but that did not stop him from using them to arrive at the conclusion that bombing North Vietnam's POL targets would seriously hamper its ability to infiltrate men into the South. Rostow's faith in his interpretation of the

[8] Ball interview.

[9] Report on the United States Senate Hearings, *The Truth About Vietnam*, p. 357.

1944 bombing of Germany was so strong that he discounted "conventional intelligence," which predicted that the bombing would have minimal impact on North Vietnam's willingness to support the insurgency in the South.

It is not possible to attribute the behavior of these policymakers to intellectual obtuseness. For the selection of superficial analogies, the clinging to one's preferred analogy, and the inability to accord discrepant information the weight it deserved occurred too consistently and to too broad a range of individuals to be explained this way. Critics who lament that the policymakers knew too little history might ponder if a more distinguished and knowledgeable group of officials has since been assembled by any president.

Policymakers' reactions to analogy-consistent and analogy-discrepant evidence are better explained by the psychology of analogical reasoning. Decision-makers sometimes may be forced to acknowledge differences, but they tend to continue to emphasize the "enormous similarities" captured by their analogies. Cognitive psychology has little trouble explaining this tendency to emphasize information consistent with one's chosen analogies. Information that can be fitted into existing "knowledge structures" is easier to process, store, and recall. The disproportionate availability of recent historical events, top-down processing, and the phenomenon of perseverance have the net effect of making policymakers treat analogy-consistent information with kid gloves while information inconsistent with their preferred analogy is either ignored or mauled.

From the perspective of the psychology of analogical reasoning, the judgmental mistakes made by the users of analogies derive from the same processes that allow them their judgmental successes at other times. To accept this view perforce makes one more pessimistic than most students of "learning from history" have hitherto been. For if analogical reasoning in foreign affairs is as problem-laden as the case of the Vietnam decisions shows, and if cognitive psychologists are right in claiming that these problems are a result of the simplifying strategies human beings use to process information, policymakers are caught in a bind. There is always a glimmer of hope that a George Ball may rise to the occasion. Such a policymaker would not only challenge the specious analogies he or she sees; he or she might propose better ones and perhaps even suggest, as Ball did, how they could be tested. Yet such mavericks, as the case of Ball shows, will have difficulty convincing other policymakers to transcend their preferred analogies or the dominant analogies of their time.

Has "Vietnam" become the dominant analogy of our time? Judging from the way Vietnam has been invoked in virtually every post-1975 debate about U.S. commitments to the Third World, one would think so. Judging from the unceasing attempts of historians and policymakers to draw lessons from America's failure in Vietnam to illuminate the present—much as their predecessors drew lessons from the 1930s and 1950s to make sense of the threats of the 1960s—one arrives at the same conclusion. Vietnam seems to have assumed the spot that its predecessors, the Korean and Munich analogies, have done so much to prepare it for: the "reigning analogy" of its time.

But there is a critical difference between Vietnam and its predecessors. The lessons of Vietnam are as diverse and contradictory as the emotions raised by the war.[10] Among this plethora of lessons, two have been especially influential in structuring the foreign policy debate in the United States in the last two decades. I refer to the two opposing meanings of "no more Vietnams."[11] Many Americans—most though not all of them critics of the war—counsel against intervening in civil wars à la Vietnam. For these critics, "no more Vietnams" means that the United States should abstain from intervening in areas of dubious strategic worth, where the justice of both the cause and of the means used are likely to be questionable, and where the United States is unlikely to win. This disposition against intervention—whether for strategic, moral, or pragmatic reasons—has led some to label this view as the "Vietnam syndrome."

The other interpretation of "no more Vietnams," held by a smaller but very influential segment of American society—many of whom supported the war, fought in it, or held command positions in it—rejects the presumption against intervention. Motivated by the perceived responsibilities of a superpower and by reactions to the postrevolutionary atrocities in Indochina, this group also does not want another Vietnam. But by this it means taking steps to ensure U.S. victory in future wars. In particular, it warns against imposing unrealistic constraints on the military.[12] Some, like Norman Podheretz, argue that the repressive methods of Hanoi in the postrevolutionary years justified the U.S. intervention in retrospect; the mistake the United States made was not to have fought harder. That the United States lost because it chose not to fight harder, not because the war was unwinnable, has increasingly come to be the view of

[10] See Fromkin and Chace, "What *Are* the Lessons of Vietnam?" for an especially good survey of the different lessons learned by different American policymakers. See also the essays in Pfeffer, *No More Vietnams?*; Anthony Lake, ed., *The Vietnam Legacy: The War, American Society, and the Future of American Foreign Policy* (New York: New York University Press, 1976); and Braestrup, *Vietnam as History*.

[11] See Fromkin and Chace, "What *Are* the Lessons of Vietnam?" pp. 733–43, for an analysis of the role of these two views in the foreign policy debates of the 1980s.

[12] A survey conducted in 1980 found that 82 percent of the Vietnam veterans believed that the war was lost because they were not allowed to win (cited in Karnow, *Vietnam*, p. 15). See also Westmoreland, *A Soldier Reports*.

this group. The lesson it takes, then, is that it was the imposition of unrealistic constraints on the military by civilians unschooled in modern warfare that led to the defeat in Vietnam. If only the harsher options had been chosen, Hanoi might have been compelled to negotiate sooner or perhaps even capitulate. "No more Vietnams" therefore implies removing these constraints and doing whatever is necessary to win in future conflicts.

Throughout the 1970s and 1980s these two lessons—the Vietnam syndrome and the massive force syndrome—were pitted against one another. Opponents of the Nixon administration's involvement in the Angolan civil war and critics of the Reagan administration's policies in Lebanon, El Salvador, and Nicaragua continually warned about the danger of getting bogged down militarily in other peoples' civil wars. Proponents of these policies countered that the policies were necessary to prevent these countries from going the way of South Vietnam. This dissension troubled many observers. Even the most insightful attempt to pin down the lessons of Vietnam concludes that the final tragedy of Vietnam is that it has produced no common, unifying lesson that can be applied to future problems. As the authors, David Fromkin and James Chace, put it:

> The Munich pact was a disaster, but at least the Western world recognized it as such and learned that it would be a mistake to commit the same error again. The lesson of Munich can be misapplied—but the point is that it can also be *applied*. The lessons of Vietnam, if there is one, cannot be applied because we still do not agree about what happened. Far from helping to clarify policy issues in Central America or the Middle East, appeals to the lessons of Vietnam merely compound a conflict about current policy with an argument about history. Reference to Vietnam, therefore, is at this point divisive rather than unifying.[13]

Some may argue that Fromkin and Chace spoke too soon. Has the successful use of force in Grenada (1983), Panama (1989), and the Persian Gulf (1990–1991) not shown that those empowered to make decisions have internalized and indeed applied the second lesson of "no more Vietnams"? Recent administrations, it seems, have been careful to pick their conflicts and then do what is necessary to win.[14] In fact, in the aftermath of expelling the Iraqis from Kuwait by use of overwhelming force, Presi-

[13] Fromkin and Chace, "What *Are* the Lessons of Vietnam?", p. 746.

[14] Secretary of Defense Caspar Weinberger's November 1984 statement on the six criteria for the use of military force is the most systematic expression of this all-or-nothing approach. See David Twinning, "Vietnam and the Six Criteria for the Use of Military Force," *Parameters* 15 (1985): 10–18, for a summary and analysis of these criteria.

dent George Bush claimed that the United States had also kicked the Vietnam syndrome.[15]

Thus it seems that the second interpretation of "no more Vietnams"—the overwhelming force syndrome—has indeed been internalized and applied. The Bush administration's military strategy during the war against Iraq is an interesting indicator of this. Although President Bush's definition of the situation may have been partially informed by the Munich analogy—with Saddam Hussein portrayed as "Hitler revisited"—his military strategy seems entirely consistent with the second interpretation of "no more Vietnams." [16]

During the course of the Gulf conflict, Bush publicly assured the nation that it would not be "another Vietnam." Of course the president was justifying his policy, but, as our analysis of the Vietnam analogies suggests, what is used in public to justify is also usually used in private to analyze. The little we know about the private deliberations of the administration indicates that the president also repeatedly told his advisers, as well as the leaders of Saudi Arabia, that there would be "no more Vietnams."[17] By this Bush meant that the United States would not fight with one hand tied behind its back should war come.[18]

A quick mental juxtaposition of what Bush did in 1991 and what Johnson did in 1965 is revealing: Bush did virtually everything Johnson did not in 1965. Bush called up the reserves at the start of the crisis, he sent nearly half a million U.S. troops to Saudi Arabia in six months (Johnson gradually sent the same over three years), and he was of course willing to use the air power to "bring the enemy to his knees" as soon as the war started. The United States indeed prevented a repetition of Vietnam: it used massive force right from the start, and it succeeded in driving the Iraqis out of Kuwait.[19]

[15] *Weekly Compilation of Presidential Documents* (Washington, D.C.: U.S. Government Printing Office, 1991), February 25, 1991, p. 183.

[16] See ibid., August 13, 1990, p. 1217; and October 22, 1990, p. 1594, for references to the 1930s and Hitler. See ibid., December 3, 1990, p. 1949; January 14, 1991, p. 15; and January 21, 1991, p. 51, for "no more Vietnams."

[17] See Bob Woodward, *The Commanders* (New York: Simon and Schuster, 1991), pp. 307, 339, 347, and 355.

[18] Ibid., p. 339.

[19] Saddam Hussein and his advisers may not have realized that there were two opposing meanings of "no more Vietnams" in the United States. Or, even if they realized that, they could not guess which lesson influenced whom. Thus a possible explanation for Hussein's bravado throughout the Gulf crisis might be that he genuinely believed that faced with over 400,000 Iraqi troops in Kuwait and southern Iraq, the United States, would, remembering Vietnam, back away from an actual war. The United States would not want to risk the high casualties it had suffered during the Vietnam War. Hussein was right in that many Americans, including congressmen and antiwar protesters, took the latter view; he was wrong in that the few who counted—Bush and his advisers—took the opposite view, namely, "no

However, the prominence of the massive force syndrome during the Gulf crisis does not mean that it has emerged as the dominant or consensual interpretation of "no more Vietnams." For the other interpretation—the Vietnam syndrome—has also influenced the thinking of recent administrations. The forays into Grenada and Panama do not merely suggest the triumph of massive force; they also indicate that policymakers were careful to enter those conflicts they were sure of winning. This effect of the Vietnam syndrome is more clearly seen in the restraint exercised by the Reagan administration in Central America. For all its anxieties about Soviet expansionism and for all its desire to roll back communism in the Third World, the Reagan administration refrained from pursuing military options in Cuba, El Salvador, and Nicaragua. These threats, from the administration's perspective, were much greater than those posed by a communist takeover in Grenada, yet it intervened only in the latter. Since the United States has traditionally not been averse to the use of force in its "own backyard" to get it the outcomes it wants—witness the dispatch of marines to Nicaragua in 1912 and 1927, the overthrow of Jacobo Arbenz of Guatemala in 1954, the abortive Bay of Pigs invasion of 1961, and, of course, the landing of U.S. marines in Santo Domingo in 1965—the restraint of the 1980s needs explanation. The fear of getting into another civil war in which the United States might not win is probably a major part of the explanation.[20]

The restraining effect of the Vietnam syndrome was not absent during the Persian Gulf War either. Opponents of the war—a minority of the public and the majority of congressional Democrats—invoked this lesson to emphasize the dangers of intervention. This lesson probably had little impact on Bush's definition of the situation, since Iraq's action was a clear-cut invasion, not a case of troops infiltrating to support one side in a civil war. The Vietnam syndrome, however, may have encouraged the administration to ask itself tough questions about the stakes of the conflict and about whether it was underestimating the enemy. In other words, the syndrome may have exerted its impact through its presumption against intervention; Bush and his advisers, however, concluded that the stakes and the possibility of victory were high enough to justify war.

More important, once the decision for war was made, the Vietnam syndrome might have warned of the dangers of carrying the fight too far.

---

more Vietnams" meant no more fighting with one arm tied behind one's back. None of the military actions taken by the Bush administration prior to the start of Operation Desert Storm could shake Hussein from his "no more Vietnams" schema.

[20] In the one case where U.S. troops were sent as "peacekeeping forces"—Lebanon—the Reagan administration quickly withdrew the forces after a terrorist bomb killed over 240 soldiers. Staying on, it was feared, would endanger the lives of the remaining troops and might also engulf the U.S. in the Lebanese civil war.

That is one reason why the Bush administration was reluctant to march into Baghdad or to help the Kurds and the Shiites to overthrow Saddam Hussein. Getting involved in such a civil war might be extremely messy, just as Vietnam was. In other words, both lessons of "no more Vietnams"—the Vietnam syndrome and the massive force syndrome—may have informed the Bush administration at different points in the war. One lesson played a role in influencing the choice of "overwhelming force," and the other lesson played a role in the quick termination of the war.

The minor purpose of this speculative analysis is to suggest how the idea of Vietnam might have affected the policy choices of the 1980s and 1990s. The larger purpose, however, has been to underscore the point made by Fromkin and Chace earlier, that the lessons of Vietnam remain divisive and contradictory, and that it is probably premature to claim that the Vietnam syndrome has been kicked. Consequently, a consensus about the lessons of Vietnam comparable to that which obtained for the lessons of Munich or Korea remains elusive. That, I would like to suggest, is not necessarily for the worse.

That is not necessarily for the worse because our analysis of the Korean and Munich analogies suggests that the power of historical analogies is in part a function of how deeply ingrained they have become in the official and public mindset. When their lessons become part of the unspoken and spoken lore, when there is only one consensual interpretation, their premises and their relevance become matters of dogma that few will see fit to question. At that point, analogies step beyond their roles as heuristic devices for discovering facts and explanations and assume the roles of explanations and facts themselves. Scientists have always found analogies indispensable in discovering new explanations, but their inferences from analogical reasoning have always been put to experimental tests. In contrast, America's Vietnam decision-makers were unable or unwilling to put their analogical inferences to tests, such as those proposed by George Ball. The Munich and Korean analogies were not used as heuristic devices for suggesting and entertaining tentative interpretations of the nature of the problem in Vietnam; instead, they became the dominant schemas through which much else was viewed.

If there had been less of a consensus about the lessons of the 1930s and 1950s, perhaps the analogy of Dien Bien Phu might have had a fighting chance. It might have compelled policymakers to take a closer look at the local realities at work in Vietnam. Such scrutiny might reopen questions—and perhaps suggest fresh answers—about the nature of the struggle in Vietnam, the prospects of achieving American aims at an acceptable cost, and the reactions of allies and adversaries to the nonintervention options. It is not that the lessons of Dien Bien Phu would have provided correct answers to these questions, for its answers would need to be "tested" (in ways suggested by George Ball) just as the answers provided by other analogies would need to be (but never were). It is that there was so strong a consensus about the lessons of Munich and Korea and their relevance to Vietnam that the lessons of Dien Bien Phu failed to provoke new questions about the fundamentals.

Writing about a different set of ideas, Gelb and Betts once argued that "the strength of a political philosophy lies in the questions it does not have to answer."[21] This insight is surely applicable to the role of the Korean and Munich analogies in the 1960s; just as surely, it is not yet applicable to the Vietnam analogy. But there is growing interest in extracting a unifying lesson from Vietnam, if the examples of President Bush and Fromkin and Chace are any indication. The final implication of our analysis, however, casts doubt on the desirability of such a consensual lesson. For our analysis suggests that when historical analogies have the strength, and when they command the acceptance that Gelb and Betts write about, they are also at their most dangerous. Analogies that are immune to critical questions, such as Korea and Munich in the 1960s, are unlikely to serve as a basis for genuinely productive analyses. Analogies that invite too many questions, such as the Vietnam analogy in the 1970s and 1980s, may be divisive, but at least they encourage their users to seek their answers elsewhere. That is probably for the better.

[21] Gelb and Betts, *Irony of Vietnam*, p. 181.

Bibliography

Interviews

Ball, George. July 23, 1986, New York City, New York.
Bundy, McGeorge. April 10, 1986, New York City, New York.
Bundy, William. April 11, 1986, Hofstra University, New York.
Hilsman, Roger. April 9, 1986, New York City, New York.
MacPherson, Harry. April 11, 1986, Hofstra University, New York.
Roche, John. July 5, 1986, Medford, Massachusetts.
Rostow, Walt. November 17, 1986, Austin, Texas.
Rusk, Dean. August 21, 1986, Athens, Georgia.
Schlesinger, Arthur. April 10, 1986, New York City, New York.
Sullivan, William. July 23, 1986, New York City, New York.
Thomson, James. October 31, 1986, Cambridge, Massachusetts.
Unger, Leonard. August 13, 1985, Medford, Massachusetts.

Archival Materials

Lyndon Baines Johnson Library, Austin, Texas

Cabinet Papers
Declassified and Sanitized Documents from Unprocessed Files (DSDUF)
Meeting Notes File
National Security File (NSF)
- Country File, Vietnam
- Files of McGeorge Bundy
- Memos to the President
- Name File
- National Security Council Histories
- National Security Council Meetings

Office Files:
- Horace Busby
- Harry McPherson
- Bill Moyers

Oral History Collection Transcripts:
- George Ball
- William Bundy
- Clark Clifford

Papers of:
- McGeorge Bundy
- William Bundy
- Clark Clifford
- John McNaughton

David Nes
Walt Rostow
Paul Warnke
William Westmoreland
Reference File
Tom Johnson's Notes of Meetings
White House Central Files—Confidential File
Vice Presidential Security File

John F. Kennedy Library, Boston, Massachusetts

National Security File (NSF)
Countries File, Vietnam
Meetings and Memoranda
Regional Security File, Southeast Asia
Staff Memoranda
Oral History Collection Transcripts:
Walt Rostow
Maxwell Taylor
President's Office Files (POF)
Countries File, Vietnam
Staff Memoranda

Public Documents

The Pentagon Papers: The Defense Department History of United States Decisionmaking on Vietnam. Senator Gravel Edition. 4 vols. Boston: Beacon Press, 1971.

U.S. Department of Defense. *United States–GVN Relations.* 12 vols. Washington, D.C.: U.S. Government Printing Office, 1972.

U.S. Department of State. *Department of State Bulletin.* Washington, D.C.: U.S. Government Printing Office, 1961–66.

———. *Foreign Relations of the United States, 1952–54.* Vol. 13, *Indochina.* Washington, D.C.: U.S. Government Printing Office, 1982.

———. *Foreign Relations of the United States, 1952–54.* Vol. 12, *East Asia and the Pacific.* Washington, D.C.: U.S. Government Printing Office, 1984.

———. *Foreign Relations of the United States, 1961–63.* Vol. 1, *Vietnam.* Washington, D.C.: U.S. Government Printing Office, 1988.

Weekly Compilation of Presidential Documents. Washington, D.C.: U.S. Government Printing Office, 1990, 1991.

Books and Secondary Sources

Abelson, Robert. "Script Processing in Attitude Formation and Decision-Making." In *Cognition and Social Behavior*, edited by John Carroll and John Payne, pp. 33–45. Hillsdale, New Jersey: Lawrence Erlbaum Associates, 1976.

Abelson, Robert, and John Black. Introduction to *Knowledge Structures*, edited by James Galambos, Robert Abelson, and John Black, pp. 1–20. Hillsdale, New Jersey: Lawrence Erlbaum Associates, 1986.

Abelson, Robert, and Ariel Levi. "Decision Making and Decision Theory." In *Handbook of Social Psychology*, vol. 1, *Theory and Method*, edited by Gardner Lindzey and Elliot Aronson, pp. 231–309. New York: Random House, 1985.

Abelson, Robert, et al., eds. *Theories of Cognitive Consistency: A Sourcebook* (Chicago: Rand McNally, 1968).

Acheson, Dean. *Present at Creation*. New York: W. W. Norton, 1969.

Alba, Joseph, and Lynn Hasher. "Is Memory Schematic?" *Psychological Bulletin* 93 (1983): 203–31.

Allison, Graham. *Essence of Decision: Explaining the Cuban Missile Crisis*. Boston: Little, Brown and Company, 1971.

Allison, Graham, and Morton Halperin. "Bureaucratic Politics: A Paradigm and Some Policy Implications." In *Theory and Policy in International Relations*, edited by Raymond Tanter and Richard Ullman, pp. 40–79. Princeton: Princeton University Press, 1972.

Ambrose, Stephen. *Rise to Globalism*. New York: Penguin Books, 1984.

Anderson, Craig A., Mark Lepper, and Lee Ross. "Perseverance of Social Theories: The Role of Explanation in the Persistence of Discredited Information." *Journal of Personality and Social Psychology* 39 (1980): 1037–49.

Anderson, Paul A. "Justifications and Precedents as Constraints in Foreign Policy Decision-Making." *American Journal of Political Science* 25 (1981): 738–61.

Art, Robert. "Bureaucratic Politics and American Foreign Policy: A Critique." *Policy Analysis* 4 (1973): 467–90.

Axelrod, Robert. "Schema Theory: An Information Processing Model of Perception and Cognition." *American Political Science Review* 67 (1973): 1248–66.

Ball, George. "How Valid Are the Assumptions Underlying Our Viet-Nam Policies?" *The Atlantic Monthly* 320 (July 1972): 35–49.

———. *The Past Has Another Pattern*. New York: W. W. Norton, 1982.

Bassett, Lawrence J., and Stephen E. Pelz. "The Failed Search for Victory: Vietnam and the Politics of War." In *Kennedy's Quest for Victory: American Foreign Policy, 1961–1963*, edited by Thomas G. Paterson, pp. 223–52. New York: Oxford University Press, 1989.

Beck, Robert. "Munich's Lessons Reconsidered." *International Security* 14 (1989): 161–91.

Berman, Larry. *Planning a Tragedy: The Americanization of the War in Vietnam*. New York: W. W. Norton, 1982.

———. *Lyndon Johnson's War: The Road to Stalemate in Vietnam*. New York: W. W. Norton, 1989.

Billings-Yun, Melanie. *Decision against War: Eisenhower and Dien Bien Phu, 1954*. New York: Columbia University Press, 1988.

Black, Max. *Models and Metaphors*. Ithaca: Cornell University Press, 1962.

Blaufarb, Douglas. *The Counterinsurgency Era: U.S. Doctrine and Performance*. New York: Free Press, 1977.

Blight, James, and David Welch. *On the Brink: Americans and Soviets Reexamine the Cuban Missile Crisis*. New York: Hill and Wang, 1989.

Braestrup, Peter, ed. *Vietnam as History: Ten Years after the Paris Peace Accords*. Washington, D.C.: University Press of America, 1984.

Bransford, John D., and Marcia K. Johnson. "Consideration of Some Problems of Comprehension." In *Visual Information Processing*, edited by William Chase, pp. 383–438. New York: Academic Press, 1973.

Burke, John P., and Fred I. Greenstein. *How Presidents Test Reality: Decisions on Vietnam, 1954 and 1965*. New York: Russell Sage Foundation, 1989.

Butinger, Joseph. *Vietnam: The Unforgettable Tragedy*. New York: Horizon Press, 1977.

Butterfield, Herbert. *History and Human Relations*. London: Collins, 1951.

Cantor, A., and W. Mischel. "Traits as Prototypes: Effects on Recognition Memory." *Journal of Personality and Social Psychology* 35 (1977): 38–48.

Chanda, Nayan. *Brother Enemy: The War after the War*. New York: Harcourt Brace Jovanovich, 1986.

Charlton, Michael, and Anthony Moncrieff. *Many Reasons Why: The American Involvement in Vietnam*. New York: Hill and Wang, 1978.

Clark, Margaret, and Susan Fiske, eds. *Affect and Cognition*. Hillsdale, New Jersey: Lawrence Erlbaum Associates, 1986.

Clifford, Clark. *Counsel to the President: A Memoir*. New York: Random House, 1991.

Clodfelter, Mark. *The Limits of Air Power: The American Bombing of North Vietnam*. New York: Free Press, 1989.

Deibel, Terry L., and John Lewis Gaddis, eds. *Containing the Soviet Union: A Critique of U.S. Policy*. Washington, D.C.: Pergamon-Brassey, 1987.

Divine, Robert. *Roosevelt and World War II*. New York: Pelican Books, 1970.

"Documentation: White House Tapes and Minutes of the Cuban Missile Crisis." *International Security* 10 (1985): 154–203.

Duiker, William. *The Communist Road to Power in Vietnam*. Boulder, Colorado: Westview Press, 1981.

Eckstein, Harry. "Case Study and Theory in Political Science." In *Handbook of Political Science*, vol. 7, *Strategies of Inquiry*, edited by Fred I. Greenstein and Nelson W. Polsby. Reading, Massachusetts: Addison-Wesley, 1975.

Eden, Anthony. *Full Circle: The Memoirs of Anthony Eden*. Boston: Houghton Mifflin, 1960.

Eisenhower, Dwight. *Mandate for Change*. New York: Doubleday, 1963.

Ellsberg, Daniel. *Papers on the War*. New York: Simon and Schuster, 1972.

Erskine, Hazel. "The Polls: Is War a Mistake?" *The Public Opinion Quarterly* 34 (1970): 138–41.

Fairbank, John K. "How to Deal with the Chinese Revolution." *New York Review of Books* (February 17, 1966).

Fallaci, Oriania. *Interview with History*. Translated by John Shepley. Boston: Houghton Mifflin, 1976.

Feldman, Shel, ed. *Cognitive Consistency: Motivational Antecedents and Behavioral Consequents*. New York: Academic Press, 1966.

Fischer, David Hackett. *Historians' Fallacies*. New York: Harper and Row, 1970.

Fiske, Susan, "Schema-triggered Affect: Applications to Social Perception." In

Affect and Cognition, edited by Margaret Clark and Susan Fiske, pp. 55–78. Hillsdale, New Jersey: Lawrence Erlbaum Associates, 1982.

———. "Schema-Based versus Piecemeal Politics: A Patchwork Quilt, but Not a Blanket of Evidence." In *Political Cognition*, edited by Richard Lau and David Sears, pp. 41–53. Hillsdale, New Jersey: Lawrence Erlbaum Associates, 1986.

Fiske, Susan, and Shelley Taylor. *Social Cognition*. Reading, Massachusetts: Addison-Wesley, 1984.

FitzGerald, Frances. *Fire in the Lake: The Vietnamese and the Americans in Vietnam*. Boston: Little, Brown and Company, 1972.

Friedberg, Aaron. *The Weary Titan: Britain and the Experience of Relative Decline, 1895–1905*. Princeton: Princeton University Press, 1988.

Fromkin, David, and James Chace. "What Are the Lessons of Vietnam?" *Foreign Affairs* 63 (1985): 722–46.

Gaddis, John Lewis. "Was the Truman Doctrine a Real Turning Point?" *Foreign Affairs* 52 (1974): 386–402.

———. *Strategies of Containment: A Critical Appraisal of Postwar American National Security Policy*. New York: Oxford University Press, 1982.

Gelb, Leslie, and Richard Betts. *The Irony of Vietnam: The System Worked*. Washington, D.C.: Brookings, 1979.

Gentner, Dedre. "The Mechanism of Analogical Learning." In *Similarity and Analogical Reasoning*, edited by Stella Vosniadou and Andrew Ortony, pp. 199–241. Cambridge: Cambridge University Press, 1989.

George, Alexander. "The 'Operational Code': A Neglected Approach to the Study of Political Leaders and Decision-Making." *International Studies Quarterly* 13 (1969): 190–222.

———. "The Causal Nexus between Cognitive Beliefs and Decision-Making Behavior: The 'Operational Code' Belief System." In *Psychological Models in International Politics*, edited by Lawrence Falkowski, pp. 95–124. Boulder, Colorado: Westview Press, 1979.

———. *Presidential Decisionmaking in Foreign Policy: The Effective Use of Information and Advice*. Boulder, Colorado: Westview Press, 1980.

George, Alexander, David Hall, and William Simons. *The Limits of Coercive Diplomacy: Laos, Cuba, and Vietnam*. Boston: Little, Brown and Company, 1971.

George, Alexander, and Timothy J. McKeown. "Case Studies and Theories of Organizational Decision Making." *Advances in Information Procession in Organization* 2 (1985): 21–58.

Gibbons, William. *The U.S. Government and the Vietnam War*. Parts 1, 2, and 3. Princeton: Princeton University Press, 1986, 1989.

Gilovich, Thomas. "Seeing the Past in the Present: The Effect of Associations to Familiar Events on Judgments and Decisions." *Journal of Personality and Social Psychology* 40 (1981): 797–808.

Goldman, Eric F. *The Tragedy of Lyndon Johnson*. New York: Alfred A. Knopf, 1969.

Goldstein, Judith. "The Impact of Ideas on Trade Policy: The Origins of U.S.

Agricultural and Manufacturing Polices." *International Organization* 43 (1989): 31–72.

Graff, Henry F. *The Tuesday Cabinet: Deliberation and Decision on Peace and War under Lyndon B. Johnson*. Englewood Cliffs, New Jersey: Prentice Hall, 1970.

Haas, Ernst. *When Knowledge Is Power: Three Models of Change in International Organizations*. Berkeley: University of California Press, 1990.

Halberstam, David. *The Best and the Brightest*. New York: Random House, 1972.

Hall, Peter. Introduction to *The Political Power of Economic Ideas: Keynesianism across Nations*, edited by Peter Hall, pp. 3–26. Princeton: Princeton University Press, 1989.

Halperin, Morton. *Bureaucratic Politics and Foreign Policy*. Washington, D.C.: Brookings, 1974.

Harriman, Averell. "Leadership in World Affairs." *Foreign Affairs* 32 (July 1954): 525–40.

Hastie, Reid. "Schematic Principles in Human Memory." In *Social Cognition: The Ontario Symposium*, edited by E. T. Higgins, C. Herman, and M. Zanna, 1:39–88. Hillsdale, New Jersey: Lawrence Erlbaum Associates, 1981.

———. "Social Inference." *Annual Review of Psychology* 34 (1983): 511–42.

———. "A Primer of Information-Processing Theory for the Political Scientist." In *Political Cognition*, edited by Richard Lau and David Sears, pp. 11–39. Hillsdale, New Jersey: Lawrence Erlbaum Associates, 1986.

Henry, John, and William Espinosa. "The Tragedy of Dean Rusk." *Foreign Policy* 8 (Fall 1972): 166–89.

Hermann, Charles. "Changing Course: When Governments Choose to Redirect Foreign Policy." *International Studies Quarterly* 34 (1990): 3–21.

Hermann, Charles, Charles Kegley, and James Rosenau, eds. *New Directions in the Study of Foreign Policy*. Boston: Allen and Unwin, 1987.

Hermann, Charles, and Gregory Peacock. "The Evolution and Future of Theoretical Research in the Comparative Study of Foreign Policy." In *New Directions in the Study of Foreign Policy*, edited by Charles Hermann, Charles W. Kegley, and James N. Rosenau, pp. 13–32. Boston: Allen and Unwin, 1987.

Herring, George. *America's Longest War: The United States and Vietnam, 1950–1975*. New York: John Wiley and Sons, 1979.

Herring, George, and Richard Immerman. "Eisenhower, Dulles, and Dienbienphu: 'The Day We Didn't Go to War' Revisited." *Journal of American History* 71 (1984): 343–63.

Herzog, Werner. *Screenplays*. Translated by Alan Greenberg and Martje Herzog. New York: Tanam Press, 1980.

Hesse, Mary. *Models and Analogies in Science*. Notre Dame, Indiana: University of Notre Dame Press, 1966.

Higgins, E. Tory, and John A. Bargh. "Social Cognition and Social Perception." *Annual Review of Psychology* 38 (1987): 369–425.

Hilsman, Roger. *To Move a Nation*. Garden City, New York: Doubleday, 1967.

Hoffman, Robert. "Metaphor in Science." In *Cognition and Figurative Lan-*

guage, edited by Richard Honeck and Robert Hoffman, pp. 393–418. Hillsdale, New Jersey: Lawrence Erlbaum Associates, 1980.

Hoffmann, Stanley. *Gulliver's Troubles, or the Setting of American Foreign Policy*. New York: McGraw-Hill, 1968.

———. *Primacy or World Order: American Foreign Policy since the Cold War*. New York: McGraw-Hill, 1978.

Holland, John H., Keith Holyoak, Richard Nisbett, and Paul Thagard. *Induction: Processes of Inference, Learning, and Discovery*. Cambridge: MIT Press, 1986.

———. "Foreign Policy Decision-Makers Viewed Psychologically: Cognitive Processes Approached." In *Thought and Action in Foreign Policy*, edited by G. Matthew Bonham and Michael Shapiro, pp. 10–74. Basel: Birkhauser, 1977.

Holsti, Ole, and James Rosenau. *American Leadership in World Affairs: Vietnam and the Breakdown of Consensus*. Boston: Allen and Unwin, 1984.

Holyoak, Keith and Paul Thagard. "Computational Model." In *Similarity and Analogical Reasoning*, edited by Stella Vosniadou and Andrew Ortony, pp. 242–66. Cambridge: Cambridge University Press, 1989.

Honeck, Richard, and Robert Hoffman, eds. *Cognition and Figurative Language*. Hillsdale, New Jersey: Lawrence Erlbaum Associates, 1980.

Hoopes, Townsend. *The Limits of Intervention*. New York: David McKay Company, 1969.

Hung, Nguyen Tien, and Jerrold Schecter. *The Palace File*. New York: Harper and Row, 1986.

Jervis, Robert. *Perception and Misperception in International Politics*. Princeton: Princeton University Press, 1976.

———. "Cooperation under the Security Dilemma." *World Politics* 30 (1978): 167–214.

———. "Political Decision Making: Recent Contributions." *Political Psychology* 2 (1980): 86–101.

———. "Cognition and Political Behavior." In *Political Cognition*, edited by Richard Lau and David Sears, pp. 319–36. Hillsdale, New Jersey: Lawrence Erlbaum Associates, 1986.

———. "Representativeness in Foreign Policy Judgements." *Political Psychology* 7 (1986): 483–505.

Johnson, Lyndon B. *The Vantage Point: Perspectives of the Presidency, 1963–1969*. New York: Rinehart and Winston, 1971.

Kahin, George McT. *Intervention: How America Became Involved in Vietnam*. New York: Alfred A. Knopf, 1986.

Kahin, George McT. and John W. Lewis. *The United States in Vietnam*. New York: Dial Press, 1967.

Kahneman, Daniel, Paul Slovic, and Amos Tversky. *Judgment under Uncertainty: Heuristics and Biases*. Cambridge: Cambridge University Press, 1982.

Karnow, Stanley. *Vietnam: A History*. New York: Viking Press, 1983.

Kattenburg, Paul. *The Vietnam Trauma in American Foreign Policy, 1945–75*. New Brunswick, New Jersey: Transaction Books, 1980.

Keane, Mark T. *Analogical Problem Solving*. Chichester, West Sussex: Ellis Horwood, 1988.

Kearns, Doris. *Lyndon Johnson and the American Dream*. New York: Harper and Row, 1976.

Kelley, Harold. "The Warm-Cold Variable in First Impressions of Persons." *Journal of Personality* 18 (1950): 431–39.

Kennedy, Robert F. *Thirteen Days*. New York: New American Library, 1969.

Khong, Yuen Foong. "From Rotten Apples to Falling Dominos to Munich: The Problem of Reasoning by Analogy about Vietnam." Ph.D. diss., Harvard University, 1987.

———. "Seduction by Analogy in Vietnam: The Malaya and the Korean Analogies." In *Institutions and Leadership: Prospects for the Future*, edited by Kenneth Thompson, pp. 65–77. Lanham, Maryland: University Press of America, 1987.

Kissinger, Henry. *A World Restored*. Boston: Houghton Mifflin, 1957.

———. *White House Years*. Boston: Little, Brown and Company, 1979.

Kolko, Gabriel. *The Roots of American Foreign Policy: An Analysis of Power and Purpose*. Boston: Beacon Press, 1969.

———. *Anatomy of a War: Vietnam, the United States, and the Modern Historical Experience*. New York: Pantheon Books, 1985.

Krasner, Stephen. "Are Bureaucracies Important? Or Allison Wonderland." *Foreign Policy* 7 (1972): 159–79.

Kuhn, Thomas. *The Structure of Scientific Revolutions*. Chicago: University of Chicago Press, 1962.

Kuklick, Bruce. "Tradition and Diplomatic Talent: The Case of the Cold Warriors." In *Recycling the Past: Popular Uses of American History*, edited by Leila Zenderland, pp. 116–31. Philadelphia: University of Pennsylvania Press, 1978.

Ky, Nguyen Cao. *Twenty Years and Twenty Days*. New York: Stein and Day, 1976.

Lakatos, Imre. "Falsification and the Methodology of Scientific Research Programmes." In *Criticism and the Growth of Knowledge*, ed. Imre Lakatos and Alan Musgrave, pp. 81–196. Cambridge: Cambridge University Press, 1970.

Lake, Anthony, ed. *The Vietnam Legacy: The War, American Society, and the Future of American Foreign Policy*. New York: New York University Press, 1976.

Lakoff, George. *Metaphors We Live By*. Chicago: University of Chicago Press, 1980.

Larson, Deborah Welch. *Origins of Containment: A Psychological Explanation*. Princeton: Princeton University Press, 1985.

Lau, Richard, and David Sears. *Political Cognition*. Hillsdale, New Jersey: Lawrence Erlbaum Associates, 1986.

———. "Social Cognition and Political Cognition: The Past, the Present, and the Future." In *Political Cognition*, edited by Richard Lau and David Sears, pp. 347–66. Hillsdale, New Jersey: Lawrence Erlbaum Associates, 1986.

Lebow, Richard Ned. *Between Peace and War: The Nature of International Crisis*. Baltimore: Johns Hopkins University Press, 1981.

Leites, Nathan. *A Study of Bolshevism*. Glencoe, Illinois: Free Press, 1953.

Lindzey, Gardner, and Elliot Aronson. *Handbook of Social Psychology*, vol. 1, *Theory and Method*. New York: Random House, 1985.

Lomperis, Timothy. *The War Everyone Lost—and Won*. Baton Rouge: Louisiana State University Press, 1984.

Lowenthal, Abraham. *The Dominican Intervention*. Cambridge: Harvard University Press, 1972.

Lunch, William, and Peter Sperlich. "American Public Opinion and the War in Vietnam." *The Western Political Quarterly* 32 (1979): 21–44.

MacFarquhar, Roderick. "The End of the Chinese Revolution." *New York Review of Books* (July 29, 1989): 8.

McGuire, William. "The Current Status of Cognitive Consistency Theories." In *Cognitive Consistency*, edited by Shel Feldman, pp. 2–46. New York: Academic Press, 1966.

McVey, Ruth. *The Calcutta Conference and the Southeast Asian Uprising*. New York: Cornell University Interim Report Series, 1958.

Mandler, Jean. *Stories, Scripts, and Scenes: Aspects of Schema Theory*. Hillsdale, New Jersey: Lawrence Erlbaum Associates, 1984.

Markus, Hazel, and R. B. Zajonc. "The Cognitive Perspective in Social Psychology." In *Handbook of Social Psychology*, vol. 1, *Theory and Method*, edited by Gardner Lindzey and Elliot Aronson, pp. 137–230. New York: Random House, 1985.

May, Ernest. *"Lessons" of the Past: The Use and Misuse of History in American Foreign Policy*. New York: Oxford University Press, 1973.

Mayer, Arno J. "Greece, Not Munich." *The Nation* (March 25, 1968): 407–10.

Means, Gordon P. *Malaysian Politics*. Singapore: Hodder and Stoughton, 1976.

Mefford, Dwain. "Analogical Reasoning and the Definition of the Situation: Back to Snyder for Concepts and Forward to Artificial Intelligence for Method." In *New Directions in the Study of Foreign Policy*, edited by Charles Hermann, Charles Kegley, and James Rosenau, pp. 221–44. Boston: Allen and Unwin, 1987.

Miller, George. "The Magical Number Seven, Plus or Minus Two: Some Limits on Our Capacity for Processing Information." *Psychological Review* 63 (1956): 81–97.

Nathan, James, and James Oliver. *United States Foreign Policy and World Order*. Boston: Little, Brown and Company, 1976.

Neustadt, Richard, and Ernest May. *Thinking in Time: The Uses of History for Decision-Makers*. New York: Free Press, 1986.

Nisbett, Richard, and Lee Ross. *Human Inference: Strategies and Shortcomings of Social Judgment*. Englewood Cliffs, New Jersey: Prentice Hall, 1980.

Nixon, Richard. *RN: The Memoirs of Richard Nixon*. New York: Grosset and Dunlap, 1978.

Nolting, Frederick. *From Trust to Tragedy*. New York: Praeger Books, 1988.

Odell, John S. *U.S. International Monetary Policy: Markets, Power, and Ideas as Sources of Change*. Princeton: Princeton University Press, 1982.

Paige, Glenn. *The Korean Decision: June 24–30, 1950*. New York: Free Press, 1968.

Paterson, Thomas, ed. *Kennedy's Quest for Victory: American Foreign Policy, 1961–1963*. New York: Oxford University Press, 1989.

Pepitone, Albert. "Some Conceptual and Empirical Problems of Consistency Models." In *Cognitive Consistency*, edited by Shel Feldman, pp. 258–97. New York: Academic Press, 1966.

Pfeffer, Richard J., ed. *No More Vietnams? The War and the Future of American Foriegn Policy*. New York: Harper and Row, for the Adlai Stevenson Institute of International Affairs, 1968.

Podhoretz, Norman. *Why We Were in Vietnam*. New York: Simon and Schuster, 1982.

Porter, Gareth, ed. *Vietnam: The Definitive Documentation of Human Decisions*. Vol. 2. New York: Coleman Enterprises, 1979.

Powell, Charles, James Dyson, and Helen Purkitt. "Opening the 'Black Box': Cognitive Processing and Optimal Choice in Foreign Policy Decision Making." In *New Directions in the Study of Foreign Policy*, edited by Charles Hermann, Charles Kegley, and James Rosenau, pp. 203–20. Boston: Allen and Unwin, 1987.

Purtill, Richard. *Logical Thinking*. New York: Harper and Row, 1972.

Pye, Lucian. *Guerrilla Communism in Malaya*. Princeton: Princeton University Press, 1956.

Race, Jeffrey. *War Comes to Long An*. Berkeley: University of California Press, 1972.

Read, Stephen J. "Once Is Enough: Causal Reasoning from a Single Instance." *Journal of Personality and Social Psychology* 45 (1983): 323–34.

Richardson, J. L. "New Perspectives on Appeasement: Some Implications for International Relations." *World Politics* 40 (1988): 289–316.

Ridgway, Matthew. *Soldier*. New York: Harper and Row, 1956.

Robinson, Donald, ed. *The Dirty Wars: Guerrilla Actions and Other Forms of Unconventional Warfare*. New York: Delacorte Press, 1968.

Robinson, Frank, and Earl Kemp. *The Truth About Vietnam: Report on the U.S. Senate Hearings*. San Diego, California: Greenleaf Classics, 1966.

Rosati, Jerel. "Developing a Systematic Decision-Making Framework: Bureaucratic Politics in Perspective." *World Politics* 33 (1981): 234–52.

Rosch, Eleanor. "On the Internal Structure of Perceptual and Semantic Categories." In *Cognitive Development and the Acquisition of Language*, edited by Timothy Moore, pp. 111–44. New York: Academic Press, 1973.

Ross, L., M. R. Lepper, and M. Hubbard. "Perseverance in Self Perception and Social Perception: Biased Attributional Processes in the Debriefing Paradigm." *Journal of Personality and Social Psychology* 32 (1975): 880–92.

Rostow, Walt W. *The Diffusion of Power: An Essay in Recent History*. New York: Macmillan Company, 1972.

Rovere, Richard. *Affairs of State: The Eisenhower Years*. New York: Farrar, Strauss, and Cudahy, 1956.

Rumelhart, David. "Schemata: The Building Blocks of Cognition." In *Theoretical*

Issues in Reading Comprehension, edited by Rand Spiro, Bertram Bruce, and William Brewer, pp. 33–58. Hillsdale, New Jersey: Lawrence Erlbaum Associates, 1980.

Rumelhart, David, and Andrew Ortony. "The Representation of Knowledge in Memory." In *Schooling and the Acquisition of Knowledge*, edited by Richard Anders, Rand Spiro, and William Montague, pp. 99–135. Hillsdale, New Jersey: Lawrence Erlbaum Associates, 1977.

Rusk, Dean. "The President." *Foreign Affairs* 38 (April 1960): 353–69.

———. *As I Saw It*. New York: W. W. Norton, 1990.

Schank, Roger, and Robert Abelson. *Scripts, Plans, Goals, and Understanding*. Hillsdale, New Jersey: Lawrence Erlbaum Associates, 1977.

Schlesinger, Arthur M. Jr. *The Bitter Heritage: Vietnam and American Democracy, 1941–1966*. Boston: Houghton Mifflin, 1967.

———. Review of *"Lessons" of the Past*, by Ernest May. *The Journal of American History* 61 (September 1974): 443–44.

Schnabel, James. *Policy and Direction: The First Year*. Washington, D.C.: Office of the Chief of Military History, United States Army, 1972.

Schoenbaum, Thomas J. *Waging Peace and War: Dean Rusk in the Truman, Kennedy, and Johnson Years*. New York: Simon and Schuster, 1988.

Schulzinger, Robert. *American Diplomacy in the Twentieth Century*. New York: Oxford University Press, 1984.

Seymour, Charles, ed. *The Intimate Papers of Colonel House*. 4 vols. Boston: Houghton Mifflin, 1926–1928.

Shafer, Michael D. *Deadly Paradigms: The Failure of U.S. Counterinsurgency Policy*. Princeton: Princeton University Press, 1988.

Short, Anthony. *The Communist Insurrection in Malaya, 1948–60*. London: Frederick Mueller, 1975.

Shulman, Marshall. *Stalin's Foreign Policy Reappraised*. Cambridge: Harvard University Press, 1963.

Simon, Herbert. "How Big Is a Chunk?" *Science* 183 (1974): 484–88.

———. *Models of Bounded Rationality*. 2 vols. Cambridge: M.I.T. Press, 1982.

Snyder, Glenn and Paul Diesing. *Conflict among Nations*. Princeton: Princeton University Press, 1977.

Snyder, Richard, H. W. Bruck, and Burton Sapin. *Foreign Policy Decision-Making: An Approach to the Study of International Politics*. New York: Free Press, 1962.

Spiro, Rand, Paul Feltovich, Richard Coulson, and Daniel Anderson. "Multiple Analogies for Complex Concepts: Antidotes for Analogy-induced Misconception in Advanced Knowledge Acquisition." In *Similarity and Analogical Reasoning*, edited by Stella Vosniadou and Andrew Ortony, pp. 498–531. Cambridge: Cambridge University Press, 1989.

Steel, Ronald. "Cooling It." *New York Review of Books* (October 19, 1972): 45.

Steinbruner, John. *The Cybernetic Theory of Decision*. Princeton: Princeton University Press, 1974.

Stevenson, Adlai. "Korea in Perspective." *Foreign Affairs* 30 (April 1952): 349–60.

Summers, Harry. *On Strategy: A Critical Analysis of the Vietnam War*. Novato, California: Presidio Press, 1982.

Tang, Truong Nhu. *A Vietcong Memoir*. New York: Harcourt Brace Jovanovich, 1985.

Tatu, Michael. "Moscow, Peking, and the Conflict in Vietnam." In *The Vietnam Legacy*, edited by Anthony Lake, pp. 19–34. New York: Pegasus, 1976.

Taylor, Telford. *Munich: The Price of Peace*. New York: Vintage Books, 1979.

Tesser, A. "Self-generated Attitude Change." In *Advances in Experimental Social Psychology*, edited by L. Berkowitz, 11:289–338. New York: Academic Press, 1978.

Tetlock, Philip. Review of *Political Cognition*, edited by Richard Lau and David Sears, *Political Psychology* 8 (1987): 139–44.

———. "Learning in U.S. and Soviet Foreign Policy: In Search of an Elusive Concept." In *Learning in U.S. and Soviet Foreign Policy*, edited by George Breslauer and Philip Tetlock, pp. 20–60. Boulder, Colorado: Westview Press, 1991.

Thayer, Thomas. *War without Fronts: The American Experience in Vietnam*. Boulder, Colorado: Westview Press, 1985.

Thomson James. "How Could Vietnam Happen? An Autopsy." *The Atlantic Monthly* (April 1968): 47–53.

Thompson, Robert G. K. *Defeating Communist Insurgency: The Lessons of Malaya and Vietnam*. New York: Praeger Books, 1966.

———. *No Exit from Vietnam*. London: Chatto and Windus, 1969.

Thompson, W. Scott. "Lessons from the French in Vietnam." *Naval College Review* (March/April 1975): 43–52.

Truman, Harry. *Memoirs*. 2 vols. Garden City, New York: Doubleday, 1955–1956.

Turley, William. *The Second Indochina War*. Boulder, Colorado: Westview Press, 1986.

Tversky, Amos, and Daniel Kahneman. "Judgment under Uncertainty: Heuristics and Biases." In *Judgment under Uncertainty: Heuristics and Biases*, edited by Daniel Kahneman, Paul Slovic, and Amos Tversky, pp. 3–20. Cambridge: Cambridge University Press, 1982.

———. "Availability: A Heuristic for Judging Frequency and Probability." In *Judgement under Uncertainty: Heuristics and Biases*, edited by Daniel Kahneman, Paul Slovic, and Amos Tversky, pp. 163–178. Cambridge: Cambridge University Press, 1982.

———. "Subjective Probability: A Judgment of Representativeness." In *Judgment under Uncertainty: Heuristics and Biases*, edited by Daniel Kahneman, Paul Slovic, and Amos Tversky, pp. 32–47. Cambridge: Cambridge University Press, 1982.

Twinning, David. "Vietnam and the Six Criteria for the Use of Military Force." *Parameter* 15 (1985): 10–18.

Vertzberger, Yaacov Y. I. "Foreign Policy Decisionmakers as Practical-Intuitive Historians: Applied History and Its Shortcomings." *International Studies Quarterly* 30 (1986): 223–47.

Vosniadou, Stella, and Andrew Ortony, eds. *Similarity and Analogical Reasoning*. Cambridge: Cambridge University Press, 1989.

Waltz, Kenneth. *Theory of International Politics*. Reading, Massachusetts: Addison-Wesley, 1979.

Walzer, Michael. *Just and Unjust Wars: A Moral Argument with Historical Illustrations*. New York: Basic Books, 1977.

Weinberg, Gerhard. "Munich After Fifty Years." *Foreign Affairs* 67 (1988): 165–78.

Westmoreland, William. *A Soldier Reports*. Garden City, New York: Doubleday, 1976.

Whiting, Allen. *The Chinese Calculus of Deterrence*. Ann Arbor: University of Michigan Press, 1975.

Winograd, Terry. "A Framework for Understanding Discourse." In *Cognitive Processes in Comprehension*, edited by Marcel Just and Patricia Carpenter, pp. 63–88. Hillsdale, New Jersey: Lawrence Erlbaum Associates, 1977.

Wolfers, Arnold. *Discord and Collaboration*. Baltimore, Maryland: Johns Hopkins University Press, 1962.

Woodward, Bob. *The Commanders*. New York: Simon and Schuster, 1991.

Zagoria, Donald. *Vietnam Triangle: Moscow/Peking/Hanoi*. New York: Pegasus, 1967.

Zashin, Elliot, and Phillip Chapman. "The Uses of Metaphor and Analogy: Toward a Renewal of Political Language." *Journal of Politics* 36 (1974): 290–326.

Zinn, Howard. *Vietnam: The Logic of Withdrawal*. Boston: Beacon Press, 1967.

Index